Journalism Ethics and Regulation

Third Edition

Chris Frost

Head of Journalism
Liverpool Screen School,
Liverpool John Moores University

Longman
is an imprint of

PEARSON

Harlow, England • London • New York • Boston • San Francisco • Toronto • Sydney • Singapore • Hong Kong
Tokyo • Seoul • Taipei • New Delhi • Cape Town • Madrid • Mexico City • Amsterdam • Munich • Paris • Milan

Pearson Education Limited
Edinburgh Gate
Harlow
Essex CM20 2JE
England

and Associated Companies throughout the world

Visit us on the World Wide Web at:
www.pearsoned.co.uk

First published 2000, as *Media Ethics and Self-Regulation*
Second edition published 2007
Third edition published 2011

ISBN: 978-1-4082-4468-5

British Library Cataloguing-in-Publication Data
A catalogue record for this book is available from the British Library

Library of Congress Cataloging-in-Publication Data
Frost, Chris, 1950-
  [Media ethics and self-regulation]
  Journalism ethics and regulation / Chris Frost. -- 3rd ed.
    p. cm.
  Originally published under the title: Media ethics and self-regulation.
  Includes bibliographical references, webliography, and index.
  ISBN 978-1-4082-4468-5 (pbk.)
1. Journalistic ethics. 2. Reporters and reporting. 3. Press law. I. Title.
  PN4756.F76 2010
  070.4'3--dc22

                                                    2010039999

10 9 8 7 6 5 4 3 2 1
14 13 12 11 10

Typeset in 9/12pt ITC Giovanni Std by 3
Printed and bound in Great Britain by Henry Ling Ltd, at the Dorset Press, Dorchester, Dorset

WITHDRAWN

Journalism Ethics and Regulation

PEARSON

We work with leading authors to develop the strongest educational materials in business and media studies, bringing cutting-edge thinking and best learning practice to a global market.

Under a range of well-known imprints, including Longman, we craft high quality print and electronic publications which help readers to understand and apply their content, whether studying or at work.

To find out more about the complete range of our publishing, please visit us on the World Wide Web at: www.pearsoned.co.uk

Brief Contents

Contents

Abbreviations

AP	Associated Press (a US news agency)
ASA	Advertising Standards Authority
BBC	British Broadcasting Corporation
BCC	Broadcasting Complaints Commission
BSC	Broadcasting Standards Commission (or Broadcasting Standards Council. The Council became a Commission, amalgamated with the BCC, in 1997)
BSE	Bovine spongiform encephalopathy
CJD	Creutzfeldt-Jakob disease
EBU	European Broadcasting Union
ECU	BBC's Editorial Complaints Unit
ESC	BBC Trust's Editorial Standards Committee
GBNE	Guild of British Newspaper Editors (now the Society of Editors)
GPCC	(BBC) Governors' Programme Complaints Committee
IBA	Independent Broadcasting Authority
IFJ	International Federation of Journalists
IoJ	Institute of Journalists or Chartered Institute of Journalists
IRN	Independent Radio News
ITA	Independent Television Authority
ITC	Independent Television Commission
ITN	Independent Television News
NCTJ	National Council for the Training of Journalists
NPA	Newspaper Publishers' Association
NS	Newspaper Society
NUJ	National Union of Journalists
Ofcom	Office of Communications
PA	Press Association (a news agency supplying national and international news to regional newspapers and broadcasting stations)
PC	Press Council
PCC	Press Complaints Commission
PPA	Periodical Publishers' Association
Pressbof	Press Standards Board of Finance
QC	Queen's Counsel
RA	Radio Authority
SDNS	Scottish Daily Newspaper Society
SNPA	Scottish Newspaper Publishers' Association
SoE	Society of Editors
TMAP	Teenage Magazine Arbitration Panel

Acknowledgements

ACKNOWLEDGEMENTS

Dedicated to my wife Vanessa and my children Emma, Julia and Alice.

I would also like to thank the helpful people at the NUJ, the PCC, and all those who have given me permission to reproduce material from their publications.

Publisher's Acknowledgements

The publishers would like to thank Chris Frost for his dedication and skill in producing this third edition.

The publishers would further like to thank the panel of reviewers whose constructive comments on previous editions helped towards shaping this one.

We are grateful to the following for permission to reproduce copyright material:

Tables
Table 6.1 from Privacy, the public and journalism, *Journalism*, Vol. 1(2), Table 4, pp. 145–69 (Kieran, M., Morrison, D. and Svennevig, M. 2000), copyright © 2000 by M. Kierna, D. Morrison and M. Svennevig. Reprinted by Permission of SAGE.

Text
Extract Appendix.1, *PCC Code of Practice*, from *Editors' Code of Practice* (Editors' Code of Practice Committee 2009) http://www.editorscode.org.uk/the_code.html, Extracts from the Editors' Code of Practice reproduced by permission of the Press standards Board of Finance Ltd., 21 Lansdowne Crescent, Edinburgh, EH12 5EH; Extract Appendix.2 from NUJ Code of Conduct (National Union of Journalists); Extract Appendix.3 from *Code of Practice for Press Council, Ireland*; Extract Appendix.5 from *Declaration of Principles on the Conduct of Journalists* (International Federation of Journalists); Extract Appendix.6 from *Ofcom Broadcasting Code*, Office of Communications (Ofcom), October 2009 http://www.ofcom.org.uk/tv/ifi/codes/bcode/; Extract Appendix.6 from *BCI Code of Programme Standards*, reproduced by permission of the Broadcasting Authority of Ireland; Extract Appendix.7 from *TMAP Guidelines*, Teenage Magazine Arbitration Panel; Extracts on page 109, pages 109–110 from *PCC Annual Report*, Press Complaints Commission (PCC 2008); Extract on page 145 *PCC Code of Practice*, from *Editors' Code of Practice: Section 6 – Children* (Editors' Code of Practice Committee 2009) http://www.editorscode.org.uk/the_code.html, Extracts from the Editors' Code of Practice reproduced by permission of the Press standards Board of Finance Ltd., 21 Lansdowne Crescent, Edinburgh, EH12 5EH; Extract on page 169 from Open door The readers' editor on ... the cautionary tale of a citizen hoaxer *The Guardian*, 27/03/2006 (Mayes, I.), http://www.guardian.co.uk/media/2006/mar/27/pressandpublishing.comment/print, Copyright Guardian News & Media Ltd. 2006; Various extracts from Royal Commission Reports, Acts of Parliament, Parliamentary Committee Reports, Government consultation papers, and similar: Crown Copyright material is reproduced with the permission of the Controller of HMSO and the Queen's Printer for Scotland; Parliamentary material is reproduced with the permission of the Controller of HMSO on behalf of Parliament.

In some instances we have been unable to trace the owners of copyright material, and we would appreciate any information that would enable us to do so.

Introduction

This third edition was written in an attempt to continue to improve and update what I hope has been a useful source of knowledge and understanding for both students of journalism and practitioners. Its production from its early roots almost 20 years ago to this latest edition has covered some significant developments in journalism ethics and changes in the way journalism is regulated.

The idea of this book first came to me those 20 years ago because I was having great difficulty finding suitable texts about journalism ethics to recommend to my students. A number of 'How to ...' journalism books contained a little advice about standards and good practice but most were of the breezing-through style which mirrored ethics teaching on most journalism courses until very recently and so it seemed a good idea to produce something that could help students develop their ethical thinking.

So I started the first edition, conscious that I was treading on largely virgin territory, for while there were several good books on ethics from US authors, hardly anyone in the UK had previously produced a book on ethics. This was mainly because most journalism until then had been taught on relatively short training courses and it was only with the introduction of undergraduate programmes in journalism in the early nineties that journalism teachers were able expand their teaching to include ethics.

There were a large number of books written by Americans for Americans. In the USA, journalism has been an area for serious study and informed and educated practice for some considerable time. But the differences of approach there, particularly the implications of the First Amendment to the Constitution and the power this gives to the media, meant that interesting and important though many of these books were, they were of limited value to British journalists and journalism students. Lambeth's *Committed Journalism* (1992), Klaidman and Beauchamp's *The Virtuous Journalist* (1987), Meyer's *Ethical Journalism* (1987) and *Media Ethics* by Christians et al. (1998) are all books that I found instructive to read and am happy to recommend. However, the differences in culture and background between the USA and the UK mean that their perspective tends to waver in and out of focus, leaving the reader faintly confused. Too much is taken for granted. The American journalist's ethical roots are firmly bedded in the First Amendment and no further manuring is required. Of course many a cynic will say the British journalist already has his or her ethical roots firmly bedded in manure and that it will require the ethical equivalent of dynamite to move many of them away from the 'don't let the facts get in the way of a good story' style of journalistic morality but I hope things are improving and there is some evidence that most journalists attempt to aim for high standards.

Journalism books in the UK until very recently were very practical in nature. Mansfield's *The Complete Journalist* (1935) was one of the few early UK books on journalism and this was joined in 1950 by *The Kemsley Manual of Journalism* (Hadley et al.), produced to support the Kemsley Editorial Plan, a revolutionary training scheme for journalists in Viscount Kemsley's newspaper group. *The British Press*, by Robert Sinclair, was published in 1949 and this looked at ethics and the personal conduct of journalists. But its approach was very general and it is now more interesting for the light it casts on the journalistic ethics of the time than for the usefulness of its advice.

The National Council for the Training of Journalists was started in 1952 by employers' groups, trade unions and editors and on the back of this steady formalisation of journalism training, the early 1960s saw a sudden flourishing of books about journalism. While they were all solid primers on journalistic work, there was little about ethics. It is the growth in three- or four-year undergraduate courses that has done the most to expand thinking about journalism ethics in the educational establishments. A three- or four-year course allows the time to develop a critical discussion of standards in journalism in a way that was impossible before. The tradition on the one-year courses was to discuss ethical issues as they arose in the students' practical work. However, students often came to believe that ethical problems were rare and involved lengthy debate instead of being pervasive, often requiring instant decision against deadline. An excellent example of a journalism textbook produced before undergraduate programmes became popular is *Practical Newspaper Reporting* by Geoffrey Harris and David Spark which was the standard primer during the 1980s and 1990s. This was first written in 1966 for the NCTJ and a second edition was published in 1993 (and reprinted in 1994). By then the Press Complaints Commission had been launched and with it, an industry Code of Practice. This was included as an appendix in the book and a new Chapter 19 had been included on ethics. It was entitled 'A Note on Ethics' and that is all it was: two and a half pages about issues. The first page is largely about the new PCC and the subsequent pages bring up matters raised by PCC complaints covering issues such as addresses, freebies, illustrations, plagiarism and promises. This is not to criticise the book, which was typical of its type and time, but to draw some conclusions about the general view of ethics at the time (less than 20 years ago).

The first UK books on ethics were published in the early 1990s (Andrew Belsey and Ruth Chadwick (eds) (1992) *Ethical Issues in Journalism and the Media*, London: Routledge; and Elliott Cohen (ed.) (1992) *Philosophical Issues in Journalism*, Oxford: OUP). These contained essays on elements of journalistic ethics that were very useful. However, as a series of essays, they lacked cohesion, nor were they specifically aimed at journalism students.

Journalistic ethics have only very recently become a seriously regarded subject for study by practitioners and journalism academics in the UK (see Stephenson and Bromley 1998: Chapter 10). A two-hour session on a wet weekday afternoon half-way through a one-year course was very much the standard teaching for would-be journalists until towards the end of the 1980s and early 1990s. Even now there are few one-year courses that do more than a couple of sessions. A letter from the NUJ's Ethics Council to scores of colleges teaching journalism, offering guest speakers on the subject, saw only a handful of responses. In a letter to journalism colleges in 1996, the late Sir David English, then Chairman of the PCC's Code of Practice Committee, drew attention to a report from the National Council for the Training of Journalists about their National Certificate Examination which claimed that many trainees seemed unaware of the provisions of the PCC's Code of Practice. 'There was even a suggestion by trainees that the code could be disregarded if a better story was the result,' reprimanded Sir David in his letter. He pointed out that this was a matter of grave concern, and asked trainers to make clear to students what the Code of Practice had to say. But the people taking this exam were working journalists with about two years' experience on a newspaper in addition to their training course. It is to be hoped that things have improved a lot since then and that Sir David's successor both in the editor's chair at the *Daily Mail* and as Chair of the PCC Code Committee, Paul Dacre, does not need to send out a similar letter and there is some evidence that there is that sort of improvement in standards.

Things in the industry and journalism education have change enormously since 1990. We now have the internet and all that brings to journalism and information dissemination. The average journalist is now a graduate; many have been on courses that now discuss ethics, using this or one or more of the other excellent books available, such as Keeble, Harcup or Sanders, and the regulation system has changed considerably, particularly for broadcasting. Because of all this change, I felt it was time to revisit the book, to note the developments and changes made within the industry and to try to draw in some of the research that has taken place in those 20 years. It should be remembered that any book of this sort is only a snapshot of the collective thinking of journalists and that this is constantly changing. There are some areas where the issues are clear, but others where thinking is in a state of change. It is this debate within the industry and the wider public that is important and which I attempt to identify.

There is a difficult balance to be struck when writing a book of this sort. I hope it will be read by practitioners, both students and professionals, who want to gain a clearer insight into their work, as well as academics seeking to discover why a body of intelligent people who often claim to be driven by pure and noble motives seem to fail both so often and so publicly. To achieve this aim, I have tried to offer discussion, debate and advice on ethical journalistic practice derived from the experience of many journalists, the case studies of the key regulatory bodies with the under-pinning of moral philosophers through the ages and I hope you will be able to use it to develop your own set of ethical tools to guide you in your professional behaviour. My campaign for higher journalistic standards needs the support of all the journalists it can get because any move towards a more ethically-based journalism must be driven by journalists if it is to be sustained. For too long, too many journalists in the UK have tended to shrug their shoulders and assume morals are for someone else and then wonder why there are calls for legislation on such issues as payments to witnesses, and privacy. [Regular rows about media intrusions into the lives of celebrities such as David Beckham, Ashley Cole, Max Mosley or John Terry have raised public concern about the way the press so often intrudes into the private lives of public figures. Calls for legislation are made at regular intervals and are widely supported by the public even if the government fears the press too much to consider their introduction.] Clearly, in the light of such widespread public interest and concern, journalists cannot ignore or remain indifferent to the ethical aspects of their profession. The industry has been lucky. While there have been some outrageous invasions of privacy, they have not been so sustained as to force a government to act, particularly a government so concerned with its media image as Tony Blair's. But the willingness of such figures as the Prince of Wales and Tony Blair to complain to the PCC about invasions of their children's privacy as well as the jailing of Clive Goodman shows that the pressure on the media has stepped up a gear or two. There must also be concern about the creeping of legislation into the area of protection of privacy. Law and changing opinion have made it easier to prohibit the publication of names under the guise of protecting privacy.

We have a choice in the UK. Either we will have to have legislation to deal with the excesses of the media, particularly the tabloid press, or journalists will have to get their act together and start to behave responsibly. Journalists can only do this if they are educated to consider the issues raised by their work. All too often the general consensus seems to be that ethical issues are a once-in-a-blue-moon problem – crises that pop up from time to time requiring considerable thought before a decision is made. This, of course, is not the case. Ethical problems are dealt with almost on a minute-by-minute basis in journalism. They happen so regularly that many of the decisions are part of the natural working pattern and receive no particular conscious thought process. If we make an ethical decision not to steal, we do not need to revisit that decision every time we encounter something that is not nailed down. But the habitual thief does not have such an easy time as his or her decisions (which must be taken on every occasion) are not ethical but entirely pragmatic: Is the item worth stealing? Is the physical effort required worth it? Am I likely to be caught? Many journalists seem to go through the same logistics-only processes in their work. Shall I invent this part of the story? Is the mental and physical effort required worth it? Am I likely to be found out? Only the punishments for those caught out seem markedly different. Time in prison for the thief, a slap on the wrist from the PCC or Ofcom and possibly disciplinary action by the editor for the journalist. Only by making the moral decision not to invent stories in the first place can the journalist avoid mental turmoil of this sort during the writing of every story.

Of course journalists are often under pressure, or at the very least perceived pressure, from others, such as editors, to stretch ethical elasticity to its limits and sometimes beyond. There have been suggestions that print journalists should have the PCC's Code of Practice written into their contracts of employment and the PCC has already asked proprietors to do this for editors. This idea does spark some questions. For instance, if a contract of employment contains the Code and an editor instructs a journalist to pursue a story in a way that requires breaching the Code, can the editor then sack the journalist for breaching it? What if the journalist refuses to follow the instruction? Can he or she be sacked for insubordination? How can journalists be expected to adhere to a code which they have not been involved in drawing up? The PCC Code of Practice is agreed by editors only and neither journalists nor their representatives are consulted about the process. The National Union of Journalists believes that journalists should have the right to refuse assignments if they believe the assignment will breach the code of practice. This is a view that was supported by the Culture, Media and Sport Select Committee in its 2003 review of the PCC, although it changed its mind in the subsequent 2007 and 2010 reviews. That some journalists at least feel obliged to push the limits of ethical nicety was underlined by the Clive Goodman affair when the *News of the World*'s former royal editor was jailed for illegally hacking mobile phone messages. The part played by his editor, Andy Coulson, who quickly resigned, and other *NoW* executives will probably never be fully known thanks to what the Culture, Media and Sport Select Committee described as collective amnesia in its 2010 report. Re-examining the affair it said in its report:

> The readiness of all concerned – News International, the police and the PCC – to leave Mr Goodman as the sole scapegoat without carrying out full investigations is striking ... We have repeatedly encountered an unwillingness to provide the detailed information that we sought, claims of ignorance or lack of recall, and deliberate obfuscation. We strongly condemn this behaviour which reinforces the widely held impression that the press generally regard themselves as unaccountable and that News International in particular has sought to conceal the truth about what really occurred.
>
> (HoC 2010: 7)

Broadcast journalists are more constrained than colleagues in print in that they are obliged to adhere to standards of fairness and accuracy that are laid down in law. This may be a reason why our TV and radio is often less likely than a tabloid newspaper to intrude on a celebrity's privacy.

Many journalists and editors seem to believe that others can do the job of taking moral decisions for them; that they can continue to behave badly and avoid new legislation if they get the public relations right. Many editors and other commentators seem to believe that by having a PCC that is seen to work by government and public, there will be no need to bring in laws. But a self-regulatory system can only work if the editors want it to work. At the moment they do – but often for the wrong reasons. Many seem to want to be ethical only when it is marketable. Few editors and proprietors seem keen to employ ethical journalism if it interferes in any way with their position in the market and their ability to make profits. In a market-dominated culture that has dispensed with social responsibility, I find it difficult to understand why anyone should be surprised that our newspapers give priority to profit over ethics, circulation over public responsibility. We can count on one hand the number of times over the past ten years that the press has restrained itself for entirely unselfish motives.

Broadcasting has a better reputation, but even this is slowly being eroded as the market becomes the dominating factor and digital TV spreads competition and the fight for audiences. The public service broadcasting ideal and the need for high-quality commercial television is being diluted by the increase in the number of channels. We are in the era of 'cheap is best' because it is all about profit. Ethics come a very poor second when the journalist is under constant pressure to get the story regardless in order to boost circulation or viewing figures. We should also consider why it is acceptable to have legislative control of broadcasting ethics but not of print. What is it about newspapers that suggests self-regulation is good enough when we are told that only statutory regulation will do for broadcasting?

Unless a journalist's understanding of ethics and journalistic morality is firmly rooted, then he or she will have neither the educational background nor the inclination to stand up for what he or she believes is journalistically right against the pressures of profit and a threat to career development. Even with a strong ethic to support them, journalists will still, on occasion, go for the sensational or invasive story. I hope that after reading this book, they will at least think about it and know why they breached their ethics in the name of profit, career ambitions, malice or whatever and will be able to decide whether it was worth it.

The structure of the book

This book is planned to lead the reader through the elements of journalistic morality in a way that I hope is helpful and informative. It is run in two major sections. The first looks at journalistic ethics while the second looks at regulation in the UK and elsewhere.

The journalism ethics section opens with several chapters discussing the nature of ethics and attempting to provide the tools needed for the practitioner to make sensible judgements. The second half of this section discusses a number of issues, often using case studies as guidelines. It would have been good in these chapters to show how the philosophical guidelines introduced in earlier chapters can be used, but lack of space makes it impossible to do that in every case. The section starts in Chapter 1 with a short appreciation of some of the classical philosophers from the early Greeks to the modern day. I believe that while these philosophers may seem a long way from modern journalism, their thinking can help us come to some conclusions about the way journalists work and how moral philosophy can be best applied to questions of journalistic standards. It is very difficult to discuss journalism ethics without being aware of what journalists are trying to do and so Chapter 2 looks at what news is, how journalists identify it and why news is abstractly different from the event it is describing. It also examines what interests people and helps to sell newspapers and magazines. The freedom of the press is probably one of the most abused clichés in the English language. Raised almost exclusively on occasions when there has been an abuse of that freedom, it is at the root of the journalist's need for ethics. Chapter 3 looks at the links between morality and a free press and how society often uses the law to enforce elements of morality. In the chapters that follow I look at a range of professional issues that help explain how society has developed Western-style journalistic ethics. In Chapter 4 the relationship between the press and the public is explored while examining what makes a good journalist. Chapter 5 attempts to examine the complex relationship between truth, accuracy and objectivity.

Chapter 6 looks at privacy and intrusion. Privacy has been the fastest growing area of ethical concern over the past fifty years and the one that draws the most confused attention from the public. Celebrity revelations sell news. Intrusive reality TV shows such as *Big Brother* attract big audiences, but people still think the press is too intrusive and there seem to be growing demands to strengthen respect for privacy despite the fact that much celebrity revelation is freely provided by the celebrity themselves and then consumed by those calling for more privacy.

Chapter 7 looks at reputation and the fast-developing changes in both our understanding of reputation and its effects on journalists, while Chapter 8 reviews general news-gathering and the ethical dilemmas this can pose, from harassment through to deceit and pretence in gathering information. Vulnerable groups in society require particular care in news-gathering and their problems are covered in Chapter 9. Chapter 10 looks at the particular problems of publication and broadcast. This covers issues such as manipulation and watersheds. Chapter 11 covers the problems of harm and offence; issues of taste and decency, and deciding what is right to publish or broadcast. Chapter 12 looks at a range of dos and don'ts – issues that need to be considered in day-to-day working that spin out of the issues mentioned in other chapters.

Chapter 13 switches the reader to the second section of the book, moving from ethics to regulation. This chapter identifies different regulation systems and explains how they work.

Chapter 14 provides a history of print regulation in the UK and is followed by Chapter 15 on broadcast regulation. Chapter 16 introduces the concept of codes of conduct and how they work in the UK.

Chapter 17 examines press and internet regulation systems in the UK and Ireland and how these bodies operate. Chapter 18 does the same for the broadcast regulators in the UK and Ireland. In the final two chapters, 19 and 20, the examination of regulation is expanded to other countries and the future. I consider the problems raised by the growing opportunities for journalists to work across international borders, the use of new technology and of course the huge developments in the World Wide Web and spin-off technologies such as Facebook and Twitter and their impact on the future for ethics, journalism ethics and regulation.

I hope I have produced something that is readable, interesting and helpful. Throughout the text there are some exhibits, case studies, tables and figures to help to illustrate the major points. Most of all I hope this book will help explain why more emphasis should be put on good journalistic ethics if we are to avoid more bad media regulation. High standards of journalism can only be found from within, not imposed from without. Journalism can only improve if journalists and editors themselves are allowed to take ethics seriously.

Chapter 1

What are ethics?

This chapter discusses:

- Morality and the need for professional ethics

- Some of the theories identified by classical thinkers on morals

- How the key moral theories can be applied to journalism ethics

Ethics is defined by *The Concise Oxford English Dictionary* as 'the science of morals, treatise on this, moral principles or rules of conduct' (1964: 415). The word comes from the Greek *éthikos* meaning 'of or for morals'. Morals are described by the same dictionary as being concerned with 'the distinction between right and wrong'. This comes from the Latin *mos* (pl. *mores*) which means 'a measure or guiding rule of life; as determined not by the law but by men's will and pleasure' (Lewis and Short 1900). Clifford G. Christians et al. define ethics as: 'The liberal arts discipline that appraises voluntary human conduct insofar as it can be judged right or wrong in reference to determinative principles' (1998: 7).

In practice, ethics is a way of studying morality which allows decisions to be made when individuals face specific cases of moral dilemma. At their most praiseworthy, the journalist's tussles are going to be between the right of the public to know and some other moral tenet – perhaps the invasion of an individual's privacy – which would militate against publication. This right of the public to know springs from the theory of representative, democratic government. Mill (1991: 245) tells us:

> There is no difficulty in showing that the ideally best form of government is that in which the sovereignty, or supreme controlling power in the last resort, is vested in the entire aggregate of the community; every citizen not only having a voice in the exercise of that ultimate sovereignty, but being, at least occasionally, called on to take an actual part in the government, by the personal discharge of some public function, local or general.

In his excellent essay supporting this view, Mill makes it clear that correct and detailed information about how the country is run is an important prerequisite for any person involved in taking political decisions and this must surely apply, even if the decision taken is only how to vote every few years.

However, all too often the right to know is used as an excuse to publish circulation-boosting journalism. Whether this is designed to appeal to readers' prurient natures or pander to their prejudices does not seem to matter as long as there is a profit to be made from increasing sales.

Why do we need morality?

If we lived in a world that contained no other people, would we need to be moral? If no other entity existed and we were totally alone would our day-to-day existence contain any need to modify our behaviour in order to do what was morally right? How could we steal? There would be no one to murder or insult. The only person offended by our violence, bad language and behaviour would be ourselves. Those who believe in a deity would of course still say that morality was important, that God had laid down moral rules which must still be followed. But even those who do not believe in God would find it morally repugnant to do some things. Chopping down all the trees in the world, even if no one else was there, would be an act that many would consider to be immoral. Morality would still be an important consideration in your life in such circumstances; it would just have very different rules. Without anyone else, entirely marooned, there would be far fewer moral dilemmas to solve. Moral dilemmas are the penalty of our involvement with society, the price we pay for the benefits of living in close proximity with others. At one end of the spectrum this involves adhering to the law; at the other, being courteous and respectful to others.

Many philosophers have wondered why we have morals and where they come from. There seem to be three main theories. The first of these (and perhaps the oldest) is religion. Most religions have a code of morality connected to them, usually passed to the people from God through a prophet. These morals are usually enforced by some notion of reward in the afterlife for adherence, or damnation for continually breaking the code.

The second theory is that morals are a pact with society that allows us to gain the benefits of living with others. These are taught to us by our parents and others and are initially enforced by our parents and, later, more subtly but just as strongly, by society at large. Very few of us continue to do something that society generally thinks is wrong and opposes, certainly not that strand of society with which we bond. The final theory is that we are moral because we are naturally attuned to doing the right thing – that somehow we instinctively know what is right and wrong and that even if we were not taught how to behave, we would still instinctively behave well. This seems unlikely. One only has to watch young children for a short time to realise that their behaviour is entirely self-centred and only becomes more moral over time as they are trained by their parents and society.

Some elements of unacceptable social behaviour are identified as damaging enough to a society for the whole of that society to insist on their suppression. If, for example, we were to allow murder or serious violence to be used as methods of solving disputes, the benefits of society would soon cease for many people and day-to-day living would become largely unbearable. 'Might is right' is fine when you are one of the mighty, but none of us are mighty all of the time. It is in all our interests to ensure that we all adhere to the rules and that those who don't are punished. Because of the potential for breakdown, many societies formalise the rules under which that society exists. These become the laws of that particular society and allow it to lay down penalties for transgressors. The death penalty is the most extreme penalty society can impose for serious crimes whereas prison is generally seen as a milder form of punishment. The law is good at providing support for those moral dilemmas with which we are all in agreement, but is far less good at dealing with moral dilemmas about which there is considerable debate. The law is for saying what we must do or must not do; it is not good at saying what we ought to do or not do. The law can tell me that I mustn't kill or be violent to a member of my family if they annoy me, but it can't tell that I ought to be kind and generous to them whenever possible. This doesn't stop the law trying to regulate what we ought to do, of course, just that these tend to be the kind of laws that are more difficult to enforce. Laws about alcohol use, smoking and recreational drugs, for instance, throw up considerable differences of opinion within society. These are areas where someone's personal morality can conflict quite strongly with the law. One person might want to limit the hours when drink can be sold, but be quite happy about legalising cannabis; another might feel that it's not the state's business to decide when one can have an alcoholic drink but feel that all other recreational drugs should be illegal.

Laws normally apply to the whole of society but there are some actions that can only be perpetrated by certain people in certain positions. Some of these actions are so important to society that they require legislation. For instance, corruption of officials or politicians only involves a few people in powerful positions but the corruption may affect many other people. Consequently we enshrine such matters in our legal system. Other issues, a doctor's impropriety with a patient, for instance, may affect individuals but do not directly damage society and consequently are not enshrined directly in law. This is where professional ethics become important. A doctor who has an affair with a patient may be deemed to have breached professional ethics; he or she has not broken the law. A journalist is in the same position. For example, if he or she takes advantage of a situation and does not deal fairly with those to whom he or she owes loyalty (e.g. revealing a source who wishes to remain anonymous), then it is unlikely that society will suffer directly but the individual might well suffer. There are a wide range of issues in which journalists are involved that are not subject to the law but must be considered from an ethical viewpoint.

Why do journalists need professional ethics?

The concept of an ethical journalist may seem to be a contradiction in terms. The phrase 'you shouldn't believe all you read in the papers' sums up the attitude of many people. A reasonable definition of a *good* journalist is 'someone who gathers, in a morally justifiable way, topical, truthful, factually-based information of interest to the reader or viewer and then publishes it in a timely, entertaining and accurate manner to a mass audience'. However, all too often journalism falls far short of this ideal. Nor is this necessarily a description that would be used by all journalists to describe excellence in the profession. Many colleagues would describe a good journalist as having the professional virtues of 'getting the story' – the ability to find an interesting story, research it and return it to the news centre by the deadline. How the news was gathered and sourced, together with the degree of accuracy, would seem to be secondary considerations in this definition of a 'good journalist'. 'Don't let the facts get in the way of a good story' is an instruction that has been heard in more than one newsroom.

The suggestion that journalists are more concerned about the story than how they get it, or whether it is truthful, highlights the pressures under which those in the profession work. Commercial pressures to provide the most interesting stories combine with tight deadlines to make journalists more single-minded than perhaps they should be. Essentially this is an argument of functionality. Is a good journalist one with high principles or one who brings his employer, within the deadline, stories that will boost circulation? The reader may say the former even though they add support to the latter every time they buy a newspaper or tune in to a news bulletin. All too often a journalist can forget his or her loyalties to the reader in the rush to show loyalty to his or her employer.

But a good journalist surely needs to be both. In order to win the reader's trust, a journalist must show time after time that stories are accurate and truthful and this will involve ensuring they are gathered fairly. Gathering stories without due regard to professional morals and printing them without regard to truth might work well for a short period, but since the purpose of journalism is to report the truth, the trust a reader has for the journalist would soon evaporate and this means that the journalistic vehicle would become useless.

Many journalists believe that they should be trusted by their readers and that this is the mark of good journalism. But that trust must be earned and the only way to ensure trust from anyone is to never let them down. If you are always providing readers with stories that have been gathered fairly and are presented to them accurately and honestly to reveal as much truth as is possible, then readers will come to trust the journalist. No other method will work as well or stand the test of time.

Classical theory

Our moral obligations can be explained by a number of different theories, some of them overlapping and some completely at odds with one another. Some of these theories can help journalists try to determine the morality of their professional actions. I will consider a few of the more important theories and their implications for journalism. There are many other leading philosophers whose work I have ignored as being either derivative or less easy to apply directly to professional morality.

Aristotle

Aristotle (d. 322 BC) was a Greek philosopher who believed that the function of human beings was to pursue happiness or Eudaimonia. 'Eudaimonia is often translated as happiness, but that can be misleading. It is sometimes translated as flourishing. Which although slightly awkward, has more appropriate connotations' (Warburton 1998: 18). To achieve happiness, Aristotle said, one should live moderately. His theory is known as the 'golden mean'. He argued that one should live neither to excess nor to frugality but in moderation somewhere between the two. Aristotle's theory is extremely useful provided you can decide what is excess and what is frugality and where the mean lies. Bravery, he tells us, is a virtue that lies somewhere between the extremes of cowardice and rashness. When Aristotle talks about a mean, however, he is not talking about an average. To take the example of drinking: it is not to say that at one extreme is drinking far too much alcohol or at the other drinking none at all and that taking an average of say four units of alcohol a night is the mean. Aristotle contended that the right mean may well vary from person to person or even occasion to occasion. So there are people who say it is wrong to drink alcohol but they are often accused of being too self-satisfied and sanctimonious to be considered morally good. Nor are they necessarily acting in their own best interests as certainly some health research shows that a drink every now and again is good for you. Refusing to drink a toast to peace or friendship in Western Europe at a gathering of European delegates because you do not believe in drinking alcohol could be perceived as being mean-spirited. On the other hand, few people would see drinking fifteen units of alcohol every night of the week as acceptable for a whole variety of reasons. It is also bad for your health. Most would regard having a drink now and again as the 'golden mean'.

Aristotle also believed that one had to learn to be virtuous. Virtue was not something that was given to all automatically. It explained why children and animals had not achieved Eudaimonia.

> Virtue, then, being of two kinds, intellectual and moral, intellectual virtue in the main owes both its birth and its growth to teaching (for which reason it requires experience and time), while moral virtue comes about as the result of habit ... From this it is also plain that none of the moral virtues arise in us by nature; for nothing that exists in nature can form a habit that is contrary to its nature. For instance, the stone which by nature moves downwards cannot be habituated to move upwards, not even if one tries to train it by throwing it up ten thousand times ...
>
> (Aristotle 1980: 28)

A problem with Aristotle's theory about the mean, however, is that there are some virtues that seem to be absolutes. Truth, for instance, does not seem to be a virtue to be delivered in moderation. Either one is truthful or one is not. It is in its failure to address the issue of moral absolutes that Aristotle's theory is seen to be deficient.

Religion

> Jesus answered, 'The first is, "Hear, O Israel: the Lord our God, the Lord is one; you shall love the Lord your God with all your heart, and with all your soul, and with all your mind, and with all your strength." The second is this, "You shall love your neighbour as yourself." There is no other commandment greater than these.'
>
> (Mark 12: 29–31)

Religion is the basis of much moral teaching in the world. The West has been mainly influenced by Judaeo-Christian ethics whereas much of the Arab and North African world has seen Islam as a strong and uncompromising influence. In India, Hinduism is a powerful religious and social system, which includes the use of the caste system as the basis of society.

Although theoretically religious moral teaching requires a belief in God to underpin it, this seems in practice to be unimportant. In Britain, and indeed most Western countries, Christianity has become so entrenched within the culture that much moral teaching and thought comes from it without being based on active belief. Our fundamental structures of right and wrong, good and evil tend to be based on the Bible's teachings.

While its use by Christians is understandable, many people in the West who claim not to believe in God also use this ethical system to underpin their moral values, if only because they have absorbed the established cultural moral underpinning without much thought as to its origins. Christians accept the entire teaching. However, those who do not believe in God seem to be able to accept the guidance on living a good life without the religious belief and to use it as an ethical system.

The main criticism of religion as an ethical system is the need for faith. What if God is not a loving and moral God? Using religion, we judge our moral code by our own interpretation of God (be that personal or cultural) and what he expects of us and not vice versa.

Ethical egoism

Aristotle's view that people should behave so as to achieve happiness is challenged by some philosophers as being fundamentally flawed. To do what is right because it makes us happy is just self-interest, they claim. Talking about the duty to be truthful, German philosopher Immanuel Kant (1993: 15) says that 'To be truthful from duty is, however, quite different from being truthful from fear of disadvantageous consequences; in the first case the concept of the action itself contains a law for me, while in the second I must first look around elsewhere to see what the results for me might be connected with the action.' Kant believed that morality is measured by the human will; if our will to do something is good, then the action is moral. But to do something because the consequences of not doing it might be damaging to ourselves is merely self-interest.

Writing about the ideas of Plato, H.A. Prichard (1949: 110–11) goes further and proposes that what Socrates must have meant in 'introducing the subject of the Idea of good' was 'that in all action what we are striving to bring into existence is – not what is good but – what is really good for us, or for our own good'. He goes on to say: 'If we accept the idea we shall be involved in very awkward consequences. For we shall then be forced to allow (1) that there is really no such thing as a conscientious action or a benevolent or a malevolent action, and also (2) that there is really no difference in the motive between the acts of a so-called good man and those of a so-called bad man' (ibid.: 112).

Ethical egoism suggests that all morality is in reality merely self-interest. If doing my duty either brings good consequences or simply makes me feel happier because I have done my duty, then surely my action is indistinguishable from self-interest?

Utilitarianism

> Utility, or the Greatest Happiness Principle, holds that actions are right in proportion as they tend to promote happiness, wrong as they tend to produce the reverse of happiness.
>
> (John Stuart Mill 1991: 137)

Utilitarianism or teleology is also widely accepted in the West as an ethical system. Jeremy Bentham (1748–1832) and John Stuart Mill (1806–73) are usually credited as being its most significant proponents. Utilitarians believe that an action that produces an excess of beneficial effects over harmful ones must be the right one. Certainly this a system that has considerable appeal for journalists. It justifies, for example, ruining the life of a children's home superintendent by exposing him as a child abuser on the basis that it has saved children of the future from a good deal of misery and brought some small measure of justice to children (perhaps now adults) who have suffered at his hand in the past.

One problem with utilitarianism is that it depends on who makes the decision. For instance, one could justify the killing of a homeless down-and-out who has no family in order that his organs could be donated to several desperately ill patients on the basis that several people could live with consequent benefits to their families for the loss of only one life. But this depends on each unit of happiness being the same, something Friedrich Nietzsche (1844–1900) condemned ruthlessly. He believed that some people were more important than others. Writing about the English utilitarians in less than complimentary terms, he said:

> Not one of all these ponderous herd animals ... wants to know or scent that the 'general welfare' is not an ideal, or a goal, or a concept that can be grasped at all, but only an emetic – that what is right for one cannot by any means therefore be right for another, that the demand for one morality for all is detrimental to precisely the higher men, in short there exists an order of rank between man and man, consequently also between morality and morality.

> (Nietzsche 1973: 139)

One can argue not only that one person is more important than another but also that actions have different perceived values. For instance, money given to a beggar has more significance, in moral terms, when that money comes from a poor student than from a millionaire. Utilitarianism also does not require any measurement of the motive of the action. Provided the consequence is an increase in the sum of happiness, an evil act can be justified.

Kant: the categorical imperative

The German Immanuel Kant (1724–1804) is a highly significant figure in modern philosophy. He helped to develop the concept of deontology or duty ethics. Kant believed that a moral act was one that denied self and followed only obligation. If I have promised to meet someone tonight then I am morally obliged to do that regardless of my inclinations. If, however, I have made no such promise, then I am free to follow my inclinations. But whatever I do would be merely a matter of taste and not a moral act.

Kant went on to develop the theory of universalisability. This determines that: '[I] ought never to act in such a way that I could not also will that my maxim should be a universal law' (Kant 1990: 18). Kant identified three different sorts of actions, or imperatives, that are useful in identifying how moral actions work.

The first is technical imperatives. A good journalist must be able to take a quick, accurate note and many learn shorthand in order to accomplish this. This is a technical imperative: they have a good shorthand note. Next Kant identified hypothetical imperatives. These are concerned only with prudential action, or those actions that it would be sensible (but not necessarily moral) to take. If you were about to be run over by a car, then a hypothetical imperative would be: 'To avoid being run over, run fast to your left.' This would be a prudent action and has no moral component. On the other hand, it is a duty to maintain one's life and so there may well be an element of the final imperative contained here. Categorical imperatives enjoin action completely without qualification; they deal solely in absolute duties; duties carried out solely because the will has determined that these types of actions are moral actions. This deontological approach to morals means that if one has determined a categorical imperative that one must not lie, then that is what one should do regardless of the circumstances. Kant's theory allows the development of a set of universal laws that are a form of moral code. This system can be used by journalists to develop a linked set of categorical imperatives around professional practice. This is the basis for codes of conduct or practice.

Kant also believed that one would have to examine the motives of a person to see whether their behaviour was good or bad. Their intentions are more important than the act itself, certainly more important than the consequences in terms of morality. If they acted solely from a sense of duty and not out of self-interest, then their action could well be morally justifiable no matter what the consequences. If a journalist were to report something that was not true, despite thorough checking (perhaps he or she had been lied to), then the journalist could not be blamed for the consequences, even if these were damaging. He or she would have been behaving morally in printing the truth as he or she had determined it to be.

However, Kant's formulation does not handle conflicts of interest well. For example, if a journalist were asked by police to suppress the story of a kidnap in order to protect the victim's life, how could the journalist not publish when it should be a categorical imperative to publish known information; yet to protect someone's life when such protection is required must surely also be a categorical imperative? Since much of the ethical debate within the media is balancing the right to publish against some other right, such as a person's right to privacy, Kant is not always that helpful, although his theories do allow the building of codes of practice.

Kant believed that every person had equal value and the same right to have their view taken into consideration. He thought that the end did not justify the means. Only by acting from duty could one be said to be acting morally, and the consequence was not something that could always be foreseen. Prichard does not think Kant's use of the categorical imperative gets us out of the difficulty of moral decision making, however. We can't use the excuse of a 'moral command' to force us to act morally: 'it should be noted that the summary attempt to elucidate the nature of moral obligation by the analogy of law ... is only mischievous, because it represents our being morally bound to do some action as if it were our being commanded to do it' (Prichard 1949: 95).

Others find Kant difficult because of this inflexible and absolute nature of categorical imperatives. The NUJ's code of conduct, for instance, says that a journalist must never reveal the identity of a confidential source of information. While many journalists stick by this absolutely, there are some who feel that it is not possible to be so inflexible. Nick Martin-Clarke, for instance, gave evidence against a former confidential source who he claimed had confessed a murder to him (http://www.bjr.org.uk/data/2003/no2_martinclark, accessed 11 January 2010). What conditions might tempt you to go back on a promise to a source?

Ross

The philosopher Sir William David Ross (1877–1971) was a deontologist and took the view that we all have duties of fidelity. In other words, we are bound by our own words or acts. If we sign a contract, we are duty-bound not to break it. If we make a promise, we are bound to keep it. He also believed in the concept of reparation. If you do 'wrong' you are duty-bound to undo the wrong and make good the damage as far as possible. This duty extends to gratitude. If someone performs a good act for you, you are under an obligation to return the favour at some point. Ross believes that this duty of gratitude can extend to friends, relatives, employers and employees.

Ross's ideas have a direct application to journalism as it can be said that journalists have a duty of gratitude to readers, advertisers, employers and so on. We will use this view of duty a lot throughout this book, although I will refer to it more often as a duty of loyalty as I think this better describes the relationship. I might be grateful that you are reading this book, but I do not see that

that entails me in any duty. But my loyalty, induced by that duty of gratitude, will mean that I will produce the most accurate, informative book that I can.

Ross also talks about other duties:

- *Beneficence* – our duty to improve the lot of others.
- *Justice* – we all have a duty to see that people get what they deserve, whether this is pleasure or punishment.
- *Self-improvement* – we have a duty to try to improve our own condition of virtue, intelligence or happiness.
- *Non-injury* – our duty not to hurt others or allow them to be hurt if we can prevent it.

Ross chaired the first Royal Commission into the press in 1947.

The language of morals

The former [objectivists] lay stress on the fixed principles that are handed down by the father, the latter [subjectivists] on the new decisions which have to be made by the son.

(R.M. Hare 1995: 77)

Much of the ethical debate over the last century has revolved around the analysis of the language of morals and what the words 'good', 'bad', 'ought', 'right', 'wrong' and so on mean. A number of theories have been developed by philosophers such as G.E. Moore, A.J. Ayers and R.M. Hare which attempt to shed some light in the area of value words and our use of them. Most of these theories are essentially theories about theories and as such require much supportive argument. However, Table 1.1 summarises the main ideas. To put some of the theories in Table 1.1 into context, let us look at a dilemma and how the various theories would address it. I promise a friend that I will meet her in town at six o'clock. Is it acceptable to break my promise in order to rescue someone from a burning building, thus making me late for my appointment? A motivist might say 'yes' as my motive for breaking my promise would be to save a life or 'no' if my duty was to keep my promise. Consequentialists believe that only the consequence of the act is significant. Therefore, a consequentialist might say 'no' as the consequence of braving the flames would be to break my promise or 'yes' as the consequence is to save a life. A deontologist believes that the act of promising to do something performs an act which by its very nature obliges one to carry it out regardless of the consequences. I have promised to meet my friend at six o'clock; if I do not do so I am breaking my promise (no matter what the excuse) and that is not acceptable. From this viewpoint a journalist would automatically be acting immorally if he or she did not gather truthful information and disseminate it to the public because, by the nature of the act, that is what journalists should be obliged to do. Clearly deontologists need to be careful with their promises!

What is a right? Why do people have them?

The importance of laws and ethical matters to society has already been discussed but another issue that is often talked about is that of rights. 'I know my rights,' we say. The United Nations Declaration of Human Rights was written following the horrors of the Second World War and was closely followed by the European Convention on Human Rights. The UK government included these rights into UK law with the Human Rights Act 1998.

The Concise Oxford English Dictionary describes rights as 'being entitled to privilege or immunity, thing one is entitled to' (1964: 1075). However, rights are not things we have automatically and in

Table 1.1 The language of morals

Naturalism	If a moral judgement can be reduced to some other branch of science, then ethics must be naturalistic. In other words, if I do something 'good' in order to please someone else, then that is a matter of psychology rather than ethics.
Non-naturalism	If ethics is a true branch of science by itself with its own laws, if the world contains moral elements in the same way it has physical elements, then ethics must be non-natural. Followers of religion see morality in this way: morals are not a branch of science, but the divine will of God. These people are non-naturalists.
Emotivism	Emotivists claim that all ethics are about how people feel, not in the sense of feeling right or wrong, or indeed any real evaluative phrase at all. Emotivists believe it is impossible to verify moral judgements scientifically.
Subjectivism	A subjective theory of morals is one in which ethical judgements are neither true nor false or if those judgements are true or false they are always individualistically applicable to the psychology of the person who utters them. If I believe that it is wrong to steal, but you believe it is all right, then we are both right although I may well disapprove of your actions. All we can argue about is how we feel about the act, not the moral questions of the act itself. Your right to believe your beliefs would be as valid as mine because there are no provable precepts, only individual psychology. This takes on an important role when comparing international sets of ethics, particularly in journalism.
Objectivism	An objective theory is one that is not subjectivistic. It allows holders to say that there can be a set of guiding principles which will hold true for all, and we can then debate the rights and wrongs of an issue and not just how we feel about it.
Motivism	Motivists believe that only the motive for an action needs to be considered when looking at whether it was a moral act. Even if the act leads to disastrous consequences, if the motive was pure, then the action was a moral one. Kant believed that it was immoral to tell a lie to hide a friend from a mad axe-murderer even if the consequence was that the friend was later found and killed.
Consequentialism	Consequentialists are little concerned about motivation. Provided the act has good consequences, it is moral. The end justifies the means.
Deontology	Deontologists believe that the very words themselves carry an obligation. They believe that neither the motive nor the consequences are of significance, only the nature of the act itself. If you promise to do something, then the obligation contained in the word 'promise' leads to a duty to fulfil the act no matter what the circumstances. This has particular relevance when we look at the punishment of crime. Do we punish the motive, the consequence or the act? We punish the act, but use the motive and consequence as mitigating factors. It is against the law to steal, but stealing a few items of food from a major supermarket to feed one's hungry children would not be punished as severely as stealing thousands of pounds from gullible investors (one would hope!).

many areas of the world breaches of human rights are commonplace. Human rights in this country are ours by agreement – a pact we have with the authorities of the country in which we live but it is important to understand that these are inalienable rights and cannot be removed. They exist purely by virtue of the political system in which we live. In many countries that right is underscored by a constitution or a 'bill of rights' which lays down the rights or special privileges citizens can claim while listing the responsibilities that follow from them. By living in a democracy, however structured, a complex structure of rights and obligations is built up. For instance, we have a right to be considered innocent until proven guilty, if we should happen to face accusations in a court of law, because the law grants us that right. In exchange, we are obliged to live in peaceful coexistence with our neighbours under the law. If our neighbour annoys us, we don't punch him on the nose, we take him to court. We give up our right to punish wrongdoers ourselves, to those we elect or appoint for the purpose. We also give up our ability to escape punishment in return for protection under the law. There are a number of other rights that we have which all have consequent duties that we are obliged to fulfil to ensure that others have their rights.

The idea of human rights grew up with the theories of democratic government in the seventeenth century. Thomas Hobbes (1588–1679), a British philosopher, believed that the only form of rule must be authoritarian as he believed this was the only way to have firm control and peace. Life in 'the state of nature', according to Hobbes, 'is solitary, poor, nasty, brutish and short'. The way to improve matters was for people to stick to the rules, to abide by 'covenants of mutual trust'. But, said Hobbes, these covenants must be enforced by an absolute power as only 'the terror of some punishment' would keep men to the covenants. Hobbes argued that this power should be a single person, probably the king, as then his self-interest would be directly tied to the country, as a single person would not have internal conflicts, compromise secrecy or change decisions depending on who turned up to debate and vote.

Those who opposed these views pointed out that once one has an absolute power, then there is no turning back to having control over the covenants. Having given absolute power to someone, they then have absolute power to ensure one can't change one's mind. An absolute power almost always crushes any dissent. There are plenty of examples of such absolute powers around the world and changing them proves to be extremely difficult whether from without or within, as we found to our cost in Iraq.

John Locke (1632–1704) argued differently. For Locke, the state of nature is one in which a man who is wronged by another has the right to punish him. However, since Locke accepted that there are several reasons why this may not work, he believed men should come together and give up their right to escape punishment by authorising society to punish them, and therefore gain the right to have those who transgress against them punished by those elected so to do. By agreeing to give up our right to escape punishment, we allow the law to be enforced when we might be strong enough to enforce it ourselves, ensuring that others are punished at times when we might be too weak to arrange punishment ourselves. Locke pointed out that for this to work there must be law above all and that tyranny – absolute power – of any sort must therefore be wrong. Locke said that the only sensible way to live was to give up the right to escape punishment and determine the law in return for appointing people who determined the law and ensured that those who broke it were punished. As part of this compact, the people gain rights. These are not privileges, granted to them by the government, because this would imply that these rights could be taken away for misbehaviour or simply at the whim of the government. This would make a mockery of such rights as the right to a fair trial or to be presumed innocent until proven guilty. Our pact was solely to give up our ability to escape punishment in favour of the opportunity to appoint the lawmakers.

John Stuart Mill (1806–73) supported this view, saying that there was no difficulty showing that the best form of government is one that is 'vested in the entire aggregate of the community; every citizen having not just a voice ... but being called upon to take an actual part in the government, by the personal discharge of some public function local or general' (Mill, *On Liberty and Other Essays*).

Perhaps the most important exponent of rights was Thomas Paine (1737–1809) who wrote *Common Sense and the Rights of Man*. Paine was an Englishman who fled first to France and then America because of his unpopular republican views and was influential in the growth of American civil rights and the development of both the French and American revolutions and subsequent building of their republics. He believed that rights grew out of nature, but that we had to surrender some of these natural rights of intellect, mind or religion on entering society, exchanging them for 'civil rights': 'He deposits this right in the common stock of society, and takes the arm of society, of which he is part, in preference and in addition to his own' (Paine 1993: 90). For this to happen all men had to be equal, with equal rights from birth that should equally be supported by their civil rights. No man could be raised above another without the application of the law fairly applied to all.

Both Locke and Paine believed that people who are appointed to make and uphold the law should be responsible to those who appoint them. It is at this stage that the media becomes important as it has a significant role to play in ensuring that those appointed to draw up the law answer to those who appoint them. In a Hobbesian media there is no need to challenge and test government. It could not inform voters as there would be no voters. There would be little point in criticising or challenging a leadership that had absolute power, first, because that power would be certain to crush this act of dissent and, second, because there would simply be no purpose in it. Much better to pretend that things were fine and only talk about the good in life rather than point out that there were lots of things wrong about which you could do nothing. There would almost certainly be a media of entertainment and a news service providing information and limited education. But it would not be attempting to mediate between government and governed. It would be tightly controlled by the absolute power and so, while it would need to have some thought about professional practice, many of the ethical issues required of a media operating in a Western-style democracy would not be required. In a rights-based society, however, Paine said that the people of England had three fundamental rights:

1   to choose their own governors;
2   to cashier them for misconduct;
3   to frame a government for themselves.

(Paine 1993: 64)

This right to choose our own leaders, to kick them out of office if needs be and to frame our own government, and to be involved in policy making even if only by being involved in the debate, does require a fully functioning, questioning media. It would clearly be impossible for us all to quiz politicians on their views and policies, but we can be informed through the media in all its forms.

This view of the inalienability of human rights and its importance to democratic systems of government has permeated much of the radical political thinking of the past three hundred years. Much of the US constitution can be identified as coming directly from the theories of Locke and Paine (indeed Paine was directly involved with the likes of Jefferson in writing it), while much of Western political democracy is based on their theories. The human rights that are now codified in the European Convention on Human Rights are fairly extensive, but the ones that apply mainly to our consideration of journalism include the right to:

- freedom of speech;
- freedom of conscience and opinion;
- a fair trial;
- be presumed innocent until proven guilty;
- be free from discrimination;
- respect for private and family life; and
- the right to free elections.

Human rights are often enshrined in law. Human rights in the UK are ours by virtue of the Human Rights Act 1998 and the European Convention on Human Rights. In many countries human rights are upheld by a constitution or a 'bill of rights' which identifies the rights of its citizens as part of that constitutional contract between state and individual. The laws to which citizens must adhere because they have agreed to give up their opportunity to avoid punishment are drawn up by those we elect to govern, whom we can remove if sufficient of us agree that they are not governing as we would wish. By living in a democracy, however organised, our rights should be protected by the law; for instance, we have a right to be considered innocent until proven guilty if we should happen to face accusations in a court of law. In exchange, we live in peaceful coexistence with our neighbours under the law and accept that if we don't, we will be obliged to face that court and explain ourselves and accept the court's judgment. It is to provide a forum to debate how this should work and to inform us about how our leaders have lived up to their promise that is one of the media's most important jobs. We need freedom of speech, and from it freedom of the media to protect our rights and our democracy.

Further reading and support material

There are a number of books examining the different approaches that can be taken to ethics and moral reasoning. Harman Gilbert (1977) *The Nature of Morality: An Introduction to Ethics* (Oxford, Oxford University Press) is a useful introduction to some of the ideas outlined above and this can be augmented by P. Singer (1994) *Ethics* (Oxford, Oxford University Press). There are numerous books examining the arguments of Kant, Aristotle, Bentham and Mill, among others, and these can be found in any reasonable bookshop or library. For an excellent explanation of the rights of man, it's still difficult to beat Thomas Paine (1993) *Common Sense and The Rights of Man* (London, Phoenix Press).

Chapter 2

News: towards a definition

This chapter discusses:

- What makes a news story

- Why it is important to understand news in order to grasp journalism ethics

- How news, as demanded by today's audiences, poses particular ethical dilemmas

The media are full of information: reviews, listings, features, profiles, forthcoming events, sports, advertisements and news. Media consumers expect this information to follow ethical norms and yet sometimes it doesn't. Why is this?

In order to understand some of the temptations that lead journalists, on occasion, to behave unethically, and particularly to distort and twist the truth, we need to know what it is that makes something newsworthy and therefore attracts the journalist's attention in the first place. What is it about an event that makes it stand out as newsworthy when there are scores of other events or pieces of information that someone, somewhere, would like a journalist to use on the news? Until we know what a newsworthy event is, it is very difficult to understand the problems, both practical and ethical, facing the journalist who wishes to report newsworthy events.

Practical problems

There is a difference between a newsworthy event and news. A newsworthy event will not necessarily become news, just as news is often about an event that is not, in itself, newsworthy. We can define news as an event that is recorded in the news media, regardless of whether it is about a newsworthy event. The very fact of its transmission means that it is regarded as news, even if we struggle to understand why that particular story has been selected from all the other events happening at the same time that have been ignored. News selection is subjective so not all events seen as newsworthy by some people will make it to the news. All journalists are familiar with the scenario where they are approached by someone with the words 'I've got a great story for you'. For them, it is a major news event, but for the journalist it might be something to ignore.

One of the problems with evaluating news decision-making is that news is analog rather than digital. We cannot say 'this is news and this is not' for each event we come across, as a particular event's newsworthiness varies depending on the circumstances surrounding it and the target audience group. For instance, to find a bag abandoned in a hotel lobby is probably not newsworthy – it might be surrounded by others with its owner trying to check out at reception – but to find a bag abandoned in a quiet corner of a railway station might well demand more urgent action and become a news story. Whether an event is used as news may also depend on other criteria, such as the space available in a paper or bulletin or the number of other good stories about. Government spin doctors have been known to issue press releases containing bad news on days they know the media will be full with news of a royal wedding or other major news story.

There are many factors that influence the choice of good news stories. Threshold criteria must exist to separate events that make it into the news from those that do not. Some of the threshold criteria for news are the circumstances surrounding the medium (see Exhibit 2.1).

Exhibit 2.1 Threshold criteria for news

Space: A newspaper with only a few pages will have a higher threshold than one with a lot of space to fill. The less space available, the more newsworthy the event must be to make it into the newspaper. Broadcasting regularly has a higher threshold than newspapers because it has less space.

Logistics: Several observers have identified the physical difficulties of putting a news report together as an important criterion in its selection. Paul Rock explains in a chapter called 'News as Eternal Recurrence' that:

> in place of the random search [for news], news gathering takes routine forms ... Journalists position themselves so that they have access to institutions which generate a useful volume of reportable activity at useful intervals. Some of these institutions do of course make themselves visible by means of dramatisation, or through press releases and press agents. Others are known regularly to produce consequential events. The courts, sports grounds and parliament mechanically manufacture news which is effortlessly assimilated by the press. (In Cohen and Young 1973: 64)

News is more likely to be reported from places where reporters are already working. An editor cannot afford to have reporters sitting around twiddling their thumbs waiting for unpredictable events. It is more likely, therefore, that a report from a criminal court will be used rather than a newsworthy event from a source that cannot be predicted, even if the unpredictable event is more newsworthy as measured by other objective criteria.

Time: Time plays an important part in any news-gathering operation both in terms of getting the story and in terms of when the event became newsworthy. An event must be topical within the period of publication. No newspaper wants to carry a story that has happened earlier than the publication of the previous edition. A radio or TV bulletin prefers to update the news given on the last bulletin while a website will get the news out as soon as possible.

Philip Schlesinger, in *Putting Reality Together: BBC News* (1978), supports the above ideas by identifying time constraints and logistics as reasons why journalists alter the threshold requirement for a newsworthy event to become news.

What do other people think is news?

The criteria listed above affect the choice of news stories but are mainly to do with the medium in which the stories are to appear. However, there are other factors that distinguish the events that become news from those that do not.

One of the first groups in the UK to define 'news' was the Royal Commission on the Press of 1947–49 (the Ross Commission). It said:

> There are, however, certain elements common to all conceptions of news. To be news an event must first be interesting to the public, and the public for this purpose means for each paper the people who read that paper, and others like them. Second, and equally important, it must be new, and newness is measured in newspaper offices in terms of minutes.
>
> (1949: 103)

The Commission went on to list items of interest identified in a questionnaire as follows: sport; news about people; news about strange or amusing adventures; tragedies; accidents; crimes; 'news whose sentiment or excitement brings some colour into life' (1949: 104). In the 1960s, Alastair Hetherington, editor of *The Guardian* newspaper, drew up a list of news priorities for new staff, which contained the seven factors outlined in Exhibit 2.2. Although Hetherington's list is of some use for media decision making, it is not as helpful as it could be for understanding news; it is the distillation of his considerable experience and professional skill.

Exhibit 2.2 Alastair Hetherington's news priorities

- **Significance**: social, economic, political
- **Drama**: excitement, entertainment
- **Surprise**: unpredictability, newness
- **Personalities**: royalty, showbusiness
- **Sex**: scandal, crime
- **Numbers**: scale of the event
- **Proximity**: the geographical closeness of the event

There are many other ideas about what news is: 'When a dog bites a man, that is not news, because it happens so often. But if a man bites a dog, that is news' (John B. Bogart, City editor, *New York Sun*, 1873–90); 'News is People'; 'News is what they talk about down at the local pub'; 'News is something someone wants to keep secret'. While all descriptions like these have an element of truth and wit, they are not much help in sorting news from other information. After all, what if, for instance, the dog carries a strange new disease that is transmittable to man by biting and has only been recognised by medical science that week? The unusual element in the story means this certainly would be news.

So what about academics? Have they done any better? Johan Galtung and Mari Ruge were among the first academics to try to explain news. Their work is substantial and influential. It underpins the thinking of John Hartley in *Understanding News* (1982) and is used by John Venables in *What is News?* (1993) and was revisited as a major theory of news by Harcup and O'Neill (2001).

Galtung and Ruge originally published their research in the *Journal of International Peace Research* in 1965. It was a study of the presentation of the Congo, Cuba and Cyprus crises in four foreign newspapers, looking at the structure of foreign news. An extract entitled 'Structuring and Selecting News' was published in *The Manufacture of News: Deviance, Social Problems and the Mass Media*, edited by Stanley Cohen and Jock Young (1973). Galtung and Ruge saw news broken down into two categories: general news value and news values of particular importance to Western media (see Exhibit 2.3).

Harcup and O'Neill draw on these last two lists to develop a more up-to-date version of their own that suggests that potential items must fall into one or more of the following categories:

The power elite: stories concerning powerful individuals or organizations;
Celebrity: stories concerning those already famous;
Entertainment: stories concerning sex and show business;
Surprise: stories containing an element of surprise;
Bad news: conflict or tragedy;
Good news: stories with positive overtones;
Magnitude: stories perceived as sufficiently significant;
Relevance: stories perceived to be relevant to the audience;
Follow-ups: stories about matters already in the news;
Media agenda: stories that fit the news organization's own agenda.

(Harcup and O'Neill 2001: 279)

Useful though these lists are, they are all attempts to identify news from experience, or observation of what actually ends up in a newspaper or news broadcast. They identify a series of criteria that help explain why those stories became news, that is why they were in the newspaper or broadcast, but they do not explain why they were chosen in the first place by the news selectors out of the thousands of events that also fulfil the criteria but were ignored; nor do they fully explain why readers buy the eventual product. It's also worth remembering that while Galtung and Ruge's list is used extensively in recent textbooks to explain why events are newsworthy and still has some relevance, news values (in terms of what is now significant in terms of sales) have changed enormously over the past forty years. Even a cursory examination of a newspaper of the 1960s and a modern newspaper shows that now there is far less international news, far fewer stories about politics, less industrial news and more gossip, more sport and more entertainment and celebrity news. This change is not well explained by Galtung and Ruge or Harcup and O'Neill. Nor are we able to tell from Galtung and Ruge's analysis which stories were chosen by the news editors of their samples and which news was ignored. We are unable to compare other events that happened at that time but did not make the newspapers, not for reasons that were in Galtung and Ruge's list but by reason of other criteria which we may not know.

More helpful in our development of an analysis of why events become news are criteria identified by John Venables. He comes to the conclusion that 'change' and 'security concerns' are 'the fundamental factors which motivate attentiveness in an audience' (1993: 34). Although some changes are good, they all have threatening implications. Learning to deal with change requires intelligence and planning. He goes on to describe the importance of change: 'Without change, information cannot be interpreted as news. Change is important because it involves uncertainty, which in turn generates attention and concern' (ibid.).

Exhibit 2.3 Galtung and Ruge's news criteria

The list of general news values relies on logical categorisation:

Frequency. The timespan of an event affects how it is used. If an event takes much longer to unfold than can be handled by the publication frequency of the media concerned, then it is 'marked' by the issuing of reports or sub-events.

Threshold. The size of a story. John Hartley explains this: 'There is a threshold below which an event will not be reported at all (the threshold intensity varies in intensity between, for instance, local and national news)' (1982: 76).

Unambiguity. Clear-cut events that require little explanation are more likely to be used as news.

Meaningfulness. An event which coincides with the cultural assumptions of the journalist or the target audience is more likely to be used. (There is a tie-in with *unambiguity* here – a meaningful event is less likely to be ambiguous.) This is a similar criterion to Hetherington's *significance* (Exhibit 2.2).

Consonance. Something that accords with the media's preconceptions is more likely to be reported. It also works the other way around: an event is more likely to be reported in accordance with the preconceptions of the reporter.

▶

Unexpectedness. Also appears on Hetherington's list as *surprise* (Exhibit 2.2).

Continuity. If an event is already making news, then it is likely it will continue to make the news.

Composition. An event might make the news even though it is not in itself that newsworthy, merely to balance the media presentation. In other words, a weak foreign story might be added to a radio bulletin merely to balance the home-and-away elements of the bulletin.

There are a further four news values of particular importance to Western media:

Elite nations. They believe there is a bias in Western media towards reporting events in the first world. This is also hinted at by Hetherington in *proximity* (Exhibit 2.2), but is not quite the same thing.

Elite persons. The activities of those perceived as important are of more interest than the activities of people considered less socially significant. Hetherington talks about *personalities* (Exhibit 2.2).

Personalisation. Events being presented as the actions of a particular person, e.g. 'Blair backs Bush in Iraq', to invent an example.

Negativity. The view that bad news is 'good' news. Only news that is negative is used in the media. A complaint supported by Martyn Lewis, the television news reader, who campaigned some years ago for a good news channel.

Change is a key determiner of news, but we are talking here of step changes, not gradual change. If a plane is in the sky one minute and then crashed on the ground the next, that's a change. If a production plant is in full production one minute and then due to close the next, that's a change; if a motorway has cars bowling along at full speed one minute and then piles of wreckage strewn across the road the next, that's another change, and they are all newsworthy. Anything that will change someone's life is potentially newsworthy as we are all nervous of change to some extent, even though we know change can be both good or bad.

Familiarity or meaningfulness is another factor that is identified by Galtung and Ruge and other commentators that needs to be carefully considered. The more familiar the subject of an event, the more interested we are in it. Venables tries to put this the other way around and talks about the boundary of relevance. By this he means 'the limits of which are determined by our ability to understand and model our relational links with others and therefore their relevance to our own security concerns' (Venables 1993: 34). Galtung and Ruge identify it as meaningfulness. These concepts are linked to cultural assumptions and understanding. We understand the way things are done within our own cultures and are able to make assumptions about them that make it easier for us to identify if we are interested in them and therefore if they are news. Outside our own cultures, we may not so easily understand the dynamics of a particular story. We may need to have explained why an enmity exists, or why apparently disparate groups of society are allies. Our understanding of health delivery in the UK, for instance, is posited around a universal health service that is free at the point of delivery. For this reason, the fierce debate over healthcare in the US that followed the election of Barack Obama was not well covered in the UK as we are unfamiliar with concepts such as health insurance, hospital bills and prescription drug advertising on TV. To have to explain these concepts in every story would take more space or time than most editors were prepared to give and so the stories tended to be about the inter-party rows and Obama's chances of getting the legislation he sought.

All the observers, academics and practitioners discussed (except Venables) categorise what is news but there is little consideration of what we mean by newsworthiness. There are many journalists who have developed their sense of what is newsworthy, their 'nose for news', by copying the reactions of more experienced colleagues. We can hardly be surprised if a new reporter decides that something is newsworthy if it makes the news editor happy or excited. Unfortunately this empirical approach has the same drawbacks as all observational views on news-gathering. Observation alone is never enough by itself to deal with new circumstances. What happens when a new news editor takes over in the office and seems to work by different criteria? Are there really different criteria or has the inexperienced journalist merely misunderstood them? Students on journalism courses often find it frustrating when one tutor seems to advise leading with this angle while the next tutor appears to favour that angle. In fact, when the two tutors talk, their apparent differences quickly disappear and an agreed angle normally appears. Journalists need to test their hypotheses about news criteria under a number of different circumstances if they are to become more efficient at news selection.

The Royal Commission used the word 'new' to indicate that the news item is recent. Since this can easily be confused with the word 'news', I will use 'topical' to indicate newness in the rest of this chapter. But remember, newness to a monthly magazine will not be the same as newness to a daily newspaper or a website, which will have different views of newness from a radio bulletin with an hourly schedule. Some events continue over a long period and so remain topical. Wars, for instance, remain topical despite their extended life-cycle. All events are subsets of other events. The Second World War was a subset in the flow of European political history. The retreat of the British Army from Dunkirk was a subset of the Second World War. We could no doubt find subsets of Dunkirk. Each of these would be handled in different ways by publications with different publication frequencies. A magazine that only publishes every ten years, assuming there were such a thing, might lead its 1940s edition with a story about the Second World War headlined: 'European clash leads to global war: Allies triumph.' Weekly papers of the period looked at the retreat from Dunkirk in its totality, while radio bulletins and daily papers of the time broke that episode into subsets.

Almost everyone, academic and practitioner alike, agrees that there has to be a new or topical element for an item of information to be news. There is also widespread agreement that news needs to interest the public. In modern terminology, the general public is known as the target group and what the Ross Commission called 'the people who read that paper and others like them' would now be described as the target readership. This is a subsection of the general population that can be clearly identified, whether they actually read that publication or not. The *Daily Mail*, which has a clear view of its target readership (one of the reasons why it is successful), aims at women, aged 25–50, who are, or aspire to be, middle to upper middle class with a traditional view about life and therefore a propensity to see their purpose as family carers, even if this is manifested in a career which will provide financial security for the family. The difficulties arise when we start to consider precisely what it is that is of interest to the target group. We can easily draw up a list of items that interest different target groups: sex, war, crime, health and so on, but this is still based on observation. We need to move beyond pure observation and start to look at what makes for newsworthiness – or, what might be a better description in the context in which we are working, what attracts readers.

For this is one of the main difficulties. Academics and serious commentators regularly express their concern about the dumbing down of news, and newspapers in particular. They are concerned that newspapers should be the serious-minded imparters of information to the general public in the constant political debate that is central to democracy. Unfortunately, the average reader is less interested in such issues unless they can be persuaded by the newspaper that this has a direct effect on their lives. What does have a direct effect are stories that are about security change that directly impinge on them and those they care about, and those that directly or indirectly effect how they live their lives. When it comes to this second category, I believe that gossip and its impact on readers is often underplayed by commentators, many of whom attempt to limit news to its public sphere context where its purpose is to develop debate and aid decision making in the public forum. In fact, most readers want to apply intelligence they can gather directly to their own lives and this means being concerned about issues that directly affect their decision making and their moral approach to living. This means that gossip plays a much stronger part in the ordinary person's life than many commentators would like, and that news is focused on making issues easy to understand (even if they're not).

Consequently stories about moral behaviour, whether of ordinary people or celebrities, are important to readers, together with stories about tax, living costs, mortgages and anything that potentially affects their earning and spending power (such as redundancy, immigration, work changes, cheap imports, energy costs and transport). Some papers carry this to extremes with the *Daily Express*, for instance, formulaically running front-page stories about tax, mortgages, house prices, immigration, crime or pensions, unless there is another story that absolutely has to claim the front page.

The reason for this is clear – newspapers are there to make money and they must keep their sales figures up if they are to keep their ad revenues high. The same is true of commercial television. Although it has a public service obligation to provide news and current affairs, commercial providers will always have one eye on the viewing figures.

People are interested in gossip, particularly celebrity gossip, and many anthropologists and psychologists say that gossip is important to a society and that its role is often underplayed (see Gluckman, Spacks, Hermes, Allport and Postman, and Dunbar). So while gossip in newspapers is widely condemned either as intrusive or as evidence of 'dumbing down', in fact it may well play an important role in determining society's norms. In a society where direct person-to-person contact is now less important than social networks and the mediated contact of websites, TV, radio, magazines and newspapers, it should be no surprise that the peer and hierarchical concerns about our colleagues and neighbours have been replaced by celebrities so that our gossip is no longer so much about our neighbours and our 'betters' but about those we see regularly on TV and in the newspapers, whether celebrities or fictional characters.

Talking about one's friends, neighbours and relations is probably as old as language, but Tebbutt, and Rosnow and Fine identify the term 'gossip' as being derived from the old English term *godsibb* meaning 'god-parent' (Rosnow and Fine 1976: 86; Tebbutt 1995: 19). This term became extended over the years to mean female friends of the mother who would gather at the birth and chatter idly among themselves.

Hermes believes that gossip has gathered a bad reputation over the years, to the point where most people consider it either trivial or malicious:

> It is considered a typical women's pastime and is often taken to be highly malicious talk about persons who are not present. Academic sources underline that gossip creates in-groups and out-groups and that it is a social menace ...
>
> (Hermes 1995: 119)

Hermes believes there are three varieties of gossip published in magazines: malicious gossip and scandal, friendly stories about celebrities and friendly stories about royalty (1995: 118). Much of the gossip in newspapers follows a similar pattern.

Rosnow and Fine (1976) offer several definitions for the meaning of gossip:

The unabridged Random House dictionary gives rumor as a synonym for gossip, which it defines as 'idle talk'. Niehoff, however, has suggested drawing a distinction between 'positive gossip' and 'negative gossip,' and preserving rumor as a synonym for the latter expression. Cooley writes that rumor deals with events and gossip deals with people, but Thomas and Znaniecki have qualified this distinction slightly in arguing that rumor deals only with important events and gossip deals with trivial personal occurrences.

(Rosnow and Fine 1976: 83)

There seem to be two main themes to gossip: first, that it can be positive or negative and, second, that it is almost always trivial and without consequence, unless it is malicious. Rosnow and Fine certainly identify positive and negative gossip but emphasise that this is not really essential to its definition (1976: 87). They define gossip as

news about the affairs of another, to one's own memoirs or confessions, or to any hearsay of a personal nature, be it positive or negative, spoken or in print. In that shadowy area between gossip and rumor, where the significance of the message is unclear or debatable, either term will suffice. The question now posed is how something characterized as trivial can be of value as a social resource.

(Rosnow and Fine 1976: 87)

There are two further elements to gossip identified by Spacks. One is the character of the exchange of information: Spacks believes that no more than two or three can 'engage in what I call a serious gossip' (1986: 4) and she believes that the level of gossip deteriorates as the group expands. It is certainly axiomatic that only a limited number of people can gossip, and close observation of groups in social settings such as pubs will show that a group of six or more friends will usually split into sub-groups of three or four in order to talk, although these sub-groups may change membership regularly over a period.

The second element is that the gossip always 'involves talk about one or more absent figures' (ibid.). One might question a friend or exchange confidences, but discussion about an absent subject is gossip.

Hermes identifies gossip, certainly when it comes to reading gossip magazines, as a pleasurable pursuit:

Some of the women's magazine readers ... do occasionally read gossip magazines ... and enjoy their unpretentious, undemanding stories. Others are fascinated, but express puzzlement at their fascination or defend their taste for this low-level genre by making it clear they are aware of this low status and that they are not taken in by the magazines and what they write.

(Hermes 1995: 122)

Rosnow and Fine also point out that gossip is not always seen as being entirely bad. They give an example from Lumley in which in 1888 'The girls of North Hall, Newnham, debated the question whether life without gossip would be worth living'. They came to the conclusion it would not and the principal defended this decision (1976: 86).

Many anthropologists now see gossip as playing an important part in a number of social and community roles. Dunbar believes that primates use their social intelligence to form complex alliances with each other. He has found considerable evidence to suggest that the normal size for a human social grouping is between 100 and 200, with a natural grouping being in the 120 to 150 range (1992: 30). He believes that a group that size could only be maintained if humans had moved away from more typical primate group activities such as grooming which limits interaction to two, to language in which a 1 : 2.7 ratio could be achieved: one talker and 2.7 listeners – well within Meyer's 'good gossip' limits, suggesting as it does an average group of between three and four. Dunbar takes this a stage further and suggests that the way men and women use gossip could suggest that:

> language evolved in the context of social bonding between females ... The suggestion that female–female bonding, based on knowledge of the relationships of other individuals, was more important fits much better with views about the structure of nonhuman primate societies where relationships between females are all important. That conversations allow us to exchange information about people who are not present is vitally important. It allows us to teach others how to relate to individuals they have never seen before. Combined with the fact that language also makes it easy to categorise people into types, we can learn how to relate to classes of individuals rather than being restricted to single individuals as primates are in grooming.
>
> (Dunbar 1992: 31)

So communication may well have started or gained impetus in order to gossip, because it was a useful survival tool and that continues to be the case as gossip can help us to place people into types and groups, making it easier to understand them and to deal with them on a day-to-day basis. Gossip can help prevent us making damaging mistakes, speeds up the development of relationships and refines our understanding of what is socially acceptable in our community.

Gluckman (1963: 312) supports this with a case study that shows how insiders use gossip to ensure their position within the community by using the lack of knowledge of outsiders against them. Tebbutt also explains how women's gossip was used to hold together communities at the turn of the nineteenth century (1995).

Tebbutt, Hermes, and Rosnow and Fine identify gossiping as being something that is often seen as a women's pastime. Where men are involved in gossip (and Rosnow and Fine point out that 'one need not search very far to find gossipy men' (1976: 83)), the description is different. Men are usually described as being involved in 'shop talk' or 'shooting the breeze' (Rosnow and Fine 1976: 82), the implication of this being that men's gossip is of more worth than that of women. Tebbutt also identifies this trend and points out that women tend to be patronised, where their voices are documented at all, as 'a second class version of "real" language' (1995: 1). She agrees that where men's talk 'performs the same function as women's gossip it is simply called something else' (ibid.). This may help explain why gossip is not seen as being important despite much research which shows that gossip, whether direct or mediated in the newspapers, is important. Where gossip becomes important in everybody's opinion, it is simply called something else: networking, personnel intelligence, politics or background information. Professionals attend conferences and meetings, for instance, as much for gossip about peers as for the subject matter of the conference.

Several authors identify (if only in passing) the aspirational nature of gossip. The ability of gossip to define clear groups of people, insiders and outsiders – what Paine calls 'we groups' (1967: 278) – has been identified by several writers (Tebbutt, Rosnow and Fine, Gluckman, Shibutani, etc.). Gluckman expands on this theme by pointing out that the more exclusive the group, the greater the amount of gossip (1963: 309). He gives, as an example, groups whose social status becomes so exclusive that they tend to become hereditary and then it also becomes necessary to gossip not only about present members of the group but also the dead members. These high-status groups, whether hereditary or professional, are adept at excluding parvenus by using gossip:

> old practitioners of a subject can so easily put a comparative newcomer into his place, can make him feel a neophyte. They have only to hint in a technical argument at some personal fact about the person who advanced the theory discussed, to make the eager young student feel how callow he is.
>
> (ibid.)

This ability to retain exclusivity among a high-status group by using gossip to exclude is often reversed by gossip magazines and newspapers so that they could be seen as providing this exclusive gossip to low-status 'wannabes' who would then feel they were 'in the know' and could take their 'rightful' place as part of the high-status group.

Because gossip is important to media consumers and because we seem to be endlessly fascinated by celebrities and gossip about their lives, it is not surprising to find that newspapers use substantial amounts of gossip.

A survey of one day's newspapers chosen at random found that gossip was present in all the newspapers. There were differences: the tabloids concentrated on popular celebrities such as David Beckham or *X-Factor* contestants, while the quality papers carried such stories with a much narrower gossip context such as the story about two directors of New Look (a fashion chain) announcing they were having an affair. However, both stories were gossip.

Not surprisingly, many of the same stories appeared in all the newspapers. There was one particular story in *The Sun* that set it apart from the other papers. All of the first three pages contained a picture story about the visit to Disneyland of David Beckham, wife Victoria Beckham and their son Brooklyn. Despite this major spread of gossip, *The Sun* was still matched by the *Star* for the quantity of gossip. One of the main stories of the day in all the newspapers was the progress of a young girl (Sally Slater) who had had a heart transplant. A popular gossip story for the broadsheets was the opening of the Tate Modern gallery. This did not appear in the tabloids apart from a short piece in the *Daily Mail*. The gossip in the tabloids was almost always about celebrities such as: Les Dennis, the Beckhams, Eva Herzigova, Elle Macpherson, Sir Elton John, Mike Tyson and stars from the *Coronation Street* TV soap. A story about a maths teacher who had apparently absconded with a female pupil was also widely used.

There are three clear categories of newspapers when it comes to the percentage of news within the space available. *The Sun*, the *Mirror* and the *Star* carry the least (31–35 per cent), the *Daily Telegraph*, the *Daily Mail* and the *Daily Express* carry 46–53 per cent while the rest all carry 81–83 per cent news.

Table 2.1

Newspaper	Circulation	Editorial as percentage of total space	News as percentage of editorial	Gossip as percentage of editorial	Features as percentage of editorial
Independent	225,372	55.7	82.9	10.8	6.3
Guardian	397,704	51.4	81	6.2	12.8
Star	517,000	49.7	34.4	48	17.6
Times	723,689	47.2	81.6	17.1	1.3
Telegraph	1,035,615	57.5	52.4	15	32.6
Express	1,096,862	59.7	52.8	17.1	30.1
Mirror	2,274,324	55.4	35.1	25.8	39
Mail	2,371,421	59.2	46.1	28.8	25.1
Sun	3,497,563	50	31.4	47.8	20.8

Note: Papers for 11 May 2000. First 21 pages only

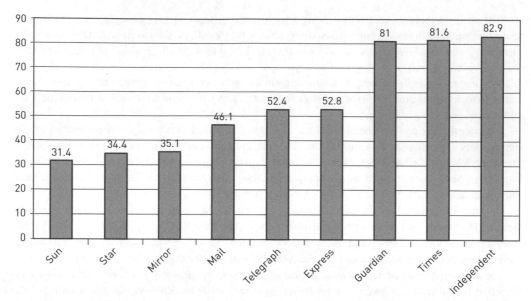

Figure 2.1 News as a percentage of editorial space

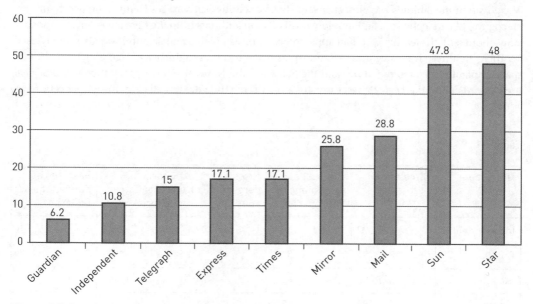

Figure 2.2 Gossip as a percentage of editorial space

The surprise here is the relatively low count for the *Daily Telegraph*. Despite its broadsheet tradition, its news count is only on a par with the mid-market tabloids.

The measure for gossip breaks into groups. The first, the low circulation broadsheets (*The Guardian* and *The Independent*), have relatively low amounts of gossip. The *Daily Telegraph* once again joins the mid-market *Daily Express*, this time with *The Times* for the second group of papers that have between 15 and 17.1 per cent gossip. The third group is the *Mirror* and the *Daily Mail* with 25.8–28.8 per cent. Fourth, and top of the gossip league, are the *Star* and *The Sun* with almost identical figures of 47.8 per cent and 48 per cent.

With the exception of the *Star*, the amount of gossip a paper contains is directly in proportion to its circulation. It would be wrong to identify this as the only factor affecting circulation, but it clearly has an effect.

Although the survey was limited to one day, it supports the hypothesis that the amount of gossip, in the red tops at least, far outweighs the amount of other news. The surprise was the mid-market papers and particularly the *Daily Telegraph*. The *Daily Telegraph*'s circulation approaches that of the *Express* and is easily ahead of its other broadsheet rivals, but it does this with a much higher gossip quotient than the other broadsheets. Indeed, its gossip quotient is very close to that of the *Daily Express*, whose circulation it lagged at the time by only 61,000. The biggest surprise was that with the exception of the *Daily Star* (whose circulation is about a third to a quarter of what would be expected for its content) and *The Times*, charting gossip against circulation shows a surprisingly straight line. This suggests that the amount of gossip does indeed have a direct effect on the sales of newspapers. Of course gossip is almost certainly not the only criterion affecting circulation. *The Sun* picks up many readers with its sports coverage, while the *Daily Mail* targets a female audience with great success. Design, presentation, marketing, news choices and writing styles must all play a part in the approach, but the type of news covered has a major impact and gossip is popular with readers. There is no reason to suppose that these news choices are any different for broadcasting or online publishers and they certainly make good use of celebrity gossip, particularly on channels and websites aimed at younger audiences who because of their relative immaturity and inexperience may be keener than older people to discover what is socially acceptable with their peers and role models.

The problem with gossip as a central part of the news agenda is that it involves intimate details of people's lives and this may involve the invasion of privacy that so many people claim to abhor. On the one hand, the public complains that newspapers in particular are far too intrusive, yet on the other they increasingly jostle for intimate details of the lives of the celebrities. Even ordinary people are no longer immune with magazines such as *Chat* using real-life tales to draw audiences. These magazines are now appearing in the PCC's list of adjudicated cases more often: one complaint made against *Chat* concerned Sylvia Payne, who had been convicted of unlawful sex with a member of her own family after sleeping with her teenage son. An MP complained that she had been paid for her story. The magazine accepted that payment should not have been made and the PCC upheld the case (http://www.pcc.org.uk/cases/adjudicated.html?article=MzkzNw== accessed 22/1/10). In another case *Closer* magazine ran a story headed 'I was drunk when I went into labour' that concerned a women who had not realised she was pregnant and had drunk during the pregnancy, sometimes to excess, but claimed the magazine had distorted and exaggerated her story. The Press Complaints Commission agreed the story was exaggerated and that the magazine had fabricated quotes from the complainant and upheld the complaint http://www.pcc.org.uk/cases/adjudicated.html?article=NTc3MA== accessed 22/1/10).

News and ethics

As we have seen above, the increasing market orientation of news-orientated media has meant that all but the public service broadcasting sector have been more concerned with chasing audiences than presenting what many call quality news. The days when reporters got stories because they were good stories that people ought to read have now almost completely gone and stories are now gathered because they will interest the target audience and tempt them to buy the magazine or newspaper. These marketable stories are desirable enough to tempt journalists to behave unethically more often than would be the case were their motives for pursuing the story less tainted with commercialism.

Celebrity is now a major selling point for a newspaper or magazine. Publications such as *Hello!* or *OK!* are prepared to pay hundreds of thousands of pounds for picture spreads of an A-list celebrity's wedding. Cheryl Tweedy of *Girls Aloud* and footballer Ashley Cole allegedly set up a £1 million deal for the coverage of their wedding by *OK!* magazine (Millar 2006: 3). An interview with a major star of sport, screen or TV is very hard to come by and can take months to set up. Fees are sometimes paid and copy approval is the norm. This is where the star's public-relations managers are able to select the pictures to be used with the interview and to read the interview, giving approval and, if necessary, making amendments of 'fact'. This means that A-list stars are able to determine which media carries their words and pictures, where that appears, and that the story maintains their carefully-crafted image. Stars are often heard complaining about intrusion into their privacy: Michael Douglas and Catherine Zeta Jones won a privacy case in the UK courts for what they claimed was an invasion of privacy at their wedding by a celebrity magazine.

Such major stars are not only able to limit their appearances to key media with copy approval but they are also able to sufficiently protect their privacy to ensure that those are the only stories that get out. B- and C-list celebrities are obliged to seek media exposure lower down the feeding chain in more salacious magazines or newspapers, but still the principles are the same. Many of the so-called snatch pictures of celebrities used in *Heat* or red-top papers are carefully posed to ensure maximum publicity for the star involved. People from Oscar Wilde down have produced witty quips to the effect that there's only one thing worse than having people talking about you and that's to have them not talking about you. As most press relations experts will tell you, there's no such thing as bad publicity.

With celebrity ruling the news agenda, and manufactured news ruling celebrity, it can be no surprise that the temptation is there for a journalist, working for a publication that is not on the A-list celebrity's reading requirements, to bend the rules themselves to get work.

It is all very well for the elite – politicians, academics, intellectuals and others – to complain about the dumbing down of newspapers, the replacement of serious political discussion, international news and mind-broadening information with celebrity titbits, but while commerce is the driving force for the media, the media will continue to provide people with what they want and that often means celebrity gossip. Living in a modern democratic society where education and advancement is available to all means that we can all aspire to be wealthy and famous and that this is no longer purely the prerogative of a preordained elite. The growth of celebrity and the removal of any qualifications for celebrity means that anyone can become a celebrity – it's available to all, but we can only become a celebrity if others are prepared to bow down and worship. For this reason alone, the cult of celebrity shows no sign of abating, many of them exposing the downside of celebrity, the stars' struggles with weight, with lovers, with life in general. Many people want to read about or watch the lives of celebrities, lives we either assume are much better than our own or hope that they may actually be in some ways so much shallower that we can enjoy sneering at them. Either way our lives can be measured against theirs to ensure we are not stepping so wildly outside the norm, that our social security is endangered by setting ourselves up for ridicule by our peers.

So news is a combination of a number of factors. In the final analysis, it is about attracting an audience; about selling newspapers, magazines or building an audience for radio, TV or website. First and foremost, a story must be of interest to the target audience if it is being selected as news. At the height of the Haiti earthquake for instance as most newspapers talked of the dead and dying and the failing relief effort, the *Daily Express* splashed on a proposal for a tax on sweets and snack wrappers. So *targeting* is critical. *Familiarity* is another important element of news to ensure our audience is interested in the story. Things about which we know nothing or are outside our experience do not attract media consumers and are in any case difficult to present.

Timing is important too and a story must be *topical*, although journalists and PRs are adept at finding ways of making old news topical if it suits them. 'A spokesman commented today ...' may well mean the story is several days old, but a recent comment has made it topical. News should also be *truthful* although, as we see later in the book, this is not always the case and, anyway, is not always easy.

News involves *change*. A clearly defined difference in states from period of publication to the next. Gradual change rarely becomes news, but lose your job, close a factory, win an election, sink a ship, crash an aircraft, or see a major fall of snow or the destruction of an earthquake and these are all news. *Security concerns* are also news, if we consider security in the widest sense from where we live to the money in our pockets through to our social standing and reputation as identified in gossip.

Further reading and support material

A good general book about news and its meaning is John Hartley (1982) *Understanding News* (Routledge, London). John Hartley discusses Galtung and Ruge's influential paper which can be found in Johan Galtung and Mari Ruge (1973) 'Structuring and Selecting News', in Stanley Cohen and Jock Young (eds) *The Manufacture of News: Deviance, Social Problems and the Mass Media* (Constable, London). A different approach can be found in John Venables (1993) *What Is News?* (ELM Publications, Huntingdon). Logistics have a significant impact on what is identified as news and this is discussed by Philip Schlesinger (1978) *Putting Reality Together: BBC News* (Constable, London). Although this is over thirty years old, it still identifies the problems and, if anything, the issues it raises are even more important today.

Chapter 3

Morality of reporting

This chapter discusses:

- The freedom of the press and its conflicts with journalism

- The moral pressures journalists face working in a business attempting to both make money and inform

- The dichotomy between freedom of expression and freedom to publish

There are a number of moral issues that are relevant to all forms of media which underline some of the justifiable fears that many people have about the media as commercial institutions. Although this chapter looks at these issues from the point of view of journalism and the journalist, it is worth remembering that they affect the whole of society and they are not just the preserve of editors and journalists.

Press freedom

Much has been written about the freedom of the press and its 'duty' to inform the public. This duty is often expressed in terms of the public's right to know in a democratic society, for instance, if someone elected to a position of authority and trust is betraying that trust by accepting bribes. However, in practice, this duty to inform is often used to justify publication not only of information relevant to that person's public office (e.g. the taking of bribes), but also of details of their private life (e.g. a sexual liaison) which may have no direct relevance to the carrying out of their public responsibilities, and only serve to satisfy the public's prurient curiosity and boost circulation or viewing figures. It is this central dilemma of press freedom that is examined in this chapter.

Press freedom follows from the human right to freedom of expression and opinion and the right to receive information. These are some of the key rights that started a development of ideas among forward thinkers such as John Locke in the 1600s. The ideas gained ground over the course of the eighteenth century with supporters such as John Wilkes, Thomas Paine and later John Stuart Mill. Paine's ideas took hold in the United States and were reflected in its new constitution, and other countries also started to allow further freedoms.

Locke's view of government was that it should be a communal affair, that men should come together to give up their right to escape punishment by authorising society to punish them, thereby gaining the right to have those who transgress against them punished. Following from this, men also gave up the right to determine the law to those they appoint. Those so appointed would be responsible to those who appointed them. Because people have voluntarily given up their ability to escape punishment, they gain rights; as these have not been granted by society but are earned as society's part of the arrangement, society cannot remove them.

Thomas Paine further developed this thinking about rights – still seen during this period as dangerous, even subversive thinking – and he identified that equality was central to thinking about rights:

> ... men are all of one degree, and consequently that all men are born equal, and with equal natural rights, in the same manner as if posterity had been continued by creation instead of generation, the latter being only the mode by which the former is carried forward; and consequently every child born into the world must be considered as deriving its existence from God. The world is as new to him as it was to the first man that existed, and his natural right in it is of the same kind.
>
> (Paine 2000: 88)

Paine showed that natural rights developed into what he called civil rights. He points out that men do not enter society to be worse off than in the natural state; they belong to society to ensure their natural rights are better secured. Natural rights, he explained, are the rights of mind and intellect that man, when acting as an individual for his own comfort and happiness, has 'the power to execute it is as perfect in the individual as the right itself' (ibid. 90). Civil rights, though, relate to membership of society. These are rights that have their roots in natural rights such as security and protection but are rights that man is not always able to enforce for himself. Liberty, security and protection from harm require society to guarantee these rights for him, to ensure that might does not always win out whether it comes from government, a mighty corporation, corrupt businessmen, criminals or physical abuse. Man may have the right to 'judge in his own cause' (ibid.) but if he is not able to enforce that judgment then it is largely pointless. In order to ensure that this judgment can be enforced, man deposits his rights into the 'common stock of society' using the strength of that society to enforce his rights. That society grants him nothing – his rights are inalienable, springing from that equality of common birth. Paine concludes:

> First that every civil right grows out of a natural right; or, in other words is a natural right exchanged.

> Secondly, that civil power properly considered as such is made up of the aggregate of that class of natural rights of man, which becomes defective in the individual in point of power, and answers not his purpose, but when collected to a focus becomes competent to the purpose of every one.

> Thirdly, that the power produced from the aggregate of natural rights, imperfect in power in the individual, and in which the power to execute is as perfect as the right itself.

> (ibid.)

Central to this proposal is the idea that all men are born equal, with equal natural rights. Each is as entitled as the other to expect society to give them the same protection under the law to extend their natural rights to civil rights.

Democracy and civil rights

Both Paine and Locke go on to identify that as part of this development of civil rights, the method of government is paramount. Paine identifies three styles of government, those arising out of superstition, the rule of the priesthood, those arising out of power, rule by conqueror, and those arising from the common rights of man. All the great thinkers on the rights of man go on to show that in order for man to continue to have his civil rights supported for him by society, man must be able to choose the government on the basis of reason; he must be able to select those who make and are responsible for upholding the laws as well as having the power to get rid of them. In order for there to be equality between members of society about how these people are chosen, all members of society should have an equal right to a say in who governs. This is usually carried out by having universal suffrage; elections of some sort to determine who is the people's choice.

In many parts of the world it is generally accepted that democratic representation is the best form of government. This is certainly true among European signatories to the European Convention on Human Rights.

John Stuart Mill says that there is no difficulty in showing that the best form of government is one in which supreme power is ultimately vested in the full aggregate of the community. He tells us that there are two key reasons why this is so:

> The first is that the rights and interests of every or any person are only secure from being disregarded, when the person interested is himself able, and habitually disposed, to stand up for them. The second is, that the general prosperity attains a greater height, and is more widely diffused, in proportion to the amount and variety of the personal energies enlisted in promoting it.

> (Mill 1991: 245)

In other words, people need to be involved in the democratic process – the debate and campaigns to elect and then influence politicians – in order for their views and interests to be taken into account. Only if all the special interests that people have are taken into account by those in government will the government continue to represent all. Mill identified that it would be all too easy for a government to ignore the rights and needs of a segment of society if that segment did not get their views fully represented either in the corridors of power or in the forum of public debate. Mill identifies that many see this as the politics of selfishness but he argues that while human nature tends to prefer themselves and those close to them rather than those who are more remote, it is still important to ensure that those who are remote from the executive class and so have no natural defenders are able to have their voices directly heard in government. It is also true that while the executive class may have no intention of ignoring the needs of those remote from them, they may nevertheless not fully understand the needs and desires of others and their understanding of the issue needs to be influenced directly by those involved.

The second point is more complex in that Mill is saying that individuals need the room to become self-dependent, within the rule of law, to develop their own interests either on their own or with others because, by developing themselves in terms of commercial or intellectual advancement, they will help develop the common prosperity and diffuse it more generally through society.

Positive and negative rights

Different styles of democratic governments can support rights of different kinds. These are sometimes identified as negative or positive rights. Positive rights come from traditions such as those of Jean Jacques Rousseau, a tradition more common on the continent of Europe than in the UK or US. These allow for welfare rights that expand outside the individual to include rights of welfare such as education, healthcare and the right to earn a living. The UK and US tradition is more about what are sometimes called negative rights; that government is there to protect the individual's civil rights to such things as liberty, life and the pursuit of happiness (Halstead 2005: 10).

Democracy and free speech

If democracy is to work well and we are to exercise our right to vote responsibly, then we need to be reasonably well informed so that we are able to use our vote wisely and involve ourselves in the political debates of our times.

> It is by political discussion that the manual labourer, whose employment is a routine, and whose way of life brings him in contact with no variety of impressions, circumstances, or ideas, is taught that remote causes and events which take place far off, have a most sensible effect even on his personal interests; and it is from political discussion, and collective political action, that one whose daily occupations concentrate his interests in a small circle around himself, learns to feel for and with his fellow-citizens, and becomes consciously a member of a great community.
>
> (Mill 1991: 328)

It is here that the media in all its forms has its most important role – keeping the public informed and facilitating political debate.

But we would be fooling ourselves if we believed that democracy worked this way everywhere in the Western world. All too often it seems that people are too busy, too lazy, too cynical or too preoccupied to make the effort required to be well enough informed to reach a reasoned decision on voting choices. People often vote the way their parents did, or the way they did last time, or because of their emotive perception of the party for which they 'should' be voting. However, a concern that the system doesn't really work as it should is no reason not to continue working for the ideal, and this pursuit requires the continuing flow of information about what our political masters are up to in our name. It is for this reason that it is generally accepted in most Western countries that part of the media's remit is to inform and that part of that informing role will involve them in a close scrutiny of the motives and actions of people in positions of power and trust. Of course this does not mean that the media always provides this information and political debate any more than that the reader always makes the effort to receive it. Most news media in the West are run by commercial operations and their primary aim is to sell products and make a profit – the larger the better. Their main aim is to satisfy shareholders, not consumers, and so stories about celebrities are far more likely to be used in a popular paper than stories about politics. Even when politics does make the front pages or the main news bulletins, it is likely to be about issues such as tax rises that have a direct impact on the consumer's pocket and therefore their spending power.

The public's belief in the media's ability to hold politicians to account varies wildly around the globe. A 2006 survey by the BBC/Reuters/Media Center carried out in ten countries (Nigeria, Indonesia, India, USA, Russia, UK, South Korea, Brazil, Egypt and Germany) showed that 61 per cent of the public trusted the media ahead of 52 per cent who believed politicians. Things were not so encouraging in the UK where politicians were more trusted than the media, 51 per cent to 47 per cent, or the US where 59 per cent trusted the media compared to 67 per cent who trusted politicians (http://news.bbc.co.uk/1/shared/bsp/hi/pdfs/02_05_06mediatrust.pdf accessed 25/1/10).

However, we need to remember that political systems that do not require or allow the participation of all citizens through the ballot box do not need a free media. In such a system a free media is a potential voice of dissent that is likely to cause disruption in society. Nor is a challenging media likely to be of use to the citizens themselves unless they are seeking to change the government and introduce democracy:

> But political discussions fly over the heads of those who have no votes, and are not endeavouring to acquire them. Their position, in comparison with the electors, is that of the audience in a court of justice, compared with the twelve men in the jury-box. It is not their suffrages that are asked, it is not their opinion that is sought to be influenced.
>
> (Mill 1991: 329)

But we should appreciate that even governments who face the ballot box on a regular basis will often do the best they can to control the information to which voters have access while trying to appear as though they support a free press and greater access to information.

In countries where the media is even more strictly controlled, only 'good' news about the government can be disseminated. It also means that few, if any, of the ethical problems facing journalists in a free media arise. If a journalist is limited in the sources he or she can use, is instructed by the authorities about what to write and how to write it, and how it should be used, the debate is not about ethics but about definitions. Indeed, it is debatable whether that person can be considered to be a journalist at all. Without media freedom the journalist's reason to behave in a way which may bring about direct moral conflict no longer exists. If the journalist's role is confined purely to that of entertainer or propagandist, the only criteria by which they can be judged are whether they get their work in on time and fulfil the brief provided by their political masters. Questions about matters such as invading privacy and obtaining information through straightforward means no longer apply; there is no public interest defence to obtaining information in this way and therefore no excuse to do so. There is not even an obligation to be truthful if part of a journalist's job is to distort the facts to present the government in a good light.

From this discussion it is clear that only if democratic decision making genuinely exists does a fully free media also need to exist as a reliable source of information, comment and analysis. Journalists only need to behave in a way which might be morally debatable (e.g. intrude, breach people's privacy) if they have a justification, and surely the only justification to publish such material is the citizen's right to be informed if it is in the public interest.

According to the 1977 Royal Commission on the Press, freedom of the press is 'that degree of freedom from restraint which is essential to enable proprietors, editors and journalists to advance the public interest'. However, it went on to say: 'Freedom of the Press carries different meanings to different people' (1977: 8). Thus when we talk about a free media we are not necessarily talking about the media's right to publish anything they like, but that people, including journalists, should have the right to spread information and ideas which can be justified morally in order to support the public's right to be informed – in other words, information published in the public interest, not merely information to sate the public's curiosity or desire to be entertained. This means that any pressure brought to bear on a person and his or her right to hold and disseminate ideas and information (whether from government agencies, proprietors, threats or bribes from outside agencies, including advertisers' pressure) damages the citizen's ability to have access to as wide a range of views on a subject as he or she desires.

On analysis it would seem that there is almost nowhere in the world that has a truly free media. In capitalist societies, proprietors and advertisers have a strong role in controlling what is published or broadcast, and the line the journalist takes while covering stories. Societies which are controlled by totalitarian governments, or which face strong social control from organised religion or other sources, are also constrained in a way which militates against a free press, and even in democratic societies governments will try to control the information that is disseminated about them. It is these differing social pressures and expectations which account for the diversity of ethical views found among journalists around the globe.

Freedom of the press as a development of human rights

The right to free expression in the UK is now incorporated in the Human Rights Act 1998. This is a version of the European Convention on Human Rights that covers all European citizens and is similar to the US Bill of Rights, which is a series of amendments to the US Constitution. The Human Rights Act (and European Convention on Human Rights) states:

> Anyone has the right to freedom of expression. This right includes freedom of opinion and freedom to receive or communicate information or ideas without interference from public authorities and regardless of borders. This article does not prevent states from subjecting radio or television broadcasting or cinema enterprises to a system of authorisations.

There are two key points to note here. The clause allows the right to receive information; this is not the same as 'the right to know'. I would certainly *like* to know all sorts of things, but that does not give me the right to know them. Some of them might legitimately be secret or private, some may just be unknowable and some may require some effort on my part to learn of them. However,

I should have the right to ask questions and receive information. It is not much use one person having the right to freedom of expression if no others have the right to receive that expression, provided they make some effort (such as buying a newspaper) to do so.

The second point about this right is that it does not talk specifically about freedom of the press. This suggests that there might well be a difference between personal freedom of expression and press freedom of expression. This has gained some support in UK law which identifies differences in several statutes. Libel, for instance, is defamation in permanent form while slander is transient. They are treated differently. Things are different in the USA and a number of other European countries. The US Bill of Rights states: 'Congress shall make no law respecting an establishment of religion, or prohibiting the free exercise thereof; or abridging the freedom of speech, or of the press; or the right of the people peaceably to assemble, and to petition the government for a redress of grievances.' Here the press is specifically mentioned and given the same protection as the people. The Irish constitution also protects the right of citizens to express freely their convictions and opinions and:

> The State shall endeavour to ensure that organs of public opinion, such as the radio, the press, the cinema, while preserving their rightful liberty of expression, including criticism of Government policy, shall not be used to undermine public order or morality or the authority of the State.
>
> (http://www.taoiseach.gov.ie/eng/Youth_Zone/About_the_Constitution,_Flag,_
> Anthem_Harp/Constitution_of_IrelandNov2004.pdf accessed 25/1/10)

But in the UK, that freedom of the media is not directly protected under the Human Rights Act. The Bill of Rights 1689 does allow freedom of speech and debate in parliament, but this was enacted too early for media to be a real concern as newspapers were a relative newcomer. The common law has provided some measure of media freedom and our personal rights to free expression in the Human Rights Act, as exercised through the media, gives more protection. But media freedom and personal freedom of expression are not the same. It is the right to receive information that is the true driving force behind media freedom in the UK. If we are to receive information, we must receive it from the media and so to prevent the media telling the public things, unless it is to protect some other right (reputation, privacy, life or fair trial), would be to breach the rights of many citizens to freely receive information.

When considering the justification for freedom of speech, it is difficult to come up with a better argument than John Stuart Mill, the nineteenth-century philosopher:

> We have now recognised the necessity to the mental well-being of mankind (on which all their other well-being depends) of freedom of opinion and freedom of expression of opinion on four distinct grounds which we will now briefly recapitulate. First if any opinion is compelled to silence, that opinion may, for aught we can certainly know, be true. Secondly, though the silenced opinion may be in error, it may, and very commonly does, contain a portion of the truth. Thirdly, even if the received opinion be not only true, but the whole truth; unless it is suffered to be and actually is vigorously and earnestly contested, it will, by most of those who receive it be held in the manner of a prejudice. Fourthly, the meaning of the doctrine itself will be in danger of being lost, or enfeebled and deprived of its vital effect on the character and conduct: the dogma becoming a mere formal profession.
>
> (Mill 1991: 59)

Mill makes two important points that are often forgotten by those who claim to support freedom of speech. Even if something is true, it should be challenged on a regular basis if it is not to become merely a dogma. These sorts of unchallengeable beliefs eventually are held 'in the manner of a prejudice'; no longer fully true, but often still believed. Often these are beliefs that go on to be moral panics or myths. Widely believed planks of public policy that can quickly crumble once challenged by the spotlight of informed and rigorous debate. Only by rational discussion and exchange of evidence and opinion can we truly arrive at the truth.

The second point is that the freedom to express opinion must include the freedom to express opinion that is likely to offend. If we only exchange views that are non-offensive and fit neatly into our present understanding of the world, then those who seek to dominate are able to manipulate those who only want a quiet life and prefer not to offend. History is littered with tyrants who have stamped on the views of others by claiming that what they are saying would or has offended some group or another. The point about freedom of expression is that we should speak out even if we know it might offend, not because it will offend, but because it might help to enlighten. That doesn't mean that journalists are obliged to offend, nor that there are not times when it would be more ethical to avoid offending, merely that offence, by itself, is not necessarily a good reason to avoid speaking out.

Morality and a free press

Following the news reflects and reaffirms our membership in a community of shared interests.

(Joshua Halberstam, quoted in Cohen 1992: 19)

Being part of a community brings responsibilities, yet it is only with enough information to form meaningful views that people can make sensible, well-informed decisions about those responsibilities and so play their part in the community. As the journalist's prime objective is the discovery, disclosure and analysis of the information on which others will base their views, the decisions affecting a journalist's choices about what material to publish or broadcast should have as strong a moral component as the methods used to gather that material. But often the moral decisions are not about which news to use but about whether the text concerned is news at all.

Journalists have to make choices all the time about what to put in or leave out of stories, what stories to use in newspapers or broadcasts and which sources to contact to support the stories. In Britain journalists often look at the commercial aspect of a story. They ask themselves whether a story is going to sell papers and if the story is what people want. It would be impossible for people to read every story written on a particular day, even if journalists could put their hands on their hearts and swear that they have been universal in their coverage. Consumers rely on journalists to give them the kind of information they want and journalists measure their success at doing this by readership. However, readership is not the only measure of success for most media. Total income, which includes income from advertising, sponsorship or sales, is often considered the most important yardstick. The exception to this rule is the BBC. This organisation is of course very different as it is a public service broadcaster and so has to justify its coverage on the basis of consumer needs alone, although whether this is entirely the basis is of course open to question.

A journalist needs to determine right from the start of any story the reason why he or she is covering it. If the reasons for covering it are morally, not just commercially, viable, or if the moral reasons for using the story outweigh the moral arguments against, then the journalist should aim to publish. However, it also needs to be looked at in another way: is a story not being covered because it is morally, or merely commercially, unjustifiable?

Freedom to publish

I have talked at length about the need for a free press, but the phrase 'freedom of the press' also needs to be discussed. It is a phrase used often by politicians, broadcasters and newspaper proprietors who want to use press freedom for their own ends, and therefore their definitions of 'freedom of the press' will differ. Politicians tend to see freedom of the press as the freedom to print the 'truth' about their opponents, whereas printing the 'truth' about them is interpreted as an invasion of privacy. Newspaper proprietors mean freedom to print whatever makes money, but also accept that printing stories about advertisers, if they are derogatory, might damage profits. Broadcasters want the freedom to broadcast whatever will titillate and increase audiences to improve ratings and boost advertising revenues.

In some countries, for example Sweden, the USA and Australia, there are very few limits on what may be printed or broadcast. Only decency and public acceptability prevent publication. However, in the UK, while supporting media freedom, we have taken the view that there should be limits on what may be printed for a number of reasons. These limits are quite extensive and come under the following headings:

- Coverage of criminal proceedings
- Protection of individual honour (defamation)
- Protection of commercial confidentiality
- Invasions of personal privacy
- Security and defence
- The public good (decency and good taste)
- Public order
- Prevention of terrorism

It seems to many that in the UK freedom of the press is under attack as the number of newspaper proprietors continues to fall, allowing fewer outlets for alternative views. Furthermore, the proprietors who remain have reduced the number of papers they produce. There are far fewer national, regional and local papers than there were a few years ago. In broadcasting, there are more stations, but they are owned by fewer people and tend to have less commitment to news. On the other hand, the number of websites has spiralled. Some are very good, although these are often linked to existing mainstream news providers. Others do little more than further confuse by failing to distinguish between comment, news, campaigning, public relations, spin and opinion.

Why the media are in business

It is important to remember that most media in a market economy are not in business because of high and lofty ideals; they are there to make a profit for their owners and shareholders. This means that costs need to be kept to the minimum, concomitant with providing a saleable product, while keeping revenue, through selling advertising space and the product, as high as the market can bear. It is a pressure of a market economy that if a revenue-generating idea proves to be successful, other entrepreneurs will move in to exploit the profit potential, reducing the amount of revenue available to all until the number of competitors in that marketplace neatly matches the number that can exist and still provide a reasonable return on capital invested. This means that any serious interest that commercially-driven broadcasters and publishers have in information is entirely based on its potential to develop revenue and therefore ultimately to make profits. Never has this been clearer than over the past couple of years with the credit crunch leading to massive cost cutting, closures of newspapers and industry-wide concern about how to make news websites pay.

With profit as the motive for owning and running news media, it can hardly be surprising that proprietors, and therefore editors, want to present news that costs as little as possible to gather, and yet provides the largest audience and thereby the highest revenue return possible. In-depth investigative stories based around issues are not the highest-profile stories. They are also some of the most risky in terms of libel suits. With libel laws in Britain being some of the most repressive in the world, a court system that is extremely costly and juries which, at the moment, are highly unsympathetic to the media, it is a brave editor who will stick his or her neck out to run an investigative story about sharp practice in the City and risk a law suit which could cost several millions rather than a kiss-and-tell exposé of some celebrity. This need to go for the cheapest option has led to a reduction in quality news and investigations with more news media chasing the same stories as everyone else because it's cheap and easy. Nick Davies in his book *Flat Earth News* expands on this theme, exposing some of the real problems facing the industry.

Morality and society

Most societies in the world feel strongly about some area of media ethics and ensure appropriate behaviour by legislating in that area. It is perfectly legitimate for societies to reach a consensus about what is acceptable for the media to publish or, more usually, not publish as they need to protect the civil rights of their citizens that we have discussed above. Nearly all societies, for instance, prevent the publication of defence information that could put at risk the nation's security. In some societies, privacy is very important and so the law covers privacy, whereas in others the presumption of innocence and the right to a fair trial is paramount and there the law will cover that and perhaps make no mention of privacy.

The emphasis that societies place on matters such as privacy and the way they deal with them differs greatly. For example, in France, the law covers a wide range of issues that are dealt with by other countries in their press codes of ethical conduct. It is no surprise therefore that France, with its tough constitution and laws, has a limited code of journalistic conduct while Sweden, which has practically no legislation in the area of ethical media activity, has a strong code and regulatory media council that is taken very seriously by practitioners.

Where there is strong law in a country for one area of journalistic morality, it often happens that the journalists in that country cease to see that area as a moral problem at all, except in very general terms. For instance, in Britain, journalists are restricted in what they report on criminal proceedings by a number of statutes. The 1981 Contempt of Court Act lays down that once someone has been arrested, or a warrant has been issued for their arrest, nothing may be published or broadcast which 'creates a substantial risk that the course of justice in particular legal proceedings will be seriously impeded or prejudiced' providing the proceedings are 'active'. This is called 'strict liability contempt' because there is no need to prove that there was any intention to prejudge a trial, only that there was a substantial, serious risk to an active proceedings. Should there be evidence that the matter was published intentionally to prejudice proceedings, then the older common law definition of contempt of court could still be used.

Once a matter comes to a trial the media can report provided it is a fair and accurate report of public legal proceedings published contemporaneously and in good faith. In addition, the court can make orders to hear evidence in private in certain circumstances and it is also, under section 8 of the 1981 Act, a contempt to 'obtain, disclose or solicit any particular statements made, opinions expressed, arguments advanced or votes cast by members of a jury in the course of their deliberations in any legal proceedings'. This means that British journalists tend to think of the issue of covering court cases in terms of the law rather than morality. Whereas a US journalist might take an ethical decision when considering whether to interview a jury member or talk to a witness before a trial, a British journalist would not even consider interviewing a juror about that particular case as he or she would know this could be illegal and therefore pointless.

If a journalist is obliged by law to do, or not do, a certain action, then there can be no feeling of moral obligation. This is a prudential decision: a decision to avoid punishment, not a moral decision, a question of deciding what is right and what is wrong. In practice this seems to have the effect of eventually eroding a person's consideration of the underlying moral principle that applies in that particular area. Doubtless the same would be true for journalists if the laws of contempt of court were removed. Present loopholes in the law are used at every opportunity for a story regardless of the ethical considerations, so, if the laws were removed, journalists would certainly have a field day with court coverage.

Morality and commerce

Another important factor in the ethical debate is market forces. Most Western journalists work in a marketplace to some degree or another. Even if their media output is being consumed by a captive audience (public service broadcasters, for instance, or journalists working for fixed circulation publications), they still end up working to performance criteria which have audience approval as a major component. This inevitably puts pressure on the journalist to follow market-driven journalism rather than adhering to an ethical value system. Journalists will then often deceive themselves that they are doing the right thing by publishing a story which by any other standard would be considered unethical. Essentially this is an issue of loyalty. To whom does the journalist owe loyalty? Is it the employer, the consumer, the advertiser, the law, or some other authority?

The drive to improve circulation or viewing figures can tempt a journalist to use a story that morally-driven caution might have persuaded him or her not to have used. This shows loyalty to the employer; a chance for the company to boost profits by improving circulation or viewing figures and self-serving ambition. A journalist who is loyal to an employer and helps to boost profits is bound to be a more marketable talent. For the same reason, some journalists may allow themselves to back away from a story out of loyalty to the company or an advertiser or both. They may go along with an instruction not to cover a story because it concerns a major advertiser or potential advertiser, even though the journalist may feel that morally the readers should be told about the advertiser's questionable practices.

Morality and the consumer

Sometimes journalists will consider the consumer only when making 'moral' judgements. The argument is often put forward that a particular item has been published because the consumer wants to read it and therefore it must be accepted that it is morally right to publish. The reader has bought the edition of the paper or magazine and, because of the direct link between consumer and circulation, there is the proof that the newspaper was right to publish the item. However, the journalist or publisher is then upset when the decision to publish is attacked as being immoral and tries to blame the reader for acting immorally by buying the product: if the consumer had not wanted this article, he or she should not have bought the publication.

This argument was raised in connection with the press coverage of the relationship between Diana, Princess of Wales and her friend Dodi Al-Fayed, and the backlash against the press that followed their deaths. Max Hastings, the editor of the *London Evening Standard*, put forward the argument that editorial judgement was driven solely by market considerations. As news and photographs of the princess raised circulation figures, newspapers were right to publish them and would only cease when the public no longer wanted them. The late Sir David English, then chairman of the PCC Code of Practice Committee, considered that the public reaction against the press at that time was a warning: 'Public opinion ... was telling us loud and clear that we needed to look to our laurels' (PCC 1997: 15). Journalists and editors are often tempted to blame the consumer for buying the newspaper or magazine containing unethical material. If people didn't buy it, goes the argument, journalists would not run the stories. But the consumer cannot be blamed for buying a publication that contains material that is unethical for the following reasons:

- The consumer may be entirely unaware that the publication contains unethical material.
- Even when a consumer is aware that a publication contains material which is at the centre of moral controversy, he or she cannot be expected to make an ethical judgement until they have seen the article or pictures in question.
- A journalist uses the material knowing that many will be unable to resist buying something over which there has been so much fuss – if only to find out what everyone is talking about.
- The moral judgement about whether or not to use the material is the journalist's alone and is not a decision that can or should be shared with the consumer. The consumer's moral judgement that they ought not to be reading that story cannot encompass the moral judgement about printing the material in the first place.

As the case of the Princess of Wales illustrates, debates about morality often centre around invasion of privacy. Journalists no longer debate whether it would be morally right to use this story or that image, but look merely at the commercial implications, as the view expressed by Max Hastings highlights. The question raised concerns about whether more people will buy the paper than will be put off if a particular story or picture is published.

The rights to freedom of speech and access to certain information apply as equally to journalists as they do to private citizens. Journalists have always resisted attempts to make them different, partly because if the media were to have special privileges it might also be expected to have special obligations. However, this is not the case throughout the world and in some European countries journalists have special rights and special rights of access to information unavailable to the general public. In Belgium, for instance, journalists have special travel rights and cut-price telephone calls. In Portugal, journalists have special rights of access to government sources of information and a legal right not to be coerced into acting against their consciences, while in both Portugal and Italy, journalists cannot work for the media without being registered and obtaining a press card. France, Britain, Luxembourg and the Netherlands all have national identity card schemes in cooperation with the police. These are voluntary and you can operate as a journalist without them, but they do make working in dramatic situations such as demonstrations, riots and disasters much easier.

The right to a free press needs to be handled with considerable care. People's reputations, possibly even their lives, could be at stake when journalists are probing into areas which, without the justification of the public interest, would normally be left alone. In such instances professional morality becomes crucially important. Without the concepts of freedom of speech and the protection of democracy, a journalist would find it almost impossible to justify underhand methods of gathering information such as those involved in the *Guardian* 'cod fax' episode (Case study 3.1).

Case study 3.1 Professional morality and the public interest

It would be naive to suggest that every covert investigation carried out by a journalist could be completely justified by freedom of speech and the public interest. However, some stories of major public interest can only be exposed by using deceit or trickery. Long focal lenses and bugging devices, false identities and theft have all been used in order to obtain stories.

The Guardian newspaper, intent on showing that Jonathan Aitken, a Conservative MP, was corrupt, was trying to prove that Mr Aitken had stayed at the Ritz Hotel in Paris at the expense of Mr Mohammed Al-Fayed, the hotel's owner. Mr Al-Fayed, also the owner of Harrods, was cooperating with the newspaper and Mr Peter Preston, Editor-in-Chief of *The Guardian*, had no wish to reveal that he was the source of the information and had therefore breached client confidentiality. Instead, *The Guardian* sent a fax to the hotel on House of Commons notepaper, purporting to be from Mr Aitken asking about the bill.

Was the story worth the deceit? Peter Preston didn't think so later on when he apologised to the Commons Privileges Committee for sending the 'cod fax', saying it was a 'stupid and discourteous thing to have done'. 'The committee concluded that Mr Preston and *The Guardian* were 'guilty of unwise and improper conduct' (*The Independent*, 25 January 1996).

The trouble with freedom of speech is that it is rights-based, not virtue-based. It is not possible to measure an excess or frugality of freedom of speech. Freedom of speech is an absolute; either you have it or you don't. If freedom of speech is removed in even the smallest part, then it risks being removed almost in its entirety. That is not to say that there should not be limits placed on the average work of the journalist, but it has to be understood that any limitation on freedom of expression has to be justified, because otherwise it is a restriction that could eventually lead to the loss of that freedom. Of course if I were to damage someone's reputation I would have breached their human right to a reputation and then it is only reasonable that that person should be able to lay suit against me and pursue me through the courts for damages. For this reason I would need to take care that I did not put myself or the news provider I worked for at risk. Other rights granted under the appropriate convention also need to be considered when measuring whether one should fully press freedom of expression. People's right to privacy, liberty, security, fair trial and presumption of innocence could all be adversely affected by my using my freedom of expression and opinion. This is why the freedom of the media is not directly the same as the freedom of the individual. My right to freedom of expression when I am there to answer directly for my views can be entirely open and only if I can be shown to have acted with malice, or have recklessly set out to deceive or blacken someone's name without regard for the consequences of my actions should there be legal repercussions. But when I express opinions that can be heard or read by millions, without my being there to take the blame, when my views can reach a wide audience instantly, other safeguards are felt to be required by society. I must handle such power far more responsibly, and society should have the power to be able to insist that I can defend my decision to publish what I have to that wider audience. But otherwise, the free press is an extension of freedom of speech.

There are four main areas of a journalist's work in which professional morality may place a limit on freedom to publish or broadcast. They are:

- The limits that are placed on what information is gathered.
- The limits that are placed on how that information is gathered.
- The limits that are placed on what information is published.
- Guaranteeing the quality of the information that is published.

Limiting what information journalists can gather

It is confusing and concerning that many people in Britain, and indeed in several other countries, appear to support freedom of speech and a free press while supporting censorship on specific matters. In a *Times/Mirror* Center (now the Pew Center) for the People and the Press survey taken in 1994 a worryingly low 52 per cent of Britons said they supported a free press (the lowest of all the countries surveyed). Yet 71 per cent of respondents in Britain favoured censorship to discourage terrorism, a similarly high figure to those who would welcome censorship to restrict portrayals of explicit sex (72 per cent). Many might say this is because of the high levels of terrorism in this country, yet both Spain and Italy, which face similar problems, had much lower numbers of respondents calling for censorship (62 per cent and 42 per cent respectively) (see Table 3.1).

The 1987–95 British broadcast ban, which prevented the broadcast of the voices of certain politicians, particularly those from Sinn Fein, the political wing of the Irish Republican Army (IRA), was a relatively thin edge of an extremely dangerous wedge. Although there were many who believed that removing the 'oxygen of publicity' would stifle the IRA and therefore reduce the violence, there is no evidence that this was the case; indeed it defies logic. Violence is often the last resort of those who are otherwise unheard. Censoring the views and opinions of those who believe they have legitimate grievances or complaints is an almost guaranteed way of ensuring that they start using more direct and often violent methods. The present upsurge of Islamist terrorism and protest around the world is an argument for listening more closely, not for restricting freedom of the media. Accepting the principle that there are certain people in society who do not have the right to speak or be heard purely on the basis of who they are is essentially no different to gagging anyone whose opinions are not welcome by the ruling group. Not acknowledging this is to live in ignorance of, or indifference to, the evidence presented by scores of tyrannical governments around the world who have imprisoned journalists, political opponents and others who have voiced opinions that were not welcome. Society should not be preventing coverage of Muslim extremists or the BNP in the news media for fear of what they might have to say for only the oxygen of publicity will expose them for what they are, not a conspiracy of silence and censorship. By debating, challenging and presenting counter-arguments society can work through the problems, isolating those whose extremism is purely opportunistic and protecting and assisting those with real grievances.

So, despite a worrying lack of support, free speech and a free press in Britain are essential to the free style of democracy that we all seem to favour, whether by choice or apathy, and, because

Table 3.1 Support for censorship to discourage terrorism or displays of explicit sex

Country	Terrorism	Explicit sex
Canada	68	65
France	82	67
Germany	61	67
Italy	42	43
Spain	62	49
United Kingdom	71	72
United States	60	59

Source: Data from the Pew Center

of this, the journalist needs to take care that he or she does not step over the invisible mark that divides responsible reporting from licence to allow editorial choice to become censorship.

Should there be any limits set on the information journalists gather? The government certainly thinks there should be and a number of laws are in place preventing journalists from researching stories involving some issues. The Official Secrets Act 1989 is one of these. The Act makes it an offence for a journalist to enquire into any government business that could be deemed sensitive without the approval of a minister of state. Of course, this is not the only law that governs what information journalists may gather. There are various Acts limiting the information a reporter may gather on crime. The Contempt of Court Act 1981, Sexual Offences (Amendment) Act 1976, Criminal Justice and Public Order Act 1994, Criminal Justice Act 1991, Criminal Evidence and Youth Justice Act 1999, the Terrorism Act 2000 and others all limit what information can be either gathered or published.

Inevitably, there are also ethical issues to be considered when gathering information and these can place limits on a reporter. They are mainly concerned with issues of privacy and intrusion. For instance, exactly how much information should a journalist be entitled to gather about an individual?

Limiting how journalists gather information

There must also be limits to the way journalists obtain their information. For example, paying criminals for their stories is seen as unacceptable by the public in most countries. Society takes the view that criminals should not profit from their crimes and so the idea of a newspaper or broadcast station paying a criminal for his or her story is one that upsets many people. Intruding into private places, harassing people and deceit are also methods of obtaining information which are usually seen as unacceptable unless they are 'in the public interest', as illustrated by the *Guardian* investigation into politicians taking free hospitality (Case study 3.1).

Limiting what information journalists can publish

There are some limits on the information that can be published by news sources in even the most free of societies. Protecting the reputation of citizens, preventing excessive invasions of privacy and intrusion, protecting the innocence of those facing court proceedings are all rights protected under the UN Declaration of Human Rights, clause 12 and, if only for this reason, citizens expect state support for their rights. Most countries have laws of defamation and some, like France, have privacy laws. There have been defamation laws in Britain since the reign of King Alfred, who used to have the tongues of slanderers cut out. Countries which do not have laws about issues such as privacy (Germany, the UK and Sweden) usually have codes of conduct in these areas.

Many individuals and public figures have complained about excessive press intrusion into matters they feel should remain entirely private and many have called for tougher laws to protect their privacy (see Case study 3.2).

Of course, the media should have some right to invade a citizen's privacy, provided there is a justification of public interest in the affair. This can be loosely defined as the public's right to receive information about something which is being done privately by someone and which is against the general or specific interests of society.

Guaranteeing the quality of information published

A journalist and his or her publisher must be answerable to their consumers for the quality of information that they provide. Clearly truth and accuracy have a part to play in guaranteeing the quality of information (see Chapter 5). All journalists and editors have an obligation to be honest with their public about the quality of information provided. However, this guarantee of quality of information is not something that can be instantly provided and some news outlets can be considered more reliable than others.

Case study 3.2 Privacy and press freedom

Privacy is a key human right identified in the Human Rights Act 1998. It has helped redefine the limits on intrusion into privacy in the UK.

One of the key recent cases (2008) involved Max Mosley, the then president of the International Formula One Racing Federation. The *News of the World* carried a story about him, including pictures and video on its website, claiming that he indulged in a sadomaso-chistic sex session with prostitutes in a Chelsea apartment. The *News of the World* claimed that the orgy had had 'Nazi overtones' and they claimed that it was this aspect, bearing in mind that Max Mosley is the son of Blackshirt leader Oswald Mosley, that made the case of public interest. However, the court was not convinced and consequently Mr Justice Eady said that the claimant had a reasonable expectation of privacy, particularly for the publi-cation of the video and photographs:

> There was bondage, beating and domination which seem to be typical of S and M behaviour. But there was no public interest or other justification for the clandestine recording, for the publication of the resulting information and still photographs, or for the placing of the video extracts on the *News of the World* website – all of this on a massive scale. Of course, I accept that such behaviour is viewed by some people with distaste and moral disapproval, but in the light of modern rights-based jurisprudence that does not provide any justification for the intrusion on the personal privacy of the Claimant.
>
> (http://image.guardian.co.uk/sys-files/Media/documents/2008/07/24/
> mosley_v_news_group.pdf accessed 25/2/10)

He awarded costs to Mr Mosley and damages of £60,000.

This sparked considerable controversy, even leading some media people and politicians to question whether the courts were abusing the Human Rights Act and whether it should be repealed. *Daily Mail* editor Paul Dacre condemned Mr Justice Eady and 'the wretched Human Rights Act' telling the Society of Editors in a speech in 2008:

> Since time immemorial public shaming has been a vital element in defending the parameters of what are considered acceptable standards of social behaviour, helping ensure that citizens – rich and poor – adhere to them for the good of the greater community ... the press ... has the freedom to identify those who have offended public standards of decency ... and hold the transgressors up to public condemnation.
>
> (http://www.pressgazette.co.uk/story.asp?sectioncode=1&storycode
> =42394&c=1 accessed 25/1/10)

When should our natural right to privacy be contravened by someone else's natural right to free expression? At what stage does comment on behaviour we feel has gone beyond acceptable standards become intrusion?

A recent survey by the BBC, Reuters and Media Center of the levels of trust the British public places in the media has shown an increase in levels of trust over the early years of the new millennium. However, trust in British media is still low compared to that in many other countries. National television is most trusted with 82 per cent of adults trusting it, followed by 75 per cent trusting national newspapers. Despite the increase, Britain was still the only country where more people were likely to trust the government than the news media (Smith 2006b: 14).

That national TV should top the poll is not a surprise. The BBC World Service, for instance, has a superb reputation worldwide and when changes were suggested in 1996, these were strongly opposed by many who saw the new practices as damaging to the service's unrivalled reputation for unsensationalised, accurate and balanced coverage which had been built up in more than fifty years of broadcasting. The then BBC Director General John Birt had planned to cut back programme making drastically, while moving the radio newsroom to a combined newsroom in West London. This would have meant sharing with domestic services and therefore introducing a slightly different approach to the news-gathering. The move was opposed by the former World Service Managing Director, John Tusa, the novelist P.D. James, a Conservative peer and former BBC governor, John McCarthy, Mark Tully and Sir George Solti, to name just a few. A mass lobby was held outside Parliament on 2 July 1996 (*Journalist*, August/September 1996: 9). At around the same time in 1996, a sub-editor who was sacked from the *Sport* for allegedly making up quotes was reported in *The Journalist* (the NUJ's magazine) as saying: 'We did this all the time. I have invented quotes for her often before ...' (*Journalist*, August/September 1996: 8). The BBC World Service and the *Sport* can be seen as spanning the range of reliability in the British media, from a news service relied on by state leaders to one that is not taken seriously. Yet both have a place in the media market and both employ journalists who take their work seriously.

The decisions journalists make about the extent of their research, and the extent to which they correlate sources, depend on the needs of their audience. The quality of information they provide will vary depending upon the market and its requirements. For instance, readers of the *Sport* appear only to require titillation from stories that do not need to be honest, truthful, accurate or balanced. Their view of the world will only be changed peripherally by what they read and they are unlikely to base decisions of any importance on the stories and information contained in the *Sport*. However, even though readers are unlikely to believe any particular story, the continued diet of stories of a such a titillating nature about supposedly sexually available women might damage their view of the world and be more likely to lead them to hold women in low esteem. Academics are still researching the notion that our view of normality is affected by what we see in the media, but most of the work is centred on fictional violence rather than supposedly factual stories. It seems to me that the debate about whether *Reservoir Dogs* or *Tom and Jerry* alter our views about the acceptability of violence is an entirely different one from whether a consistent diet of supposedly truthful stories about the sexual antics of other people affects someone's view of what is normal. Publications which do not rely on stories that are true and accurate are not confined to the UK. *Weekly World News* is an American publication that contains truly fantastical stories. Some of the greatest front pages include such shockers as 'Society matron commits suicide – after breaking wind at swanky dinner party' (*Weekly World News*, 26 November 1996: 27) and 'Doc throws up in heart patient's surgical opening – and kills her!' (*Weekly World News*, 22 November 1994: 19). Clearly, the journalist is giving the readers what they want and boosts circulation by so doing. The audience wants largely titillating fiction and that's what is provided. The quality of the information content is very low, but the entertainment value is high.

While this formula works reasonably well with extremes such as the *Sport* and the *Weekly World News*, the majority of news providers lie somewhere in the middle. They want to provide their audience with entertaining stories but they also want those stories to have credibility so that the consumer will continue to consider them as a competent supplier of news. It is here that the temptation grows to provide stories that are not as thoroughly supported by sources as they should be because they are entertaining to the target audience. For a paper such as *The Sun*, which is bought for its entertainment value rather than its ability to inform with a high degree of credibility, it is easier to print stories that are not so well sourced. For *The Guardian*, which draws an audience that requires a high degree of credibility to its information, an entertaining story that withstood only a cursory analysis would be very damaging to its sales. Its readers would soon switch to another publication if its stories were regularly proved to be wrong.

Exhibit 3.1 Testing the credibility of news stories

There are two main ways that we can check the information we are given by news outlets:

1   We can test it against our knowledge, our experience of the outlet, and scepticism.
2   We can test it by accessing primary sources and checking the information.

For instance, if a tabloid newspaper reported that a Home Secretary was going to legalise cannabis, we might well, as readers, be sceptical. After all, politicians of all parties have long supported the banning of drugs for recreational use. The paper that the story appears in may not have a good reputation for total accuracy and may well have distorted whatever element of truth there is in order to get a better story. However, if a broadsheet was running the same story, it would be more likely to make us accept the story. This is partly because we would be given more information from a wider range of sources, together with a more detailed analysis of the issue, which might well make the story more convincing. Perhaps the new Home Secretary is a libertarian from the far right of the party who believes there should be no restrictions on the sale of drugs provided their purity is assured.

Television and radio news would be able to go even further in convincing us to accept the story. A short introduction and a quick interview with the Home Secretary saying, 'I believe that making drugs illegal is counterproductive. It sets up a criminal sub-class and robs the Treasury of potential billions in excise revenue. I intend to legalise them all tomorrow and set up a drugs consumer bureau which will ensure the quality of all drugs on sale' might well shock and surprise the electorate but would leave no doubt about the veracity of information. It is the ability to hear, or see and hear, the prime sources that helps make broadcasting so potent in news reporting. While we need to remain aware of the ability of the reporter to pick and choose the sound bites used, we are still able to confirm for ourselves that the words were used and we can make our own minds up about whether the person who spoke them was telling the truth and meant what he or she said.

The need to guarantee the information that a source provides raises the following ethical issues for the journalist (these are considered in detail in the chapters indicated):

- Guaranteeing sources for information (Chapter 7).
- How those sources are reported (Chapter 7).
- The reporting of comment as fact (Chapter 5).
- Image manipulation, including video and film editing (Chapter 6).

- Playing fair with interviewees, e.g. using material on/off the record (Chapter 4).
- The selection of news (Chapter 2).
- Bribes and corruption of sources and reporters (Chapter 11).
- Protection of sources (Chapter 11).

It is important to remember that the issues discussed in this chapter will arise only in a democratic society which respects and values freedom of speech. In a country which no longer allows free speech and a free press there will be laws limiting the amount and the quality of information that can be published. What information can be gathered and published is already controlled for the journalist and editor. The only ethical consideration remaining to journalists working in such countries is how to regulate the way information is obtained. But this is really a sterile debate because with strict limits on what information a journalist can gather and what he or she can publish, how they gather it is not likely to be a problem area. The law or the government has taken over the main duties of ethics. However, in a democratic society ethical considerations become an important aspect of the journalist's work. The driving force for the ethical debate within the media is to help journalists perform to the standards needed and expected by the culture in which they work, despite the restrictions laid down by the same culture, either directly by its social expectations or indirectly by government edict.

Chapter 4

The good journalist

This chapter discusses:

- The meaning of the term 'a good journalist'
- The separation of publishing, broadcasting and journalism

What is a good journalist? There is no one answer to this question. The kinds of attribute that would be valued by colleagues would not necessarily be the same as those sought by the public or consumers. For instance, an editor would probably value reliability and the ability to produce exciting stories to a deadline. The reader, however, might think that above all a journalist should be highly principled and truthful, even though they appreciate the exciting or controversial stories he or she has written. How then does the journalist decide what is good journalism? Which aspects of a journalist's work are the most important? And how should journalists approach the stories they cover? We need to look at how journalists work in order to help explain why they take some of the decisions they do, and to offer ethical guidance that might help journalists improve their decision making.

What is a good journalist?

Some people have attempted to produce a definition of a good journalist. David Randall tells us there is only 'good or bad journalism' (1996: 1). Dismissing liberal journalism, Western journalism and a host of other adjectival journalisms, he goes on to produce a list that he claims describes the 'good' journalist. The list is too long to print here and it does little to help us to decide what a good journalist is, although it certainly contains a number of the functions that most people would happily ascribe to a 'good' journalist. Randall believes that this list is universal, and condemns the cultural differences that can easily be spotted between journalists across the world as being evidence of bad journalism. It seems to me that there are several definitions of a good journalist, depending on where you are standing in both a global and hierarchical sense.

If I were a newspaper editor employing a journalist, I would certainly have a firm idea of the qualities I was seeking in a good journalist. They would include:

- An ability to recognise a good news story.
- An ability to find stories that would attract readers.
- An ability to persuade people to talk to them about their experiences.
- An ability to take a good note.
- A willingness to work hard and put in long hours.
- An ability to write well.
- Punctuality.
- Trustworthiness and reliability.
- The ability to use the word processing system used by the newspaper.
- Honesty with their expenses.
- Someone who did not demand an excessive salary.

If you look in the *Guardian* media section or the *Press Gazette* – the journalist's trade magazine – you will find jobs advertised for reporters that list many of these qualities, or at least imply them.

However, if we were to ask a newspaper reader what they would look for in a good journalist, we would see some different answers. So long as the journalist found interesting, dramatic and truthful stories and wrote them up well, his or her punctuality, knowledge of a particular computer system, or willingness to work long hours for poor pay would be of little concern to the reader. The people featured in the stories would seek yet a different set of qualities. They would want the journalist to be capable of taking a good note, to be accurate and to write well. They would also want punctuality, reliability and honesty. Of course prioritising characteristics can be in the journalist's best interest. While a journalist is never going to be paid more than an editor can afford for a journalist, one who combines workaday values such as reliability and punctuality with professional virtues such as the ability to track down a good story is more employable and is more likely to earn better pay.

Clearly, it is possible to produce a list of characteristics that a good journalist should possess, as David Randall has done, but it is up to each individual journalist to decide which of them are important and which should have priority. The journalist has a moral duty to decide which characteristics he or she will choose to display while doing their job and to make an evaluative choice about which qualities are more important. It is tempting to think that one can display a different set of values at different times: one set in the office for the editor and another out on the job with a contact. But this is not really possible. The drive to be loyal to an editor may make a journalist choose to sensationalise a story in order to make it seem more exciting and therefore more saleable, but this cannot be achieved while still pretending to choose accuracy for both the reader and the contact. A journalist can either satisfy a moral directive to be accurate or make his or her newspaper more marketable by building up a story beyond the point where accuracy can be guaranteed.

So far I have been talking about moral goodness, but there are other forms of action and it is often difficult to separate these from the moral actions that are the main concern of this book. Kant identified this when he talked about there being three types of imperatives. Categorical imperatives are about morality – actions done for no other reason than the rightness of the action. But Kant identified two other sorts of actions. The first of these is the hypothetical imperative. This is a prudential action. If we are crossing the road and a bus comes hurtling towards us, we would hurry to get out of the way, because otherwise we risk pain, injury or death. It is possible to say that this action is good, but it is not a categorical imperative carried out solely because the act itself is good. It is only carried out because the action leads to a desirable outcome: in this case saving our life and also not putting others at risk or even causing them upset, but in other circumstances we might stand firm in front of the bus because our intended outcome is to force it to stop. There is nothing inherently good in either standing or not standing in front of the bus: only the desired outcome can determine what we should do. A categorical imperative is carried out without any particular end in view; it is done solely because it is the right thing to do, regardless of outcome. An action done solely to achieve the desired outcome as motive is a hypothetical imperative, just as when hammering nails one endeavours to keep thumbs and fingers clear of the hammer; our purpose is to keep our fingers safe from injury. At other times we might be obliged to put fingers in the way of the hammer, in order to hold a nail for instance, so that the outcome determines our behaviour, not a moral principle.

The second imperative identified by Kant is the technical imperative. This is the rule of skill that does not ask whether the purpose is reasonable or good, it only asks what must be done to attain it. A good carpenter knows how to ensure his or her fingers are not struck while hammering a nail, but whether the nails are used to hold together some useful piece of joinery or as some macabre torture is not the issue. Equally, for a journalist there are a number of skills the acquisition of which is essential if one is to become a good journalist, but that does not mean such a good journalist is necessarily a morally good journalist. Good writing skills can be used to write lies as well as truth; the ability to draw information from people during an interview can be used for both justice and defamation. A journalist's technical skill is no indicator of their moral calibre. This type of imperative is solely about function. We call a knife that is capable of cutting well a good knife, but it has no decision-making powers – we decide where it will cut and what. The same is true of the journalist. The amoral journalist may be a good journalist in the sense that they can write well, take a good shorthand note and persuade sources to divulge information they would rather keep secret but they will not be moral in that they would always do as directed whether that is good or bad.

So there are three principles: 'rules of skill, counsels of prudence or commands (laws) of morality' (Kant 1990: 33). All of them apply in the day-to-day work of the journalist. Of course a poor journalist may not even have sufficient moral fibre to become a good journalist in the technical sense; they will be too idle to put in the hard work required to master shorthand, interview technique, writing and production skills. So the first step to becoming a good journalist in the full sense of the word is mastery of the technical skills, but technique without the inclination to apply moral judgement through the use of a code or some other method is not sufficient.

Journalistic duty

Categorical imperatives are an important decision-making tool. They are the foundation of codes of conduct and often fit well into the way that journalists work. Endeavouring to be truthful and accurate are clear categorical imperatives and do not require any interpretation, or concern about consequence. A journalist should attempt to tell the truth because it is the moral thing to do; we can justify it through logic and do not need to consider what the consequences of our action might be. But there are other ethical dilemmas that do not fit so easily into this 'never mind the consequences' style of decision making.

Some ethical issues require a consequential approach. Conflicting imperatives might mean that the journalist has to follow through potential situations. If keeping a promise means telling a lie, or if telling the truth might put lives at risk, or informing the public about what they deserve to know means invading someone's privacy, then there are other factors that need to be taken into account. One of the key factors is loyalty. This could be described as duty or obligation, but since this duty or obligation could, under different circumstances or mindsets be as easily applied to one group as another, with different outcomes, I prefer to describe it as loyalty. Loyalty is a difficult concept. It has often been seen as something that is an obligation that should be accepted without debate. Loyalty to country, for instance, is something that is required under certain circumstances whether agreed with or not. The approach of much of the US media in the immediate aftermath of 9/11 made it clear that dissent from the position 'my country right or wrong' was not well-received within the United States. Loyalty to flag and country was expected and rational debate about what that might mean, and whether it was right, was not acceptable. Loyalty is not a value that should become a categorical imperative. We should never agree to attach our loyalty to a particular group regardless of the circumstances. So in this way, it cannot be a true duty or obligation as our loyalty has to be constantly rethought as the circumstances and potential consequences change. We can therefore use our perception of our loyalties at any given time to help us decide where our duty or obligation lies and, within the changing circumstances, which consequences we would find acceptable.

Deciding to whom you owe loyalty is an important component of working out what you should do in any moral dilemma. Clearly, the journalist is working in a field in which there are a number of potentially conflicting loyalties. For instance, journalists have contractual duties as employees, they have professional duties, and duties of general public responsibility. It follows that the journalist's obligation to choose how he or she performs their work may depend on whom they feel most loyalty towards: the reader, the employer, or some other figure. The following groups are ones towards whom a journalist may owe a loyalty under certain circumstances. Some are clearly of more significance than others.

The reader, viewer or listener

Maintaining trust with readers means dealing fairly with them by providing them with the information they want in a truthful and timely manner. This raises a number of questions such as how do journalists decide what information readers want; how do they ensure truthfulness? Since most of the moral components of the good journalist's approach hinge on loyalty and fair dealing, the journalist who deals fairly with sources and readers, refusing to trick them or lie to them, stands a better chance of behaving morally than a journalist who treats them with contempt.

The editor

Find and produce stories that sell and which do not get the editors into trouble with consumers, complaints commissions, etc., and editors will be happy. Since keeping the editor happy is usually good for one's career, whether in terms of money, ambition or simply more pleasant working conditions, this loyalty may well take precedence over others. It is probably fair to say that loyalty to the editor is generally the most significant to many journalists. The editor has the power to dismiss a journalist and so many journalists do what they feel is necessary in order to please the editor. This loyalty of course extends down through the management structure and so loyalty to the news editor or chief reporter is an extension of loyalty to the editor.

The advertiser

Advertisers will be upset when, having paid thousands of pounds for a major campaign in a newspaper or with a broadcast station, they find that the journalists on the same outlet are running derogatory stories about their products. Their objections inevitably get back to the editor and may be bad for business, and bad for the career of the journalist concerned. Although this loyalty rarely outweighs that to the reader, it does happen and we need to be aware of its potential to distort news selection and to limit the complete truthfulness of a report. Some journalists like to think that the advertiser plays no part in their thinking about story choice and coverage, but over an extended period that is both naive and unlikely. However, most journalists would prefer to limit loyalty to advertisers, viewing the attempts of advertisers to influence coverage as crass commercialism. There are exceptions, of course, and Charles Wintour told the Royal Commission on the Press that it was not wrong to give some degree of preference to stories which advertise 'provided their products are good – and they are unlikely to waste money advertising unless they are ... those that help keep our own shop open are entitled to a little extra limelight' (Royal Commission on the Press 1977: 105). The Commission had been investigating the influence of advertising, saying that in the past the press had been heavily criticised on the grounds that advertisers exercised too much influence on the content of newspapers. Such accusations had been one of the reasons for setting up the Commission, but the Commission found little evidence that this was happening. It had received evidence of 'one or two complaints of attempts to silence criticism'. It saw such threats as deplorable although it agreed 'it is easy to see why advertisers should resent it when they are subsidizing with their payments a publication which attacks them or their products or service' (ibid.).

The proprietor

The proprietor is not only concerned about keeping the advertisers happy but is also keen to boost circulation. He or she may also have private areas of concern (be they political, commercial, or private) that he or she would like to publicise or hush up. Rupert Murdoch, for instance, likes BSkyB satellite television to be promoted in other News International products, such as *The Sun*.

He is also prepared to protect his commercial interests by refusing to publish things he fears might be damaging. Consider the refusal to publish a book by the former governor of Hong Kong, Chris Patten. Mr Patten had been commissioned to write a book, *East and West: The Last Governor of Hong Kong*, by one of Murdoch's publishers, HarperCollins. In January 1998, they told him that the first six chapters did not meet 'reasonable expectations' and also leaked a story to a Sunday paper that the book was 'boring'. Mr Patten sued for breach of contract and shortly afterwards received an unreserved apology and an undisclosed financial settlement. He signed a new contract with Macmillan – not a Murdoch company. The *Daily Telegraph* reported:

> A joint statement issued by lawyers for both sides said: 'It should be publicly recorded that HarperCollins have unreservedly apologised for and withdrawn any suggestion that Chris Patten's book was rejected for not being up to proper professional standards or for being too "boring". They accept that these allegations are untrue and ought never to have been made ...'
>
> An internal memo, disclosed by *The Telegraph* last week, made clear that the book was dropped at Mr Murdoch's instigation because of its 'negative aspects'. It has been widely assumed that he did not wish to compromise his satellite television interests in China by publishing trenchant criticism of the regime in Beijing.
>
> (*Daily Telegraph*, 7 March 1998)

The story was also an embarrassment for the Murdoch-owned *Times* newspaper which had not covered it. Raymond Snoddy, the media editor of the paper, had to admit that the paper had made an unacceptable error in failing to report the row over the book.

> He said there had been no conspiracy and that he had not been 'leant on' to ignore the story that HarperCollins, the publishing house owned by Mr Murdoch's media group, abandoned plans to publish the book because it criticised China. But Mr Snoddy, widely regarded as one of Britain's most authoritative media journalists, said that the lack of coverage had inevitably resulted in his own reputation, and probably that of *The Times*, being damaged.
>
> He told Radio 4's Medium Wave programme that he believed it to be 'completely obvious' that the decision to ditch the book stemmed from the threat to Mr Murdoch's economic aspirations in China.
>
> (*Daily Telegraph*, 2 March 1998)

Parliament and the law

A journalist should generally abide by the law and has a responsibility to Parliament as the central law-making body. Parliament and the law, in theory at least, are the representation of the will of the people in the society in which journalists live. Of course this does not mean that journalists have to obey blindly. A healthy dose of scepticism for those in power and the laws they make can ensure that lawmakers have always to justify what they do. But it does mean that journalists cannot behave morally without due regard to the laws and standards of the society in which they are working. Of course, this may mean different standards in different societies. For instance, a female journalist working in a Muslim country might need to change her Western style of dress to avoid offending the local people from whom she is expecting to obtain stories. This is a moral issue in the sense that it is good professional practice. It is much more difficult to get stories from shocked and outraged interviewees than those who merely think you are a slightly eccentric foreigner.

Keeping a loyalty to the law and the society that makes it can present extra problems to a journalist. If, during the researching of a story, we come up with evidence of a crime, should we provide the information to the police, even if it means exposing a source or losing the story? A colleague had covered a run of stories about a severely disabled little girl who had no arms and legs. The paper had campaigned to raise money for her so he was shocked, when covering court one day, to see her father on trial for handling stolen goods. These were substantial, requiring fourteen lock-up garages. The colleague had a dilemma. Should he run the story about the man, making the link to the little girl, or should he spike the story? He decided to submit copy and the editor used it. The reporter received death threats for his pains, but his loyalty to the law meant he could not cover it up, and his loyalty to readers and editor meant he was obliged to make the link between man and daughter in the story.

Regulatory bodies

A regulatory body such as the Press Complaints Commission demands some loyalty, even more so if the body is voluntary and self-regulatory, as is the PCC. If journalists and editors ignored the PCC's codes and its judgments, the PCC would become an irrelevance. And as the PCC would be replaced by a statutory body, something many journalists and editors would not welcome, there are also political reasons for supporting it.

Contacts

Journalists need to deal with their contacts as fairly as possible, telling them who they are, what they intend to do and how they intend to do it. It is in the journalist's best interests to deal with contacts fairly. A contact who has been tricked will probably not speak to that journalist again. A journalist who abuses trust by printing lies or half-truths is not dealing fairly with the contact and is not a 'good' journalist. This is particularly true if the journalist has promised to keep the contact's name secret.

Himself/herself

It is important that a journalist is loyal to him- or herself. If journalists are not clear about their reasons and motives for handling stories in the way they do, then work will eventually become very difficult. A journalist has personal desires and ambitions, and often dependants to whom he or she also owes loyalty. Working long hours, for instance, may well support the loyalty felt towards the editor and proprietor but would not be appreciated by a partner or children. The journalist's loyalty to self and family also extends to minimising danger. Covering dangerous assignments may well show loyalty to the reader and editor, but shows little loyalty to self and family. A journalist should ensure that work in war zones or other dangerous places or work on stories that might carry risk of injury or death is carried out with minimum risk. In some instances, this might mean refusing the assignment altogether.

Other journalists

Most journalists feel some loyalty towards colleagues working for the same employer. However, even journalists from other media or employers deserve some level of loyalty, whether that is expressed through membership of a union such as the National Union of Journalists, support for the NUJ's Code of Conduct, or is a more general sense of loyalty with members of the same profession.

Journalists work as a team, but in competition. They work with journalists for their own paper or broadcasting station but will be in competition with journalists from other outlets, or even, on occasions, from their own organisation. This means they will often do things to mislead other journalists or put them off the scent of the story. For instance, papers run what are known as 'spoilers' to ruin the circulation-boosting effect of an opponent's scoop. A journalist will rarely share information with another journalist, whether it is a contact, a direct quote or another piece of information. The exceptions are on a colleague-to-colleague basis in situations such as press conferences or sports matches where a moment's inattention can mean missing what has happened. Journalists who know each other will then often help each other out. Refusing to share information with a competitor is justifiable provided you do not expect help from them in the future.

Technology has helped change some of the more competitive aspects of journalism. The days when fighting to get your hands on the only telephone was an important part of the job have gone. Lines of communication remain very important to journalists but, with the arrival of the mobile phone, broadband and wi-fi, it is no longer necessary to queue up to phone copy over the only working public telephone within a ten-mile radius.

Separation of publishing, broadcasting and journalism

Journalists are not so directly driven by profit as newspaper proprietors and broadcast stations. They are, of course, concerned that the organisation they work for should continue to operate (as they do not want to lose their jobs) but as long as the journalists feel they are providing their employer with stories that will interest readers, and so continue to make their newspaper, website or broadcast station successful, then they have fulfilled their function.

Media proprietors are only really interested in the morality of the final product; the means of achieving it are of less importance. Journalists' decisions need to be made before this. They need to be aware of the moral issues surrounding the stories they are pursuing and how they are pursuing them. As discussed, by the time the story is published they may have already considered several different moral problems, starting with whether to cover the story at all. Journalists need to consider the level of protection they can give to a source, the veracity of the information they are being fed and how they would support that information and how far they can morally go in gathering evidence. Only when they have the story does the publisher become involved, yet this is often too late.

The early PCC Code of Practice concentrated largely on publication only. Whereas, because it had been set up by journalists themselves, the NUJ Code saw the need to control journalism and the way journalists behaved, the PCC Code, because it had been established by editors and publishers, concentrated on what was published. The changes that have been introduced since the Code was first written have tended to dilute this concentration on publishing, with the emphasis turning towards news-gathering. This process was speeded up by the death of the Princess of Wales and the subsequent public outcry over her perceived hounding by the press. The strengthened Code attempted to introduce more controls on the gathering of news and this meant that more clauses needed to include the defence of the public interest. Similarly the BBC Editorial Code and Ofcom's code are about broadcasting generally and not all of it applies to journalism. These are codes for broadcasters covering everything from product placement to children in shows. Consequently there are elements that do not fully cover what journalists do. This is less so for the BBC who have seventy years' experience. The problem here, and it's replicated by Ofcom, is that the code is so long that one only really uses it as a reference tool, when one is certain there is already a moral dilemma.

Chapter 5

Truth, accuracy, objectivity and trust

This chapter discusses:

- The importance of truth-telling in journalism
- The difference between truth and accuracy and their importance to the journalist
- Objectivity, balance and fairness
- The importance of trust for a news outlet

No matter what cynics may say, in the final analysis, journalism is about truth-seeking. It is about presenting facts that have been properly researched and checked and put together in an attempt to present readers or viewers with a coherent factual story about an issue or event that will be of interest. This is not to suggest that every story in every media outlet is absolutely true or even accurate. Many stories contain elements that are wrong or made up for all sorts of reasons, but it must be recognised that journalism is about presenting facts and that anything in a news outlet that is not factual is not journalism, although it may well be entertainment masquerading as journalism.

Journalism and the media that carries it will only be trusted by consumers if it is consistently truthful. A media outlet that produces factual errors, or misleads and does not correct the mistake as soon as possible will gradually lose the trust of consumers. A media brand that is not trusted might still sell, because its material is seen as entertaining, but it will only ever attract a smaller audience seeking pure entertainment.

There are two main reasons why the journalism presented in a media outlet or broadcast might not be truthful: pressure of time or resources can limit a journalist's ability to get to the story and a desire to increase readership can make it very tempting to present a story that is interesting, but not actually accurate or truthful. Both of these are serious problems, not only because individual journalists are faced with these dilemmas the whole time, but also because these are institutionalised problems. News organisations are businesses and the pursuit of greater profit leads organisations to cut costs, reducing resources and making it more likely that news desks will not have sufficient resources to follow up stories appropriately as they have fewer journalists. Inevitably, editors keen to increase circulation will then be more receptive to stories that interest readers and so will be likely to attract sales even if these stories are not entirely truthful. Of course, in order to minimise potential embarrassment, many of these stories are not about serious issues or events that could be quickly sourced and denied but are interesting stories about people in places that are not easy to trace, or concern events that are difficult to deny, of which the 'World War Two bomber on the moon' story in an early edition of the *Sunday Sport* is an extreme example.

The truth is a difficult concept to pin down but nearly all commentators agree that the search for it is one of the main purposes of journalism. The popular TV show *The X Files* claimed 'the truth is out there' which implied that it existed, but that it was not something that any one person possessed. Truth by its nature is fragmented and it is unlikely that any one us will ever see the whole Truth.

Those who believe in God consider him to be a major part of the truth, but atheists are not in a position to accuse believers of lying, merely that they are wrong or mistaken. Atheists do not believe, but have no evidence to support their viewpoint, any more than those who believe are able to show concrete evidence in favour of a deity, although there is plenty of evidence to show that religion exists; we only have to look at the disturbingly high number of people who have died defending their religion or because of religion to confirm that.

It is probably the moral nature of truth that should concern us here rather than truth in the metaphysical sense. We can all understand the meaning of truth when it comes to telling the truth rather than lying and it is this level of truth that most people want from journalists.

Morality and truth

Journalists should seek out the truth just as any rational person does, by examining evidence from a variety of sources, testing it, checking it and then putting it together with other bits of evidence to produce stories for publication or broadcast. All of this has to be done to tight deadlines with limited resources and a constant temptation to cut corners; to take someone's word for it or to believe what a source says without checking against another source.

The quality of information offered to consumers is inevitably as variable as the sources from which it comes and so a major part of a journalist's work in gathering material for publication or broadcast from a news source is to determine how reliable this information is. This can be done by testing the information against known facts or other sources. If the information is known to the journalist to be totally accurate, for instance, the journalist actually saw a politician crash his car into a wall, then that is an accurate fact that can be reported. But, when information comes from another source that is not so reliable, and which cannot be confirmed from sources that are more reliable, the journalist has to make an assessment about whether to pass this information on to the consumer. Should he or she report claims (to extend the fictitious example above) that the young woman seen fleeing from the politician's car was a prostitute? Should the report mention that the politician had allegedly been drinking at a party shortly before the accident? The reliability of sources as well as the reliability of their evidence should both be checked. The BBC is in no doubt:

> All BBC output, as appropriate to its subject and nature, must be well sourced, based on sound evidence, thoroughly tested and presented in clear, precise language. We should be honest and open about what we don't know and avoid unfounded speculation. Claims, allegations, material facts and other content that cannot be corroborated should normally be attributed.

> The BBC must not knowingly and materially mislead its audiences.
> (http://www.bbc.co.uk/guidelines/editorialguidelines/page/guidelines-accuracy-principles/ accessed 14/10/10)

It is important that the journalist handles information from an untrustworthy or unreliable news source with care to ensure the consumer is not to be inadvertently misled. In this sense 'unreliable' means news sources which provide inaccurate or misleading information, information which is biased, or that present comment and propaganda as fact. Unfortunately, virtually all news sources, by their very nature, provide information that is distorted, either because of pressure of time or resources or because of a deliberate desire to deceive. This why it is so important to check one source against another. Politicians will always want to suggest that their ideas are right or that their opponents are wrong. Does this mean they tell lies? It depends on the individual. Very few people, and politicians are no exception, tell the whole truth all of the time. Sometimes we will lie to protect a friend or relative. At other times, our view of an incident will be coloured by our own best interests. It is difficult to imagine someone (politician or not) who could lie the whole of the time without being detected very quickly. If consumers are to be able to identify which politicians are lying (or at least putting a favourable gloss on the truth) at any given time, they need to be able to test the information they are fed by the journalist to analyse critically the words of the politician.

Journalists have to take the middle ground when dealing with people. They should be sceptical about everyone, seeing them as neither good nor bad but merely human. This does not mean that a journalist has no duty to follow up information that shows a person to be lying. Quite the reverse. It means listening and watching carefully, picking up on the small signs that can help show someone has something to hide, and listening for inconsistencies and refusing to believe at face value what they are told. People do not tend to lie outright. It is too easy to be found out. Rather they use sentence forms that can have several meanings. They evade the questions. They twist and turn in the hope that the journalist will not notice. For instance, the question 'Did you take a bribe for £100,000?' might elicit the response '£100,000? Of course not, my dear fellow. Would I still be sitting around London with that kind of holiday money in my bank account?' This straightforward denial of the charge stands up to little sceptical scrutiny. Assuming the speaker is telling the absolute truth, and we have no way of checking that, the only things we know for sure are that the speaker is in London and that any bribe he received was probably not for £100,000. We can guess that any bribe taken was for less, otherwise he would, by his own admission, be on holiday. Clearly, we need to ask further questions. It is for this reason that Jeremy Paxman is considered to be a good interviewer: he is not afraid to keep asking the same question until he either gets an answer or it becomes clear that the interviewee is unable to answer truthfully and the viewer can make their own mind up about what that might mean.

It is a journalist's moral responsibility to check information as carefully as possible before passing it on. This raises technical issues as well as moral ones. We all regularly pass information on to others for a variety of reasons: because it's interesting, because it will make us look good in some way or because we believe it is in the interests of the person we are telling. In normal circumstances, we may not be too concerned about how carefully we check the information. Particularly in the last circumstance, if we are told something that we believe we can pass on without risk to someone, but the information, if true, could be important to that person, then we will tend to do that. This is the basis for urban myths many of which are now passed on through e-mail. We receive an e-mail warning us about some alleged scam or criminal activity and we pass it on to our friends unchecked. We do this because we identify the risk claimed in the e-mail as high, whereas the risk of passing it on if untrue is low. It's not worth the effort of checking, but not worth the risk of not passing on when that is so easy to do (Frost, C. 2002: 222–8). But a journalist has to leave this normal behaviour at the office door. Such stories might be true, but need to be checked before they are used. Only if the risk is discovered to be real should the story be used.

Truth and accuracy

Sources of information are often not as accurate or as certain as we might like. A police chief dealing with a major incident may issue information to journalists which has not been checked and therefore could be inaccurate. Because he or she wants to show the media that he or she is doing a good job the information is released before it is ready. Those in authority learn very quickly that the nature of news means that a story is soon forgotten, taking false or misleading statements with it into oblivion. Everybody in the news wants to show themselves in a good light and so are likely to distort the story in some way, even if unconsciously. Again the journalist must use his or her judgement to try to spot the leaps of faith by the source of information and put them in the right context.

The case of the Brazilian Jean Charles de Menezes, who was shot dead by the Metropolitan police in the mistaken belief he was a terrorist, is a prime example of this. At the time the police issued statements leading journalists to believe that the police had no option but to shoot to kill but in later enquiries it became clear that this was inaccurate and that police chief Sir Ian Blair had known it was wrong within hours of the shooting:

> witnesses, who were inside Scotland Yard's headquarters on July 22, have told the IPCC that on the day of the shooting planning and discussion took place based on the assumption that an innocent man had been killed.
> (http://www.guardian.co.uk/frontpage/story/0,,1726676,00.html accessed 14/7/06)

Although the need to be aware about the accuracy of information has been stressed, we should not assume that all outlets claiming to issue news actually do so or that their customers are unhappy about the poor quality of information supplied. Consumers are often willing to be told stories that are amazing, funny, surprising and just plain entertaining, even if they don't always believe them to be true. There are many publications around the world that carry such stories.

The People of 6 October 1996 carried the story 'Elvis is alive' on its front page. The *Weekly World News*, published in the USA but with an international circulation, is always full of unbelievable tales such as 'Couple with 8-inch tongues marry!' complete with pictures (*Weekly World News*, 14 June 1994: 1). More and more of the celebrity-based stories of which the media are so full these days are also invented; designed to boost the exposure of the celebrity and provide entertainment for the media consumer. Urban myths and hoaxes are another way of entertaining by passing on stories that sound true, but aren't. They are plausible tales that cannot be properly sourced as they are almost impossible to trace back to their origins. Yet people enjoy hearing them, hence their popularity on the World Wide Web.

If a media outlet is just aiming to entertain readers in this way, then it does not need to provide accurate information because that is not what its market wants. Most people, however, buy into information systems because they want high-grade information, not just entertainment, and any media outlet that claims to be an information provider and wishes to maintain its market would do well to justify the veracity of its sources. Any product that does not supply what its market requires, in this case accurate information, is soon going to go out of business. This does not mean the media never deals in inaccurate information. One of the prevailing dilemmas for the journalist is whether to publish stories of the 'Rumours have been denied …' sort. Publishing such a story gives it credence, but sometimes the rumour is already widely known and believed and so requires the record being set straight.

Very often consumers need and want to know about information that cannot be easily verified as being truthful. Much political reporting is of this sort. If, for example, one politician says that poor teaching is responsible for our children being ill-educated, while another says it is a lack of resources and a third says our children are actually the best educated in the world, it would not be surprising if a journalist reported this story as a row between politicians, only briefly mentioning their points of view. The only thing we can be certain is true is the row. The rest lies in the field of opinion, usually based on untested facts and one-sided statistics. It would be foolish, and indeed dangerous, for journalists to pretend that they can provide enough accurate information for the consumer to come to a firm conclusion. It is important, however, that we know that a debate about education has been started. If the Secretary of State for Education then becomes involved in the debate, making a 30-minute speech on how out-dated teaching methods are responsible for past failures in the education system in the UK and that new ideas are to be introduced, we can report that as the minister's view. No journalist is going to be able to devote the time and resources required to track down in detail all the theories and see whether the academic literature bears out the Education Secretary's view, but journalists can approach educational experts and political opponents for their views as well as looking for obvious inconsistencies in the speech, and use those as the basis of the story. In other words, a good story would be about the new methods of education, why the Secretary of State is intending to introduce them and why old methods have been used for so many years, possibly ignoring the advice of the experts. While it would be accurate to report just the Secretary of State's speech, it would not be truthful to report only that. A journalist has a duty to set such a report in context for the consumer.

Accuracy is a word that causes much confusion in journalism. People expect the media to be accurate so that they can reassure themselves that their model of the universe, formed in part by the information the media feeds them, is accurate. Yet a considerable measure of that universal model will be formed from information that is not accurate or even truthful. Each person's model of the universe will be built around presumptions, assumptions and information that is either wrong or is at least unproved. While consumers seek accuracy, there are other criteria which are just as important. There is no point in a reporter being absolutely accurate six months after the event because this would entail sacrificing timeliness to accuracy. The journalist must do all he or she can to minimise mistakes, distortions and untruthfulness but he or she must also be aware that time is an important component of this type of information-gathering (see Exhibit 5.1).

Exhibit 5.1 Time and accuracy

I learn, from a radio report, that the road I usually take to drive home from work is blocked because, police have reported, a lorry has shed its load. I am naturally interested in this news and listen closely to gather all the information that I can. I learn that the load is unlikely to be cleared for several hours and therefore the road will remain blocked. On the basis of this information I might decide to take a different route home or, if this were not possible or considered inadvisable, I might decide to stay where I am and work late. Either way, it would not worry me if I later learned that in fact the road was blocked because a car had broken down (unless of course the updated information meant that the road was cleared much faster than would have been the case if the original story had been correct, so invalidating my decision process). Since my purpose in having the information is to use it as the basis for a decision to take a detour before being caught in the traffic jam, it does not matter much that the reason for blockage is not fully accurate.

Because of the way we treat information, not only do we occasionally accept inaccurate information, we actually need it. Making mistakes can be an important part of news reporting. While news media should aim to produce truthful information, it is as important that they get the information out quickly. Accurate information too late is of little value in news terms. For example, a journalist covering a train crash is told by the police chief that there are 60 people dead but the ambulance chief says 58, while the hospital says the number is 59. What should the journalist report? That a number of people were killed, or should he or she choose one of the numbers and try to confirm which is right later on? Of course it might be weeks before the final death toll was determined. Most consumers I suspect would prefer to know the approximate number rather than wonder what range 'a number of deaths' came into.

If we look at information-gathering from a Kantian viewpoint (see Chapter 1), the problem arises about how to draw up a universal law. It is clear from the above discussion that it would not be helpful or usefully attainable to propose that all information passed on by journalists should be accurate. The National Union of Journalists' Code of Conduct says a journalist 'Strives to ensure that information disseminated is honestly conveyed, accurate and fair', but this leaves a problem: how hard should the journalist strive? If we exchange accuracy for truthfulness, we eradicate these problems. 'A journalist should always report truthfully' allows the journalist to report potentially inaccurate or untruthful information providing he or she ensures that the consumer is able to make a judgement about how reliable the information is. If the journalist has taken every care to ensure that the information is as truthful as possible and is properly sourced so that the reader is able to decide how far they can trust the information, the journalist has surely dealt with the consumer fairly, even if the consumer's hope for completely accurate information has not been fulfilled. Furthermore, the journalist ought not to stop at only providing information from sources which are in themselves accurate, but he or she should also seek to put that information in the context of the wider truth. One can be accurate just by making a couple of telephone calls, but finding and presenting the truth often takes a lot more effort.

Readers expect that the information they are being fed is properly sourced, so journalists have a moral obligation, if they are unable to guarantee accuracy of information (although they do have an obligation to do their best to ensure accuracy), to at least ensure the reader or viewer is made aware of the source of any story and therefore the part it plays in the truth of the story. The process of belief/non-belief of the source (and therefore the information) lies with the consumer. It is the journalist's job to give them the information they need to make a rational decision, not to take that decision for the consumer. Accuracy can be seen as a market commodity. Any media outlet claiming to sell information should ensure that it is accurate so that its customers return for more. But truth is a deeper ethical commitment which goes beyond the strict commercial contract between supplier and consumer. A good newspaper executive will want to ensure accuracy in order to continue selling papers; a good journalist will want to tell the truth in order to do what's right by the consumer.

Tom Koch, in *News as Myth* (1990), gives the example of a Hawaiian judge (Shintaku) who brought in a verdict which was unpopular with the authorities. He was later rushed to hospital with injuries gained in mysterious circumstances. It suited the authorities to ascribe these to an attempt at suicide even though the evidence for this was skimpy. Press reporting at the time seemed to support this conclusion by reporting only what the authorities said:

> Reportage of the Shintaku case was based on the generally accepted journalistic assumption that attributed fact is sufficient. Editorial judgement is for the op-ed page while reporters need not and should not judge the statements of those they are sent to cover. For Samuel Johnson, however, it was precisely here that the hack showed his or her skill, probing on the basis of prior experience the limits of a single event's description ... The issue these cases raise is the efficacy of an institutionalised set of journalistic practices which presumably guarantees veracity but ultimately leads ... to the reportage of incomplete, misleading, 'false truths'.

> (Koch 1990: 9)

Journalists in this case were able to report accurately but not truthfully. Gainsaying the official verdict would have been difficult but the journalists should have attempted to show the consumer that while they had accurately reported what official sources had said, there was good reason to doubt the veracity of those sources.

Truth and objectivity

Objectivity is another value that, it seems, is highly prized and desired by consumers and journalists. Consumers often complain that journalists are not impartial or objective, while many journalists are convinced not only that they should be objective, but also that they *are* objective.

The debate about objectivity is still very much alive among journalists and academics. There are those who say journalists should be objective: Matthew Kieran, for instance, supports this view very strongly. Others are confident that objectivity is impossible and some even believe it is not desirable. Part of this debate is in semantics; it is all about the words we use. Objectivity has taken on an almost mythical status for journalists over the past century. Many journalists have been known to become upset when their professional objectivity has been questioned.

The BBC's charter, Ofcom's code and the various broadcasting laws require impartiality from broadcasters, but the Press Complaints Commission has always been happy for newspapers to be partial, provided they make a distinction between fact and comment. The NUJ also believes journalists can comment provided it is made clear when this is being done. Because our choice of words is important when working in this important yet delicate area, you should look at Exhibit 5.2 for a definition of some of the terms used and to identify how I will use them in this discussion. These terms are often used interchangeably, but they are quite distinct in their meaning and unless they are used appropriately, the debate will continue to rage.

Exhibit 5.2 Impartiality and objectivity

Bias or slant. *The Concise Oxford English Dictionary* (1964) describes bias as prejudice. Its origin is from the game of bowls where the lop-sided construction of the ball gives bias – a twist in the path it follows. Bias, as used in this book, means the deliberate slanting of a story to favour one side of the argument rather than another on the grounds of the personal choice of the writer.

Balance. The idea that the journalist can and should present equally two sides of an argument.

Comment. An explanatory remark or criticism. 'Comment' in journalistic terms can range from the expert opinion of a correspondent to the unwarranted insertion of unsupported views.

Objectivity. The most contentious description. That which is objective cannot and should not contain that which is subjective. This is often taken to mean that a journalist should not allow his or her feelings and beliefs to intrude into the article.

Neutral or impartial. Taking neither side. This does not exclude subjectivity but necessitates that the journalist stands aloof from any decision making.

Prejudice. A preconceived opinion. This differs from bias in that bias may slant a story without there being a preconceived idea. Prejudice is more likely to determine what information is gathered for a story while bias is more likely to determine how it is written and used.

Fairness. The idea that the journalist gives all sides of the argument a fair hearing as well as being fair to sources.

Having drawn up some definitions, we now need to take this further and identify which of these are important to journalists. There are several concepts involved. We must consider whether:

- There is such a thing as objectivity in the abstract.
- This objectivity is necessarily linked to truth and the truth is capable of being reported objectively in a theoretical sense.
- The truth is capable of being reported objectively in practice.
- Consumers actually want objectivity in any case.

The trouble with using a word like 'objectivity' is that it is always linked somehow to the concept of truth. The positivist views of the nineteenth and twentieth centuries have left us a legacy that suggests that if only we stand far enough back from something and try to rid ourselves of all preconceived ideas or prejudices, we will find it much easier to see the truth and that we will be able to see it objectively. This has served us well in the approaches to science and technology, allowing us to understand the physical world much better, but it does not serve so well when it comes to understanding the world of relationships and behaviour. Part of the reason for this is that our understanding of physical things can be described in terms that externalise it, make it part of the world outside us. Many of the things we are most interested in, in terms of news, however, have a large internal component. It is very difficult to report objectively on subjects such as immigration, for instance, without understanding the position of the reporter and without taking into account the views that consumers might have of it. Reporting of such stories will be handled very differently by the quality papers who are writing for an audience that would be far more open to long discursive explanations of cultural context than the readers of some of the tabloid papers who are seeking a simpler more focused report. The truth about immigration is different from one reader to another, influenced by their internal view of the impact immigration has on their life and its influence on society at large. All news reports might be giving information about immigration but the reports would be very different from each other even though all would claim to be truthful. This surely means that none are objective, since they are written from the subjective viewpoint of the reporter and include a subjective understanding of what the audience requires. This is, however, very different from suggesting there is a bias or deliberate attempt to slant the reporting in a particular way. The reporters for the various papers have probably all attempted to present their readers with the truth, and they have attempted to do so without bias, but they have not done so objectively because they will have ensured the story fits the subjective truth that their paper and its readers largely share. They will also not have been able to put sufficient distance between themselves and the subjects of the story in order to achieve that level of objectivity. Journalists do not have enough time or space in which to distance themselves.

To give another example: most people are able to identify colours, but it is reasonably clear that we do not all perceive them in the same way. Generally we all understand the term 'green' and would all identify well-watered, healthy grass as green. But as the colour green edges towards blue, it is clear that there are different opinions and some people identify that colour as blue and some identify it as green. The truth about that particular colour's identity is subjective, despite it being a fixed wavelength of light that can be scientifically measured and identified. Our eyes can be deceived by the light reflected from elsewhere on to the colour and our own internal perception of that colour. Of course our own like or dislike of a particular colour can also affect the way we view it and so, as human beings, our understanding of colour is far more than a scientific measure of its wavelength. Fashion, our development, our previous interactions with colour and the ability of our eyes to distinguish a greater or lesser range of colour is going to affect our view of the truth of colour.

We can now look at how a similar process affects our interaction with journalism. 'There are words in English printed on this page' is a statement that is unlikely to cause a reaction more significant than a cautious nod of the head; there seems little cause for argument. There is a page, there are words; those who read English will recognise those words and that their use is consistent with English grammar and usage. The words now stand for themselves, and your ability to understand what the words appear to represent could arguably be said to be truthful, and even objective. But the purpose of putting words on a page is not to present a textual design; it is to communicate a message and it is here that objectivity breaks down. My involvement in the message and the processes involved in your understanding of it mean that the message contained in the words is entirely subjective. The truth of the message, assuming there to be one, has changed by being understood by you. But this is to ignore the physical evidence of the page and the print that can also be seen by others, even if they interpret the same message in a different way. In other words, the issue is whether there is any objectiveness in my meaning of the words, your understanding of the words or only in the imprint of the words themselves on the page.

We can say pragmatically, and with evidence, that the page exists. We can prove to other people that the page exists by showing it to them. However, that is the last objective truth we can show them. You cannot prove that the meaning you take from this page and these words is the same as the meaning I intended to give them or the same as the understanding someone else has. I hope that those understandings will be very similar, otherwise I have failed in my task as a communicator of ideas, but I would be foolish to think that I would have been able to transfer exact and identical understandings of a complex issue through anything I could write. I can only hope to present a perspective that would allow you to come to a closer understanding of how I view what is happening.

The concept of objectivity is further complicated by the practicalities of news-gathering. Which stories are covered and how they are covered are more likely to be affected by practical and logistical pressures than by careful consideration of the philosophical niceties of objectivity. The ability to access a story, for instance, can have a direct effect on how objective or even truthful a reporter can be. There was much concern, quite rightly, during the Iraq war about reporters being embedded with troops. This limited the ability of reporters to access news from sources other than a particular group of soldiers.

Reporters attempting to cover a major disaster may often find their access limited to all but a small area because of safety, travel difficulties or the straightforward inability of an area in such crises to handle the large number of correspondents who often follow such crises from around the world. Often, for instance, reporters will be filing from miles away from the event, totally reliant on video rushes sent by an agency over whom that reporter has no control.

Truth and impartiality

Many people have claimed that the good journalist should hold up a mirror to the world to allow the viewer to see things as they really are. But it can be argued that this advice has two flaws. First, none of us sees things in mirrors as they really are. We view ourselves according to our own prejudices; some will see a gorgeous creature smiling back, while those with lower self-esteem may see a less appealing reflection. More importantly, the mirror argument also makes the assumption that the reporter adds no distortions or unconscious changes to the image in the mirror. This is unlikely. Journalists may not deliberately remove a wart or minimise the grey hair, as some painters may, but they inevitably concentrate on one feature more than another, or they may even deliberately choose to minimise a feature which might otherwise add unnecessary confusion.

Matthew Kieran criticises the view that objectivity is not possible, saying it has become 'increasingly fashionable, within cultural, media and even journalistic circles, to dismiss claims concerning objectivity' (Kieran 1998: 23). He goes on to argue for impartiality, concatenating it with objectivity:

> Good journalism aims at discovering and promoting the audience's understanding of an event via truth-promoting methods. This is indeed why impartiality is important. For a journalist must aim to be impartial in his considered judgements as to the appropriate assessment of particular events, agents' intentions, why they came about and their actual or potential significance. A failure of impartiality in journalism is a failure to respect one of the methods required in order to fulfil the goal of good journalism: getting to the truth of the matter.
>
> (Kieran 1998: 34)

He talks about objectivity in news-reporting almost as an alternative word for impartiality. But the two are very different. Certainly a journalist who aims at the truth, and most commentators are agreed that this is what should be happening, should try to be impartial. A good journalist should not be attempting to present one side as being more important than another. But I hope such a journalist would not be so deluded as to assume that this means they would, or even could, be objective.

Hartley used Lewis's map analogy to explain his ideas about the interpretation of truth and meaning: 'A map organises, selects and renders coherent the innumerable sense impressions we might experience on the ground. It does not depict the land ... Clearly a map is an abstraction from reality ...' (Hartley 1982: 15). A totally objective map would be so large as to cover the country it purported to map, inserting every feature to be found in the real thing and so becoming indistinguishable from the real thing. In order to be used as a map, it must reduce the detail and thus interpretation is needed. A road map of the UK may well be entirely truthful and useful to road users, but it would be of little value to someone walking in the Lake District where roads are sparse. The truth in any map is subjective because it is based on a decision-making process rationally reached by the map-maker to provide a useful map for a certain section of map users.

Like the map-maker, the journalist is never in the position of being able to present the whole picture. If a journalist is covering a plane crash, how much detail would he or she need to know about plane manufacture, safety-testing procedures, production of aviation fuel, airport procedures, the private lives of passengers and crew members, the method of training pilots, and so on? The journalist has to draw a line somewhere or no copy would ever be filed. The instant a journalist decides that he or she has enough information to file a story, objectivity is out of the window; the editing process has begun and subjectivity is in. But that should not mean that impartiality goes out of the window as well, for that would mean the journalist abandoning the search for truth. There is a world of difference between looking for the truth and expecting to find it. Looking for the truth requires impartiality, reporting requires acknowledging you have failed to find it.

With newspapers and broadcast stations perpetually short of space, with time pressing on the reporter and the importance of getting the story as quickly as possible, there are a range of physical and practical problems which will prevent objective reporting. Reporters have to decide to whom they will speak and editors have to select what to publish in order to make deadlines and produce newspapers and news programmes.

Does the argument that objectivity is probably not possible mean that we should not pursue it? After all, the whole truth is probably never possible, or only in a limited way, but we still pursue that. There are some very good reasons why even the pursuit of objectivity (as opposed to impartiality, balance or fairness) is not desirable. Objectivity is often seen as standing well back from the problem – taking the man-from-Mars approach, working as though the reporter were an anthropologist reporting on a strange and unknown tribe. But this is not what reporting is about. It is detailed reporting of day-to-day events by people deeply involved, expert even, in that society and culture to people who are also members of that culture.

Theodore L. Glasser offers some insight into the practical problems of the pursuit of objectivity by journalists. He believes that:

> Objectivity in journalism is biased in favour of the status quo; ... against independent thinking; it emasculates the intellect by treating it as a disinterested spectator. Finally objective reporting is biased against the very idea of responsibility; the day's news is viewed as something journalists are compelled to report, not something they are responsible for creating ... Objectivity in journalism effectively erodes the very foundation on which rests a responsible Press.

(Glasser 1992: 176)

Martin Bell puts a similar case from the viewpoint of a highly experienced practising journalist:

> I am no longer sure about the notion of objectivity, which seems to me to be something of an illusion and a shibboleth. When I have reported from the war zones, or anywhere else, I have done so with all the fairness and impartiality I could muster, and a scrupulous attention to the facts, but using my eyes and ears and mind and accumulated experience, which are surely the very essence of the subjective.
>
> (Bell 1998: 16)

From these standpoints it seems likely that even an attempt at balance, to put 'both sides' of the argument may limit the journalist's ability to attempt the truth. Many viewpoints may legitimately shed light on a story whether this is a political party, a campaign group, people involved in the dilemma, those with experience of similar past events, and so on. How is a journalist to evaluate who is best to speak on an issue and who will offer what evidence?

We also need to ask ourselves whether objectivity is what the consumer wants. I am confident that the consumer wants the media to have made selections both in what stories are used and how they are used. Taking the above into account, it seems clear that anyone seeking objective reporting in practice has four areas of concern:

- The pursuit of objectivity is biased in favour of the status quo.
- The pursuit of objective reporting is biased against independent thinking.
- The pursuit of objective reporting is biased against responsible reporting.
- Objective reporting by its very nature is almost impossible and is in any case undesirable.

Let us look at why this is the case. First, the pursuit of objectivity is biased in favour of the status quo, such as the courts and public authorities, because that is where reporters inevitably tend to go when seeking stories (see 'logistics' in Exhibit 2.1). However, if we only give the views of the court and Parliament, for instance, as being the objective truth, we only represent society from one point of view. It is a common failing of much reporting that only establishment or elite sources are used.

Second, often this very limitation on the use of sources is seen as somehow being objective. The very act of attempting to be impartial leads some journalists to limit independent thinking for fear that using unusual sources or contacts would be seen as abandoning impartiality. How can a journalist use creative intellect to advance a story, make unusual connections or talk to different people to widen their readers' view of a topic and still remain objective? Surely this is just an admission that there is a wider story and that no one could ever get to cover it all. But the reporter who strives to be impartial and pursue the evidence of truth wherever it is to be found, while understanding this does not open the box to total and objective truth, is bound to provide a wider truth. Martin Bell, perhaps one of the most successful and certainly best-respected journalists of his generation, says:

> it is my experience that the campaigners and crusaders tend to find what they are looking for, ignoring inconvenient evidence to the contrary and the unstructured complexity of what is actually out there. Rather I have found it useful to do the opposite and seek out the unfavoured spokesmen of unpopular causes, whether the Afrikaners of South Africa, the loyalist paramilitaries in Northern Ireland, or the Serbs in Bosnia; they will often hold the key to a conflict and its possible resolution.
>
> (Bell 1998: 16)

Third, if a journalist is able to say 'it's not my fault, I have to report this story because my obligation is to provide impartial or objective reports', it can give a misleading impression to the consumer. It is quite common for a statement made by a person or group to be used as the basis for a story, despite the reporter knowing or suspecting that the information is misleading or even untrue. Many journalists do not want to risk destroying a good story by discrediting the statement, but will use it on the grounds that it is a fact that the words were said 'by a spokesman', even if they are untrue.

Finally, trying to be objective is undesirable in that it tends to lull the reporter into writing only about what is immediately observable, using traditional and well-tested sources which are themselves supposed to be objective. When reporting a council meeting, for instance, one might think that by taking the argument for the motion, together with an argument against and the officer's briefing speech, and adding to it the outcome of the vote, this would result in a rounded impartial report. But of course this may not be the case. What if one of the speakers was mistaken, lying or simply speaking about the wrong agenda item? What if the officer's briefing was misleading because he or she was incompetent or corrupt? The article might well be objective about the debate, but it would be woefully inaccurate and misleading about the issue. It might also miss two or three much better stories that might have emerged if the reporter had been more concerned with presenting a full picture to the reader than an objective one.

There is also the view that objectivity is not even that desirable. Martin Bell talks of the journalism of attachment. This is not, he says, the same as campaigning or crusading journalism:

> By this I mean a journalism that cares as well as knows; that is aware of its responsibilities; that will not stand neutrally between good and evil, right and wrong, the victim and the oppressor. This is not to back one side or faction or people against another. It is to make the point that we in the press, and especially in television, which is its most powerful division, do not stand apart from the world. We are part of it. We exercise a certain influence, and we know that. The influence may be for better or for worse and we have to know that too.
>
> (Bell 1998: 16)

Bearing in mind the duty to the reader to present truthful information, then, a journalist should endeavour to be fair (and therefore impartial in the sense of not taking sides) in his or her reporting, presenting to the reader a fair representation of what has happened, who said what, putting it into context and, where possible, a context of what is true, what is reliable and what is not. For instance, if a group called Smokers for Health existed and issued a press release saying that latest research, paid for by the group and carried out in their own laboratories, shows smoking not only to be safe, but also positively beneficial to health, then objective reporting might require the publishing of this amazing revelation. A reporter determined to be fair and to present truthful information to the reader might dig a bit deeper, carry the same story but with additional information. He or she would add that Smokers for Health is funded by a cigarette manufacturer and carried out its research in an impoverished part of the world, paying its 'guinea pigs' with resources such as food and water that were unavailable to the rest of the local population, and then leave the reader to decide why the survival rate for smokers was better.

Balance and impartiality

While considering impartiality and objectivity we need to consider balance. Is this the same as impartiality (see Exhibit 5.2)? Journalists and the public often assume this to mean balance between the political parties, whether this is as simple as providing 30 seconds' coverage to each party, 100 words to all sides, or something a little more sophisticated in terms of balancing over a period of time, an election campaign for instance. The broadcasting laws in Britain require news and current affairs to provide a balance between parties or candidates over the period of an election: each candidate in a particular constituency (local or national) should receive about the same amount of air time.

For the most part, balance is difficult to achieve. This is the notion that both (or more) sides should have equal time and equal space to put their arguments. This balance, or fairness, is fine when two sides of the political divide are explaining their policies and the defects of their opponents' policies. But are we really suggesting, in an article or report about child abuse, that for every social worker or police officer talking about the problem, we would have a child abuser extolling its virtues? If a journalist is reporting on a story that focuses on good and evil, should both sides get an equal share of neutral reporting? Searching for the truth would certainly involve a good journalist talking to paedophiles or organisations supporting paedophiles, if such exist. Only by discovering the views of those so deeply concerned with the problem can we start to understand it. But I don't think anyone would suggest that the paedophiles' views should be put to balance the views of those who condemn paedophilia – only to help explain them.

Balance is not a juggling act between establishment sources. While all the mainstream political parties are debating an issue from one point of view, is it either sensible or impartial only to cover those views? If all the major parties are in debate about the minutiae of a Terrorism Bill, is impartiality about giving the different parties' views or is it about finding those who oppose the Bill altogether as well? Clearly, journalists need a wider concept than impartiality or neutrality in order to be fair to the consumers and to all those involved in the argument. Fairness, honesty and justice are required because these are the only concepts that allow journalists to look up to higher ideals than something as drab and unhelpful as objectivity. Objectivity, even impartiality maybe, requires diffidence, dispassion, an ability to step outside the society in which we live. Even if this were possible for a journalist, would anyone be interested in listening to or reading his or her reports?

Sensationalism

An avoidance of sensationalism is often given as the reason for the pursuit of truth and objectivity in reporting. As we have seen before, newsworthiness is, partly at least, about material that will sell a newspaper or broadcast to people seeking information. Following on from that, we need to consider why it seems that many journalists cannot bring information of an event to the consumer accurately and devoid of sensation.

There is little sensationalism in ordinary stories of the sort that usually fill our newspapers and the stories are generally accurate (within the limits that can be explained by tight deadlines and the explanation of topicality as a major criterion of the news judgement). If the information is easy to obtain, is detailed and the sources are credible, then there is little chance of the story becoming sensational. Journalists can supply all the information the consumer requires without stepping outside the wealth of accurate information easily available to them. However, with a big story things are different. Big changes, or matters that give people considerable anxiety about their security, raise the desire for information. People will take as much information as news outlets can give them. A big story will bring a heightened desire for news and the information requirement of the average consumer can soar. Additional consumers can also be drawn in. People who ordinarily do not buy newspapers suddenly start doing so in order to find out more.

If formal news sources are unable to provide enough information to satisfy consumers, then there is no way newspapers involved in a vicious circulation war are going to let that stop them making the most of their ability to capture consumers. People are prepared to pay for information whether the paper has it or not. Newspapers may well carry stories from dubious, informal sources, knowing that the information is not well sourced, in order to provide enough copy for the consumer. If reliable sources, authorities such as the police or other emergency services, are not able or are unwilling to give information, this is not an excuse that a newsdesk, determined to fill a special edition, is likely to accept. Reporters will be obliged to use less reliable sources, witnesses whose motives in giving evidence may be less honest. Where there is an absence of reliable information, rumour quickly develops and this may make it into the paper. Classic cases include the reporting of the death of Princess Diana. Early reports claimed that the speedometer of her car jammed at 120 mph (*Daily Mail*, 2/9/97 page 8). This was completely untrue, according to the later police reports, and also defies logic, as it is impossibly fast in an urban area, even on a motorway. It's possible that this mistake developed out of a reporter forgetting that speeds in France would be measured in kph: 120 kph being much closer to the speed the police finally reported.

This happens less often in broadcasting as the generally fixed length of news bulletins reduces the opportunity to use additional material. However, stories such as the 7/7 bombings, the 9/11 attacks, the death of Diana, Princess of Wales and the Haiti earthquake can change even that. Bulletins were extended to cover the London terrorist attacks and the attacks on the twin towers, while the Princess's death and funeral received massive coverage from newspapers and broadcasters, even when there was nothing more to add.

Case study 5.1 The funeral of Diana, Princess of Wales

The death of Diana, Princess of Wales, in August 1997 shocked the world and her funeral received massive coverage from both newspapers and broadcasters. The coverage continued even when there seemed to be nothing more to add.

The funeral took place on Saturday 6 September and broadcasters felt obliged to broadcast all afternoon, long after the funeral had ended, forcing them to show repeats of selected items from the funeral, footage of the funeral cortège on the motorway, and interminable interviews with various pundits. None of this added any new information, yet broadcasters felt it necessary to carry on and viewers felt obliged to stay with the coverage.

On the following Monday the newspapers were full of pictures and reports of the funeral, despite the massive live viewing figures on the Saturday and extensive coverage by the Sunday papers. It seemed that people were willing to take as much information as they could get about such an important story.

Some newspapers that are covering big stories and are unable to supply enough information to satisfy the reader find that additional information can be built on the top of a relatively spurious incident. The whole story is driven by sensation and built on rumour. Figure 5.1 illustrates how the unfulfilled information requirement of consumers is pandered to by sensation, rumour and fiction. It is impossible to give true measurements to such an illustration, so this is merely an attempt to explain graphically what happens in such situations. When the interest level of the target group of readers exceeds the available news, then a risk area for sensationalism is created and filled with stories that are designed to appeal to the target group's appetite for information about that particular subject.

With a relatively un-newsworthy story, the information available far outstrips the interest level of the target group (Figure 5.2). In this case, the only decision for an editor is what information to leave out of the story to ensure that the information offered to the reader matches closely the information required. There is no risk area for sensationalism with this type of story.

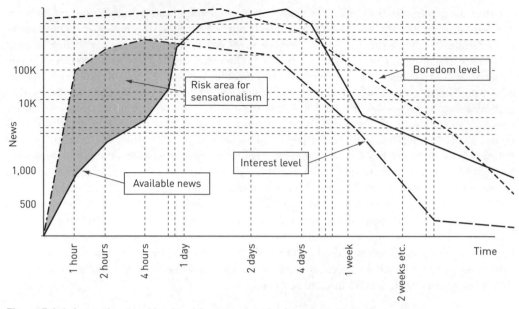

Figure 5.1 Information-tracking in a big story of major interest to the target group

Because even a tightly targeted consumer group will not all want exactly the same information in a story, some information overload is needed to ensure the editor has fulfilled all the consumers' requirements. This is why the information requirement and boredom threshold (the point at which virtually all consumers have moved on to read something else) are some distance apart in Figures 5.1 and 5.2. The need for information overload may mean providing up to 100 per cent more information than one person requires to cover the personal variations between consumers.

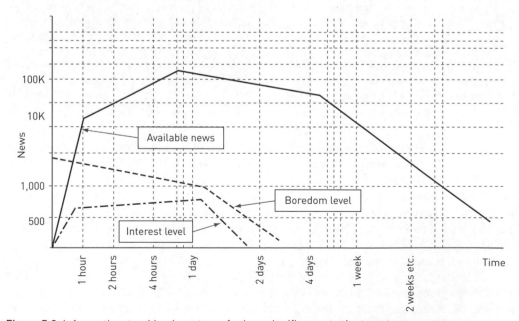

Figure 5.2 Information-tracking in a story of minor significance to the target group

From an ethical point of view, the major trouble area is where the interest level and the boredom threshold exceed the news available. Consumers seek more information, and rather than risk them moving to another paper, a journalist can be tempted into trying to fill the gap (shaded in Figure 5.1). As explained, this is the area in which sensationalism lives, and it is the place where the clash between journalism as a social service and the news media as a commercial enterprise is at its most vivid.

We should also be aware that journalists are not the only ones with a need to get their story out. The early reporting of important stories means that local sources do not have the full details. They may have been misled or they may want to portray themselves in a good light, knowing that mistakes were made, about which they want to keep quiet. Police sources at Hillsborough led *The Sun* to run a story about Liverpool fans that was completely wrong and still damages *The Sun*'s circulation in Liverpool sixteen years on. *The Sun* attempted another apology as recently as 2005. The killing of Jean Charles de Menezes in Stockwell tube station in 2005 was another case where the story initially given by the police was completely at variance with the story as finally revealed by a series of inquiries.

Media scares

Another type of story that dances with the truth that has become much more prevalent over the past few years is the media scare. As I identified in an earlier chapter, one of the reasons people want news is to inform them about the risks in their lives and how to deal with them. We are concerned about our security and about change. When an issue of major importance is reported, sales of newspapers rocket and access to other media increases. It is clearly in the interests of the media to have more such stories. Recent cutbacks in editorial staff in all news media means that often when a big story does come up, the news desk must commit a large part of its resources to covering the story. It is not then in a position to carry other stories and is obliged to stick with the one major story regardless of whether it continues to be worthwhile. Combined with this, there are a number of factors likely to tie individual reporters in with particular stories. They have nurtured specific contacts, built up expertise and can easily file a lot of copy very quickly. They are no more anxious to move on than their news desks. With all the major news centres concentrating on the same story, there is no danger that they will be scooped from elsewhere so competitive pressure is also limited. This can lead to a situation where it is in almost everyone's interests to build the story up beyond its real value. This happened with the swine flu epidemic. The story was first identified when there was insufficient information to be clear about its danger. The World Health Organisation (WHO) acted quickly as the media stoked up stories about millions dying but within six months there were stories explaining that the pandemic had been much less dangerous than predicted and that we were left with millions of doses of unwanted vaccine (Britain may sell or donate swine flu vaccine because of over-supply) (http://www.dailymail.co.uk/news/article-1241725/Britain-sell-donate-swine-flu-vaccine-supply. html accessed 01/02/2010). Various commentators were quick to condemn first the WHO for having 'faked' the pandemic and then the drug companies for hyping it up for bigger profits and finally the government, for getting it wrong ('After this awful fiasco over swine flu, we should never believe the State scare machine again'; http://www.dailymail.co.uk/debate/article-1242479/ CHRISTOPHER-BOOKER-After-awful-fiasco-swine-flu-believe-State-scare-machine-again.html accessed 01/02/2010). Christopher Booker, the author of this comment piece, had identified the hallmarks of media scares in a book published in 2007. Media scares, he said, could be identified by the following attributes:

- A real problem becomes exaggerated.
- The threat must be universal.
- Must be a strong element of uncertainty.
- Threat must be scientifically plausible.
- Scare must be promoted by the media.
- Crisis as threat is acknowledged by the government.
- Finally the truth emerges.

(Booker and North 2007: 164)

Such scares must be promoted by the media as part of their development as it is only when the media builds the scare up that the government feels obliged to act. No government could have refused to buy all the flu vaccines it could back in August 2009 as the media would have crucified any minister who refused to buy vaccine and was later proved wrong. Booker and North go on to identify a number of scare stories that failed to live up to their hype including salmonella in eggs, BSE and foot and mouth disease. They also express their concerns that supporters of the case for anthropogenic climate change often massively and dangerously overstate the case in the way identified by Booker and North's media scare hypothesis.

Policing the truth

Although consumers ask for accuracy, journalists, as we have already considered, can only offer an honest presentation of the information they have gathered, checked as best they can, together with its sources, always remembering that a journalist will have a professional interest to give the consumer as much accurate information as possible. This dichotomy presents journalists with a problem when it comes to codes of conduct. Should they draw up a universal law about accuracy, one that is either so full of caveats and qualifying phrases it becomes almost worthless, or should they draw up a clause they know they cannot follow? Both the NUJ and the PCC opt for the former, producing accuracy clauses full of caveats such as '*strive to ensure* the information he/she disseminates is fair and accurate' (NUJ) or from the PCC a negative approach, '*Take care not to* publish inaccurate, misleading or distorted material'. Of the two, I prefer the positive emphasis even though this is, of necessity, qualified. Ofcom is quite clear about reporters' 'obligation to accuracy and impartiality'. The BBC is just as definite: 'The BBC is committed to achieving due accuracy. This commitment is fundamental to our reputation and the trust of audiences, which is the foundation of the BBC.' (http://www.bbc.co.uk/guidelines/editorialguidelines/page/guidelines-accuracy-introduction accessed 14/10/2010). This approach means that TV broadcasts will often withhold information because they are unable to guarantee its accuracy. When transmission does finally take place, it is often to report that the newspapers have reported that such and such has happened. This allows the TV programmes to maintain accuracy without having to guarantee the actual story. This is a double-edged sword for television. It means that reports are believed, but it also means that stories are lost because they have to have a higher grade of accuracy than newspapers.

Interestingly, the BBC's new *Editorial Guidelines* seem much more interested in impartiality, and seem to treat both accuracy and truth as a way of guaranteeing impartiality rather than a direct loyalty to the viewers or listeners. 'Impartiality lies at the heart of public service and is the core of the BBC's commitment to its audiences. It applies to all our output and services... We must be inclusive, considering the broad perspective and ensuring the existence of a range of views is appropriately reflected.' (http://www.bbc.co.uk/guidelines/editorialguidelines/page/guidelines-impartiality-introduction accessed 14/10/10).

They remind producers about matters such as distinguishing between primary and secondary sources, warning of the dangers of using cuttings and library sources which might be out of date, the difference between mechanical accuracy and a regard for a wider truth. They also advise producers that it is good practice not to run a story from a news agency unless it can be substantiated by a BBC correspondent or another agency. The BBC is also well aware of the importance of naming sources so that viewers can form their own judgement about the evidence. Reconstructions can be a good way for TV to illustrate what has happened, but the guidelines give appropriate warning about how to handle these events: 'Reconstruction should be identified clearly so that no-one is misled.' The same criteria should be used by both papers and broadcasters when using models to stage events, or when library film or pictures or computer graphics are used. Captions with phrasing such as 'The couple in happier times', 'The couple on holiday earlier this year', 'Actors play members of the gang', 'A computer simulation of the attack', far from detracting from the action, add a sense of credibility and authority without losing the sense of drama.

The BBC's guidelines may be comprehensive, but they are far from being a universal law or a golden mean. The BBC is often seen as authoritative but slightly dull. A good part of this is its inability to broadcast information which is *likely* to be accurate but which they cannot substantiate.

This is not to say that I have any answers of my own. 'A journalist shall take every care in an attempt to ensure the information he/she provides consumers is as truthful as possible' is as close as I can get. The wording allows for errors but stresses truthfulness. In many ways this is much better than the mere adherence to accuracy demanded by the other codes. It accepts that truth is the more important aim. If journalists are behaving honestly, trying to report the truth, then they should not object to occasionally admitting an honest mistake. In this circumstance, printing a correction is the right thing for the 'good' journalist to do.

Corrections and right of reply

A correction is used to amend an incorrect fact or false impression that might otherwise blemish the full truth the journalist was aiming to provide the consumer. It is not the same as a right of reply. A reporter should always be prepared to print a correction, and possibly an apology, when he or she makes a mistake or falls short of his or her own standards of truthfulness and the expectations of the consumer. If someone is small enough to make a mistake, they should be big enough to apologise for it. Both the NUJ and the PCC accept this and both have clauses which call on editors and journalists to publish corrections of significant errors promptly and with due prominence. The BBC also considers it important to admit mistakes: 'We should normally acknowledge serious factual errors and correct such mistakes quickly, clearly and appropriately. Inaccuracy may lead to a complaint of unfairness. An effective way of correcting a mistake is saying what was wrong as well as putting it right' (http://www.bbc.co.uk/guidelines/editorialguidelines/page/guidelines-accuracy-correcting-mistakes accessed 14/10/10).

The Press Complaints Commission upheld a complaint against a newspaper which refused to print a correction on a matter of fact. The *Burton Mail* carried a story about a coach colliding with a car. The coach owner complained that his coach was stationary at the time and that the story was therefore misleading. The paper accepted that but did not print a correction or apology. The PCC said it was surprised that the editor had not resolved such a straightforward matter. 'While the newspaper may have been given the wrong information by a third party, Clause 1 of the Code clearly states that "a significant inaccuracy ... once recognised must be corrected, promptly and with due prominence". The editor had failed to comply with this requirement, resulting in a breach of the Code' (http://www.pcc.org.uk/cases/adjudicated.html?article=Mzk4MA== accessed 14/7/06).

A right of reply allows people who think an inaccurate impression has been given about them in an article to seek a response to put the record straight. Many codes of conduct include a right of reply as well as an obligation to print corrections. The fact that a right of reply exists in many countries under statute and works relatively uncontroversially suggests that it should not be a problem to a journalist to print a reply from people who feel they or their ideas were not presented as truthfully as was possible. Again, the NUJ and the PCC agree on this issue and suggest a right of reply should be offered. They differ slightly on what should be offered and why. The PCC only offers replies to inaccuracies. Clause 2 of its Code says: 'A fair opportunity for reply to inaccuracies must be given when reasonably called for' (http://www.pcc.org.uk/cop/practice.html accessed 14/7/06). The NUJ calls for the right of reply to people criticised, whether or not there was any inaccuracy, provided the issue is of sufficient importance.

The majority of complaints to the PCC are about accuracy (62.1 per cent over the period 1991–2008, 71.4 per cent in 2008), but there is a small proportion about the right to reply (2.2 per cent from 1991 to 2008). Most of these complaints are resolved with the editor and few are adjudicated. Of course this is how it should be; many newspaper editors will quickly correct mistakes once the matter has been brought to their attention, particularly if it has been brought to their attention on PCC-headed paper. The only surprise is that more don't correct from the first complaint.

Image manipulation

This is an extension of the need to report truthfully. If a picture or video is taken and then manipulated physically or electronically to show something different, the consumer is not receiving a truthful impression of events. A couple of examples illustrate the damage done to the media's credibility by manipulating images. *The Sun* carried a front-page story about a monk who had fallen in love with a woman and was being asked to give up his vocation. The picture they had obtained showed the monk in ordinary street clothes walking next to the woman, but with a reasonable distance separating them. The paper admitted in 1993 that the picture was manipulated in order to change his clothes to those of a monk's habit. The impression given by this front-page picture, which was cleverly and undetectably manipulated, was entirely different from the reality. *The Sun* admitted in an official statement: 'We have superimposed the monk's habit to make it clear to the readers that the story is about a monk.' In another example, deputy Labour leader John Prescott had his beer replaced by champagne in a picture used by the *Daily Express*. In another famous example, the website of *Sepah News*, the media arm of Iran's revolutionary guard, ran pictures of missile launches in July 2008. One of the four missiles is a digital copy to cover the fact that one of the missiles failed to launch. Examples of a number of famous manipulated pictures throughout history can be found at http://www.cs.dartmouth.edu/farid/research/digitaltampering/ (accessed 5/2/10).

Television is also capable of giving the wrong impression. Electronic manipulation by computer or editing can completely alter the viewers' perception of events. During the 1984 miners' strike in Britain, in the crucial political battle between the government of Margaret Thatcher and the miners, public opinion was vital. The miners were seen as doing an important job and were viewed sympathetically by ordinary people. They were also well supported by other trade unionists. But if it could be shown that the strikers were unreasonable or violent, public sympathy would soon ebb away. Several major battles between miners and police damaged the miners' case badly; the television coverage consistently showed the miners' attacks as happening first and the police's 'defensive retaliation' following. Many miners, however, claim that this was a distortion. They say that the police always attacked first, attempting to provoke a violent reaction. Did TV companies, for whatever reason, distort the reality by editing the tape to show the 'truth' as happening as the government claimed, rather than the 'truth' as perceived by the miners? It is probably now impossible to find a truly unbiased witness to give us a credible answer, yet this simple example shows how easy it is to distort the picture to present a new 'truth'.

Digital image processing also allows TV to create images that are impossible to differentiate from reality. Many feature films and commercials use these techniques to provide us with fictional or constructed realities that are impossible to distinguish from reality. The *BBC Editorial Guidelines* warn that viewers must not be misled into believing that they are seeing something which is 'real' when in fact it is a creation of a graphic artist.

The Swedish code of conduct has a strong clause on image manipulation: 'Making a montage, retouching a picture by an electronic method, or formulating a picture caption should not be performed in a such a way as to mislead or deceive the reader. Always state, close to the picture, whether it has been altered by montage or retouching. This also applies to such material when it is filed' (Swedish Press Code 1995). The NUJ agreed at its 1996 conference to campaign 'for the adoption of a world-wide convention for the marking of photographs that have been digitally manipulated'. At its 1998 conference the union decided to change its code of conduct to specifically outlaw the practice of digital manipulation: 'No journalist shall knowingly cause or allow the publication or broadcast of a photograph that has been manipulated unless that photograph is clearly labelled as such. Manipulation does not include normal dodging, burning, colour balancing, spotting, contrast adjustment, cropping and obvious masking for legal or safety reasons' (NUJ Code of Conduct 1998). The NUJ later amended the code to give pictures and words the same level of requirement for truth and accuracy.

Audio manipulation

Radio is not immune to the opportunity to manipulate how reports are perceived. Adding an additional soundtrack can alter how the report is perceived whether the additional soundtrack is music or effects. Adding sound effects to give the impression that a piece is recorded somewhere different is something that should not be done lightly. Adding a soundtrack to give the impression that a piece was recorded in a faraway jungle instead of a studio in a Midlands town, for instance, would be to mislead the audience. Equally, adding a music soundtrack would mean adding a mood to the piece that would be inappropriate unless the piece was actually about music.

Impartiality and bias in broadcasting

Impartiality and bias are the big divide as far as TV and newspapers are concerned. Newspapers do not see it as part of their brief to be impartial whereas it is an important ethical area for broadcasting. I've used the point from the *BBC Editorial Guidelines* before, but 'Impartiality is at the heart of the BBC'. Both history and the law go into making sure that impartiality is a major cornerstone of British factual broadcasting. The Broadcasting Acts insist on it and it is a major regulatory purpose of Ofcom and the BBC.

This means that broadcasting has a duty to be fair to all sides of an argument. This may involve more than two sides. It is perfectly possible that a controversial issue has four or five major strands with protagonists supporting and opposing different strands all at the same time. Television producers must ensure not only that each protagonist gets equal air time, but also that the major strands of the debate get a fair hearing. Political matters are particularly sensitive but, again, just giving each major party equal time may not be enough. Discussions on the environment, for instance, might involve the Green Party as well as the three main parties. European debates might involve the Referendum Party. These specialist interests should bring new arguments and points of view to the debate. For instance, all three major parties were in favour of staying in Europe in 2010. To get views from a party which wished to pull out (or at least implied that it would be prepared to pull out) one would have to talk to the UK Independence Party. Newspapers, on the other hand, are almost always biased and have no legal obligation to present news impartially. They do, however, have an obligation to tell the truth and this should limit the amount of slanting possible, although there is no obligation on a newspaper to present all sides of an argument. While some are better than others at presenting a range of views, very few present all the facts all of the time. It is necessary to read a number of papers and listen to the news if one is to get a balanced view of the news.

Comment

This sub-section of impartiality is slightly different in that comment in the media is common currency. Whether it is reviewing a film or a book, describing the performance of a sporting team or player, or analysing the ideas of a politician, journalists in all media are commenting about things and presenting their opinions to the consumers. There is nothing wrong with the presentation of comment in the media provided everyone is clearly aware that those views are the opinion of the writer or broadcaster and are not to be taken as fact.

Many newspapers, radio stations and TV channels rely on opinionated writers or presenters to outrage or cheer up their readers or listeners. Indeed, publication of strong and controversial opinion without the need to present a single supporting fact is the historical birthplace of modern journalism, which sprang to cynical middle age from the cradle of political partisanship. Only if comment is mixed in with factual reporting in an attempt to mislead or distort should the journalist beware. Again, truthfulness is damaged if the consumer is led through a series of opinions under the guise of truth.

The BBC and other broadcasters have a legal obligation to be impartial and this can give rise to problems with comment programmes. The *BBC Editorial Guidelines* say that such programmes involve special obligations. Such programmes must be signalled in advance to the audience and editors must ensure that comment does not misrepresent opposing viewpoints. The *Guidelines* suggest that it may be appropriate to offer an opportunity to respond and that it may be inappropriate for regular presenters and reporters to present personal views on such programmes.

The PCC Code of Practice has a clause on comment: 'Newspapers, while free to be partisan, should distinguish clearly between comment, conjecture and fact.' The NUJ Code says that a journalist 'upholds and defends the principle of media freedom, the right of freedom of expression and the right of the public to be informed' and that a journalist 'differentiates between fact and opinion'. Ofcom's code only calls for news to be impartial, which has some place in this section although partiality is not the same as comment.

Chapter 6

Privacy and intrusion

This chapter discusses:

- A right to privacy in our personal lives

- The moral problems of intrusion into personal privacy

- The development of privacy as a matter of public concern

- Intrusion as a moral dilemma

Privacy is one of the more controversial areas of professional ethics. Many of the big ethical debates of the past fifty years have been about intrusions into privacy and the way journalists have handled them. There has been a steady growth in the desire for privacy since the Second World War which is matched by a rising desire to know more about the celebrities that have become a central part of many of our lives.

What is privacy?

'A society which permits individuals to choose how they are to lead their lives is one which will recognise the choice of privacy' (Lord Chancellor's Department 1993: 9). Invasion of privacy is the journalistic ethical issue that probably most concerns the public. It is certainly the issue that has underlined many of the major debates on the press of the past twenty years or so. Privacy is recognised by psychologists as a basic human need, a drive almost as powerful as sex, hunger and thirst. We all need privacy and we need to be in control of the flow of information about our private selves. It is often said that information is power, but it is just as true that control over information is power. Human dignity, certainly in part, requires the ability to control information about ourselves and if we are to have a right to dignity, we need a right to respect for privacy.

There are some other concepts that we need to consider when looking at privacy. They are related and are often confused. The most private condition is secret. We all have areas we want to keep private, but not all of us see those as secret. Secret means keeping the information from everyone, or at least from all but a small, chosen group. We often go to considerable effort to protect secrecy as releasing secret information could damage our security. Privacy is not so closely guarded as secrecy. Private information is information that we don't necessarily want others to know, but is not a secret. Often this level of information would not seriously damage a person should it reach the public domain, but we might prefer that it shouldn't because it would give others more information about us, and therefore more power over us, than we would prefer. For instance, my choice of music or food is not a secret and if it got into the public domain I would not be too upset – surprised perhaps, but not upset. However, I would probably prefer that it didn't as it would give strangers the feeling of a greater level of intimacy than I would prefer. This brings us to a related concept, that of intimacy. Intimacy is the sharing of private information with someone you trust or someone with whom you are attempting to develop a relationship. This intimacy, the sharing of private information, is used to build relationships. At the level of acquaintance, we would not share much in the way of private information. Friends would know a good deal more.

There exist a number of theories about privacy and related concepts and we should examine them. Archard (1998: 83) claims that 'Privacy has to do with keeping personal information non-public or undisclosed.' He goes on to explain that some classes of information might be considered private by some, but not others. This is quickly proved. Ask any friend to give you some private information. You will find that the type or class of information given is very varied. One friend might be happy to share her weight, another might not and instead would choose to let you know her salary. Another friend might be happy to let you know his favourite colour, while another would only say he likes lager. It is probably reasonable to assume that the closer a person's private details are to the cultural norm, the happier they would be to share the information. The more different the information, the more privately the information is held.

Parent expands Archard's view about personal information a little but the essentials remain the same: 'Privacy is the condition of not having undocumented personal knowledge about one possessed by others' (Parent 1992: 92). She qualifies this, saying that this should mean facts that most individuals in a given society do not want widely known about themselves. This is an interesting qualification as it suggests that there is information that is not private, even though we might not tell anyone about it, simply because it is not in that class of information that a given society believes should be private. But that distorts the nature of privacy. Surely if I decide information should not normally be shared, it is private, regardless of what my culture says. Of course, I am more likely to keep information private if my culture sees that as a class of information that should generally be kept private.

Wacks talks about privacy being the use or abuse of personal information about an individual: this personal information being facts, communications or opinions which that individual might regard as intimate or sensitive. This is a development on the previous theories as it is now not concerned with the information itself but the usage of it by others (Wacks 1995: 23).

Sissella Bok introduces a more complex theory on privacy. This does not concentrate solely on the information held and whether it is in the public domain or not and therefore whether it is private or not, but she considers who controls access to the information:

> Being protected from unwanted access by others ... Claims to privacy are claims to control access to what one takes – however grandiosely – to be one's personal domain.
>
> (Bok 1982: 10–11)

Judith Innes believes that privacy is dependent not on the information itself, but on the motivation for keeping things private or revealing them. This takes privacy into a wider arena. Remember, we are not necessarily talking about secrets here, but private information. Secrets are things we do not want others to know and we go to some lengths to keep them secret. We either share the information with no one, or at most a small number of trusted people; trusted either because we believe them to be trustworthy, or because we believe they have a very strong motive of their own to keep the matter secret.

Innes believes we must reject what she calls separation-based definitions of privacy or a definition that defines privacy as not being looked at or listened to. She gives the example of someone locked in a room – they would have privacy, but it would be an undesirable privacy that they would seek to end. If privacy is about controlling access, then that same person has no privacy, as they do not control access: someone else has the key. Both these definitions fail then, because no one would seriously suggest that this was a true measure of privacy or its removal. The TV show *Big Brother*, for instance, is not about privacy, but about revelation, which is not the same thing at all.

Privacy is more closely linked to intimacy, information that we only share with those we trust and with whom we want to build a bond. Fried talks about the commodification of intimacy:

> close relationships involve the voluntary and spontaneous relinquishment of something between friend and friend, lover and lover. The title to information about oneself conferred by privacy provides the necessary something ... intimacy is the sharing of information about one's actions, beliefs, or emotions which one does not share with all, and which one has the right not to share with anyone.
>
> (Charles Fried as cited by Innes 1992: 82–3)

This does not go far enough for Innes. She believes that intimacy must have a special meaning for this commodification to work. For her, privacy hinges on the motivation of imparting information, not the act itself. This links into intimacy. If I share information about myself that I consider to be private, in terms of developing an intimate relationship, then I have the right to consider this information private. If I release it in order to make money or to make myself famous, then my motivation was not to develop an intimate relationship, but to develop a public relationship. In Innes' theory, privacy protects a realm of intimacy:

intimate matters draw their intimacy from their motivational dependency ... To claim that an act or activity is intimate is to claim that it draws its meaning and value from the agent's love, liking, or care.

(Innes 1992: 90)

So, for Innes, privacy is all about our motivation in intimate relations. Something that is done out of intimacy might well be private, while the same action done for money or fame would not.

Her theories help explain why seemingly private actions can be brought into the public realm, because the motivation is to develop a public persona or to make money. Kiss-and-tell stories, for instance, might well be entirely arranged for money or fame and are not private acts. The problem is that for ordinary people, these acts are private, because their motivation in normal relations is to develop an intimate relationship. Since most people do these things for reasons that should allow them to keep those actions private, there is a level of confusion about whether they should be private just because they are those sorts of actions.

Of course this may work in reverse. Because journalists spend a lot of time these days printing stories that apparently invade privacy because the acts revealed were motivated by the search for fame and money, they may no longer be entirely certain that some acts should remain private because their motivation is the search for intimacy.

Some people believe that there is now a sea change in understanding on privacy that is developing a generational shift between young and old, a dividing line that occurs at 30. Marina Hyde writing in *The Guardian*, said: 'Gradually, older generations are having to adjust to the notion that not only do younger people not really care about privacy; they often don't even comprehend the idea of it' (http://www.guardian.co.uk/commentisfree/2007/nov/10/comment.blogging accessed 10/2/10). Pointing out that many young people now feel that fame is a basic human right, with appearances on television talent shows being the modern equivalent of youth club, she describes the new exhibitionism and goes on to warn that this cultural shift has serious dangers that will leave young people immensely exposed. This view of generational changes in privacy were supported by an Irish blogger, Damian Mulley, when addressing a conference organised by the Irish Press Ombudsman in January 2010. Describing the policy change at Facebook to default all material to public, he suggested this was the way the young generation expect things to be. Despite this claimed shift in the understanding of privacy, there is a clear increase in complaints to the PCC and Ofcom about privacy and a rising view that the media should not be exposing people's identity and private business. The link seems to be the level of control. It might be fine for me to post pictures of myself involved in whatever activities I enjoy, along with suitable and often intrusive comments, but it's not all right for the media to pick up on them and publish them more widely. This can lead to serious problems where Facebook happily publishes pictures or details of the private moments of family and friends with little thought to the protection of their privacy only for them to be deeply upset when they suddenly become a major news story and their pictures or private details are picked up from their Facebook page.

I mentioned earlier that we are less concerned about revealing intimate details if they fit firmly into what we believe to be society's norms and, conversely, the further they diverge from the norm, the less likely we would be to divulge this to all but our most intimate relations. To take sex lives as an example. No one is going to be concerned about admitting to enjoying monogamous heterosexual relations. Homosexuals are likely to be a little more choosy about who they share that information with as are those who have more than one sexual partner at a time. Those who have very unusual sexual practices such as bondage or rubber fetishism are going to confess that to only a very limited audience. This protection of privacy depending on the extent of deviance from the norm means we have to have a very clear understanding of what the limits of our society's norms are.

In order for us to understand the limits of those norms, we gossip and exchange information about our view of society and its boundaries of behaviour. Those of high status and celebrity can be role models whether they want to be or not; we look at their lives as desirable and see them as desirable and therefore as social boundary shapers. We not only want to know what they are doing in the intimate areas of their lives, but also may need to know in order to help us understand what is or is not acceptable to society generally. This may be why many of the fiercest recent rows about privacy have involved footballers. Their heady lifestyles fuelled by high salaries, adulation and youth mean that the only limitations on their behaviour are social acceptability.

While 'seven out of ten of all complaints made to the PCC concern inaccuracy in press reporting' (PCC, 1995: 7), the complaints that cause the most controversy are the invasions of privacy. 'Privacy complaints represent a key component of our work', the PCC said in its 2008 annual report. Most codes of conduct, and certainly the NUJ's, the PCC's, the BBC's *Editorial Guidelines* and Ofcom's, are concerned with privacy. However, writing a universal law to cover privacy is very difficult if we are to allow for the public's 'right to be informed'. There are too many variables around the circumstances of each invasion of privacy to allow for hard-and-fast rules. This must be particularly true if what we are attempting to measure is a person's motivation, something that nearly always remains opaque and impenetrable. When it comes to assessing whether to use a story which appears to invade someone's privacy, Clifford Christians et al. (1998: 111) advocate three tests for the journalist:

1   Decency and fairness is non-negotiable.
2   'Redeeming social value' should be used as a criterion for deciding when to invade privacy.
3   The dignity of the person should not be maligned in the name of press privilege.

There have been many serious invasions of privacy by the British press over the years and these breaches, especially those involving Princess Diana, have led to an outcry to introduce some form of legislation.

The right to respect for privacy

A number of countries around the world already have legislation to prevent invasions of privacy. France has specific laws. Others, such as Belgium, Finland or Italy, have clauses in their constitutions that protect the private rights of citizens. The UN Declaration of Human Rights also has such a clause, as does the European Convention on Human Rights.

People's concern with invasions of privacy is a fairly recent phenomenon. Very little was written about privacy until the end of the last century possibly because this only becomes an issue of concern when communities start to become large enough for us to have some element of privacy and the ability to protect it. One of the earliest definitions of privacy is Thomas Cooley's (1888) 'the right to be left alone', as cited in Warren and Brandeis' treatise on privacy. Concern over invasions of privacy started to grow in Britain, and elsewhere in Europe, after the Second World War. As radio and television gradually took over the alerting element of hard news from newspapers, the tabloids increasingly published gossip and with it increased the number of stories involving invasions of privacy. The first British Royal Commission on the Press in 1947–49 says hardly anything about the invasion of privacy. It is concerned with monopoly ownership and accuracy. By the late 1960s and early 1970s, however, it was firmly on the agenda. The Nordic Conference on the Right of Privacy (1967) came to the conclusion that:

> The right to privacy is the right to be let alone to live one's own life with the minimum degree of interference. In expanded form this means:

The right of the individual to lead his [*sic*] own life protected against:

(a) Interference with his private, family and home life;
(b) Interference with his physical and mental integrity or his moral and intellectual freedom;
(c) Attacks on his honour and reputation;
(d) Being placed in a false light;
(e) The disclosure of embarrassing facts relating to his private life;
(f) The use of his name, identity or likeness;
(g) Spying, prying, watching and besetting;
(h) Interference with his correspondence;
(i) Misuse of his private communications, written or oral;
(j) Disclosure of information given or received by him in a condition of professional confidence.

(Committee on Privacy 1972: 327)

In 1972, a committee was set up in Britain under the chairmanship of the Rt Hon Kenneth Younger. This investigated the need for privacy legislation. They found, as had others before them, some difficulty in defining precisely what was meant by 'privacy'. 'The majority of us regard the "Justice" Committee's conclusions as one more indication, and a highly significant one, that the concept of privacy cannot be satisfactorily defined' (Committee on Privacy 1972: 17). The 'Justice' Committee's conclusion says:

We have therefore concluded that no purpose would be served by our making yet another attempt at developing an intellectually rigorous analysis. We prefer instead to leave the concept much as we have found it, that is as a notion about whose precise boundaries there will always be a variety of opinions, but about whose central area there will always be a large measure of agreement.

(ibid.: 18)

This Committee came to the conclusion that there were risks in placing excessive reliance on the law in order to protect privacy. It recommended that the then Press Council should codify its adjudications on invasions of privacy and that the then Programmes Complaints Commission – the forerunner of the BCC – should have its power extended to handle complaints about privacy.

The 1947–49 Royal Commission on the Press also came to the conclusion that the law was no place for privacy: 'Quite apart from the fact that we consider the Press Council a better forum for establishing rules of conduct for the press in relation to invasions of privacy, we think it would reduce its status and importance if its jurisdiction over this area of activity were to be removed' (Royal Commission on the Press 1977: 187). The Calcutt Report on Privacy and Related Matters, set up by the government in 1989 and reporting in 1990, came to similar conclusions, but decided that the Press Council should be replaced by the PCC. It recommended against a statutory tort of infringement of privacy but did want to see the introduction of a criminal offence for physical intrusion. Any person able to prove intrusion would be able to prevent the publication of an article gathered in that way. Taking photographs and the placing of surveillance devices without consent should also be an offence. A public interest defence was available.

The House of Commons' Heritage Committee also examined the issue and came to the conclusion that a protection of privacy bill should be introduced. In 1995 the Heritage minister finally reported that the government had been unable to formulate wording and therefore was not intending to introduce such a bill.

The Government has long recognised that there is, in principle, a case for the introduction of such offences ... The Government has, however, so far been unable to construct legislation which, in practice, would be sufficiently workable to be responsibly brought to the statute book. It has no wish to introduce bad legislation. It therefore has no immediate plans to legislate in this area.

(Department of National Heritage 1995: 9)

The Labour government made it clear shortly after its election in 1997 that it also favoured self-regulation and did not intend to introduce privacy legislation. It did, however, introduce the Human Rights Act 1998 in order to bring the European Convention on Human Rights into UK law as required by the European Commission. This gave UK citizens a right to privacy in UK law for the first time (we had always had access to our Convention rights in the European Court of Human Rights):

Everyone has the right to respect for his private and family life, his home and his correspondence. There shall be no interference by a public authority with the exercise of this right except such as is in accordance with the law and is necessary in a democratic society in the interests of national security, public safety or the economic well-being of the country, for the prevention of disorder or crime, for the protection of health or morals, or for the protection of the rights and freedoms of others.

(Human Rights Act 1998, chapter 42 schedule 1)

In order to benefit under the Human Rights Act one must show that one's rights have been curtailed and seek relief through the courts. The Act specifically prevents restraint of publication unless 'the court is satisfied that the applicant is likely to establish that publication should not be allowed' (Human Rights Act 1998, chapter 42 clause 12). The court is also specifically obliged under the Act to have particular regard to the Convention's right of freedom of expression if the material seems to the court to be journalistic, literary or artistic material and the extent to which publication of the material is in the public interest, and with regard to any relevant privacy code. It is generally accepted that this is a direct reference to the PCC Code of Practice; Ofcom's privacy code is required by statute. The Human Rights Act produced a very significant change in the approach taken to the behaviour of the media by the law and by the public. A series of significant cases followed through the courts and these will be examined later in this chapter. In 2003 the Select Committee on Culture, Media and Sport met to discuss 'Privacy and Media Intrusion'. It examined problems with the PCC and looked closely at the working of various regulatory bodies. Because Ofcom, the Office of Communications, had only just started its role of regulating broadcasting, not much was said by the committee about this body. But it had plenty to say about the PCC (see Chapter 17). The committee concluded that there should be a privacy law:

On balance we firmly recommend that the Government reconsider its position and bring forward legislative proposals to clarify the protection that individuals can expect from unwarranted intrusion by anyone – not the press alone – into their private lives.

(House of Commons Culture, Media and Sport Committee 2003: para. 111)

In a mirror of the same debate ten years before, the government quickly made it clear that it had no intention of introducing a privacy law. Two subsequent Culture, Media and Sport Select Committee reports on regulation and standards of the press, one in 2007 and the next in 2010, continued the committee's support for self-regulation and, in 2010, specifically ruled out legislation on privacy. The history of privacy in the UK is summarised in Exhibit 6.1.

Exhibit 6.1 The history of privacy in the UK

Privacy has a relatively short history in the UK and there was little concern about it until widespread literacy made reading about your fellow citizens a possibility and photography made picture intrusions a reality.

1926   The Judicial Proceedings (Regulation of Reports) Act limited what could be written about divorces. This was one of the first pieces of legislation determining what could be written about people's personal lives.

1933   The Children and Young Persons Act 1933 prevented the reporting of the identity of children (aged 10–14) and young persons (aged 14–17) as alleged offenders or witnesses in magistrates' courts.

1937   Both proprietors' and journalists' organisations passed formal resolutions condemning methods of news-gathering which caused distress to private persons.

1947   The 1947 Royal Commission on the Press paid little attention to privacy. It was suggested to the Commission that intrusions into the privacy of individuals, especially those who have suffered bereavement, was an abuse that should be corrected by legislation. The Commission felt it would be 'extremely difficult to devise legislation which would deal with the mischief effectively and be capable of enforcement' (Royal Commission 1949: 170) and that it was up to the industry to make condemnation of bad practice effective. The General Council of the Press (as suggested by the Commission) would have a role to play here.

1961   The 1961 Royal Commission on the Press said nothing about privacy. However, a bill was put before Parliament by Lord Mancroft in the same year to protect a person from any unjustifiable publication relating to his private affairs and to give him rights at law in the event of such publication. It was given a second reading but was withdrawn at the end of the debate to go into committee.

1967   Mr Alexander Lyon MP introduced a bill to protect persons from any unreasonable and serious interference with their seclusion of themselves, their family or their property from the public. The bill was introduced as a ten-minute bill and there was no second reading.

The Nordic Conference on the Right of Privacy was highly influential in developing some of the main concerns about privacy.

1969   Mr Brian Walden MP introduced a bill to establish a right of privacy, to make consequential amendments to the law of evidence and for connected purposes. His bill was withdrawn after the second reading debate.

1970   The first stab at a privacy law was attempted by the Justice Committee which investigated privacy and the law and reported back to Parliament.

1972   The Younger Committee on privacy concluded that: 'Privacy is ill-suited to be the subject of a long process of definition through the building up of precedents over the years since the judgments of the past would be an unreliable guide to any current evaluation of privacy' (Committee on Privacy 1972: 206). On the other hand, it pointed out that without precedent the law would remain 'an ill-defined and unstable concept' (ibid.) as it was first formulated. In the end they agreed to three things:

- The restatement of the law of breach of confidence.
- The introduction of laws banning electronic bugging.
- The introduction of a new tort of publication of information gained unlawfully.

A minority report by Mr Alexander Lyon MP favoured the addition of a civil tort for invasion of privacy. He had already introduced a bill to attempt this in the past. Mr D. Ross also issued a minority report favouring a general right of privacy along the lines of Mr Brian Walden's bill (see 1969 above).

1974   The Rehabilitation of Offenders Act 1974 made it an offence to detail an offender's criminal past after a suitable period of rehabilitation had elapsed.

1976   The Sexual Offences Act 1976 made it an offence to name the victims and accused in rape cases.

1977   The 1977 Royal Commission discussed privacy but decided this was not within its remit.

In February, Mr Tom Litterick MP attempted to introduce a Freedom of Information and Privacy Bill. It did not get past its first reading.

1984   The Data Protection Act 1984 was agreed, giving protection to the privacy of personal data held on computers. The 1992–96 Conservative government had intended to allow government institutions to share computer-held information in a way that is barred under the present Act. This was opposed by those concerned about government invasions of privacy. On the other hand, newspaper editors were becoming concerned about the use of the Data Protection Act 1984 as a way of preventing the release of information. They were concerned that changes in the Act could tighten up their access to information about people.

1988   A Right of Privacy Bill was introduced to the house by Mr William Cash MP to 'establish a right of privacy, to make amendments to the law of evidence, and for connected purposes'. This would have allowed for civil action and had a public benefit defence. Proving that something is for the public benefit is not the same as proving it to be in the public interest. The bill did not receive a second reading.

The Sexual Offences (Amendment) Act 1988 removed the right of the accused in rape cases to have his name kept confidential. The right of the victim to keep her name confidential was also brought forward to the moment an accusation was made rather than when the case came to court, as had previously been the case.

1989   A Protection of Privacy Bill to establish a right of privacy against the unauthorised use or disclosure of private information and for connected purposes was introduced into Parliament by Mr John Browne MP. This bill made breaching privacy a civil offence with a public interest defence. It was withdrawn after the committee stage but before the report stage. Breach of confidence law does have some part to play in privacy. The law was best defined in 1990 by the Master of the Rolls Sir John Donaldson in a judgment *Attorney General* v *Guardian Newspapers*.

The Children Act 1989 raised the age at which minors could be identified to 18.

1990   The Calcutt Committee on privacy and related matters recommended that a law should be introduced making physical intrusion an offence, but did not call for a privacy law.

1992   The Sexual Offences (Amendment) Act 1992 widened the range of victims who are legally entitled to keep their names secret. Both men and women who were the victims of sexual assault, buggery, incest, under-age sex or indecent conduct towards a child now had the right to keep their names secret.

1993   Calcutt looked at privacy and press self-regulation and reported in January, recommending that the government look at introducing a tort for infringement.

The Heritage Committee discussed privacy and reported in March. They decided that a protection of privacy law should be introduced, with a public interest defence, but that this would apply to all citizens, covering invasions of privacy on a wider basis than just publication.

1994   The government announced that it had postponed indefinitely plans for privacy laws, despite issuing a consultation paper on privacy.

1995   In July, the Heritage Secretary, Mrs Virginia Bottomley, presented the government's response to the consultation paper to Parliament. There should be no privacy legislation. A few changes to the PCC were suggested, otherwise matters were to remain as they were.

1996   Diana, Princess of Wales won an injunction to prevent a freelance photographer approaching within 300 metres. Many newspapers, particularly the *Daily Mail*, tried to take the moral high ground by condemning the photographer for his methods and claiming not to use his pictures.

1997   The death of the Princess of Wales brought howls of general protest about the alleged intrusions of the press. Lord Spencer tried to relaunch his campaign to introduce a privacy law, but was refused by the government who said that it was not the time to rush into things. The government announced it intended to introduce the European Convention on Human Rights into UK law, which some saw as privacy law by the back door.

1998   In February, Lord Irvine of Lairg, the Lord Chancellor, proposed a new law of privacy that would allow for prior restraint by the PCC and the payment of compensation to those whose privacy was breached. He was immediately rebuked by the Prime Minister as being out of keeping with the agreed Cabinet line and ordered to reaffirm the government line in the Lords. A week or so later, Tony Blair told the House of Commons that he had taken personal charge of the Human Rights Bill in an effort to prevent a 'back door' privacy law.

The European Convention on Human Rights was introduced into law via the Human Rights Act 1998. Following its introduction, a number of test cases were heard that have started to produce a slightly different view of privacy.

The Data Protection Act 1998 also caused some concern now that most newspapers and broadcast operations use computers for writing stories and storing information.

2002   Two young women with whom footballer Garry Flitcroft had an affair told *The People* their story. The Appeal Court agreed that this was their right and that Flitcroft had no right to expect these relationships to be confidential. The court also agreed that there is a public interest in publishing material of interest to the public and that therefore some invasions of privacy are justified.

2003   The House of Commons Culture, Media and Sport Committee called for a new law on privacy following hearings on Privacy and Media Intrusion. The government quickly responded, saying it would not introduce a privacy law.

2004   The House of Lords overturned an Appeal Court decision over Naomi Campbell. Campbell had been reported and pictured by the *Daily Mirror* attending a meeting of Narcotics Anonymous. Although both sides accepted that the newspaper was entitled to report her attendance as she had previously denied taking drugs, the House of Lords found that it was not entitled to go into so much detail or use pictures of her treatment.

2006   The PCC amended its code of practice to include a clause about suicide to avoid intrusion into private grief in such circumstances.

The Appeal Court upheld the High Court's view on the *McKennitt* v *Ash* case that Ash had intruded on Loreena McKennitt's privacy and granted Ms McKennitt relief.

2007   The Culture, Media and Sport Select Committee examined the cases of Kate Middleton, the then girlfriend of Prince William, and her continual harassment by photographers. It also looked at the conviction and jailing of *News of the World* Royal Editor Clive Goodman for conspiracy to intercept communications by tapping into royal mobile phone answer phones alongside wider concerns about newspapers using private investigators to obtain personal data illegally. However, the committee decided that 'to rely exclusively on the law would afford less protection rather than more'.

2008   Max Mosley, the then president of the Formula 1 Association, was awarded £60,000 by the courts for the *News of the World*'s invasion of his privacy in accusing him of taking part in a 'sick Nazi orgy'. Video of his assignation with five prostitutes involving sadomasochism was broadcast on the paper's website.

2010   The House of Commons Culture, Media and Sport Select Committee reported its views on privacy. Following on from the Mosley case the Committee decided against a mandatory pre-notification, recommending instead that the PCC Code should make it a requirement for journalists to notify the subject of a story before publication subject to a 'public interest' test. The committee also agreed that it was not the time for privacy legislation.

The Coalition government is elected agreeing to 'establish a Commission to investigate the creation of a British Bill of Rights that incorporates and builds on all our obligations under the European Convention on Human Rights, ensures that these rights continue to be enshrined in British law ...' It is not clear whether this will affect privacy rights.

The present law affecting privacy

There is no general right of privacy in UK law according to the Master of the Rolls, Lord Neuberger, in a speech given at Eton (http://www.judiciary.gov.uk/docs/speeches/mor-privacy-freedom-expression-28042010.pdf). He points out that this was confirmed by the Court of Appeal in the Gorden Kaye case and reaffirmed by the House of Lords in *Wainwright* v *Home Office*.

In that case the Lords were invited to find that the Human Rights Act 1998 had introduced a right to privacy into English law. The invitation was flatly rejected. The Lords would not declare that there was as a consequence of the 1998 Act '*a previously unknown tort of invasion of privacy*' in English law. In doing so they were acting, as Lord Hoffmann had it, consistently with the jurisprudence emanating from Strasbourg. How? Because as he put it, Strasbourg has held that the article 8 right to respect for privacy does not require a State to provide a high level, general, privacy law.

(ibid: 6)

However, although there is no general right to privacy in the UK, the right to respect for privacy has led the courts to develop a number of rights to allow for legal enforcement of the right to respect for privacy, particularly breach of confidence which had been developed so that there no longer needs to be a confidential relationship between the parties in the dispute leading to a tort of misuse of private information. Lord Neuberger said:

> When assessing such a claim a court must first decide whether the claimant has established whether there is a reasonable expectation of privacy in respect of the information of which disclosure is threatened. If there's a reasonable expectation, the next issue is whether disclosure can be justified. Is disclosure in the public interest for instance? Is the information already in the public domain? Would an order barring disclosure be both necessary and proportionate? That is where the considerations set out in article 8(2) and 10 [of the Human Rights Act] come into play. And where they are both in play neither has precedence over the other. When considering the conflict between the two the court is required to do three things: first, it must intensely scrutinise the comparative importance of the specific rights claimed in the particular case; it must then consider the justifications set out for interfering with or restricting each right; and finally, the court must consider the proportionality of the proposed interference or restriction.

(ibid: 7)

It is the law of confidence that is perhaps being used most often by the courts as a way of protecting privacy. This is perhaps not too surprising considering the clear link between our desire to protect privacy and intimacy, as identified above. If we are to protect our intimacy, and it seems to be the main reason why privacy is important, then our confidential dealings with others are often at the heart of that.

The law of confidence was redefined by Sir John Donaldson in 1990. Since then there have been a number of important cases brought, seeking relief from invasions of privacy but ending up slightly reshaping the laws of confidence. These all serve to confirm that there is a right to the confidentiality of information maintained in this country. Sir John Donaldson's view was that 'Since the right to have confidentiality maintained is an equitable right, it will (in legal theory and practical effect if the aid of the court is invoked) "bind the conscience" of third parties, unless they are bona fide purchasers for value without notice …' However, he qualifies this by saying that 'the right will be lost or, at all events, the courts will not uphold and enforce it, if there is just cause or excuse for communicating the information', and 'the right will also be lost if the information, which is subject to a right of confidentiality, is published to the world by or with the consent of the confider, but it will not necessarily be lost if such publication is by the consent or with the consent of the confidant …' (Lord Chancellor's Department 1993: 57). In the case of *X v Y*, Mr Justice Rose restrained the publication of a story obtained from health service workers which named two doctors with AIDS. He said that the public interest in preserving the confidentiality of hospital records outweighed the freedom of the press to publish such information. In a later case, the courts upheld an order restraining the *Mail on Sunday* from publishing the memoirs of a nanny who had looked after the Blair's children on the grounds that a duty of confidence was owed in these circumstances. Further cases that are examined in more detail later on have also changed the view on privacy. The Michael Douglas/Catherine Zeta Jones case, the Naomi Campbell case and the Anna Ford case have all added further strength to a growing raft of laws that are adding impetus to a right to privacy.

There are also other laws in addition to confidence, defamation and malicious falsehood, providing a patchwork protection of people's private lives. The Data Protection Act 1998, for instance, makes it an offence to use personal information gathered for one purpose for another. So a company that gathers information about you in order to provide a service and bill you for it, cannot then sell or give that information to another company or a newspaper or broadcaster without your permission. To do so would be illegal.

It is illegal to intercept communications without the consent of one of the parties. So reading letters or taping telephone calls during transmission are both illegal. The Data Protection Acts 1984 and 1998 put limits on the use of data held on computers and give rights to the people whom the data concerns. The 1998 Act gives people the right to find out what is being held on computers about them, particularly 'sensitive personal data':

(a) the racial or ethnic origin of the data subject,
(b) his political opinions,
(c) his religious beliefs or other beliefs of a similar nature,
(d) whether he is a member of a trade union (within the meaning of the Trade Union and Labour Relations (Consolidation) Act 1992),
(e) his physical or mental health or condition,
(f) his sexual life,
(g) the commission or alleged commission by him of any offence, or
(h) any proceedings for any offence committed or alleged to have been committed by him.

(Data Protection Act 1998, section 2)

This could have given problems to journalists writing investigative stories, so journalism is specifically excluded as one of 'the special purposes':

(a) the purposes of journalism,
(b) artistic purposes, and
(c) literary purposes.

(Data Protection Act 1998, section 3)

Section 32 of the Act specifically excludes processing of such data if it is undertaken with a view to publication.

Court reporting can sometimes protect a person's privacy where a judge has ordered that names should not be used. This usually applies to juveniles so that their privacy is maintained, but it can apply to other cases. Rape victims and victims of certain other sex offences are granted anonymity under the Sexual Offences (Amendment) Acts 1976 and 1992. The government published a bill in 2006 proposing that coroners could gain the power to keep the names of victims or some interested party anonymous.

The Conspiracy and Protection of Property Act 1875, although intended to apply only to industrial disputes, could be brought to bear to prevent others from persistently following or watching or besetting a person's house, or place of work, or business, with a view to compelling them to do or not do something which he/she has a right not to do or to do.

The Rehabilitation of Offenders Act 1974 offers very clear protection for the privacy of former criminals. When their offence is considered 'spent', after a suitable period of rehabilitation, we may no longer write about their conviction or crime.

The Broadcasting Acts 1990 and 1996 and the Communications Act 2003 are of more concern to journalists as these give the most control on privacy of any legislation. The Office of Communications (Ofcom) was set up under the 2002 Office of Communications Act with powers derived from the Communications Act 2003 to protect audiences from infringement of privacy.

Limits on divorce reporting were set by the Judicial Proceedings (Regulation of Reports) Act 1926 and later Acts. The Magistrates' Courts Act 1980, the Children Act 1989 and the Children Act 2004 also limit coverage of private family matters being dealt with by the courts, although the Anti-social Behaviour Act 2003 calls for publicity of those issued with orders. Scotland is very different from England when it comes to privacy and the Scottish Law Commission in 1977 argued that there is scope in Scottish law for the development of a remedy for unjustifiable infringement of privacy. The Criminal Evidence and Youth Justice Act 1999 adds further constraints on the publication of the identities of minors in court cases whether victims, witnesses or alleged offenders. The Regulation of Investigatory Powers Act (2000) makes it illegal to intercept communications in transit whether postal or a public telecommunication system. The Coroners and Justice Act (2009) allows anonymity of investigation and witnesses under certain circumstances.

The language of privacy

One of the major debates around privacy is whether the notoriety or celebrity of a person forces them to accept a lesser right to privacy than others. Since we are talking about a general human right here, the view must be that all are entitled to privacy of their home life. However, those who have gained celebrity or notoriety will have inserted more of their home life into the public domain than others and so are faced with having more of their private life examined in public than others. This is not to say that the argument, often developed by the tabloids, that once someone becomes a public figure their lives are totally open to intrusion is correct. But it does mean that having gained celebrity, status, fame or money on the basis of a public life, the media does have the right to examine that life where conflicts might apply. This can involve a wide range of people and not just celebrities, the royal family or politicians. For example, there is almost certainly a public interest defence for invading the privacy of a local head teacher if it can lead to the truthful revelation that he has been downloading child pornography on to his computer or that she has been misappropriating for personal use money allocated for the education of the children at the school. This is a person who has been granted a privileged position and so has specific responsibilities to the children at the school, their parents and the community to live up to certain standards, and those people are entitled to know if this is not happening. In the instances above, the events are also criminal offences, but what if we choose another example which does not include criminality? Imagine a priest who is found to be having an affair. Not illegal, but again it is not what is expected and the press might well be justified in publishing this in the public interest. Although it intrudes into the priest's private life that intrusion may well be justified because the priest is a leader of social moral behaviour – a role model whether he likes it or not – for the local community and his parishioners in particular. His public life must involve his private behaviour more readily than might be the case for an ordinary private citizen who makes no claims to live by a particular moral code. It is important that we know whether priests are having affairs. It is not significant to anyone other than their partners if an ordinary person is having an affair, unless we consider adultery so damaging to society that we should have a view on such affairs as, for instance, is certainly the case with incest and domestic violence.

We have to accept that privacy varies from person to person as there are some people who are less entitled to privacy over certain parts of their home life than others by virtue of the positions they hold. A number of people seek social status or reputation by holding positions or offices within their communities that carry increased levels of responsibility and therefore reduced rights to privacy. Our expectations of politicians, teachers, doctors, lawyers, clergy, to name just a few, are much higher than those of ordinary citizens. These groups carry status in society but they pay for that with reduced rights. An office manager who had an affair with his secretary would not be considered anything other than foolish, but a teacher who had an affair with a sixth-former or a doctor who had sex with a patient would, quite rightly, feel the full opprobrium of the community should his or her privacy be breached and the story published. Such publication could well be in the public interest.

The public clearly identify different groups of people as having different levels of privacy. These can be loosely identified as:

Those who volunteer for public life: These might include politicians, rock stars, film stars or those seeking celebrity on TV.

Positions of public responsibility: This would include doctors, teachers and civil servants; people who have chosen careers that mean they have some level of responsibility to the public.

Those introduced to public life by accident: This might apply to those dragged into public life against their will, victims of disasters, those who are related to celebrities or criminals.

Notoriety: These are criminals or others who make themselves notorious.

A study carried out by Matthew Kieran, David Morrison and Michael Svennevig in the late 1990s found that the public had little difficulty identifying that while children should have considerable (almost total) control over their privacy, criminals should be entitled to very little control.

False privacy

False privacy is when a complaint about privacy is made concerning information which is claimed to be false or grossly inaccurate. This is sometimes done so that the complainant can seek relief without having to prove that the material is either defamatory or false. The information might, for instance, concern something that the complainant does not want in the public arena and so would refuse to comment on its truthfulness. Normally the courts would not accept that there could be a breach of privacy if the information was false. False information should lead to a suit of libel or malicious falsehood. Privacy is an intended protection against true information that is private. However, in a ground-breaking case, the High Court ruled in 2005 that David Beckham could sue for privacy without revealing whether the claims were true.

The PCC has also considered this issue and taken a similar line, saying in its 2005 annual review that:

> There has been recent comment about the notion of 'false privacy', which litigants in a very small number of cases – one or two – have tried to introduce in order to take legal action against newspapers for intrusion into privacy without saying whether the claims that have been made about them are true or not. It would be a matter for the courts to decide whether publishing an inaccuracy can be intrusive. The Commission has not taken this view, although it has previously dealt with similar issues.
>
> (http://www.pcc.org.uk/assets/111/PCC_Annual_Review2005.pdf)

The PCC went on to quote a case where it had upheld the complaint under clause 3 (privacy) despite not knowing whether the allegation was true or not. Their view at the time was that the complainant can argue that such a story is in breach of the code in that either the story is true but intrusive and so in breach of clause 3 on privacy or inaccurate and in breach of clause 1:

> the newspaper repeated the allegations at length – resulting in an impression, whether or not the allegations were founded, about the alleged lifestyle of the complainant. This resulted in a breach of the Code in one of two ways. If the allegations peddled by the extortionist were unfounded, then the impression created by the article was misleading, breaching Clause 1 (Accuracy) of the Code. If there was substance to the allegations, then the amount of

Table 6.1

Type	A	B	C	D	E	F
Child	54	19	10	6	3	3
Patient with Alzheimer's disease	54	20	12	4	3	2
Parent of murder victim	54	24	13	4	3	2
Person with severe disability	49	23	14	6	3	2
Witness to a crime	48	28	11	6	3	2
A victim of crime	47	26	12	5	4	4
A lottery winner	46	31	10	5	4	3
A member of the royal family	16	19	22	22	12	6
A schoolteacher	13	24	17	20	17	5
A senior policeman	11	18	15	23	21	9
A senior civil servant	10	15	16	27	21	7
A businessman	9	17	21	28	17	4
A film star	8	13	21	21	10	3
A religious leader	8	12	18	23	21	11
A politician	6	10	14	28	29	11
A shoplifter	4	8	9	24	26	25
A drug dealer	3	3	5	9	20	57
A rapist	3	3	3	8	19	60

Key:
A   Right to prevent mention
B   Right to prevent transmission of personal details
C   Right to control what is said
D   Right to be told in advance but not change
E   No right to prevent, but right to comment
F   No right to change or comment

Source: Kieran, Morrison and Svennevig (2000) 'Privacy, the public and journalism', *Journalism* 1(2) 145–69, Sage, London

information provided intruded into the complainant's privacy in breach of Clause 3 (Privacy) of the Code, for which there was no justification. While the newspaper may have been acting to protect the public interest in good faith, this had been an error of judgement.
(http://www.pcc.org.uk/cases/adjudicated.html?article=MTg4Mw== accessed 9/4/10)

What would a privacy law look like?

The issues involved in trying to arrive at a legislative mechanism to protect the rights of citizens against a media that is prepared to make money by exposing the private failings of the public are very complex. The position is further muddied in Britain by having a broadcast regulatory body (Ofcom) that has a statutory duty to investigate complaints about invasions of privacy and a press regulatory body (PCC) which has no statutory duty to do anything. The BBC's *Editorial Guidelines* has a fair bit to say about privacy. This is hardly surprising as the BBC is a broadcaster and so has statutory obligations regarding intrusions into privacy.

> The BBC respects privacy and does not infringe it without good reason, wherever in the world it is operating. The Human Rights Act 1998 gives protection to the privacy of individuals, and private information about them, but balances that with a broadcaster's right to freedom of expression.
>
> (http://www.bbc.co.uk/guidelines/editorialguidelines/page/guidelines-privacy-introduction accessed 14/10/10)

There must, in a democratic society, be a defence for a media that wants to reveal what those with criminal or antisocial motives are intent on keeping secret. It is right, for instance, that the public should be told about the politicians who are fiddling their expenses or taking bribes and exposing those who are offering them because these revelations would be in the public interest. It is right that we should know what legislators are doing in our name and what they are doing with public money. But most people believe there should be limits on invasions of private life, hence the calls for legislation.

If the government were to introduce privacy legislation it would first have to decide whether an invasion of privacy should be a criminal offence or a civil wrong (or tort). If the matter falls under criminal law, then journalists could face continual challenge by the police, constantly being arrested and arraigned for alleged breaches of the law. For this reason, Parliament would be more likely to make privacy a civil offence: if your privacy was invaded, you could sue. The trouble with this is that it is likely to become a rich person's toy. Those who have put themselves in positions of higher social status may have to accept that this must make them more accountable to the society that has granted them that status. Should such people then be allowed to seek less accountability by keeping journalists away with a stream of actions for breach of privacy? Robert Maxwell used this method to good effect to protect his name until after his death by issuing defamation suits against any publication that wrote about him and forcing them to defend the actions. He would then hold up the action, as he was entitled to do, for up to five years. The defendants would have to spend many thousands of pounds keeping solicitors at bay without any recompense, either because the cases never went to court or because even when costs were awarded, they never covered the full costs accrued.

If privacy was made a civil tort in its own right, as opposed to a tort of confidentiality, there is a risk that journalists will measure a person's wealth before deciding to invade their privacy. Although it is likely that conditional fee agreements (CFAs) would be available for such torts, there would still be expenses at an early stage. In any case, the main purpose of such a tort for most people, particularly those who are rich and famous, would be to gain an injunction preventing publication. This strategy has already been identified as the strategy of choice for the rich and famous by Max Mosley. Following his successful privacy case against the *News of the World*, he is presently taking a case to the European Court in a bid to get them to oblige British legislators to introduce a law that would require all journalists to contact the subject of a story before publication. In this way, the subjects of stories would always know before publication and would be able to seek an injunction. While it is obviously good practice to contact the subject of a story and it should always be done under normal circumstances, there are occasions when it would not be in the public interest as it would mean that those who should be exposed would be able to gain an injunction, pending a full hearing, dragging out the proceedings, possibly for years. The Culture, Media and Sport Committee heard a good example of such a case in their investigation into press standards in 2009:

> In May 2009, Ian Hislop, editor of *Private Eye*, told us about a case in which he was involved: 'We attempted to run a story in January [2009] and we still have not been able to run it. The journalist involved put it to the person involved, which was an error; there was an immediate injunction; we won the case; they have appealed; we are still in the Appeal Court. Essentially it is censorship by judicial process because it takes so long and it costs so much.'
>
> The case involved Michael Napier, a former president of the Law Society, and the refusal by Mr Justice Eady to grant an injunction, on grounds of confidentiality, about the outcome of professional complaints made against Mr Napier and his firm. The Court of Appeal subsequently refused to overturn the ruling, following which Mr Napier resigned from his position on the Legal Services Board. *Private Eye* estimated that had it lost, the bill for both sides' costs would have been some £400,000; and had the case gone to the House of Lords, it would have been at risk for £600,000. The magazine said it had originally intended to publish two paragraphs on the issue.
>
> (House of Commons 2010: 17)

Injunctions awarded in cases where the aim is to protect privacy are more likely to be granted becasue the balance of convenience inevitably works in the favour of the claimant. If a judge allows publication, the genie cannot be put back into the bottle. Better to block publication pending a full hearing. A privacy law would probably make it even more likely that such injunctions would be granted.

Privacy laws would also be fairly inflexible. An example of the working of privacy law was identified in a European Court of Human Rights hearing in 2010. Criminal prosecutions were brought against a number of Finnish magazines and journalists following an incident in which a public figure and his mistress became involved in a fight with his wife in 1996. The couple entered the man's home, sparking a fight with the wife. He was given a conditional prison sentence and the mistress was fined. However, Finland's criminal code says spreading information, an insinuation or an image depicting the private life of another person, which was conducive to causing suffering, qualifies as invasion of privacy and criminal charges were brought between 1999 and 2001. Although the man was a public figure and so was not protected, his mistress was not and the fact that she was the mistress of a public figure did not change that and so she retained a right to privacy, the domestic courts decided. However, the European Court decided that as long as information concerning the mistress constituted an integral element of the man's story, the mistress could not invoke article 8 protection. A story like this shows how complicated a law on privacy would make such decisions. It would certainly mean that newspapers would be even more careful of invading the privacy of the rich and famous, to the detriment of the man in the street, who would find it much more likely that he would have his privacy invaded while the rich, famous and influential will be able to avoid exposure of their less worthy deeds with a mix of injunctions and law suits. It is therefore likely that such a law would lead to an *increase* of invasions of privacy on people whose privacy should be invaded less – ordinary people without power, money or influence – while those with these attributes will be able to bring enough pressure to bear to keep their private lives to themselves, even though the public interest may mean that their private lives should be exposed. It could also happen that invasions of privacy, whether of public or private citizens, would continue and that newspapers would happily pay the damages, but would make sure they got their money's worth by really exposing the person's private life.

We also need to consider how a law would operate. At what point would the invasion of privacy start? Could a judge be asked to consider a potential intrusion from the minute the subject first detected a journalist's presence and seek an injunction to prevent the journalist's research? How could a journalist prove that the investigation was in the public interest without doing the research required? Telling a court you think that this person might be doing something antisocial is not going to be good enough, but how can you show your case without investigation?

Intrusion and harassment

Intrusion and harassment are matters of concern during the news-gathering stage rather than at publication. Removing material from someone's dustbin, shouting at them from street corners or telephoning them late at night are all forms of harassment and are usually an unwarranted intrusion. The NUJ has clauses on this matter, as has the PCC, Ofcom and the BBC, but the one difficulty faced by the PCC is how to enforce its Code as the number of freelances used by the industry grows. While the PCC can insist that a paper which sends a staff reporter to harass someone prints an adverse adjudication of its actions, or Ofcom can demand that a TV station which broadcasts a programme containing such harassment publishes a similar adjudication, if freelance journalists are intruding, they may well not be working for any particular paper or broadcast channel and so no one can be taken to task about the matter. With the rise in freelance working, as papers and broadcast stations cut back their staff, this is likely to be an increasing problem, particularly as freelances have more to gain by being more intrusive and have a higher commercial imperative to get the story. Their loyalties are not so tightly directed to readers and they have little loyalty to editors and none to proprietors. Their loyalties must be directed to themselves, their families and, to a much lesser extent, the readers.

What do we mean by intrusion and harassment?

As with many moral judgements, one person's idea of what constitutes intrusion is another person's polite enquiry. The NUJ, BBC and PCC Codes all advise against intrusion into people's grief or shock. Ofcom's code lays down strict guidelines on practices to be followed and how to go about gathering information. There is also a code on fairness. The NUJ Code says that journalists shall do nothing which entails intrusion into private grief and shock unless it is in the public interest. The PCC's Code only says that such enquiries should be carried out with 'sympathy and discretion', although, confusingly, it does mention intrusion under its privacy clause. This can be difficult to work with as there is a public interest defence to this privacy clause. How can a reporter know if the matter is in the public interest until 'intrusions and enquiries into an individual's private life' have been completed?

We need to separate privacy and intrusion as concepts. Breach of privacy is the publication of private matters; intrusion is the way those enquiries are carried out. Intrusion can be found in far wider circumstances than in someone's private grief. Finding photographers in your back garden is an intrusion. Reporters going through your rubbish bin or standing in your kitchen are intrusions. Intrusion, according to *The Oxford Concise English Dictionary* is to 'thrust oneself uninvited'. This does not alter whether the reporter has a good reason for intruding. This is one of the reasons why the codes concentrate on grief and shock only. At any other time, the codes seem to say, the victims of the intrusion should deal with it themselves. As a way of measuring if the reporter was intrusive, the codes rely entirely on what is published and why.

We need to consider whether the ends justify the means. If a minister of the Crown is having an affair, but the press only discovers this by tracking him 24 hours a day, discovering the place where he meets his lover, breaking into that house and setting up bugs and hidden cameras, are they then morally right in claiming this exposure is in the public interest? Or is this intrusion going too far to be justified? If the answer is that the intrusion (not necessarily the publication) can be justified, does this give the media the universal right to do this to anybody at any time and then decide afterwards whether it is in the public interest to publish? And what happens on all those occasions when the person is shown to be entirely blameless? The way the story is gathered has a strong moral element that is separate from the moral element of publication but is just as important.

Ofcom says that consent must be obtained to infringe privacy unless the infringement is warranted. The BBC is quite clear where it stands on intrusion: 'The use of unattended recording equipment on private property without the consent of the owner, occupier or agent must be referred to Director Editorial Policy and Standards' (http://www.bbc.co.uk/guidelines/ editorialguidelines/page/guidelines-privacy-mandatory-referrals/ accessed 14/10/10). Even then, the Director Editorial Policy and Standards must always agree in advance and will require clear evidence that the crime has been committed by those who are going to be bugged. The BBC also condemns what it calls 'fishing expeditions': that is, there must be some evidence of wrong-doing by 'identifiable individuals' before secret recording can take place. The only exceptions the BBC allows are when filming is necessary for the purpose of showing social attitudes, and the essence of the programme is that people should behave naturally. In this case, permission to use the footage has to be obtained from the people involved. If identifiable people do not give permission, their faces should be obscured, a relatively easy task with modern digital editing.

Only 4.1 per cent of the complaints adjudicated by the PCC up to 2010 concerned intrusion, so it is not a large part of their work. However, these were only intrusions that fall into the grief and shock category. In the privacy category (12 per cent), complaints have risen in line with total complaints and some of these are certainly about intrusion. Harassment is a different category and involves 2.5 per cent of complaints.

Harassment

The acid test of harassment needs to be a clear indication from the person to be interviewed that he or she does not wish to be interviewed. Continuing to press him or her for an interview after this is for the journalist to lay him or herself open to allegations of harassment.

The *BBC Editorial Guidelines* has a full page about harassment. Doorstepping is of particular concern – the practice of reporters turning up uninvited to confront and record a potential inter- viewee without permission, usually on private property. Such invasions need permission and should only be carried out '… when there is evidence of crime or significant wrong-doing' and there is 'good reason to believe the investigation will be frustrated if a prior approach is made' (http://www.bbc.co.uk/guidelines/editorialguidelines/page/guidelines-privacy-doorstepping accessed 14/10/10). Ofcom also has a long clause on this issue.

Media scrums are also of concern to the BBC and the PCC. This is where there are so many reporters that their sheer numbers can be intimidating, even if the objects of their interest are willing to talk. The BBC is prepared to accept pooling arrangements and will withdraw if it is clear the subject is not going to appear. The PCC made it clear in four judgments against different papers covering the same issue that it did not find 'collective harassment' acceptable:

> While in this case the Commission did not find evidence to justify criticising this or any other individual newspaper, it would not hesitate to do so if in a future case it became apparent that an individual newspaper or reporter either played a leading part in unjustified collective harassment or did not desist when personally asked to do so.
>
> (PCC, Report No. 37, 1997: 12)

It is often easier to find out what the PCC believes is not harassment than the other way around. A *Sun* picture taken of 'Moors murderer' Ian Brady with a very long range telephoto lens in hospital was not harassment despite there being PCC clauses both on taking pictures in hospital and of using long-range lenses. The public interest was served, the PCC said in Report No. 31 (1995). Nor was it harassment for the *Daily Mail* to ring Judy Finnegan's mother and, on being told she did not do interviews with journalists on the telephone, send reporters to her home. Both reporters finished the interview politely on being told by Mrs Finnegan that she did not want to speak to them.

In 1984 the *Daily Mail* had a complaint upheld against it for harassment after its reporters tried to photograph and interview a woman lecturer allegedly involved with a runaway jeweller. The college alleged that the reporter and photographer refused to leave college premises when asked, and followed the woman around the college, even entering a classroom in which she was due to teach. She was forced to leave under a blanket after the photographer and the reporter parked in the car park all day near to her car.

The PCC does try to prevent harassment by a system of 'private advisory notes' that are circulated to editors and newspaper lawyers highlighting problems. The PCC explains in its 2008 annual report how the system works:

- Someone approaches the PCC because they have experienced unwanted attention from journalists or photographers, or fear they may be about to;
- We discuss their circumstances and ask a number of questions, including whether they are intending to do – or already have done – a deal with other media;
- If they have a case of potential harassment, we send an e-mail requesting that journalists or photographers cease their approaches;
- This also alerts editors to the danger of publishing a picture from a freelancer, as they are responsible for the manner in which a picture is taken;
- We never instruct editors what they can and cannot publish – we simply arm them with extra information to make their own decisions under the Code of Practice.

The effect is generally that the harassment stops or that the photographs concerned do not get published. This in turn acts as a disincentive for freelance paparazzi to continue pursuing the individual. From the editors' point of view, they also minimise the chance of a formal PCC complaint of harassment after the event, or the risk of legal action. One high profile individual who used the service in 2008, when her personal circumstances changed, was the television newsreader Natasha Kaplinsky. She said: 'When I had my baby last year, I didn't want to be followed around by photographers every time I left the house, as happened when I was pregnant. We asked the PCC to issue a private request to photographers to stop following us, and to newspapers and magazines not to use pictures of me taken when I was with my family in private time. The degree of compliance was very impressive, and I would recommend this service to anyone in a similar position.'

(http://www.pcc.org.uk/assets/111/PCC_Ann_Rep_08.pdf: 8)

The PCC gave other examples of how the system works:

- A soap star was contacted about her pregnancy. Although she had informed some of her family, friends and colleagues, she did not want it to be made public. We referred to past decisions by the PCC which had ruled that the existence of pregnancy in the first twelve weeks was private;
- A rumour was circulating that a celebrity had entered rehab. Their representative contacted us saying that it was a private matter relating to that person's health;
- Two teachers, who were in a relationship, discovered that their local paper had been sent personal information by a former partner who was seeking to embarrass them.

We pointed out that, if the paper used this material, it would be assisting in that harassment;

- A national newspaper intended to publish a story about a practising dentist who was infected with HIV and Hepatitis C. The individual made clear that he was following established protocol as to how such a situation should be handled and that there was no public interest in the wider dissemination of details of his illness.

(http://www.pcc.org.uk/assets/111/PCC_Ann_Rep_08.pdf: 8)

An Act to make stalking and other harassment an offence was introduced in Parliament in 1997. The Protection from Harassment Act 1997 says that: 'A person must not pursue a course of conduct (a) which amounts to harassment of another, and (b) which he knows or ought to know amounts to harassment of the other' (http://www.hmso.gov.uk/acts/acts1997/1997040.htm). A defence is that the conduct is reasonable or that it was pursued for the purpose of preventing or detecting crime. An offence is punishable by up to six months in prison or a fine.

Case studies

The introduction of the Human Rights Act in 1998 has led a number of celebrities and others to seek relief for alleged intrusions or invasions of privacy. Carter-Ruck, high-profile media lawyers based in London, claim on their website to being involved in 'a long line of ground-breaking confidence/privacy-related actions ... on behalf of celebrity and other high profile clients. For obvious reasons the majority of such clients cannot be named here, but they have included pop stars and members of the royal family as well as members of the general public' (http://www.carter-ruck.com/articles/index.html accessed May 2006).

While the right to privacy suggests that this should be something we can all expect, the right to freedom of expression means the two have to be balanced and the courts are often called upon to decide when the press's right to publish is being muzzled or when they are being overly intrusive.

There have been some key cases since the introduction of the Human Rights Act which have helped to develop the law in this area. Usually these have been a mix of changes in the applications of laws of confidence and data protection.

Princess Caroline of Monaco

The most significant case, in that it was a ruling from the European Court of Human Rights, concerned Princess Caroline of Monaco. The Princess was photographed by paparazzi while out shopping and on holiday and these pictures were published in German magazines. The Princess had previously tried to prevent pictures of her being published when these had been taken on private occasions but the German Constitutional Court took the view that she was a contemporary public figure who should expect pictures of herself in public places to be published, even if they were of her daily life.

The case then went to the European Court which overturned the decision of the German court, ruling that there was a distinction between reporting facts about politicians and the reporting of the private life of an individual with no official standing, particularly if the pictures made no contribution to the public interest.

The court considers that the public does not have a legitimate interest in knowing where [Princess Caroline] is and how she behaves generally in her private life – even if she appears in places that cannot always be described as secluded and despite the fact that she is well known to the public.

Even if such a public interest exists, as does a commercial interest of the magazines in publishing these photos ... those interests must, in the court's view, yield to the applicant's right to the effective protection of her private life.

(Rozenberg 2004b)

This decision is highly significant as it is the strongest ruling yet on the level of privacy a celebrity can expect to be supported by the European Court.

Naomi Campbell

The next case involved the international supermodel Naomi Campbell. This went all the way to the House of Lords for a decision and was the first privacy case so to do since the introduction of the Human Rights Act. Consequently the court's ruling is important. The *Daily Mirror*, which covered the story, had found that Naomi Campbell was secretly attending meetings of Narcotics Anonymous, despite denying publicly that she took drugs.

Five elements were identified at the court case:

1   the fact of Ms Campbell's drug addiction;
2   the fact that she was receiving treatment for that addiction;
3   the fact that she was receiving treatment at Narcotics Anonymous;
4   details of that treatment and her reaction to it; and
5   surreptitiously obtaining photographs of her emerging from a treatment session.

Ms Campbell agreed that as she had previously publicly denied using drugs, the disclosure of (1) and (2) was justified in the public interest. However, she complained that the disclosure of (3) to (5) was unjustified.

In March 2002, trial judge Morland J had found that there was a breach of confidence and had awarded compensatory and aggravated damages of £3,500. In October 2002, the Court of Appeal allowed the newspaper's appeal on the grounds that the publication of the information in categories (3) to (5) was 'within the margin of editorial judgment' of the newspaper. On 6 May 2004, by a majority of 3 to 2, the House of Lords allowed Naomi Campbell's appeal and restored the trial judge's award.

There were two, related, issues to consider: whether there was a tort of privacy and how this conflicted with the right to freedom of expression.

The Lords decided unanimously that the cause of action in breach of confidence should be expanded to provide a remedy for privacy invasion as, following the introduction of the Human Rights Act 1998, the law of confidence had absorbed the values protected by article 8 (privacy). The court decided that in any claim based on the publication of private information, there should be an objective test of 'reasonable expectation of privacy'. This sidelined the 'offensiveness' test. However, all the judges agreed that this test should be applied to a person in the position of the claimant. This could mean that even someone in a public street could expect privacy, the judges agreed, although the precise limit of this policy was not made clear. Although the House did not depart from its previous decision that there is no 'general tort of invasion of privacy', any publication of private information will be potentially actionable and the values of 'human autonomy and dignity' are now directly protected.

In discussing the balance between privacy and freedom of expression, the House felt that neither right takes precedence over the other. It was recognised both that some types of speech are of greater value than others and that there are different degrees of privacy.

When it came to applying this rule, however, Lords Nicholls and Hoffmann felt that the publications were minor intrusions into privacy and that the court should recognise a degree of 'journalistic latitude'. The majority, Lady Hale and Lords Hope and Carswell, believed that the *Daily Mirror* had gone too far and that the material was too intrusive; they felt particularly that disclosing details of therapeutic treatment could have harmful effects on the complainant and that although the case was close to the line, publication was not justified. Lawyers involved in the case later offered the following advice to journalists:

> We suggest that the following is the correct approach:
>
> In relation to a proposed publication it is necessary to consider whether it contains information in relation to which any person has a reasonable expectation of privacy.
>
> If it does, it is then necessary to consider whether a 'public interest' defence is available in relation to each element of private information.
>
> If such a defence does not apply to each element it is necessary to consider how private the information is and what type of speech is involved. If information is 'intimate', it is likely that the publication must have some 'political and democratic' value to justify publication.
>
> Photographs should be considered separately. If they depict humiliating or embarrassing events or have been obtained surreptitiously, their publication is likely to be difficult to justify.
>
> > (Hugh Tomlinson QC and Mark Thomson 2004: http://www.carter-ruck.com/articles/280504_ NewModelPrivacy.html accessed 19/7/06)

Loreena McKennitt

Another case that has developed the law of privacy involves the Canadian folk singer Loreena McKennitt. A book written by Niema Ash, a friend of hers, *Travels with Loreena McKennitt*, intruded on her privacy and was false or misleading in parts, according to the singer. Judgment was handed down on 22 December 2005 after granting an injunction restraining publication in October 2005. Mr Justice Eady decided (following the recent Princess Caroline judgment):

(a) that all persons, including those in the public eye, are entitled to significant protection of privacy, not just in relation to photographs but also other information;
(b) that disclosure of information of relationships with others can be protected even if this occurs in public and even if the other person asserts his/her right of free speech;
(c) that truth or falsity of the private information is not relevant;
(d) that the public interest defence should be subject to careful scrutiny and requires a high degree of misbehaviour and not 'mere peccadilloes of celebrities';
(e) in matters of privacy the Courts should be slow to allow public domain as a defence, and it is permissible to allow a controlled release of private information.

> (http://www.carter-ruck.com/recentwork/McKennitt_SummaryJ_03Jan06.html accessed 19/7/06)

This judgment identifies (and clarifies the law's view on) a number of issues. The first new development is that public disclosure does not free journalists from any obligation to respect privacy. Just because a confidence may have been shared with friends, for instance, does not mean it is then in the public domain to be shared with all. The law should continue to provide protection until there is nothing left to protect, said the judge.

The second element that clarifies debate about truth and falsehood is very welcome. A complainant seeking relief for privacy need no longer detail which parts of 'a long and garbled story' were accepted as true, and which were said to be false. Advice on the definition of public interest is also welcome. This makes it clear that a high degree of misbehaviour is required in order to reasonably publish 'in the public interest'. This differs quite markedly from the judgment in the Garry Flitcroft case, detailed later on. However, this is not the first time there has been a different approach to public interest, for example, the observation of Gummow J. in *SK & F* v *Department of Community Services* [1990] FSR 617, 663:

> An examination of the recent English decisions shows that the so-called 'public interest' defence is not so much a rule of law as an invitation to judicial idiosyncrasy by deciding each case on an ad hoc basis as to whether, on the facts overall, it is better to respect or to override the obligation of confidence.
> (cited in http://www.carter-ruck.com/recentwork/McKennitt_KeyExtracts_03Jan06.html accessed 19/7/06)

Ewan McGregor

Film actor Ewan McGregor was successful in gaining an injunction against photo agency Eliot Press SARL, preventing publication of photographs taken of his children on a private hotel beach while on holiday in Mauritius. The Court ordered an assessment for damages for breach of confidence, compensation under the Data Protection Act and, if appropriate, damages for invasion of privacy to be assessed.

A v *B* (Garry Flitcroft)

A (the footballer Garry Flitcroft) sought to prevent publication in B (*The People*) of kiss-and-tell stories from two young women C and D with whom he had had affairs at different times. Flitcroft did not want his wife and family to find out about the affairs. He sought the injunction to prevent publication on the grounds that there should be confidentiality between him and the young women. Mr Justice Jack decided that this was an invasion of the footballer's privacy, that he should be able to count on confidentiality and that there was no public interest in publishing. *The People* appealed. Lord Woolf, sitting with Lord Justice Laws and Lord Justice Dyson overturned the decision, saying that the footballer could be named, as the ban was an unjustified interference with press freedom. Lord Woolf went on to make it clear that there was a public interest defence in publishing what was of interest to the public. He explained that if newspapers did not publish what was of interest to people, they would soon go out of business and this would have an adverse affect on press freedom and therefore the public interest. It would be a foolish journalist who felt that this gave *carte blanche* to publish anything that interested the public, but it certainly slowed the moves towards privacy law by the back door.

Douglas and Zeta Jones v *Hello!*

One of the most important cases in terms of its perception for the media is the *Michael Douglas and Catharine Zeta Jones* v *Hello!* magazine case. The Hollywood stars had signed a contract with *OK!* magazine to allow approved pictures of their wedding to be published in the magazine. A photographer took clandestine pictures at the wedding and sold these to *Hello!* magazine for publication before *OK!* Previous rulings in the 1800s had established that the publication of pictures taken in breach of an obligation of confidence could be prevented and as the Douglases had made it clear that the function was private and pictures should not be taken, that was the case at this wedding. The point about confidentiality was quickly agreed. But was this a breach of privacy? In the end, although Lord Justice Sedley thought there was now a tort of privacy in law, the other justices equivocated and while judgment was for Douglas and Zeta Jones, this was on the grounds of confidentiality rather than that a tort of privacy existed.

Anna Ford

The TV broadcaster Anna Ford sought permission for a judicial review of a PCC decision that there was no intrusion on her privacy by the publication of pictures of her and her partner on a public, but secluded, beach abroad. Permission was refused by Silber J on the basis of the 'broad discretion' that should be given to regulators as they are better equipped to resolve such difficult matters as the balancing of conflicting rights.

CCTV footage

Another important case concerned the use of CCTV footage. A local council allowed footage from a CCTV camera of a man walking along a public street holding a knife to be transmitted on television. In fact the man, Mr Peck, was severely depressed and had slashed his wrists in a suicide attempt. He complained to the ITC and the BSC, which upheld his complaint, but the PCC dismissed the complaint. The European Court of Human Rights upheld his claim that his article 8 rights to privacy had been infringed and concluded that the UK was in breach of their article 13 requirement to provide effective remedies.

Max Mosley

The Max Mosley case involves the then President of the Formula One governing body, the Fédération Internationale d l'Automobile (FIA) and son of wartime British Fascist leader Oswald Mosley. It is an important case in that it develops a number of elements arising from previous cases but depends less on breaches of confidence evident in the cases mentioned earlier and is more directly about the *News of the World*'s intrusion and its lack of defence through public interest.

The story concerned a sadomasochistic orgy with five prostitutes. Mosley is said to have enjoyed such sessions for the past 45 years and was alleged to have been beaten until blood flowed. The *News of the World* based its story on a video taken by one of the prostitutes during the orgy and placed for a while on its website. The newspaper claimed the story was in the public interest as it had a Nazi theme but the court ruled that this was not the case. The court awarded Mosley £60,000 damages with around £850,000 costs after finding that: 'there was no public interest or other justification for the clandestine recording, for the publication of the resulting information and still photographs, or for the placing of the video extracts on the *News of the World* website – all of this on a massive scale.' Mr Justice Eady said that there was nothing 'landmark' about the case and that it was simply an application of recently developed but established principles and that Mosley could expect privacy for consensual sexual activity, 'albeit unconventional'.

News of the World editor Colin Myler said outside the High Court:

> The newspaper believed that what it published on March 30, 2008 was legitimate and lawful and, moreover, that publication was justified by the public interest in exposing Mr Mosley's serious impropriety ... This newspaper has always maintained that because of his status and position he had an obligation to honour the standards which his vast membership had every right to expect of him. The *News of the World* believes passionately that its readers deserve to be informed of when the trust placed in their elected leaders and public officials has been violated.

Mosley has continued his legal battles by going to Europe in an attempt to get the European Court of Human Rights to press the UK Parliament to introduce laws to insist journalists contact the subjects of stories prior to publication. This matter was addressed by the Culture, Media and

Sport Select Committee, which decided it should not be a matter of law, but a part of the PCC Code of Conduct with a public interest defence for non-compliance.

John Terry

England and Chelsea footballer John Terry obtained an injunction to prevent publication of details of his affair with Vanessa Perroncel, the long-time girlfriend of fellow England defender Wayne Bridge. The injunction was later revoked with Mr Justice Tugendhat saying there were no grounds for the gagging order. He ruled that freedom of expression outweighed Terry's right to suppress reporting of his affair. Although Terry is married, he has admitted previous affairs and so the judge said the potential adverse consequences for Terry were 'not particularly grave'. The judge was also concerned that, in reality, this was not a question of intrusion into privacy, but a defence of reputation and that the applicant was unlikely to be able to establish a breach of duty of confidence.

The use of injunctions, or even so-called super-injunctions, which not only prevent publication of the story, but also prevent the newspaper from reporting that an injunction has prevented them from publishing the story, has become more prevalent recently and the judge criticised Terry's lawyers for taking the view that they had become routine. Terry had sought the injunction to prevent 'people unknown' from publishing the story and this scattergun approach was criticised by the judge as it did not allow the media or any newspaper in particular to present a defence. Injunctions are of particular concern in privacy cases, as has been mentioned before. Preventing publication on the basis of the balance of convenience means courts are more likely to prevent publication in order to protect a right to privacy that has yet to be fully argued before the courts.

These developments within the law of confidence and privacy have given plenty of encouragement to lawyers to continue pursuing privacy cases for rich, high-profile clients desperate to keep control of parts of their lives once they have become famous.

Further reading and support material

Discussion about privacy and its meaning is featured in a number of books, but Julie C. Innes (1992) *Privacy, Intimacy and Isolation* (Oxford University Press, Oxford) is one of the best and most useful. Sissela Bok (1982) Secrets (OUP, Oxford) also sheds some interesting light on the concept. Two books bring the subject closer to the media: Raymond Wacks (1995) *Privacy and Press Freedom* (Blackstone Press, London) covers the subject fairly fully, but for a more up-to-date look at some of the key cases in the UK and Europe, Joshua Rozenberg (2004a) *Privacy and the Press* (OUP, London) is both readable and informative.

Chapter 7

Reputation

This chapter discusses a number of the ethical issues involved in protecting reputation including:

- What is reputation?
- Human rights protection of reputation
- Legal protection under British and Irish law
- Presumption of innocence and rehabilitation

Protection of personal honour

Who steals my purse steals trash; 'tis something, nothing; ...

But he who filches from me my good name

Robs me of that which not enriches him,

And makes me poor indeed.

(Shakespeare, *Othello*, III, iii, 155–61)

One of the key human rights is the right to a good reputation. It is identified in the Human Rights Act and the European Convention on Human Rights (albeit in a slightly back to front way) under article 10, freedom of expression: 'The exercise of these freedoms [of expression], since it carries with it duties and responsibilities, may be subject to such formalities, conditions, restrictions or penalties as are prescribed by law and are necessary in a democratic society ... for the protection of the reputation or rights of others, for preventing the disclosure of information received in confidence ...' (http://www.opsi.gov.uk/acts/acts1998/ukpga_19980042_en_3#sch1-pt1)

As the Universal Declaration of Human Rights identifies, we are all born free and equal in dignity and rights. If society is to protect the dignity at the centre of those rights then laws on defamation are essential, alongside protection of the right to respect for privacy. Only if there is good cause, such as to protect the rights of others, or in the public interest, would it be appropriate to expose a reputation as being undeserved. If we are to remain equal then preventing people from damaging reputations unfairly, whether for spite or profit, is important.

There are very few if any countries in the world that do not have laws to protect the dignity of citizens and prevent defamation. Italy includes it in its constitution while America, Britain and most of Europe, Asia and Africa have laws of libel: laws, either civil or criminal, often both, which prevent the publication of information about a person likely to damage his or her reputation among 'right-thinking' members of the society.

We put a lot of store by our status within the society in which we live. Not only does it directly affect our ability to feed, clothe and house ourselves and our families, but it goes to the very core of our being – we are our social status, if you like. Many people have committed suicide rather than face the disgrace that damaging personal revelations would bring.

There is a certain crossover with privacy here. How much can we invade a person's privacy in order to see if his or her personal honour is worthy of his or her reputation? Most laws of libel allow the publication of material about a person, providing it is truthful and has been published without malice – two important tests that no journalist should miss.

The penalties for a lost libel action can be high, with both costs and damages potentially running into hundreds of thousands of pounds. Few editors will risk a libel action if they believe the subject has the wherewithal to bring such a lawsuit unless they are entirely confident they have the evidence to back the claims made. The effects of impugning someone's reputation should never be underestimated and journalists should take all possible steps to ensure they do not do so in error or needlessly, not just because it is the morally correct thing to do, but also because it could well bankrupt the publication for which you are working. Publishing reputation-damaging information without checking it is about the worst offence a journalist can commit. However, once those tests are made and the journalist is sure the information is true, the right to publish under the law exists.

British juries have in the past shown how strongly they feel about damaging reputations by ordering the payment of fantastic sums in damages once defamation has been proved. *Private Eye* was involved in a case back in the nineties where a jury awarded Sonia Sutcliffe, wife of the Yorkshire Ripper, £600,000, leaving *Private Eye*'s astonished editor, Ian Hislop, to tell the television cameras that if that was justice, 'I'm a banana'. In another case, *The Sun* paid massive damages to rock star Elton John. They later published a front-page apology under the heading 'Sorry Elton', but it is still doubtful whether the damage done to the star by these revelations was outweighed by the payout and the apology. We spend a lifetime building up a reputation but it can be destroyed in just a few careless moments.

Although damaging someone's reputation is an ethical issue, it is one of such importance that the law has long been in place to ensure that those whose reputations are damaged improperly are able to gain some sort of recompense. The common law offences of libel and slander can be traced back for centuries in the UK. The most recent legislation is the 1996 Defamation Act. Because of this reliance on the law, many British journalists fail to see reputation as an ethical issue. Broadcast regulation in the UK places more emphasis on treating subjects of stories fairly whereas the PCC has little to say about protecting people's reputation, relying entirely on their ability to sue through the courts. Consequently the laws of defamation are incredibly important but are often looked at as barriers to wriggle around rather than ethical protections. However, if we are to fully understand ethics, it is important to understand the ethics of reputation whether regulated solely by the law, as in the UK, or by both ethics and law, as happens in many other European countries.

Reputation under the law

The law of defamation in the UK is in place to protect the reputation of individuals and some corporate bodies and while it is not my intention here to become a detailed guide to the law of defamation as it effects journalists, I do want to examine how the law of defamation works in the UK to protect reputation. The first thing to be absolutely clear about is that libel is not directly connected to truth or accuracy. You can publish plenty of untruths about people without defaming them, provided they are complimentary enough. Defamation is about damaging their reputation and reducing their human dignity and that may not hang on whether the statement is true. Whether a statement has a defamatory meaning depends on whether it is likely to make people think less of the person described. The test was described by Lord Atkin in 1936 as 'one which injures the reputation of another by exposing him to hatred, contempt or ridicule or which tends to lower him in the esteem of right-thinking members of society'. This can apply to their personal life, but also their work and professional life. You could, for instance, describe me as 'an appalling violinist, incapable of picking his way through the simplest piece of music', as I can't play the violin and so have no reputation for so doing. Apply this description to the famed violinist Nigel Kennedy, however, and it might well be seen that this could damage his reputation and so is defamatory. However, shower me with the kind of accolades about violin playing that Kennedy deserves and I could not sue, as although the compliments might be lies, they would not be defamatory and would not expose me to hatred and contempt, unless I could show that there was some sarcastic or malicious innuendo in the statements that actually exposed me to some form of ridicule despite the apparent complimentary nature of the statements.

Libel is defamation in permanent form and there is no requirement on the complainant to prove damage or loss either financial or damage to reputation as this is assumed if the words are deemed to be defamatory. The mere fact that the person's reputation has been defamed is enough. Slander is defamation in transitory form, usually word of mouth (although not broadcast which is held to be a permanent form), and here there is a requirement to prove financial damage. So, for instance, describing a trader as a crook to a would-be customer who then decides against making a purchase might be slander and could be shown to have damaged the trader financially. Malicious falsehood is another form of damage to reputation but in this case the information published must be false, published with malice and must have caused some sort of loss. So to say that a theatrical show has been cancelled even though it hasn't could be a malicious falsehood.

Malice is an important component of defamation and is described as spite or ill will, but can also cover any improper motive or attempt at personal gain. It underlines the strong ethical thread that runs through the law of defamation. All too often defamation is about damaging someone's reputation for low purposes whether that is simply to make money or is more connected with deceit, spite or some other immoral purpose. If one publishes something defamatory in good faith for morally sound reasons, then it is much easier to publish corrections and apologies if appropriate and this may go a long way to ameliorating the damage caused. But to publish something recklessly or even maliciously purely for commercial gain or for spite is morally reprehensible. Of course news organisations often publish material that damages reputations for what they believe to be morally sound reasons. Stories in 2009 about MPs and their excessive expenses were clearly defamatory to many of them, but the stories were firmly in the public interest and true and so no law suits were launched. Although the stories damaged their reputation, they were a fair and reasonable discussion of matters of public concern; it was, after all, our money they were spending.

There are two main reasons for publishing potentially defamatory material. The first is simply that freedom of expression means that we should have the right to talk about people and events that might affect our lives and, of course, we all enjoy gossiping about others. However, this may not be a good enough reason, on its own, to puncture someone's dignity and potentially damage their reputation, even if the information published is true. The second reason for publishing is that the material is in the public interest. This, as we have discussed before, goes further than merely interesting the public. We may well intrude on a celebrity's private life a little to say that they have been seen out and about with a particular person; however, to go further and damage their reputation by saying they have been having an affair with that person without a good public interest defence is to either risk a suit for privacy or one for libel. If the information is true then a suit for invasion of privacy might follow; if it is not true then the information may be defamatory and we can expect a suit for libel as it would be damaging to that person's reputation in that it would risk their marriage and suggest they were not a person their spouse (or others) could trust. Of course, if there is a public interest in exposing the affair, showing the hypocrisy of someone whose public persona is of someone who puts family first, for instance, then that might be sufficient justification.

There are several issues to consider when journalists publish or broadcast something that might damage someone's reputation. The first of these is identity. Will the person being written about be identifiable? If you use their name and address, then of course they will be. But it is more complex than that. If you write about a John Smith, and give no further details other than to go on to defame him, then any John Smith who can reasonably prove he might be the person to whom you are referring can sue, even if it isn't the John Smith for whom you have the evidence required to support your allegations. You need to ensure that the only person you are defaming is the one you can prove is doing what you allege.

The second thing that has to be proved is whether the words are defamatory. If you were to allege criminality then the words would almost certainly be defamatory, but there are other things you could write that for some people would be defamatory and possibly very damaging, but which for others would be entirely harmless. You need to examine the words carefully to see if they might damage their reputation. To say the Archbishop of Canterbury doesn't believe in God could be defamatory, but to suggest that Richard Dawkins did believe in God would also risk a law suit. If, though, the remarks are fair comment based upon true facts then that might be sound enough. The final point to consider is whether the piece was written with malice. Being able to prove that the words were written in good faith in the belief they were right won't defend against a defamation suit, but they might lessen the amount of damages or allow you to withdraw from the suit at less cost.

A journalist or editor facing a libel suit has several defences that can be used in court.

- justification;
- fair comment;
- privilege; or
- consent.

Justification is when the words written are true and can be proved to be true for every allegation of substance that is made. The problem is that although you might win in court, the cost of such a case is often not fully recovered from the other side, or they withdraw before going to court leaving you or your news organisation (or both) with substantial legal costs. Another defence is that of fair comment. If what you have said is your opinion, reasonably put without malice and based on true facts then it is unlikely a court will determine this as libel.

Privilege is perhaps the most important defence. Privilege is a legal device to allow for free and frank debate in public. MPs, councillors, those in court and other public arenas are allowed to say what they like within the rules of those public spaces without the risk of a defamation suit. An MP, for instance, can hurl abuse at the prime minister and, although he may be reprimanded by the speaker, or even disciplined by the House, he will not face a defamation suit as he has absolute privilege. Flowing from that, news organisations have either absolute or qualified privilege to report what was said, even if the words would in other circumstances be defamatory. This allows the full reporting of public debates without having to worry about whether comments are defamatory. If the leader of the opposition claims that the prime minister has invented figures to make the government look good, you can report this claim without fear that you would have to prove the allegations. However, if the leader of the opposition were to repeat the allegations outside the House, then publishing them might well leave you open to a defamation suit as quoting him or her no longer attracts privilege and so you are no longer protected from having to prove what was said.

The so-called Reynold's defence is an expansion of this where the media can be argued to have a duty to publish information because the public has an interest in receiving it. It is called the Reynold's defence after a case in the UK House of Lords brought by Irish PM Albert Reynolds against *The Times*. This gives some protection to journalists if they can prove the story was largely true, published in the public interest without malice and researched with due diligence.

Consent is also a defence. No one can sue for publishing information that they have agreed may be published or broadcast.

The cost of libel

Expense underpins the big divides between ethics and law; between what we must do (or not do) and what we ought to do (or not do). Intrusion into privacy, for instance, has long been an ethical issue, but it has only started to raise howls of anguish from editors as it has become more firmly associated with the courts and the high expense that brings. This has always been the case with defamation. Being sued for libel automatically brings costs much of which may not be reclaimable even if the newspaper or broadcaster wins the case. The minute that first lawyer's letter arrives on the editor's desk threatening to sue and the lawyers are consulted to respond, the costs start to escalate. Some news organisations employ in-house lawyers who are expert in media law and so the initial costs are not high. But many smaller newspapers and broadcasters cannot afford full-time legal assistance and so have to consult lawyers on a fee basis and things can quickly get expensive. Often it is cheapest to offer a quick apology and a small amount of damages. However, on that basis, there's no point in risking the libel in the first place and it is this that is known as 'the chilling effect'. Publications fear risking a potential law suit and so constantly play safe with their reporting.

Defamation cases are heard in the High Court before a jury. This means the cases themselves are relatively expensive to run and both sides need to employ a considerable legal team to fight the court case. Finally there is the risk of damages being awarded. Damages come in three flavours:

- *compensatory*, which aim to put the claimant in the same position as before the libel;
- *aggravated*, which is where the behaviour of the defendant has made things worse – a good reason to ensure there is no malice and that appropriate apologies and offers of amends are made; and
- *exemplary*, which is for when the judge feels additional punishment is required.

The huge damages payouts mentioned earlier in this chapter have been limited since 1995 by a Court of Appeal decision that juries should be given an appropriate lower and upper limit for damages in the judge's summing up. The highest awards in recent years were of £200,000 to two kindergarten teachers falsely accused by a local council of sexually abusing children and this is now seen as the maximum for compensatory damages. Of course, out-of-court settlements made to prevent the case reaching court could be even higher than this, although it is very rare to disclose the amount of an out-of-court settlement. Robert Murat allegedly received £600,000 from eleven newspapers over false allegations of involvement in the Madeleine McCann case according to the CMS Select Committee report (House of Commons 2010: 37). But it is not just the damages that run up the bills; it is the legal costs that often make up the bulk, which is why out-of-court settlements can be higher than payments for damages in a court case. A libel case that runs its full course can, with damages awarded and full legal expenses, run into costs of many hundreds of thousands of pounds, even millions for a big case. When Richard Desmond sued author Tom Bower over claims in his book and lost, he was left with a bill in the region of £1.25 million according to the CMS report (ibid. 61). The CMS report identifies another case reported to it by Paul Dacre of Associated Newspapers; this time, when Martyn Jones MP sued the *Mail on Sunday*:

> The *Mail on Sunday* believed it had rock solid witnesses and decided to fight the case. In the event they lost and they were ordered to pay £5,000 in damages, a relatively footling sum. The MP's lawyers claimed costs of £387,855, solicitors' costs of £68,000 plus success fees, and the barrister's fees as well. Anyway, the total with VAT and ATE insurance came to £520,000. Everything had been doubled up with the success fees and that was for damages being awarded of £5,000.
>
> (ibid. 62)

This evidence identifies several issues connected with costs; first, the enthusiasm for settling early, even if this means apologising and accepting you were wrong, even when you know you are right. Paying £10,000–15,000 with damages and some legal costs is vastly different to paying more than £500,000. The second is the introduction of the terms success fee and ATE insurance.

Conditional fee agreements, more commonly known as 'no win, no fee' arrangements, were introduced in 1990 as a way of allowing those with limited means access to the civil courts. CFAs mean that solicitors can agree to take cases for clients and will only get paid if they win the case. Because of the additional risk, they are allowed to charge a success fee of up to 100 per cent of their normal fees, meaning the defendant may not only be expected to pay their own fees, plus those of the claimant, but also the success fee. Claimants can also insure against losing the case by taking out after-the-event (ATE) insurance, in which the premium for the insurance is payable only if they win and then by the defendants as part of the costs. If the claimant loses the case, then the insurance policy pays out and covers the defence lawyer's fees and costs (and the cost of the premium). Not surprisingly, such arrangements are popular with both claimants and with lawyers because of the cost efficiency. As a law firm Carter-Ruck, which specialises in defamation and media law, points out on its website advertising its CFA scheme together with ATE insurance from Temple Insurance:

> Our CFA scheme is thus an extremely cost efficient means of funding litigation and Temple's insurance offers a highly effective means by which to manage the costs risks of litigation.
>
> (http://www.carter-ruck.com/Media%20Law/Funding.asp)

CFAs and ATE insurance make it easier for people to sue and, although aimed at those with limited means, many celebrities have used CFAs to sue newspapers. No longer do newspapers look at a person's bank balance before deciding whether they might be tempted to sue. Nor, as is often suggested, is the key question whether the newspaper can stand the story up. Often a story is newsworthy and is founded on good evidence, but the risks of facing years of legal battles at huge expense means the editor decides against the story. An important part of the CMS report concerned the costs of libel actions. The Labour government was looking seriously at how to make libel cases cheaper as it ended its term in government and the new coalition government has promised to review the laws of libel to protect freedom of speech.

Rehabilitation

One of the things to remember about defamation is that it is only possible to defame someone by damaging their reputation; if they have no reputation to damage then defamation is not possible. It is not defamation to describe someone who has just finished his third lengthy jail sentence for theft as a thief and the Civil Evidence Act 1968 supports that, allowing the media to refer to a person's criminal convictions without risk of a libel action. However, it might be defamation to describe them as something else, such as a philanderer. There may come a point, though, when it is only reasonable to assume someone has been rehabilitated and has earned their reputation back. If someone was found guilty of stealing sweets from a shop at the age of 14, is it still reasonable to describe them as a thief at the age of 52 now they are a senior figure in one of the country's leading corporations? The law considers that rehabilitation is possible and the Rehabilitation of Offenders Act 1974 allows for convictions to become spent after a certain time. This means that rehabilitated people must be treated as if they had never been convicted. This is an issue which is of increasing importance for internet publication. While newspaper files are always going to contain details of a person's court case, available for all to find, it does require a certain amount of determination to take the chance that someone will be mentioned in that particular newspaper and then to search through musty files or microfiches to find the details. Searching archives online is a breeze, and it is easy to turn up such information on people at the click of a couple of buttons and with no particular purpose in mind. This is a matter vexing many newspaper and broadcast editors as they answer the growing clamour of requests to delete material from archives. I update the position on this in Chapter 20 on the future of journalism ethics.

Malice and the democratic function

Defamation was first introduced to British law in 1275 with the offence of *Scandalum Magnatam* to protect the ruling class from criticism that might raise the people against them. The ordinary people had no role in how the country was run and so to allow them to criticise was seen by those in power as unhelpful if not downright rude and this new law, mainly of slander at that time, helped reduce criticism. Freedom of the press has been interpreted in modern times as allowing, or even requiring, the media to be critical and to initiate debate. Media in Britain, as in nearly all Western democracies, is able to report Parliament and to publish and broadcast news, analysis and opinion about politics and the performance of political leaders.

Some countries, though, still use defamation to limit discussion of government policy, the competency of government officers or issues of 'national pride'. Turkey is a useful (but certainly not the only) example of such a country that has consistently tried to limit criticism by arresting and jailing critics for 'insulting Turkishness' or 'insulting parliament'. Campaign group Human Rights Watch reported that in Turkey in 2006:

> More than 50 individuals were indicted for statements or speeches that questioned state policy on controversial topics such as religion, ethnicity, and the role of the army. The government failed to abolish laws that restrict speech.
>
> In April an Adana court sentenced broadcaster Sabri Ejder Öziç to six months of imprisonment under article 301 of the Turkish Criminal Code for 'insulting parliament' by describing a decision to allow foreign troops on Turkish territory as a 'terrorist act'.
>
> (http://hrw.org/englishwr2k7/docs/2007/01/11/turkey14845.htm accessed 4/10/07)

Many South American countries also use defamation or *desacato* (insult) laws to limit criticism of government and politicians.

In the United States, though, and some European countries, strong criticism of public figures is protected by the constitution and statute provided there is no malice in what is written. Public figures hoping to prove malice have to show that not only is the information false, but also that those who published it knew it to be false and simply did not care; this gives journalists a pretty wide leeway provided they behave reasonably responsibly. This is a much stronger defence than the UK's Reynold's defence, although there are similarities.

Criminal defamation law covering such things as sedition, obscene libel and blasphemy were removed from UK law in the Coroners and Justice Act in 2009.

Presumption of innocence

Connected to the right of reputation is presumption of innocence when faced with criminal charges. Whether we start with the UN Declaration of Human Rights or in a more lowly fashion with simple fair dealing, few in the UK would argue against everyone having the right to be presumed innocent of any crime unless proven guilty by a court of law, duly constituted for the purpose of hearing their alleged crime and deciding upon the justice of the case against them. If we are all to have equal dignity, then it is only reasonable that we should only lose our reputation for innocence if evidence has been fairly presented to prove we don't deserve it and that evidence has been accepted by a jury of our peers despite our counter-arguments.

In practice (as is often the case) this is often more difficult to achieve. Often, people appear guilty of things for which there is little hard evidence. It is tempting for a journalist to write a story that will present someone as guilty of a crime or misdemeanour. Take an example: a row breaks out at a supermarket check-out. A man becomes violent and hits another man. There is a struggle. The man who started the fight leaves the supermarket and drives off in his car. A reporter could well use this story, using the evidence from the other person involved in the tussle. This witness would of course claim that he was the injured party. He did nothing to provoke the other. An unwary reporter might be tempted to use the car's registration plate in an effort to help bring the man to justice. This would label the owner of that car as someone who involved himself in violent behaviour. This may not be the case. Perhaps the car had been stolen or borrowed. Perhaps the witness was lying to cover up his own actions.

Many countries have strict laws governing what may be written about crimes and the reporting of them both during court cases and before. Britain, for instance, has a number of laws which determine exactly what can or cannot be written about in an attempt to ensure that an accused person's reputation is not damaged before the trial and a jury is not prejudiced against the defendant. Breach of these laws is considered a very serious offence. 'Contempt proceedings are vigorously prosecuted, usually by the Attorney General, with the offender facing criminal sanctions if found guilty' (Crone 2002: 140).

But presumption of innocence is more than concern about contempt of court, important to the good practice of justice though this may be. A fair trial requires that both defendant and accuser are equal before the law with equal reputations, presenting their case through testimony and evidence so that no one is falsely found guilty of a crime. Approaches to such attempts at fair trial and presumption of innocence vary widely throughout the world. In Britain, the law is very strict, yet every detail of a criminal proceeding from the act itself to the eventual sentencing of the criminal can be and often is reported in the media in considerable detail. The British believe that justice should be seen to be done and that it is important that the case for and against the defendant's innocence be presented to the public. The tight restrictions of the law can ensure a fair trial but, as we have seen before, can leave loopholes. It is perfectly possible in Britain to cover the opening presentation of evidence by the prosecution but miss the defence's rebuttal either because other things have taken over the news agenda or because the defence is not sufficiently interesting. Britain's strong laws about what can and cannot be covered have often allowed themselves to be distorted away from the aim of presumption of innocence into being solely a protection of the court itself and a bar on bringing it into contempt. British journalists do not view presumption of innocence as an area of ethical concern because it is not listed as such in the PCC's or Ofcom's code of practice. They are worried solely about committing a contempt of court and the damage to their paper or broadcast station that this would bring. Consequently, when the law no longer applies, perhaps when a case happens abroad as it did with Madeleine McCann, British journalists are not constrained by anything as they simply forget to apply simple ethical considerations such as fairness and protecting human dignity.

In Sweden and the Netherlands, however, the opposite is the case. There are few laws restricting what can be written about court cases in Sweden, yet the code of conduct is strong. Clause 14 says: 'Remember that, in the eyes of the law, a person suspected of an offence is always presumed innocent until he is proved guilty. The final outcome of a case that is described should be reported.' Clause 15 also adds: 'Give careful thought to the harmful consequences that might follow for persons if their names are published. Refrain from publishing names unless it is in the public interest.' Swedish journalists take this very seriously and so it is unlikely that they would name people mentioned in a story that would lead to them being presumed guilty. Journalists in the Netherlands are also careful about using names in court cases until after the person is found guilty. Often only initials are used to protect the defendant's reputation, until a court decides he no longer has one. British journalism comes from a very different tradition and not publishing a name would be considered the same as failing to find a good source for a story.

Irish Defamation Act

The Oireachtas (the Irish parliament) agreed a new Defamation Act in 2009, to try to make their law more sympathetic to press freedom. The new Act identifies defamation as 'a statement that tends to injure a person's reputation in the eyes of reasonable members of society'. The Act lists the same sorts of defence as UK law: truth, privilege and honest opinion.

However, there are some interesting aspects of the new Act. First, it allows for a defence of fair and reasonable publication. This allows for material to be published in the public interest, provided it was published in good faith, in the course of a discussion of a subject of public interest the discussion of which was for the public benefit and that in all the circumstances it was fair and reasonable to publish the statement.

Second, when considering whether it is fair and reasonable, a court must consider how the publication measured up to a public interest test, but also how the publisher measured up to the Press Council's code of practice. The Act also says that a Press Council may be identified by the Act and the minister announced at the start of 2010 that the Press Council of Ireland should be so identified and this now gives some status to the ombudsman, the Council, and its code and any publication that can show it did its best to stand by the code will have some additional defence in claiming fair and reasonable publication.

Further reading and support material

Robertson, G. and Nicol, A. (2008) *Media Law* (5th edn) London: Penguin.

Banks, D. and Hanna, M. (2010) *McNae's Essential Law for Journalists* (20th edn) Oxford: OUP.

Carey, P., Armstrong, N., Lamont, D., & Quatermain, J. (2010) *Media Law* (5th edn) London: Sweet & Maxwell.

Chapter 8

Gathering the news

This chapter discusses a number of the ethical issues involved in gathering the news, including:

- Straightforward means of gathering news

- Misrepresentation and clandestine methods of getting information

- Dealing with sources of information

In Chapter 3, four key elements of ethical concern were identified: gathering the news; presenting the news; guaranteeing the quality of the news provided; and ensuring standards. These four will all be dealt with in depth over the next four chapters or so.

The first of these are of direct concern to the reporter, however junior. There is a view driven by television and the movies, that ethical issues are only ever matters of major concern, to be discussed rarely and only when some major story is on the go, but the reverse is closer to the truth. Ethical issues arise every day, often concerning small questions. Even when there are major issues of ethical concern, they often start as small issues. I doubt, for instance, that Andrew Gilligan was aware of the ethical nightmare he was unleashing when he woke one morning to do a 6.07 two-way for the BBC's *Today* programme. I'm not suggesting he would have necessarily behaved differently if he had, but it shows that from little acorns do great big ethical oaks grow.

Some of the key decisions reporters need to make concern how they will gather information for their stories. This involves both the quality of the information and the method of obtaining it, including intrusion and truth, accuracy and objectivity dealt with in earlier chapters.

Straightforward means

Straightforward means concerns the way that stories are gathered – how the source is approached and questioned about the information. The NUJ Code says: 'A Journalist obtains material by honest, straightforward and open means, with the exception of investigations that are both overwhelmingly in the public interest and which involve evidence that cannot be obtained by straightforward means' (*National Union of Journalists Rulebook*, 2010: http://www.nuj.org.uk/innerPagenuj.html?docid=25 accessed 8/2/10). The BBC has no direct clauses on misrepresentation but it does say that any proposal for deception must be referred to a senior editorial figure and the *Editorial Guidelines* do warn that there needs to be a clear public interest in order for it to be acceptable not to reveal the full purpose of a programme to a contributor (http://www.bbc.co.uk/guidelines/editorialguidelines/page/guidelines-fairness-deception accessed 14/10/10). The PCC has several clauses covering the area: clause 8, hospitals, says that: 'Journalists must identify themselves and obtain permission from a responsible executive before entering non-public areas of hospitals or similar institutions to pursue enquiries. The restrictions on intruding into privacy are particularly relevant to enquiries about individuals in hospitals or similar institutions' (PCC Code of Practice 2009: http://www.pcc.org.uk/cop/practice.html accessed 8/2/2010) while clause 10, clandestine devices and subterfuge, says: 'The Press must not seek to obtain or publish material acquired by using hidden cameras or clandestine listening devices; or by intercepting private or mobile telephone calls, messages or emails; or by the unauthorised removal of documents or photographs; or by accessing digitally-held private information without consent. Engaging in misrepresentation or subterfuge can generally be justified only in the public interest and then only when the material cannot be obtained by other means' (ibid.). The broadcast regulator Ofcom says in its content code that: 'Broadcasters or programme makers should not normally obtain or seek information, audio, pictures or an agreement to contribute through misrepresentation or deception. (Deception includes surreptitious filming or recording.) However: it may be warranted to use material obtained through misrepresentation or deception without consent if it is in the public interest and cannot reasonably be obtained by other means' (http://www.ofcom.org.uk/tv/ifi/codes/bcode/fairness/ accessed 8/2/2010). It's clear from all of these that misrepresentation, deception or clandestine devices are all methods of news-gathering that should not normally be used unless the story is very much in the public interest and there is no other way of getting or confirming the information.

Misrepresentation

One major form of subterfuge used by reporters is misrepresentation; posing as something or someone other than a news reporter. This could mean posing as a police officer (illegal) or a doctor, social worker, or some other person who has regular access to people's homes or places of business. One of the best known users of false identity is probably Mazher Mahmood, investigations editor of the *News of the World*, who has dressed as an Arabian businessman on a number of occasions to carry out stings on the great and not so good including Sophie the Countess of Wessex, Sven Goran Eriksson (England's football team manager at the time), the Earl of Hardwicke and *Blue Peter* presenter Richard Bacon (Burden 2008: 118).

Mahmood's false sheik would drive around in a Rolls Royce and stay at expensive hotels in order to convince his marks that he was able to offer lucrative business opportunities. He would then persuade them to behave illegally or unethically, sometimes pressurising them to find a supply of class A narcotics for the sheik's party before exposing them for supplying drugs.

Mahmood is not the only newspaper journalist to use misrepresentation, although the number of cases adjudicated by the PCC is very small, with none being upheld over the past four years.

Three particularly prominent cases in the UK illustrate the risks journalists run in using subterfuge as a method of gathering information. In one, the feminist writer Germaine Greer, writing in *The Big Issue*, said she was willing to share her house with anyone who was not put off by the circumstances described. A *Mail on Sunday* reporter, Martin Hennessey, dressed as a 'down and out' and took her up on her offer and then wrote about his experiences including a detailed description of Dr Greer's home and possessions. The PCC's Privacy Commissioner, Professor Robert Pinker, said in his adjudication: 'Journalists should not generally obtain or seek to obtain information and pictures through misrepresentation or subterfuge.' The paper's editor had argued that the method was justified as 'this was the only way in which the article could have been written' but the PCC rejected that argument and upheld the complaint saying that: 'The article is not about the life of a genuinely homeless person, as claimed by the editor; it is about the experience of a guest in Dr Greer's home who gained entry by subterfuge' (PCC bulletin 23 1994: 18).

This example raises two points. The first is whether there is a justification in using non-straightforward methods if the story is in the public interest. If the story were, for instance, exposing corruption or criminal activity, should a reporter feel justified in using such methods to get the story if there were no other way? The second point that requires discussion is at what stage does a story become 'in the public interest'? Does a story about how Germaine Greer treated a 'down and out' fit within the category of public interest? While there might be a story in testing whether her claim to offer a bed to any 'down and out' was true, or only hypocrisy, once the reporter had established that she meant what she said, surely he should have withdrawn and not invaded Ms Greer's privacy, using non-straightforward means to obtain a story that was arguably not in the public interest.

In the other prominent case, which was reported in PCC Report No. 33 (1996: 22), a freelance reporter working for the *News of the World* entered a school to talk to pupils and staff about a story concerning a female pupil's relationship with a teacher. The reporter allegedly claimed she was the cousin of the pupil. Was the story in the public interest? Did it therefore justify the intrusion and deceit or was it an unnecessary subterfuge? The PCC decided it was misrepresentation in that the reporter hid her identity and upheld the complaint. It is worth noting that the PCC Code now bans interviewing children under 16 about issues concerning their or another child's welfare without a custodial parent or similarly responsible adult giving consent and says pupils of any age should not be approached without the permission of the school authorities.

In another case the PCC dealt with in 2005, a reporter for the *Sunday Telegraph* posed as a client to discover whether a printing firm owned by Saudi Arabians printed the British National Party's newspaper. The reporter later phoned the firm to confirm what he had learned undercover, which the complainant claimed proved that subterfuge was unnecessary, but the PCC did not uphold the complaint, saying that while other means might occasionally be available in similar circumstances, a case would not be upheld where there were 'reasonable grounds for concluding that pursuing other means would compromise the ability of reporters to investigate matters subsequently'. The PCC also felt it was acceptable where the subterfuge was not serious and caused little harm (http://www.pcc.org.uk/cases/adjudicated.html?article=MjE2Ng== accessed 8/2/2010).

Ethical problems surrounding the use of misrepresentation can be difficult to work through as the deontological approach using codes of conduct leaves a number of questions. Is this misrepresentation in the public interest? Is it the only way to access the information? Utilitarianism works much better in these circumstances, guiding us to consider the consequences of the act of subterfuge. The effect of using subterfuge is that the reporter does something immoral (i.e., lying), and the subject of the report is usually damaged, held up to ridicule or accused of wrongdoing. Only the fact that the public ought to know more about the activities of such people justifies this behaviour. Providing the public interest is served, it may be acceptable to lie and deceive, as long as subterfuge is the only way of achieving this end. It is important that reporters and their editors remember that the subterfuge they use to obtain material is immoral (and possibly illegal) – the mere act of lying is regarded as immoral by many, regardless of whether the motive was good or the consequences beneficial. However, many others also believe that lying that leads to beneficial effects is morally acceptable.

Utilitarianists could support the use of subterfuge, provided the consequences really are to produce a story that is strongly in the public interest. Often, of course, this claim to serve the public interest is just a smokescreen to cover the fact that the story is used because it increases circulation figures. The public interest defence was used by the *Sunday Mirror* when, in 1994, it published photographs of Diana, Princess of Wales working out in a private gym taken by a hidden camera of which she was unaware. Using subterfuge is extremely dangerous because once the principle is accepted that lying and deceit can be justified by loyalty to the public interest, it is only a short step to justifying it through the reporter's loyalty to the editor or proprietor. In other words, it is but a small step from lying to get a story which is important because it is in the public interest to lying to get a story which is important because it keeps the reporter's paper from bankruptcy or holds its top position in the market. Both *can* be justified on the basis of loyalty, but whereas one may be acceptable to the public, the other may not.

Another case where the PCC did accept that there was an important point of public interest was when *The People* and the *Sunday Mirror* separately managed to gain entry to Old Trafford, the football ground of Manchester United, as stewards with only minimal security checks at the time of the so-called anti-terrorist 'ring of steel'. The stewards are responsible for ensuring weapons are not brought into the ground. Controlled Event Solutions complained to the PCC that the stories used subterfuge, but the PCC rejected the complaint saying it was in the public interest (http://www.pcc.org.uk/cases/adjudicated.html?article=MjEzOQ== accessed 13/6/06).

Clandestine listening devices and cameras

Clandestine listening devices, interception of telephone calls and the use of hidden cameras are other ways to access information that might otherwise not be available. There are two main uses for such devices: to clandestinely record or film events that would otherwise remain secret and to record events involving the reporter as evidence or to provide pictures or film. The use of pictures and film taken secretly for broadcast are dealt with in more detail in Chapter 12. What is of interest in this section is clandestine recording and filming in order to get information that could not be obtained by other means.

The PCC bans the use of hidden cameras and listening devices. It also bars the interception of private communications and the unauthorised removal of documents and photographs. However, there is a public interest defence to the use of these deceits because it may be that the only way to get information in a story that is of major public interest is by recording secretly. Only a very small number of complaints are made to the PCC about clandestine devices, typically fewer than 1 per cent. Only eight were adjudicated up to January 2010. Two of these involved secretly taping telephone conversations. In one, a complaint dealt with in 1996, a woman complained that a telephone call between her and her husband had been recorded without her knowledge or consent (but with her ex-husband's knowledge) (PCC Report 35 1996: 6). The PCC upheld the complaint, including the recording of the telephone conversation. Later, in 2000, the PCC adjudicated in another case where a reporter had taped conversations with the complainant without her knowledge and consent. The PCC said it 'did not view the recording of telephone conversations as involving the use of a "clandestine listening device"' (http://www.pcc.org.uk/cases/adjudicated.html?article=MTc5Mg== accessed on 13/6/06). This is still a troubled area of debate. Recording calls you are making for your own use is not illegal but there may be copyright problems and there certainly might be ethical problems if the tape is used as a journalistic artifact. However, despite regularly recording conversations with sources, the media had a field day when it was learnt that the then Metropolitan police commissioner Sir Ian Blair had been recording telephone conversations with ministers. *The Guardian* came to his defence with a leader condemning the 'media humbug over phone recording'. However, its news item followed the pack in taking Sir Ian to task for recording a conversation with the Attorney General, Lord Goldsmith, who was said to be 'incredibly cross and very disappointed', describing Sir Ian's behaviour as 'unethical and discourteous' (Dodd 2006) (http://www.guardian.co.uk/terrorism/story/0,,1729602,00.html).

The other complaints concerned the taking of photographs, so there is little guidance from the PCC about the use of hidden microphones or recorders, but there would be no justification for using either, without a strong public interest defence. If hiding a microphone, or 'wearing a wire' as we know it from the movies, were the only way to get evidence for a public interest story, then it might well be justifiable.

Hidden microphones and cameras are more of an issue for broadcasters who want to record conversations not just to gather information but also for transmission. Modern technology means that even very small cameras and microphones can produce quality results easily good enough for broadcast. The BBC guidelines say secret recording has to be justified by a clear public interest and used only as a method of last resort. Overuse could devalue its impact (http://www.bbc.co.uk/guidelines/editorialguidelines/page/guidelines-privacy-mandatory referrals accessed 14/10/2010). The BBC says it should only be used if there is clear documentary or other evidence of an intention to commit an offence, where an open approach would be unlikely to succeed and recording is necessary for evidential purposes (ibid.). Ofcom also says such misrepresentation should only be used in the public interest and when material cannot be reasonably obtained by other means.

Phone tapping and interception

Whilst phone tapping has been possible since the first phone went into service, it has usually been too complex to be of much assistance to journalists, but the modern mobile and static phones with their built in answering services are a different kettle of fish. The ability to access people's phone messages through their answering service is relatively easy with appropriate technical knowledge. The PCC amended its code to outlaw this a couple of years ago and forbids intercepting private or mobile telephone calls, messages or emails. Ofcom's code forbids the recording of telephone conversations without permission and although it doesn't specifically exclude the interception of phone messages there's little doubt that it would find this an unacceptable breach of privacy. In his evidence to the Culture, Media and Sport Select Committee in July 2009, the Information Commissioner, Christopher Graham, identified two ways to gather information from phone networks, often perpetrated by third parties on behalf of journalists and both of them illegal. The first method is 'blagging' where private investigators access personal information, including passwords, from confidential databases either by deception or by paying corrupt employees for the information. This is illegal under the Data Protection Act and offenders face a fine of up to £5,000 in a magistrates' court, or an unlimited fine in the Crown Court. Following the Clive Goodman case, the then commissioner called for prison sentences of up to two years to deter this unlawful trade, and this was introduced in section 77 of the Criminal Justice and Immigration Act 2008 but requires an order from the relevant Secretary of State to bring it into effect.

The other method of accessing information is the interception of communications whether that is phone tapping or some way of accessing phone messages. This is now illegal under the Regulation of Investigatory Powers Act 2000. *News of the World* royal editor Clive Goodman was jailed for four months in 2007 after being found guilty under the Criminal Law Act 1977 of intercepting phone messages with co-conspirator private detective Glenn Mulcaire, who was jailed for six months. Of course the two often go hand in hand. Passwords are blagged from databases and then used to intercept messages left on answerphones.

The Commissioner said in his report to the CMS Select Committee that he would 'continue to monitor the commission of blagging offences involving journalists and others and to bring prosecutions where the circumstances justify this.' Although blagging is illegal, it can be justified as being in the public interest (http://www.ico.gov.uk/upload/documents/library/data_protection/ notices/culture_media_and_sport_committee_evidence_20090713.pdf accessed 9/2/10).

Hospitals

Hospitals are identified in the PCC Code of Practice as being of such significance that they require a clause of their own. This follows the Gorden Kaye case, when the actor was badly injured during storms in London in 1990 and journalists from the *Sport* newspaper infiltrated his hospital room to interview him even though he was barely conscious. The clause says that journalists must identify themselves and obtain permission before entering hospitals or similar institutions. There is a public interest defence around this clause, implying that a journalist could enter a hospital without permission, or in disguise if there was a public interest reason. Such a defence would almost certainly need to be about the hospital itself rather than any of its patients. It might be arguable to enter the hospital to check out the cleanliness of the kitchens as a follow-up to a complaint, for instance, but to interview a severely injured patient is likely to breach the code.

It is not entirely clear exactly what the PCC means by 'similar institutions' but there are a wide range of public buildings that journalists may feel the need to enter from time to time. Public buildings generally fall into three categories. First, there are those that are open to the public, such as libraries, public halls, sports centres, art galleries, museums and swimming baths. These may include a number of buildings that are privately owned, but that are routinely open to the public: shopping centres, for instance. These will be accessible to journalists, although they may have specific closing times and there may be some private areas where access is limited. However, even in the private office sections of such buildings, there would not be any ethical limitation with a journalist seeking entry in order to interview a member of staff. However, the staff in such a building would have the right to escort a journalist from the premises for an excessive intrusion and taking pictures in such a building would require permission.

The second category are those that are owned by government or local authorities but are used for offices or workspaces for staff. While these may have a small public area (benefit offices, housing departments and so on) the bulk of the space will be for officers. There is nothing to prevent a journalist seeking entry here to speak to an officer, but most public buildings these days have security devices to prevent strangers entering and so it is probably easiest to ask for someone at the reception area unless there is a very good reason for attempting to enter the staff-only areas. If a journalist were found in the staff-only area, it is likely they would be escorted from the premises and any future attempt to interview someone might not be well received. Again, taking pictures would require permission and indeed it might be a breach of the Official Secrets Act to take pictures in some buildings.

The third category is buildings that are largely used by the public, but are not open access in the sense of the first category. These include hospitals, but also schools, colleges and universities. Most schools now take security very seriously. Colleges and universities are following suit but find it more difficult. It is almost impossible for an adult to enter a school without gaining permission, but journalists should in any case think twice before attempting to enter a school without permission as the PCC or Ofcom are not likely to find it acceptable. It is not acceptable to interview pupils without permission of an adult and if the head teacher or other teachers have already refused to speak, then there is not much point in rampaging around the school trying to harass them into commenting. Universities are more open. Most tend to secure sensitive areas, more to ensure expensive equipment is not stolen than to prevent contact with staff or students. Entering general areas, such as common rooms and entrance halls is generally fairly easy. Entering classrooms would mean joining the class, but otherwise, it is unlikely that you would be noticed. Again the worst that could probably happen is that the journalist would be escorted from the premises.

Hospitals, ambulances, schools, prisons or police stations are all specifically mentioned by Ofcom as being places that are potentially sensitive with regards to intrusion and that separate consent should normally be obtained before filming.

Harassment

Entering buildings to talk to people or waiting outside to approach them as they arrive or leave is acceptable behaviour, but not if it extends to harassment. The PCC, NUJ, Ofcom and BBC all have specific clauses banning harassment. It is also potentially illegal under the Protection from Harassment Act 1997. According to the Act, 'A person must not pursue a course of conduct (a) which amounts to harassment of another, and (b) which he knows or ought to know amounts to harassment of the other' (Carey and Sanders 2004: 130). This leaves the definition of harassment open, but it does not have to be physical: an approach for interview would be sufficient. However, to be called 'harassment', the behaviour would have to involve such approaches on at least two, probably more occasions. No journalist has yet faced a charge under the Act, which was designed to stop stalkers, but it is worth remembering that it is potentially illegal. In ethical terms, any person who turns down an invitation to be interviewed, could claim to be harassed if persistent repeat requests are made, or if a journalist refuses to leave private premises or continues to make telephone calls after being asked to desist. It is difficult to say at what point a firm approach becomes harassment, and it may be that a second approach to someone who has already refused may be appropriate if the circumstances have changed; but a journalist really needs to have a good justification because a second approach and a third or subsequent approach is asking to be accused of harassment.

A Nicola Shields complained to the PCC about the *Daily Record*'s harassment of her in 2009. The newspaper contacted her about her pregnancy and the possibility that a footballer was the father. She asked the paper not to contact her but was contacted by journalists on two further occasions. The PCC was surprisingly sharp in its adjudication:

> The approaches to Ms Shields in breach of the newspaper's undertakings were a clear case of harassment under the Code. It should be a relatively simple matter for newspapers to communicate internally about an individual's request not to be approached. Indeed, it happens every day on most newspapers without such confusion arising. It was therefore disappointing that the procedures of a major newspaper such as the *Daily Record* should turn out to be so lacking. The Commission expects them to be tightened up immediately so that there is no repeat of this problem.
>
> (http://www.pcc.org.uk/cases/adjudicated.html?article=NjA2MA== accessed 8/2/2010)

Taking pictures or filming without permission could also be construed as harassment, if done persistently. Taking pictures of subjects who do not want their pictures taken can be difficult. If they are on private property, then that clearly breaches most codes of practice, and photographs should not normally be taken. This is somewhat of a grey area. Until 2004, the PCC said that using long-lens photography to take pictures of people in private places was unacceptable. This implied that it was acceptable to take pictures of them in such places, provided normal lenses were used, so the Code was changed to bar pictures in private places, that is, places where there could be a reasonable expectation of privacy. The PCC has made it clear through its adjudications that this would include walled or hedged gardens, homes, restaurants and hotels – but there are grey areas. A woman complained to the PCC about the *Mail on Sunday*. She had agreed to an interview, but said she had not agreed to pictures as she was involved in a witness protection programme. The paper had taken a picture of her on her driveway and she complained that this was a place where she had a reasonable expectation of privacy. The Commission decided that the driveway was not a place where there was reasonable expectation of privacy, even though it was clear that the picture had been taken from the roadway. This would almost certainly have required a lens that was to some degree a telephoto (http://www.pcc.org.uk/cases/adjudicated.html?article=MjE4Mw== accessed 13/6/06).

Subterfuge and pictures taken in a private place can also be justified by the public interest. The *News of the World* took pictures of Carole Caplin, a close friend and confidante of Cherie Blair, in a hotel and in her gym. The newspaper said they had reports that Caplin abused her friendship for gain and that subterfuge was required to pursue the story. The PCC rejected a complaint saying that the case concerned Caplin's work, not her private life. The pictures were taken in places where she had a reasonable expectation of privacy, but that there was a public interest in taking and publishing them as they showed her engaging in professional negotiations (http://www.pcc.org. uk/cases/adjudicated.html?article=MjE3NQ== accessed 13/6/06).

Sources

Dealing with sources is one of the most difficult parts of journalism. As previously discussed, a journalist owes a loyalty to a contact or source. But reporters also have a loyalty to the audience and that means giving consumers enough information to make their own judgements about the trustworthiness of the sources the journalist is using. It may also mean using more than one source in order to confirm the same point. Since the Hutton Report and the BBC's own Neil Report, the BBC has changed its rules on sources and now tells its journalists: 'the BBC should continue to report stories based on a single source but only where the story is one of significant public interest and the correct procedures have been followed' (http://www.bbc.co.uk/info/policies/pdf/ neil_report.pdf accessed 18/7/06).

The journalist should do his or her best to ensure that the consumer gets a good range of information about the source in order to enable them to make a decision about the trustworthiness of the source. All sources will have an angle, some motive for agreeing to be the source of the story. Often this will be obvious – it improves their public image, or the image of some company, club or organisation with which they are involved. However, sometimes their motive is not so clear and the reporter must make every effort to try to show that to the consumer. The reporter also needs to be sure that the source is providing information that is genuine. Many sources like to build up the information which they are offering or even make it up altogether. Not only should the journalist do his or her best to test the information but he or she should also give the consumer as much information as possible in order to help them come to their own conclusion. Anonymous sources need to be used sometimes, but it is much better to name a source and provide details about their situation so that consumers can be more sure about their motivation.

Protection of sources

All UK codes of conduct include clauses on the need for journalists to protect confidential sources. The NUJ Code of Conduct for instance says that 'a journalist protects the identity of sources who supply information in confidence and material gathered in the course of her/his work' and that a journalist 'resists threats or any other inducements to influence, distort or suppress information'.

(http://www.nuj.org.uk/innerPagenuj.html?docid=174 accessed 8/2/2010)

Much rubbish is talked about confidential sources. Reporters are not like doctors, obliged to keep confidential all that is told to them. Indeed, the very opposite is true. Journalists are expected to reveal confidences and report everything they are told. Occasionally, however, it is necessary to get information from sources who would be put at considerable risk if it were known that they had revealed what they knew. They might, for instance, lose their jobs or perhaps face even harsher punishment. These informants might be able to help a reporter to track down a story without the reporter having to use the information actually given by the informant. In this instance, a reporter might decide to guarantee confidentiality to a source. Only if the reporter has given his or her promise, or implied a promise, does the matter become an issue of ethical honour. If reporters are to be reliable and to be seen as trustworthy to the reader, they should also be trustworthy when they give a promise. No reporter should give this promise lightly.

In some countries reporters can be instructed by a court to reveal a confidence and failure to do so can result in severe punishment. Several British journalists have gone to prison in the past for failing to reveal a source. Some countries, such as Denmark, have laws that prevent a journalist revealing a confidential source. This can work in a reverse fashion, allowing a journalist who has not sourced a story properly to pretend that the contact is strong but that he or she is unable to reveal the source as to do so would be to breach the protection of a confidentiality promise.

Protecting confidential sources has a place in most codes. Deontologists say that the rightness of an act doesn't depend on its motives or consequences but purely on the nature of the act itself. You are obliged to keep a promise by the very fact that that is what defines a promise: it is a pledge one keeps regardless of circumstance or consequence. Deontologists would say that it is no good promising to keep a contact secret and then telling a court, simply because to refuse to do so would mean a jail sentence. If you promise someone confidentiality, you must stick by that. Since it is also in the reporter's interest to stick by this promise, revealing sources is not something that happens regularly. In one celebrated UK case, Bill Goodwin won his appeal to the European Court of Human Rights over the issue.

Case study 8.1 Protecting sources

While working as a trainee reporter for *The Engineer*, Bill Goodwin was contacted by a source who gave him some useful material about the financial dealings of a major company which suggested that the company was not as successful as it would have the market believe. Acting like a good journalist, he wrote the story and then contacted the company for its comments. The company refused to comment and, shortly after, *The Engineer* received a court injunction preventing it from publishing the story and demanding to know the name of the source.

The NUJ and *The Engineer* supported Bill Goodwin when he refused to name the source. *The Engineer* paid his £5,000 fine while the NUJ helped him to fight through the courts before going to the European Court of Human Rights in April 1996 which ruled that Goodwin's human rights had been violated. This leaves the government in a difficult position but it has made it clear it has no intention of changing section 10 of the Contempt of Court Act 1981 which says: 'No court may require a person to disclose, nor is any person guilty of contempt of court for refusing to disclose the source of information contained in a publication for which he is responsible, unless it is established to the satisfaction of the court that it is necessary in the interests of justice or national security or for the prevention of disorder and crime.' Lord Mackay, the then Lord Chancellor, told the House of Lords on 17 April 1996: 'Amending the legislation is unnecessary to give effect to this judgment.'

These cases are not always easy for journalists to fight. Since the court has the right to insist on disclosure 'in the interests of justice', the journalist is forced to show that disclosure is not in the interests of justice – and this is not always easy. In the Bill Goodwin case, none of the company's assertions to the court could be challenged without revealing the name of the source – the very thing Goodwin was fighting against. In an article for *The Journalist*, the NUJ's magazine, Goodwin wrote about his court experience:

> The source must be an ex-employee motivated by revenge, I was told. The information was so sensitive, the courts decided, that unless the informant was unmasked, the company could be forced into liquidation and 400 people would lose their jobs. It was hogwash. But I could not challenge any of these assumptions, based on the flimsiest of evidence, without giving away the source's identity. And because the hearings were 'interlocutory' we could not test Tetra's hysterical assertions in the witness box.

Goodwin's case is an important one in that he was upholding the confidentiality of the source despite not having promised to do so. The promise, in this case, was implied and therefore as binding. The wording of the NUJ Code of Conduct is that 'confidential sources' shall be protected. The implication is that there are sources who are not confidential.

Much of the moral decision making in this area hinges around the making of specific promises as well as a general method of working that would mean keeping names of sources private. Since a good portion of a journalist's worth is his or her sources, it makes good professional sense to keep some sources of information secret as far as possible.

However, this is different from promising to keep a source secret. This is not always as difficult as it seems. Whistle-blowers are often reticent about revealing their names. They will give a journalist the story, but will refuse to give a name. Since the journalist now knows the information and is now only looking for a way of guaranteeing the information, it is easier to make a decision about promising to keep the name secret. There are times when keeping a source secret may not be the moral thing to do: information from someone who is about to commit a major crime or threaten life is information that may well need to be passed on to the authorities and a journalist may have to decide that he or she will breach any undertaking to keep the name of such a person secret. This is one of the reasons why this moral tussle must remain in the hands of the journalist and not the law. Only the journalist is in a position to explore the motives of the informant and decide whether his or her identity should be kept secret. The law is too unwieldy a weapon to use in this kind of decision making. There is much agreement in the industry over confidentiality. The BBC says that promises of confidentiality given to a source must be honoured. It recognises that such promises may put the journalist into conflict with the court and recommends that journalists should not enter into such undertakings lightly. Confidentiality may include blurring car number plates, providing a voice over by someone else in order to disguise the voice; pictures may need to be disguised, preferably by blurring rather than pixilation, which can be reversed. Some sources may need to have their identity disguised if material is broadcast abroad.

A good reporter should also be aware that no document, whether paper or electronic, should identify the source as a court can demand the production of documents, notebooks, tapes and videos relating to any case involving a confidential source. It is always good practice not to keep records of confidential sources and discussions alongside ordinary notes. Any such notes you are forced to keep should be destroyed as soon as possible as the court may order their confiscation and destroying material after such an order is a criminal offence in itself.

The name or ways of identifying the source should not be shared with colleagues who may be ordered to reveal it. One area of potential difficulty is the keeping of a source secret from the journalist's editor. The promise made to a source is one made by the journalist and not by the editor. The editor is not necessarily bound in to the promise. It would be a poor editor who did not support a reporter, but if faced with court and the possibility of serious legal action against the paper or broadcast station, an editor might well take a different view on what is right to do, if only because the loyalties are very different. My view would be that journalists need not tell their editor the name of the source, although they might well give the editor some detail of that person's position and if the editor does not find that acceptable, then he or she should not use the story. The editor is certainly not in a position to demand the name of the source after publi-cation just because problems have developed. The BBC takes a different view. While the *Editorial Guidelines* agree that the BBC should take care to ensure that when anonymity is promised it can be honoured, the BBC insists that when a promise of confidentiality is made, the relevant editor has the right to be told their identity: 'In cases involving serious allegations we should resist any attempt by an anonymous source to prevent their identity being revealed to a senior BBC editor. If this happens, the reporter should make it clear that the information obtained confidentially may not be broadcast' (http://www.bbc.co.uk/guidelines/editorialguidelines/edguide/accuracy/anonymoussource.shtml#2 accessed 8/2/2010). This raises a major issue as a BBC journalist needs to make this clear to the source. This also means that the promise is not from the journalist alone and this may affect the level of trust by the source.

This is part of the fall-out from the Hutton Report and it was one of the recommendations of the Neil Report that editors should be informed. The BBC's rules are clear that if there is any problem with this, then the information may not be broadcast. In other words, it is a condition of BBC employment that a reporter can only make a promise to a source that makes it clear the reporter will have to tell the relevant editor who the source is. This should not normally be a problem provided everyone is clear about it right from the beginning.

Note-taking

Note-taking is an important attribute of a good journalist and is central to guaranteeing accuracy. The Hutton Report underlined what can happen when a reporter is not certain exactly what the source has said, and the BBC has laid down very strict rules about note-taking following that, making it clear that conversations should normally be recorded (http://www.bbc.co.uk/info/policies/pdf/neil_report.pdf accessed 18/7/06).

Good journalists keep accurate notes and can then show that their stories are supported by the sources they approached. It is still generally considered in the UK that the best way to do this is with fast, accurate shorthand, and most good journalism courses still teach shorthand. However, the UK is one of the few countries to do this and so there are obviously other ways to ensure an accurate note. Changing styles of reporting have made this easier. Back in the days when news reports were often verbatim recordings of speeches often of several thousand words, shorthand was essential. T.A. Reed, writing in 1876 about journalism and the need for 120 words a minute shorthand explained:

> Let it be distinctly understood that an occasional trial for one or two minutes is valueless as a criterion of speed and accuracy. Nothing less than half an hour's continuous writing should be regarded as a satisfactory test; and even this should not give confidence if any considerable difficulty is experienced in reading the shorthand characters.
>
> (Reed 1876: 21)

Shorthand writers these days need not be so skilled. Journalism students are required to reach 100 words a minute by the National Council for the Training of Journalists, but they need only maintain this speed for four minutes. Few stories these days are longer than a few hundred words and the requirement for verbatim reporting of long speeches has virtually disappeared. Newspaper editors though still require shorthand as the most acceptable method of getting accurate quotes.

Broadcasters, of course, rely on audio or video recordings. Many print journalists also use audio recorders but, when writing stories against a tight deadline, using a recorder is difficult. The tape or digital file needs to be replayed, which takes time. Also recorders are highly fallible. Microphones fail to pick up what seemed like a strong voice, batteries can run out at vital moments and key words can be distorted by extraneous noises. Audio recorders though can be useful back-up, providing evidence to support that a particular comment was made, in case of later dispute. Modern digital recorders allow reporters to store interviews on computer, which are much easier than the boxes of tapes that we used to be obliged to keep, but broadcasters should beware of using recordings taken for note-taking for broadcast. The BBC warns its staff that any intention to use recordings taken as notes for broadcast needs to be referred to the controller of editorial policy.

Reporters without shorthand tend to develop a way of writing longhand that is quick, usually using some kind of short forms. Electronic note-taking is also possible in PDAs and pocket computers, although these are still fairly slow and cumbersome. They have the advantage of being easy to transfer to most standard word-processing packages.

Right to a fair trial

One of the key human rights is the right to a fair trial. It has long been upheld as an important part of British justice and was included in the UN Declaration of Human Rights and the European Convention. Rooted firmly in civil rights doctrine, if we are to be considered equal then if accused of a crime, we should have the right to defend ourselves and the right to have our case fairly heard before a jury of our peers who should only make their decision on the basis of the evidence presented.

Chequebook journalism

Many sections of the media make payments to informants and sources. The NUJ Code has nothing to say about this practice, but the PCC has a fairly lengthy clause banning payments to witnesses in court cases until the case is concluded. They also ban payments to convicted or confessed criminals about a specific crime or glorifying crime in general unless there is a public interest to justify payment.

The BBC also advises against paying witnesses and criminals and instructs that any proposal to do this is referred to Director Editorial Policy and Standards (http://www.bbc.co.uk/guidelines/editorialguidelines/page/guidelines-crime-criminals-perpetrators/#payments accessed 14/10/10). Nor does the BBC generally allow witnesses to be paid before a trial. There are one or two exceptions: overwhelming public interest or because the interviewee is an expert witness whose professional opinion is being sought.

Various governments have been concerned about payments made to witnesses for their stories since the Rosemary West trial. The PCC finally agreed to introduce a clause into its Code of Practice on this in order to prevent a new law being introduced.

Requests for unused material

This is not the same as not revealing sources and the issues are mainly those of protecting journalists in difficult positions. If it becomes widely known that journalists supply untransmitted video or still pictures to the police, their position on newsworthy events such as demonstrations and riots could be put at risk. Some violent elements may well seek to ensure that video and still pictures do not find their way to the police by attacking the photographers and film crews at such events.

Material that is transmitted or published is, of course, already in the public domain and there is therefore little increased risk in cooperating with the authorities. Unpublished material is a different matter. The NUJ has supported photographers facing court orders for their unpublished material by sending the material abroad to safe places provided by the International Federation of Journalists.

The BBC is also concerned and says in its *Guidelines* that it will not normally hand over untransmitted material to third parties without a court order. 'We never voluntarily allow access to unused material:

- when to do so would endanger people who work for the BBC
- or when it would make it more difficult to gather such material in the future if the requests appear to be "fishing" for evidence' (http://www.bbc.co.uk/guidelines/editorialguidelines/page/guidelines-re-use-requests-for-material/#untransmitted-material accessed 14/10/2010). The BBC says such requests must be referred to the Director Editorial Policy.

Data protection

Access to information about subjects of stories may be limited by the Data Protection Act. This prevents data collectors from passing on 'sensitive personal data', that is, any data that can give personal information about a person, including their health, mental state, sexuality, trade union membership or criminal record. This could mean, for instance, that it would be difficult to find out information about someone hurt in a road accident. Before the Data Protection Act, it was a simple job to ring the hospital and ask for a condition report. Now the information requires the approval of the subject or a person in authority, a police superintendent, for instance.

The Data Protection Act also makes it a criminal offence to access that information under certain circumstances. Following the Clive Goodman case, there were calls from the Information Officer to firm up the law here, jailing journalists if necessary in order to protect information from publication.

Chapter 9

Reporting the vulnerable

This chapter discusses ethical issues to do with those who are particularly vulnerable to media abuse. These include:

■ Children

■ The mentally ill

■ Victims of disasters

■ Suicides

■ Minority groups

If democracy and free expression rests on the third leg of equality in order to deliver civil rights to all in our protection of natural rights, journalists should be doing all they can to prevent insensitive and discriminatory reporting. This is problematic as journalists have to accept that most societies have 'haves' and 'have nots'; those with power and influence and those with little or none and that journalists may need to treat those who are more vulnerable differently to those who have power and influence.

There are groups in society who are made particularly vulnerable to media abuse or oppression because they have had their ability to control their lives substantially reduced by the circumstances in which they find themselves and there is a second group that is particularly vulnerable to media victimisation because of who they are.

Those who have their power reduced (at least temporarily) because of circumstance include victims of disaster, domestic abuse, crime (including families of those accused or convicted), the bereaved or the seriously sick or injured. This group may also include those who are badly affected by poverty and it may certainly include groups such as immigrants. It is possible to leave or join these groups and nearly all of us do, to a greater or lesser extent, at various times in our lives.

Those with limited power because of who they are include children, ethnic minorities and other minorities such as the transgendered, gay people and people with disabilities. These groups are more stable in their vulnerability with their members locked within the framework set for them by the media for their entire lives.

Both these groups at appropriate times require journalists to consider reporting their stories in as sensitive a way as possible. This also applies to the second group but this group also requires reporters to consider the elimination of discriminatory reporting. Words, pictures, expressions, including the choice of copy or video footage and its editing and use, can be crucial in deciding whether copy or video will give a truthful or misleading impression about the views, feelings or approach of a minority or oppressed group. Many a politician has seized on the scapegoat nature of a minority group to place all the problems and dissatisfaction of society at its door. From the very earliest of leaders through to the modern politician of your choice, there have always been those who have been willing to play on people's fears about other cultures.

Nor is it just politicians. Ordinary citizens are also often keen to blame minority or culturally oppressed groups for their problems or failures. Often this can be explained by ignorance or fear. If we do not know or understand the culture of a minority or oppressed group, it is easy to see its behaviour as unacceptable or 'uncivilised' and therefore not worthy of consideration or respect. Only when we come to understand another culture's ways can we start to realise that it is, like ours, only human and neither totally wrong nor totally right. It should be a part of a journalist's role to give readers the information they need to reach sensible decisions, not to play on their fears and prejudices. If journalists tell people only what they expect to hear about minority or oppressed groups then the debate about their position in society is not advanced. It is part of the journalist's duty to help advance society's awareness of such problems by providing people with a wider truth than their existing prejudices.

This determination to inform people and help them overcome their fears does not mean that a journalist cannot write material that is critical of one culture or another. Journalists need to be truthful about a society, cultural group or minority if we are to come to valid conclusions. The public needs to know why this group of people has aroused hatred in another, and the failings and good points of both, if they are to understand difficult and serious situations around the world. We can use Aristotle's golden mean here to try to set the standard somewhere between the frugality of no debate and the excess of printing every offensive piece of bigotry available. The elements of hatred and violence are often used to help define this mean into a universal law. An example of a debate where a lack of sound information stunts understanding is immigration.

Case study 9.1 Immigration

This usually thorny question has become a particular political football over the past ten years with tabloids such as the *Daily Mail*, *Daily Express* and *The Sun* being particularly vociferous in the range of stories they carry about immigrants: 'Immigrants handed 1.3m jobs in Britain' (*Daily Express* 8/2/10); 'Now migrants get VIP club' (*Daily Express* 18/2/10); 'Migrant workforce surges by 175,000 despite recession' (*Daily Mail* 9/1/09); 'Asylum seeker payouts to be cut as officials admit they are "too generous" ' (*Daily Mail* 30/7/09); 'Migrants paid off' (*The Sun* 15/2/10); 'Asylum kids' £25 pocket money' (*The Sun* 14/10/09) to give just a few examples.

This is not to say that newspapers do not have the right to debate the rights and wrongs of government policy on immigration and to take a particular viewpoint as it is an important issue that deserves proper consideration. But it is not helped by stories designed to support readers' prejudices in order to boost circulation. Immigrants are an interesting group as many of them fall under both categories identified above as they are both 'other' and temporarily, at least, vulnerable. Their new position as immigrants in a country that is culturally different to their own means they are now temporarily in difficulties despite the circumstances in which they lived previously. There are a number of reasons why people move from country to country and it would be wrong to assume that all immigrants are seeking a better life because they were in poverty in their homeland. Many were reasonably well off or influential until obliged to flee political persecution. Many of them are also from ethnic backgrounds or minorities that leave them open to discrimination.

Many codes of conduct have clauses against discrimination. As would be expected from the BBC, its *Editorial Guidelines* have excellent advice on the use of discriminatory language. This discusses terminology and methods of reporting on issues involving women, Asian, African and Caribbean people and people with disabilities. Religious groups, the aged and a range of people with differing sexual orientation also come under close scrutiny. The BBC says: 'We aim to reflect fully and fairly all of the United Kingdom's people and cultures in our services' (http://www. bbc.co.uk/guidelines/editorialguidelines/edguide/harm/portrayal.shtml accessed 23/7/06). The National Union of Journalists' Code says simply: 'A journalist shall only mention a person's age, race, colour, creed, illegitimacy, disability, marital status (or lack of it), gender or sexual orientation if this information is strictly relevant. A journalist shall neither originate nor process material which encourages discrimination, ridicule, prejudice or hatred on any of the above-mentioned grounds.' It is an attempt to tap into that golden mean with a universal law.

This approach is fairly widespread around the world, with the Swedish code representing a sound example. It says: 'Do not emphasise race, sex, nationality, occupation, political affiliation or religious persuasion in the case of the persons concerned if such particulars are not important in the context or are disparaging' (Swedish Press Code 1995). The British PCC has something similar: '(i) The press must avoid prejudicial or pejorative reference to an individual's race, colour, religion, gender, sexual orientation or to any physical or mental illness or disability. (ii) Details of an individual's race, colour, religion, sexual orientation, physical or mental illness or disability must be avoided unless genuinely relevant to the story' (http://www.pcc.org.uk/cop/practice.html accessed 21/7/06). Ofcom has a similar clause for broadcast journalists.

In some countries this issue is considered serious enough for laws to be introduced to prevent incitement to hatred. Britain has such laws. These do not apply just to the media, but their general application impinges strongly there. Broadcasting or printing material likely to incite hatred on the basis of race, colour, religion or creed is an offence. Denmark has very strong laws in this area which has led to several clashes between the authorities and broadcasters and journalists seeking to produce reports of neo-fascist excesses in that country.

Despite all these laws and codes, discrimination is still a strong strand running through much of the media. Homophobia is still widely apparent in the tabloid press and racism can also be found regularly, albeit in a slightly more muted form. This is not the place for what would be a lengthy discussion on the representation of women in the tabloid press, but there are many who find much tabloid coverage to be sexist from the 'Starbird' through to *The Sun*'s picture file on the agony page.

The PCC has come under heavy criticism over the years as it has rarely adjudicated complaints about discrimination. The tabloid press's coverage of asylum seekers saw a substantial rise in the number of complaints about discriminatory coverage over the late nineties and early noughties but only one complaint has been upheld on the grounds of discrimination where a man appeared to have been quoted as saying Britain was a 'soft touch'. The PCC has spoken with groups representing asylum seekers and done more to take complaints from third parties about accuracy and has also issued strong guidance on wording for asylum seekers.

> The Commission is concerned that editors should ensure that their journalists covering these issues are mindful of the problems that can occur and take care to avoid misleading or distorted terminology. By way of example, as an 'asylum seeker' is someone currently seeking refugee status or humanitarian protection, there can be no such thing in law as an 'illegal asylum seeker'. A 'refugee' is someone who has fled their country in fear of their life, and may have been granted asylum under the 1951 Refugee Convention or someone who otherwise qualifies for Humanitarian Protection, Discretionary Leave or has been granted Exceptional Leave to Remain in the country. An asylum seeker can only become an 'illegal immigrant' if he or she remains in the UK after having failed to respond to a removal notice. Those groups set up to support and advocate on behalf of refugees and asylum seekers can provide further clarification to journalists if required.
>
> (http://www.pcc.org.uk/news/index.html?article=OTE= accessed 21/2/10)

Several cases involving gay people have been upheld by the PCC, as well as several that were derogatory to mental health patients.

Protection of minors

The United Nations Convention on the Rights of the Child was introduced in 1989 and sets out children's rights in 54 articles. The Convention is a universally agreed set of standards and obligations that should be respected by governments. This is a legally binding convention, but is of more interest to the media for the framework it sets down and the standards it provides for the approach to children that involve ensuring special care and protection for both the child and its family and the recognition that the child should be fully prepared to live an independent life.

Four articles in particular protect children's right of access to the media and protect children from the media either when journalists deal with children through the courts or directly:

Article 3
1. In all actions concerning children, whether undertaken by public or private social welfare institutions, courts of law, administrative authorities or legislative bodies, the best interests of the child shall be a primary consideration.

Article 12

1. States Parties shall assure to the child who is capable of forming his or her own views the right to express those views freely in all matters affecting the child, the views of the child being given due weight in accordance with the age and maturity of the child.

Article 13

1. The child shall have the right to freedom of expression; this right shall include freedom to seek, receive and impart information and ideas of all kinds, regardless of frontiers, either orally, in writing or in print, in the form of art, or through any other media of the child's choice.

Article 16

1. No child shall be subjected to arbitrary or unlawful interference with his or her privacy, family, home or correspondence, nor to unlawful attacks on his or her honour and reputation.

(http://www.unicef.org/crc/)

Under the Convention, it is the duty of the state to ensure that these rights are upheld and this helps explain why so many countries have strong laws to protect minors, although many had such laws before the 1989 Convention. In the UK many of these rights are enshrined in the Children and Young Persons Act 1933 and the Children Act 1989.

There are two main elements about dealing with minors that need concern us.

1   Not taking advantage of those who may be too young to make legitimate judgements.
2   Protecting the reputation of someone who may be too young to know better.

The PCC Code of Conduct in Britain is fairly strict on the subject of children and how the media may deal with them:

(i)   Young people should be free to complete their time at school without unnecessary intrusion.
(ii)   A child under 16 must not be interviewed or photographed on issues involving their own or another child's welfare unless a custodial parent or similarly responsible adult consents.
(iii) Pupils must not be approached or photographed at school without the permission of the school authorities.
(iv)   Minors must not be paid for material involving children's welfare, nor parents or guardians for material about their children or wards, unless it is clearly in the child's interest.
(v)   Editors must not use the fame, notoriety or position of a parent or guardian as sole justification for publishing details of a child's private life.

(http:/www.pcc.org.uk/cop/practice.html accessed 14/3/10)

Despite this strong clause, the PCC does not prevent the naming of children in situations where it is their own fame or notoriety that is the issue.

The clause quoted above is built on the back of British law that largely prevents the naming of children involved in crime. There can be exceptions, at the discretion of the judge, but these are rare. The two young killers of Jamie Bulger, a young boy who was led off to be killed in humiliating circumstances, were 10 and 11 years old and the judge took the unusual step of naming them only after a guilty verdict had been delivered and, in part at least, to protect some other children whom rumour had named as possible suspects. The Crime (Sentences) Act 1997 section 45 has increased the power of judges to name young offenders if it is seen to be in the interests of justice to do so.

The naming of juveniles is another area where the law and ethics are often at loggerheads. The law generally holds that juveniles involved in criminal court cases, whether defendants, victims or witnesses, should not be named. Nor should juveniles involved in wardship hearings be named. While few people argue that this is wrong, journalists have for years gone on to name juveniles in other circumstances without a thought. However, there is evidence that that is changing. While naming juveniles who are the subject of an antisocial behaviour order, naming the children of the famous has become increasingly unacceptable. The death of the Princess of Wales brought dealings with minors into sharp relief and since then the PCC has become increasingly tougher in dealing with such complaints and has upheld a number of complaints from famous parents whose children's privacy has been invaded.

The BBC and Ofcom have even more complex rules on the use of children's identities, which become more confused when these involve criminal offences or antisocial behaviour orders (ASBOs). There are two main elements that a journalist needs to consider when dealing with minors:

1 Whether or not to name a minor in a story.
2 Whether or not to interview a minor in pursuit of a story.

The aim in point one is to ensure that a minor who makes a mistake by breaking the law or committing some other act that is both newsworthy and antisocial does not have his or her adult life blighted by this childhood mistake. This upholds the generally accepted principle that childhood is a time to learn and a time to make mistakes and that only when a certain level of maturity is reached should people be held fully accountable for their actions. All of us learn, and many of us become better people, by making mistakes. Often one can only know what is right by learning from experience what is wrong. Children nearly always end up touching the hot stove despite regular warnings from parents. How can they really understand the concepts of 'heat' and 'burn' until they have done so? There is also a potential unfairness in naming or identifying a particular child when in fact the story is more general. If the story concerns the antisocial behaviour of certain groups of children, it might well be unfair to identify one or two children as examples. Publishing a photograph can also be a way of identifying a child. In a case before the PCC in 2009, for instance, a man complained that an article headlined 'Terrorised by knife thug, 7', published in the *Scottish News of the World* on 10 August 2008, contained inaccuracies and included a photograph of his son taken without consent in breach of Clause 6. The PCC decided that while there was a public interest in reporting antisocial behaviour in communities, in this case the unsubstantiated assertions about the child's behaviour meant there was no justification for his clear identification through information in the article and a pixellated photograph (http://www.pcc.org.uk/cases/adjudicated.html?article=NjA1Nw== accessed 15/3/10).

Although no one is yet calling for new legislation to extend the prevention of naming minors beyond the courts, there are plenty who believe the media go too far. In a powerful plea for his son to be left alone, the father of a child born to a surrogate mother says:

Our mistake [in allowing a story to be written about their child's birth] has resulted in Peter receiving playground taunts about his family history ... puberty is traumatic enough without the *National Daily* making it worse ... I am not suggesting that they [journalists and editors] should censor themselves; but they must remember that innocent young children cannot answer back. They have no power and must rely upon us adults to defend their interests. Where no crime has been committed, where no great injustice is being covered up, where it is merely the interests of the newspaper that are being served –

they must think more than twice about whether to publish information that could cause damage to a child.

(George X, 1997: 15–16)

George X does not call for legislation to prevent naming, nor does he object to references to his son, provided he is not named.

The law goes to some effort to protect children involved with the courts. The Children and Young Persons Act 1933 section 49 and the Criminal Justice Act 1991 prevent the identification of alleged offenders or witnesses at youth courts if they are under the age of 18. The Children and Young Persons Act 1933 also allows judges to make a section 39 order to protect the identity of children appearing before adult courts 'whether the minor is the subject of those proceedings or is a witness to them' (Carey, 1996: 94). In family matters, the Children Act 1989 puts such cases to the magistrates' courts and specially trained magistrates. The Act states:

No person shall publish any material which is intended or likely to identify:

- any child as being involved in such proceedings, or
- an address or school as being that of a child involved in such proceedings.

(Crone 2002: 127)

The Youth Justice and Criminal Evidence Act 1999 tightened this even further by making it an offence to report any matter that might lead to the identification of an alleged offender, witness or victim under the age of 18, once an investigation into a criminal offence has started. Once the case comes to court, then it may become possible to name someone under 18 if the court thinks it is in the interests of justice so to do.

The main exception to all this are the Anti-social Behaviour Acts. ASBOs were introduced in 1998 to deal with those causing 'harassment, alarm or distress' in a local government area. They can apply to anyone over the age of 10 (16 in Scotland). The ASBO powers were beefed up by the government in 2003 to include drug-dealing and children with air guns. When an ASBO is made in respect of a child, it should normally be accompanied by a parenting order – an order for the parent to attend regular counselling sessions and to comply with requirements made in the order.

Much of the confusion about the naming of children subject to ASBOs surrounds the type of court involved. Youth courts impose an automatic ban on identifying children. In an adult court, a section 39 order has to be imposed, banning the media from identifying children. So, when an ASBO is issued against a child or young person, a section 39 order can also be imposed by magistrates. It is in these circumstances that reporters often challenge the section 39 order so that they can identity the defendant. The government has made it clear that it intends for the media to name those served with anti-social behaviour orders:

The court should have a good reason, aside from age alone, to impose a discretionary order under section 39 of the Children and Young Persons Act 1933 to prevent the identification of a child or young person concerned in the proceedings.

The applicant may resist a call from the defendant's representatives for such restrictions if the effectiveness of the ASBO will largely depend on the wider community knowing the details.

(http://www.crimereduction.homeoffice.gov.uk/antisocialbehaviour/antisocialbehaviour55.pdf
accessed 15/3/10)

Also, the Serious Organised Crime and Police Act 2005 removed automatic reporting restrictions for children and young people convicted of a breach of an ASBO so that details of the perpetrator could be made public.

As well as considering identity, journalists should also be careful while interviewing minors either for print or broadcast.

Very often children make good witnesses and can provide accurate information. They are often very observant, have better memories than their elders and have the time and inclination to put these to good use. But they can also be easily led in their desire to give a person whatever it is the child thinks he or she wants. This is particularly true in what may be to them an exciting and glamorous opportunity to be interviewed by a journalist, particularly if that interview is being televised.

To ask young people to describe something they have seen is unlikely to lead to problems but to ask children to explain their actions without an adult they trust to help and guide them is unfair. As always, discretion is required when dealing with any story involving minors. Asking school-children on the way into school what they think about having to wear school uniform might be fine, provided the head teacher is aware of the identity of the suspicious character skulking outside the school gates soliciting the pupils and has given permission to interview them. Asking them about drug dealers or bullying could put them at risks of which they are often innocently unaware.

The PCC, BBC and Ofcom all have sections in their code that warn journalists not to interview without permission. Ofcom says that:

> Due care must be taken over the physical and emotional welfare and the dignity of people under eighteen who take part or are otherwise involved in programmes. This is irrespective of any consent given by the participant or by a parent, guardian or other person over the age of eighteen in loco parentis.
>
> (http://www.ofcom.org.uk/tv/ifi/codes/bcode/protectingu18/ accessed 15/3/10)

The PCC is not so tough, but still insists that parental permission is obtained for pictures and interviews. They upheld a complaint in 2009 after hearing that a reporter for the *Daily Post Wales* had interviewed a 15-year-old girl after a serious road accident involving one of her friends. But the commission noted:

> This breach of the Code was slight. While the reporter should arguably have been able to deduce immediately, from her school shirt, that the girl may have known the victim and was under 16, he did withdraw after a brief exchange when this occurred to him. It is clear that, with the benefit of hindsight, he should have taken greater care not to engage the girl in a conversation about the accident. But nothing from the interview was published – so there was no public impact on the complainant's daughter – and the Commission was satisfied that the breach of the Code was not serious.
>
> (http://www.pcc.org.uk/cases/adjudicated.html?article=NTYwNA== accessed 15/3/10)

Children in sex cases

As well as general concerns about working with children, the PCC also tries to ensure that the victims of sexual offences are not identified. This clause was agreed in consultation with other regulators to ensure that jigsaw identification across different media was not possible. The PCC Code of Practice instructs journalists that:

1. The press must not, even if legally free to do so, identify children under 16 who are victims or witnesses in cases involving sex offences.
2. In any press report of a case involving a sexual offence against a child –
   (i)   The child must not be identified.
   (ii) The adult may be identified.
   (iii) The word 'incest' must not be used where a child victim might be identified.

(iv) Care must be taken that nothing in the report implies the relationship between the accused and the child.

(http://www.pcc.org.uk/cop/practice.html accessed 21/7/06)

Jigsaw identification is where one publication may name the accused adult, but not mention the relationship to the victim, while in another publication or radio bulletin the relationship is mentioned but the accused is not named, making it possible to identify the child victim of an incestuous sexual assault. The PCC has evolved a system for dealing with this and it takes it very seriously. The former Chairman of the Code of Practice Committee, the late Sir David English, then Chairman and Editor-in-Chief of Associated Newspapers, wrote to providers of training in journalism in February 1996, expressing concern that a number of trainees taking the April 1995 National Certificate Examination in Journalism seemed unaware of the clause on jigsaw identification:

> This is a matter of grave concern and I would ask you to make absolutely clear to those in your charge –
>
> - The code of practice is a foundation stone of successful self-regulation in newspaper and magazine publishing.
> - There is nothing optional in the code – it sets out standards of conduct and practice which all publications and their journalists must follow.
> - The provisions in the code relating to cases involving a sexual offence against a child are being applied by radio and television as well as the press. Only if we all follow the provisions meticulously, can the risk of jigsaw identification be avoided.

The jigsaw clause was a development of the old Press Council's guidelines on jigsaw identification of rape victims. This followed the Ealing Vicarage rape in 1985 in which the daughter of a vicar was savagely raped by three men who were later imprisoned. A series of reports in different newspapers led to the woman being clearly identified, even though no paper actually named her. The Press Council called a meeting with representatives from the Newspaper Publishers' Association (NPA), the Newspaper Society (NS), the Scottish Daily Newspaper Society, the Guild of British Newspaper Editors (now just the Guild of British Editors), the Association of British Editors, the BBC, ITN, IRN and individual editors of national newspapers, the Metropolitan Police, the Association of Chief Police Officers and the Association of Chief Police Officers (Scotland) to discuss the issue. The conference came up with guidelines that specified the following:

- At the time of the offence no more details leading to identification of the victim should be published than would be permissible during the trial.
- The name and address of the victim or her relatives should not be published.
- The relationship between the victim and any other person named in the story should not be published.
- Premises where the crime took place should not be identified.
- The police could ask for such information to be published for operational reasons.

(Press Council, 1989: 241)

Since these guidelines were drawn up in 1989, the law has changed again and the Sexual Offences (Amendment) Act 1992 now makes it an offence to publish the name, address or picture of an alleged victim of any sexual offence, not just rape, from the minute a complaint is made. Once an arrest has been made, the Act strengthens this to include a clause which prevents the media publishing any matter 'likely to lead members of the public to identify a person as the person against whom the offence is alleged to have been committed'.

Children and celebrity

Children whose parents are famous have come under more pressure lately and their parents have become more protective. When he was Prime Minister, Tony Blair and his wife complained about a story in the *Daily Telegraph* and the *Daily Mail* about their son Euan applying to Trinity College, Oxford. The PCC, after considering the two cases, said: '... the article was an unnecessary intrusion into Euan Blair's time at school and that it had only been published because of the position of his parents. The complaint was therefore upheld (http://www.pcc.org.uk/cases/adjudicated. html?article=MjA2NQ==accessed 15/3/10).

In another earlier story, Prince Charles decided that he had no choice but to complain after a story about Prince Harry appeared in the *Mirror* in November 1998. The Prince's anger about the invasion of his son's privacy over a trivial rugby injury was exacerbated by the *Mirror*'s claims that the Palace was trying to censor the press.

> The Prince of Wales has reported the *Mirror* to the Press Complaints Commission in an effort to protect Prince Harry's privacy at school.
>
> The spokesman said: 'The Prince of Wales has asked me to say that he is deeply disappointed by the reaction of the editor of the *Mirror* [Piers Morgan] to the simple and straightforward appeal for Prince Harry to be allowed privacy at school. We respect what Mr Morgan says about press freedom. Indeed, we support it. However, this matter is nothing at all to do with press freedom. Instead, it is everything to do with the privacy to which Harry and William are entitled during their education.
>
> We are therefore making a formal complaint to the Press Complaints Commission which, with newspaper editors, has done a great deal over the years to protect the privacy of Prince William and Prince Harry, and will ask them to deal with it.'
>
> (*Daily Telegraph*, 21 November 1998)

Some children are, of course, celebrities in their own right. This applies to the royal princes, and Prince William has found that his good looks and position have made him a target for a media keen to carve out a wider share of the teenage girl market. While coverage of him at school was reasonably muted, coverage of some of his recent tours was extensive. Celebrity of this sort is usually less of a concern than most other coverage of minors. In the main it is accepted, even welcomed. There are always exceptions of course.

Some people come to the attention of the media through no fault, or only limited fault, of their own. They are often people whose rights are more limited for some reason, or who find it difficult to uphold their rights, such as children and the users of mental health services. Journalists need to be aware that, while not all the people who fall into the groups discussed below are innocent, they are often more vulnerable and less able to protect themselves and their interests, and therefore require special consideration.

Witnesses

A journalist needs to be particularly sensitive when children are at the centre of a story, either as witnesses to a court case or as the main interviewee in a general news story. Standing in a witness box can be an ordeal for even the most self-confident adult but for a child it can be a nightmare, which is made even worse by excessive media attention. The Youth Justice and Criminal Evidence Act 1999 allows those under 17 and certain other classes of witness, including children, to give evidence behind a screen or through a video link under some circumstances and this can make it easier. The court also has the power to restrict reporting of proceedings involving persons under

18, including witnesses. Outside the witness box, using reports from children could put them at risk from threats and attempts at coercion. Care needs to be taken about naming children and good journalists will always ask themselves whether a report could put the child at risk.

Offenders

The automatic assumption is that an offending child will be protected by the law, but of course this only happens when a child is in court. A child accused of improper behaviour in other circumstances is often considered fair game by the media. For example, in the summer of 1996 there were a number of cases where children had been excluded from school but were allowed to return after their appeals were upheld. However, teachers then refused to teach these children.

In one of the early cases, a 10-year-old pupil was excluded from a Worksop school for being unruly in class. He was readmitted only after a compromise scheme was worked out:

> Teachers' union leaders, governors and local education chiefs devised the compromise scheme after five hours of talks in Worksop last night to try to break the deadlock which has closed the 190-pupil school. Under the arrangements, Matthew **** will return to one-to-one tuition under a supply teacher but will also mix with selected pupils.

> Councillor Fred Riddell, chairman of Nottinghamshire education committee, said the 'mixed menu' education would give the boy the chance to show he was amenable to classroom discipline. However, there is no chance of pupils at Manton School returning to the classroom this week. Today is the school's third day of closure.

> (*Daily Telegraph*, 31 October 1996)

The *Daily Telegraph* used his name in full in the story but I have decided it would be appropriate only to use the forename Matthew in the quote.

Many of these cases seemed to be copycat, in the sense that having seen one school take industrial action to prevent the return of a child, others followed suit. It is entirely possible therefore that the children in the subsequent cases were nothing like as unruly as the first principle-testing case. However, in each case the teachers felt the child should not have been allowed to return because he or she was too unruly to teach, while the independent panel which hears exclusion appeals felt the school was wrong to have excluded the child.

At the heart of all these cases was the debate between the school and the local authority about the standard of misbehaviour that was sufficient to merit exclusion. However, in every newspaper report, particularly in the tabloids, the focus was on the children involved. The children were named, their reputation blackened, and they were given little opportunity to put their case. The matter was made worse by television and, in several of the exclusion stories, the children were interviewed, albeit briefly. Not surprisingly, they wallowed in the unexpected attention and enjoyed their few seconds of fame. Media coverage of this sort might well damage the future of the children involved and, as the law believes a minor should not be named in criminal proceedings so that their future is not jeopardised, journalists should consider not naming a child as a reasonable practice to follow in all cases where children are portrayed in an unfavourable light.

The Sun carried a two-page feature on four children expelled from school, none aged more than 13, on 18 September 1996. It named them, alongside large pictures, and published details of the views of teachers and governors. A one-paragraph response from the mothers was the only defence for the children, yet in two of the cases the children claimed their bad behaviour was triggered by an assault from a teacher – being dragged from a classroom in one case and being picked up in another. The first four paragraphs of the feature made it clear that *The Sun* had no intention of approaching this subject in an objective way and was determined to make it clear that the children were hooligans with no redeeming features:

> When pupils used to step out of line they would get a clip round the ear or six of the best from the headmaster. But today, teachers would risk swift disciplinary action for daring to hand out such punishments. If a head teacher and his governors try to expel an unruly pupil, the parents will often rush to an independent appeals panel – appointed by the local education authority – demanding their child is taken back. *And often they get their way after evidence from all sides has been heard.*
>
> (*The Sun*, 18 September 1996: 18)

The last sentence is printed in italics in order to suggest a feeling of outrage. Yet why should we feel outraged that an independent panel has come to a decision after hearing evidence from all sides? Regardless of your views on school discipline, the fact is that *The Sun* did not give the pupils a chance to put their cases, but it did identify them and potentially damage their futures. The story would have had just as much impact without naming them.

The story is, of course, newsworthy. Teachers going on strike to prevent a child being returned to school by the legally appointed authority raises a number of political issues of which we should be aware and also raises a number of human issues which would be of interest to the average reader. With 12,500 or so exclusions in English schools in 1995 (*The Sun*, 18 September 1996: 18), it is hardly surprising that there would be a few cases where the independent appeals panels, to which the pupil and parents can take their case if they think the child was wrongly or unfairly excluded, should decide that the head teacher was wrong to exclude the child. It is also not surprising that half a dozen or so of these cases should upset the teachers who think the appeals panel has got it wrong. But does the media need to name the children involved in order to examine the issues fully? In other cases, naming works the other way around. In one case:

> A teenage tearaway who has committed a catalogue of 1,000 offences was finally sent to secure accommodation yesterday.
>
> Senior police officers in Durham had expressed their frustration that the 15-year-old – known as Boomerang Boy – was consistently freed by courts almost as quickly as he was arrested. They complained that he was back on the streets committing crime as soon as he was out of the youth court doors.
>
> (*Daily Telegraph*, 13 February 1999)

The courts then ordered that, under the Crimes (Sentencing) Act 1997, the boy could be named, but his picture could not be used (see *Press Gazette*, 26 March 1999: 8).

Victims

Journalists need to consider carefully how they approach a child who has been the victim of a crime, accident or other event. Sensitivity is extremely important and a good journalist will consider resisting the temptation to squeeze information out of a minor, even if the child is accompanied by a responsible adult. In these cases, it is often the interview itself, rather than the publication or broadcast of the child's name, that involves difficult moral decisions, although naming them should be given serious thought as well.

The PCC offered advice to journalists about identifying victims in an editorial in its October–November 1993 report. The editorial was particularly concerned with the difficulties raised by the publication of pictures and the ability to identify victims even when faces are obscured.

Editors should consider carefully whether or not their pictures offer clues, albeit unwittingly, that will allow some readers to put a name to the individual concerned. Such clues may be found in unusual hairstyles or in distinctive clothing. They may also be found in pictures that illustrate a particular relationship between the victims and family members, friends or locations. The choice of colour photography instead of black and white could also lead to easier identification in some cases.

(PCC 1993: 5)

The Commission suggested that while black and white photographs may not be the complete answer, silhouettes may reduce the probability of identification. The Commission also suggested consultation beforehand to ensure that the subject chooses hairstyle and clothing with care. The context in which the picture appears may also be an important consideration. Cropping and editing may allow a picture to be used in a way that reduces the potential for identification and electronic manipulation of pictures may also be useful.

In another PCC complaint, a mother said that the *Express on Sunday, Daily Express, Scottish Daily Mail* and *Daily Record* had all used a story about her daughter that invaded her privacy. The daughter had been diagnosed as suffering from Creutzfeldt-Jakob disease, the human form of BSE, and all of these newspapers ran stories about her and her illness which identified her. The PCC upheld the complaints against each paper, saying: 'Publication of the identity of the patient was not essential to informing the public of the vital information about the illness and diagnosis, and indeed any doubts about the diagnosis' (PCC 1997: 10).

Vulnerable adults

Although nearly all children need to be considered as vulnerable groups before writing about them, there are also a number of adults who need special consideration because they are particularly vulnerable in some way. They could be related to celebrities or notorious criminals, they could be recently bereaved or involved in some major story that has left them traumatised or they could be disabled or mentally ill.

Adult victims of crime

The only clause the PCC Code has on victims states: 'The press must not identify victims of sexual assault or publish material likely to contribute to such identification unless there is adequate justification and they are legally free to do so' (PCC Code of Practice 2005). Since, in most cases, the media is at liberty to do so, being the victim of crime is to lay oneself open to having one's privacy invaded. The BBC does not have much to say about victims, suggesting only that journalists think of ways to minimise distress.

Journalists need always to remember that victims of crime are not there by choice and rarely through any fault of their own. If the report will make things worse for the victim, then the journalist should think carefully about how the report should be handled. I discussed in Chapter 6 how most people see victims of events as maintaining a stronger right to privacy than, say, criminals.

When plans were first drawn up to make it an offence to report the name of a rape victim, many editors condemned it absolutely. Yet some thirty years later, there is little evidence that it has damaged the press's freedom to report the court cases. Except in the case of a celebrity victim, the inability to report the name makes little difference to the newsworthiness of the story, although it is worth remembering that it may have some effect on its credibility in some circumstances.

Victims of crime and disaster also need to be handled with care, although naming them is often not a problem. Getting to know the person, particularly if they come from our home town or have some other connection, is important in giving a connection between reader and subject, but the method of interview and the way the story is written or broadcast should be handled sensitively.

Case study 9.2 Reporting crime

The *Sport* had its knuckles rapped by the PCC in November 1991 for publishing an inaccurate report of a rape that could have led to the identification of the victim. The PCC says in its report:

> The *Daily Sport*'s report of a rape trial included prurient and offensive details of evidence, the publication of which was likely to cause additional distress to the victim
> ...
>
> Misleadingly it omitted an important part of the victim's evidence which made it clear that a particular act which had been threatened did not take place. By reporting her attacker's address inaccurately, the paper increased the risk that she would be identified by readers who knew her. This possibility was made more distressing by the paper's unnecessarily detailed account of the attack on her.
>
> (PCC, Report No. 4, 1991: 6)

The Commission expressed its profound sympathy with the victim and upheld the complaint.

However, the Press Council rejected a complaint from a woman that the *Redditch Indicator and the Redditch Advertiser* had irresponsibly published a picture of her when she was the subject of persistent harassment (Press Council, 1985: 166). The woman was a police officer, although this was incidental. The man pestered her with 5,000 phone calls for which he was jailed for nine months. The two local papers published pictures of her. The court had made no order not to publish photographs and the newspapers in question claimed they had no reason to know that the defendant was unaware of what the woman looked like. Although in this case it is difficult to blame the newspapers which merely made a natural assumption that the defendant knew what the victim looked like, it is a suitable cautionary tale.

Protection of victims and relatives of criminals

While those accused of crime have the right to be presumed innocent, journalists must never forget that their victims or relatives and friends are also innocent. This group of people is often dragged into the public domain through no fault of their own. Picked, often at random, to be victims, or being related to a criminal, their troubles can be magnified first by being harassed by journalists and, second, by the way their story is subsequently treated by the press or on the airwaves. The BBC has a lengthy section in its *Editorial Guidelines* about reporting crime. Much of it concerns the presentation of programmes such as *Crimewatch* and *Police, Camera, Action!* where guidance is given about the presentation of crime and violence in a way that sets it into context and makes it clear that it is an exceptional event. It covers items such as not using incidental music, taking care about camera angles and not using slow motion to linger on dramatic events. It also gives advice on interviewing serious criminals and the need to avoid glamorising their actions.

Friends and relatives of the criminal and the victim are some of the first people that journalists approach to get information. These are usually people dragged into the limelight very much against their will. Imagine the shock of Dunblane killer Thomas Hamilton's mother. Almost minutes after the police informed her not only that her son was dead, but also that he took sixteen children and a teacher with him, the media was on the telephone. No wonder she looked odd on her television interview. She was in shock. This is not so much an invasion of her privacy as merely insensitive behaviour. She is not directly involved with the crime, but with the criminal. While it would be acceptable to quiz her about her son, with the same sensitivity that a journalist would use with any grieving person, it would not be right to cause her distress. The BBC's *Editorial Guidelines* say: 'Reporting the facts about criminals may include detailing their family circumstances, but we should avoid causing unwarranted distress to their family. Also we should not imply guilt by association without evidence' (http://www.bbc.co.uk/guidelines/editorialguidelines/edguide/ crime/reportingcri.shtml accessed 15/3/10). The PCC Code of Conduct has a strong clause to cover these problems. It says: 'Relatives or friends of persons convicted or accused of crime should not generally be identified without their consent, unless they are genuinely relevant to the story' (http://www.pcc.org.uk/cop/practice.html accessed 15/3/10). This does not mean that friends and relatives can be assured of strict anonymity, because this is one of the clauses identified by the PCC as having a public interest defence, but it does mean that a paper has to have a good reason for publishing.

Mental health

The PCC in its January–February 1994 report reminded journalists that although many patients at special hospitals such as Rampton, Ashworth, Carstairs and Broadmoor are convicted criminals, a number have not committed any crime and are not detained for treatment because of an appearance before a court. It explained that the 1959 Mental Health Act requires that all such patients, criminal or otherwise, are designated 'patients' rather than 'prisoners'. The staff serve in their medical capacity and are not prison officers, even though some may be members of the Prison Officers' Association (PCC 1994: 5).

Case study 9.3 Mental health and the media

There is considerable concern among health professionals, researchers and patients about the descriptions used in the media of mental health patients and the effects these have on public perceptions (see Philo, 1996). Certainly, considerable thought and sensitivity should be applied to the terminology used. Phrases such as 'psycho', 'sicko', 'nutter', 'maniac' and 'loony' do appear regularly, especially in the tabloid press, but should never be used to describe those with mental health conditions. This was spelt out by the PCC in their January 1996 report when the *Star* was found to have committed two breaches of clause 13 of the Code of Practice (discrimination) (see Appendix 1). The first case involved a patient at Broadoak hospital who cycled up to the late Princess of Wales during a visit and asked for a kiss. The *Star* described him as 'a raving nutter' and a 'loony' (9 November 1995 and 10 November 1995). The Commission agreed that 'to describe a person suffering from a mental illness as a 'raving nutter' and a 'loony' could not in the circumstances of this case be other than pejorative in breach of clause 15 of the code' (PCC 1996: 17).

In the same PCC report, a complaint about a story in the *Star* was also upheld. The article (*Star*, 26 January 1996) reported that there had been a complaint to the patients' council about beef being served at the canteen at Ashworth hospital despite the BSE scare. The newspaper reported that 'crazies at a top security mental hospital refused to eat beef

– because it might send them MAD'. The report included a spoof menu with such items as 'bread and nutter pudding' and 'chicken in a basket case'. The PCC said: 'The commission did not accept the newspaper's response as the descriptions contained in the article were applied to all patients at Ashworth. It considered the language to be pejorative ...' (PCC 1996: 19).

The National Union of Journalists released guidelines on mental health reporting on 21 June 1997. Called 'Shock treatment', the leaflet encourages journalists to cover stories about mental health in a more enlightened way. The guidelines advise journalists to avoid words such as 'nutter' and 'psycho' and explain that those who use the services prefer to be called mental health service users or survivors rather than patients. The Health Education Authority have also issued a report, 'Mental Health and the National Press', which gives a number of recommendations. The report showed that 40 per cent of all daily national tabloid coverage and 45 per cent of all Sunday national tabloid coverage of mental health contained pejorative terms such as 'loony', 'mad' and 'crazy' (Ward 1997: 14). The report recommends that editors should avoid using stigmatising language and not use clinical terms such as schizophrenia in non-specific or derogatory ways.

Those involved in disasters

People involved in disasters, the same as those who have been bereaved, are not there by choice. Their involvement in the story has been thrust upon them and they would prefer to be elsewhere. Often they have lost a loved one or are in a situation where a loved one's life is in the balance. They may have lost their home, or their job, or both. They are at a particularly vulnerable time and often cannot think straight.

This does not mean that journalists should not interview them; they are often at the centre of a story that is of major importance, but it does mean journalists should treat them with particular sensitivity.

Media packs should be avoided and harassment should be kept to a minimum. If a person does not want to talk, the journalist should respect that and find another interviewee. Questions should be handled with particular care to ensure they do not leave the person looking foolish or indeed the journalist looking foolish.

'Would you say you were devastated?' is an insensitive question to ask someone whose family has been killed in a tsunami that flattened their home and took their job. But more gentle questions about their family or their home would allow them to talk coherently and convey to the reader or viewer the enormity of the disaster. Ofcom advises strongly against putting those in distress under pressure to take part in a programme or be interviewed unless it is warranted. Care needs to be taken about both taking and broadcasting video or audio of people caught up in such events if that results in an unwarranted invasion of privacy.

Domestic violence

The addresses of women's refuges should normally be kept confidential in order to protect the victims of domestic violence.

Suicide

Coverage of suicide is a difficult area and requires sensitivity. Journalists should avoid trying to oversimplify the story. Often suicide is the final act of a long chain of events and journalists need to make it clear that people do not normally use suicide as an answer to one problem but as an answer to a string of problems or events. The desire to get the story should not reduce it to its simple culmination. All the regulators have guidelines on suicide that advise it should be handled with great sensitivity. Reports of suicide should avoid glamorising the event or providing very graphic or technical detail of the method for fear of others copying how it was done. The PCC has upheld a number of complaints about suicide reports that were too detailed, upholding its code of practice that says: 'When reporting suicide, care should be taken to avoid excessive detail about the mthods used' (http://www.pcc.org.uk/cop/practice.html accessed 6/4/10). The BBC's *Editorial Guidelines* also warn that 'care must be taken to avoid describing or showing methods in great detail' (http://www.bbc.co.uk/guidelines/editorialguidelines/edguide/harm/suicideattempted.shtml accessed 6/4/10).

It is important to remember that there may well be close family who will read the story or see it and their feelings should also be considered.

The language of suicide also needs to be thought through and the BBC advises that the phrase 'committed suicide' can cause offence. Apart from not jumping to conclusions about the cause of death until a coroner's court has come to a decision, suicide has all sorts of moral connotations, particularly for the practitioners of some religions. Better to talk about 'taking one's life' than committing suicide.

Pictures of suicide, particularly if the method is gruesome should also be handled carefully and only done if warranted by the circumstances. The BBC insists that any proposal to broadcast a hanging scene should be referred to a senior editorial figure.

Death knocks

Death is a constant source of stories, but it is a source that needs handling with care as there is a good chance that someone will be mourning the loss of a loved one. The death knock is a visit to a bereaved person's home by a reporter seeking information about and comment on a person who has recently died. These are never easy jobs for a journalist to do, although we should not assume that such visits are always unwelcome. Often the bereaved is willing to talk about the deceased as this may be the only way they will be able to publicly describe their sense of loss. The PCC advises that 'In cases involving personal grief or shock, enquiries and approaches must be made with sympathy and discretion and publication handled sensitively' (http://www.pcc.org.uk/cop/practice.html). Ofcom has similar rules: 'Broadcasters should try to reduce the potential distress to victims and/or relatives when making or broadcasting programmes intended to examine past events that involve trauma to individuals'. Ofcom's rules go a little further than just death and include any kind of trauma, including crime. They also warn about the problems facing producers who hope to broadcast dramatic reconstructions.

Discrimination

The key thing to remember when writing about minority groups, whether they are ethnic minorities, refugees or disabled people, is to ensure you only mention their differentiating characteristics if it is vital to the story. A story about a wheelchair user not being able to access a shop because of a flight of stairs would not make sense without mentioning that the person was a wheelchair user. On the other hand, saying that someone who had been fined for speeding was Asian or an asylum seeker would be unnecessary. No journalist would mention that the person was a British citizen, or white or able-bodied. Of course, if an able-bodied person was fined for parking in a disabled parking space, then it would be important to mention that.

The PCC Code of Practice has a clause on discrimination:

12 (i) The press must avoid prejudicial or pejorative reference to an individual's race, colour, religion, gender, sexual orientation or to any physical or mental illness or disability. (ii) Details of an individual's race, colour, religion, sexual orientation, physical or mental illness or disability must be avoided unless genuinely relevant to the story.

The PCC is quite strict about taking complaints only from individuals under this clause. If you are not the person mentioned in the story, you can't complain about it.

The NUJ also has a clause on discrimination:

A journalist shall only mention a person's age, sex, race, colour, creed, illegitimacy, disability, marital status, or sexual orientation if this information is strictly relevant. A journalist shall neither originate nor process material which encourages discrimination, ridicule, prejudice or hatred on any of the above-mentioned grounds.

Ofcom and the BBC have similar clauses.

There are two key points to remember here. The first is that a journalist should not be producing material that encourages hatred or violence and the second is to only use details of a person's race, colour and so on if it is strictly relevant. The detail is of course the kind of material that might spark discrimination solely on those grounds.

Chapter 10

Deciding what to publish

This chapter examines the specific problems facing journalists involved in the editing process, including:

■   Ethical decisions about what to publish

■   Ethical decisions about what to broadcast

■   Considerations about where to publish it

■   Considerations about when to broadcast

■   Any ethical issues involved in how the material is used

All newspapers and broadcast outlets have to make regular decisions about what to publish or broadcast. Earlier chapters have looked in detail at what makes news and therefore what influences editors in their decisions on what to publish. Newsworthiness, the space available and a balance of stories all play their part in deciding what finally finds its way into a newspaper or broadcast, but the suppression or exaggeration of stories (either in the way they are written or by the way they are used) can be determined by the personal views or political stance of the editor or publisher. This is particularly true in newspapers and magazines where there is no legal obligation to remain impartial.

It is not unusual for a newspaper or magazine to follow a particular political or cultural line in its coverage. If it is to continue to hold the trust of its readers then it must attempt to be truthful and accurate, but there is little evidence that strict impartiality has any bearing on people's trust rating. Indeed, it may well be that they are more likely to trust a paper with similar cultural biases to their own, provided that the stories it does cover are accurate and that the bias is only obvious in the choice of sources and presentation and context of the material.

Suppression

Editors and journalists sometimes have to decide when not to publish a story. Brian Whitaker, in *News Limited: Why You Can't Read all About it* (1981), goes into this in depth and his book is well worth reading. In one example he explains why no local newspaper is likely to go upsetting the local status quo:

> It is in coverage of council affairs that local papers are usually at their worst. You only have to read the papers to learn that councillors are as public-spirited, well-informed, thoughtful, eloquent, dedicated and high-principled a body as you could ever hope to meet – but then a paper does have to be responsible. To reprint verbatim the speech of Councillor X, a former mayor who has served the borough for nigh on 50 years, would let the world know that the old boy has completely lost his marbles – and that would be cruel. To record the number of times the mayor has to be corrected on procedural matters by the clerk would imply that he is not fit for his office – and that would be disrespectful. To list the financial interests of all the members who get business from the council would suggest that they are out to feather their own nests – and that would be a slur. In short, to tell the truth, the whole truth and nothing but the truth about the council would be nothing less than to embark on a campaign to discredit the whole of local government – and that would be grossly irresponsible.
>
> (Whitaker 1981: 39)

Few local newspapers or radio stations are going to risk retaliatory action by local advertisers, who might damage revenue, or local dignitaries or business people, who might hit circulation figures or the ability of reporters to report on local stories. While national and some regional media outlets are better able to withstand these pressures, they have to be certain that the story (or a succession of such stories) will increase circulation more than the damage such attacks might do to revenue. Sometimes, of course, there may be a more noble reason to suppress a story. Kidnaps are rarely reported in Britain before the police have caught the perpetrators. Fortunately, this is a very rare crime in Britain anyway, but it can be argued that the responsible position taken by the media has helped. If a kidnap happens, the police will keep the media informed provided they agree only to use the story once the police approve – usually after the victim has been freed. This gives the media good information on what happened, without using the story and endangering the victim's life.

Stories are often suppressed, or the information that is known about them is limited, during wars. Defence Advisory notices (DA notices) give guidance on these matters. The Defence Press and Broadcasting Advisory Committee, made up of senior civil servants and editors from newspapers and broadcast stations gives regular guidance on security issues, but has standing guidance on military operations, nuclear weapons, communications, sensitive installations and security services (www.dnotice.org.uk). A DA notice does not prevent a newspaper or broadcast station from using the story, but does offer guidance. Of course occasionally that guidance might be that publishing the information would lead to a prosecution under the Official Secrets Act. However, often the advice is about how to publish the story without endangering people.

In the Iraq War, for instance, the media was briefed away from the front line to prevent stories about planned attacks being transmitted back home being intercepted by the enemy. Sometimes, journalists need to go along with that. For instance, a story that the army was just about to launch an attack across the front line at such and such a place with 200 men set to target a military base at X would be good copy but it would not improve the chances of those 200 soldiers returning alive. Journalists have to decide whether to protect those lives, even though it may mean using the story later or with only part of the information, or not. This is an exercise in utilitarianist logic. The high risk of harming 200 people, possibly fatally, outweighs the small rise in happiness for millions of readers in knowing the truth. But what about loyalty to the reader? Does this go by the board because of our loyalty to the subject of the story?

Sometimes, of course, stories are suppressed because they do not suit the purpose of the media outlet carrying them. The *Daily Express*, for instance, is much keener on using stories that show the Labour party in a bad light than those that are unhelpful to the Conservative party. The *Daily Mirror* takes the opposite view, while *The Sun* does not carry stories which suggest that BSkyB is anything less than the perfect TV station because both are owned by Rupert Murdoch's News International.

Advertising as editorial

A considerable amount of editorial these days seems to be advertising and this presents editors and journalists with problems. Pressure from advertisers to cover a particular story or not cover a story can put journalists on the spot over their choice of loyalties. If it puts a reporter's job on the line, it can hardly be surprising if loyalty to self and family means journalists give in to the pressure to print what they are told. If an editor is supportive, then they may well see their loyalty to the reader to tell the truth as paramount. The water becomes a good deal muddier when an advertiser takes what is known as an *advertising feature*. These can take several forms.

An *advertorial* is a small advert supported by accompanying editorial copy, usually describing the advertiser and its wares. This is an attempt to add editorial authenticity to an advertisement. The entire space, including that used for the editorial, is usually bought by the customer and then filled with the advertisement and the editorial. Often this editorial is written by a journalist. Journalists generally do not like writing these kinds of items because of the pressures to write supportive material.

An *advertising feature* or *advertising supplement* is usually editorial copy about a topic which is supported by adverts on a similar theme. The advertisers are told what the subject area of the editorial is beforehand. An advertising supplement on health and beauty in a woman's magazine, for instance, is designed to attract advertising in the health and beauty field. Occasionally, an advertising supplement is just a very large advertorial, where there is only one advertiser whose products are at the centre of the editorial material. Many of the larger retailers use this method of promoting their wares in the quality monthly magazines especially in the run-up to Christmas.

Advertising features are also often written by journalists. These do not tend to be quite so difficult as the subjects are much more general and it is easier to write something fair and truthful. Often though, there is pressure to add the names of advertisers to the copy. Sometimes copy for ad features comes from the PR or advertising agency. This has then to be edited and laid out in the newspaper's standard style. Journalists who do this work are also under pressure to present the material in a favourable light.

The increase in the number of advertising features used by the regional and national press has started to distort the way a number of reporters view their responsibilities. Constantly writing material that is, to all intents and purposes, advertising copy means that many reporters writing such features see it as their role to put the advertiser in the best possible light in an article which is intended to look like part of the editorial with all the qualities that that implies about accuracy, balance and fairness. Because the advertising feature purports to be editorial, the reporter should maintain the standards that apply to editorial. This does not always go down well with advertisers or with advertising departments who tend to see the reporter's concerns as being over-scrupulous. But where material is masquerading as editorial, then the editorial standards need to apply or the paper risks damaging its editorial reputation. Advertising features are not a problem for television, although the growth of programme sponsorship could become one. The use of brand labels in programmes is a problem, however, and although the BBC no longer goes to the lengths of obscuring brand names, it does attempt to avoid using them. The BBC's guidelines say:

> We need to be able to reflect the real world and this will involve referring to commercial products, organisations and services in our output. We must avoid any undue prominence or giving the impression that we are promoting or endorsing products, organisations or services.
> (http://www.bbc.co.uk/guidelines/editorialguidelines/page/guidelines-editorial-integrity-product-prominence/ accessed 14/10/10)

Product placement is also banned by the Ofcom code which says: 'products and services must not be promoted in programmes'. It identifies product placement as the inclusion of products or services in programmes for which there is no editorial justification for payment. So, for instance, it would be wrong for a newsreader to have a bottle of a well-known cola placed prominently on his desk, but a drama involving a character well-known for consuming a particular product would be OK. However, the government proposed lifting the ban on product placement in an announcement in February 2010. Culture, Media and Sport minister Ben Bradshaw said:

> Adherence to our current position in which UK TV programme-making cannot benefit at all from the income potentially to be generated by product placement would lead to continuing damage to its finances at a time when this crucial part of our creative industries needs all the support we can give it.

> It has become the more important to make this move now that every other EU member state, with the sole current exception of Denmark, has either allowed television product placement already or has expressed a firm intention to do so.

Advertisers also latch on to editorial by *sponsoring pages or programmes*. In broadcasting this tends to be confined to drama programmes or weather broadcasts, but it can only be a matter of time before food shows are sponsored by food manufacturers and motor shows by car makers. Newspaper pages tend to be limited in their sponsorship more by lack of opportunity than by principle. Favourites for sponsorship are the TV page, weather and wedding reports.

All of the methods mentioned above for displaying advertising as editorial copy are favoured by advertisers as it lends their adverts the authority and credibility that goes with the editorial. They become more believable. Finance companies are particularly fond of taking advertising supplements in the tabloid nationals; local papers often have ad features for local pub openings. These methods have become more and more popular over the past few years as it means adverts are more likely to be read. This adds to the journalist's fear of undue influence. If a big retailer is supporting an advertising feature, how can the journalist write a true review of that particular product? Often the product the journalist is writing about is known to the journalist only through the press information material sent by the manufacturer. How can the journalist give a fair assessment from the manufacturer's own press information?

The pressure for a journalist to write a piece that is supportive of the advertiser regardless of the real situation is extremely strong. The NUJ takes the view that journalists' duty is clear: they should write an accurate, truthful article. But loyalties are often stretched when reporters are asked to produce stories to advertising briefs. In one provincial newspaper I was told about, reporters were expected to write restaurant reviews from a copy of the menu and perhaps a quick telephone call to the restaurateur. They are also expected to ring back and read the copy over the phone for approval. Regular checks with my students over the years show that in their experience on work placements this practice is growing. This makes a nonsense of any pretence that such features are attempting to be truthful. No reporter can give a truthful report of food they have not tasted, in a review they have to approve with the advertiser. Yet readers are often misled into believing that such reports are as ethically sound as the material in the rest of the editorial sections of the paper. Most readers are unaware of the difference between editorial and advertorial copy. Both the Newspaper Society and the NUJ advise that advertorials and advertising features should be clearly marked as advertising or advertising features, and journalists involved in editing and laying out such copy should ensure this happens.

Identification

Identification of people and places needs particular care. This is an area where the PCC and Ofcom take very different views with the press regulatory body merely warning journalists not to encourage harassment and Ofcom taking a much firmer line. Identification of people is dealt with in more detail in the chapter on privacy, but identification of address and other details is about what to publish or broadcast.

Publishing names and addresses

Journalists like to use names in their stories because they add veracity to the article. Sometimes of course the name is the article. A story about something happening to President Obama may well be newsworthy whereas if the same thing happens to me, it may not be. Also, if I were to say we should declare war on Australia, then no one would do more than look at me oddly. If our prime minister were to say it, then there would be banner headlines.

David Randall explains the journalistic requirement to name people very well, with an anecdote about his first week in the job:

> by a combination of luck and my determination to make an impact [I] got on to a good story about river pollution. I went off, did the research and then rushed back to the office dreaming of the accolades that would be coming my way when I turned in the story. 'What the hell is this?' shouted the news editor when he read it. 'Where are all the names?' I had been so thrilled with the story I had forgotten to ask the names of the people I interviewed. There were lots of good quotes, but all of them were from 'worried resident', 'water engineer', 'safety inspector' etc.

(Randall 1996: 33)

Randall's story is good lesson for any young journalist to learn. But journalists need also to be aware that there are times when names do not need to be used and sometimes should not be used. It is regular practice for the police and armed services to refuse to give names of serving officers and to ask the media to refrain from publishing them. Since publication could, in some circumstances, put officers at risk from revenge attacks, most media consider complying with these requests if the circumstances seem reasonable. The media is also asked not to publish detailed addresses of such groups and it is often easier to acquiesce about an address rather than a name. Other groups may also need to have their addresses and movements treated with care. In a judgment in 1985, the Press Council upheld a complaint against the *Kent and Sussex Courier* for publishing the address of a bank security guard injured in a raid. It says: 'It was improper to publish his address, thus placing him and his family potentially in further danger' (Press Council 1985: 165).

The PCC published some guidance to editors about publishing names and addresses in its August 1992 report (see Exhibit 10.1).

Exhibit 10.1 Publishing names and addresses

The PCC places responsibility on journalists to 'discourage, and certainly not encourage, the harassment of individuals named in stories and features in their publications' (PCC, Report No. 12, 1992: 5). The PCC supported the practice of regional papers, which like to publish street names to stress the local relevance of a story, but do not publish house numbers or names in order to reduce unwanted attention and because: 'It reduces the possibility of error: if you do not publish the number, you cannot get it wrong' (ibid.).

The PCC reminded editors and other journalists to use their common sense and careful judgement on the use of addresses:

> It is true that in the case of prominent people addresses are readily available but the press is not under an obligation to make it easy for cranks and criminals by saving them the bother of researching telephone books and directories. Newspapers should not assist in identifying targets for opprobrium, far less for life-threatening attention, and there is a common-sense obligation upon editors to avoid endangering families by publishing actual addresses unless they constitute an essential part of the story.
>
> (PCC, Report No. 7, 1992: 5)

The PCC gave as an example the *Evening Standard*, London, which, after giving the address of a prominent individual's weekend home in Wales, suggested: 'He had better not tell the Welsh nationalists or they will come and burn it down' (ibid.: 6). The PCC held this to be an infringement of the person's privacy.

Perversely, the PCC decided that there had been no breach of the Code of Practice in 1999 following a complaint from Eric Forth MP and the parents of the five suspects in the Stephen Lawrence case against *New Nation* and the *Sunday Telegraph*. *New Nation* had published an article giving the suspects' addresses, together with robust comments about enhancing their 'facial features'. The PCC found that the robust comments were on a matter of public interest and dismissed complaints about harassment and incitement to racial hatred. They also dismissed complaints about invasion of privacy against both *New Nation* and the *Sunday Telegraph*, saying: 'In view of the wide reporting of the case and the fact that the information about the complainants' addresses was already in the public domain, the commission did not find that there was a breach of the code' (*Press Gazette*, 7 May 1999: 6). One can't help wondering if commissioners were swayed by concern about the opprobrium a decision to uphold the complaint would have heaped on the Commission's head.

Various groups of people and professionals who might be considered at particular risk if their addresses or their movements are published include the following:

- People in the public eye.
- Judges and magistrates.
- Police officers.
- Members of the armed forces.
- People accused of serious crimes, and their relatives.
- Aids victims and their care workers.

Ofcom also offers extensive guidelines to broadcasters, much of which is important to news-gatherers. Information giving the address of someone's home or family is not normally acceptable unless there is a good public interest reason so, unlike print journalists, it is not normal practice to use full addresses although a town is fine. Nor should broadcasters continue filming or recording if asked to stop, unless it is warranted.

Journalists should also refrain from publishing the addresses of refuges and shelters for those who have been the victims of domestic violence and abuse. This would put the people seeking refuge and the workers in the refuges in danger. Indeed, the very purpose of the refuges is invalidated if addresses are made public.

Number plates

Don't publish car registrations and other identifications. Unless there is a particular reason for publishing the registration number of a vehicle or a house number or any other identification sign, journalists should normally ensure these are pixelated in pictures or video. This is particularly the case if the registration number is of a vehicle that is of some particular significance such as belonging to a celebrity or a police officer. Not identifying cars or houses ensures that simple mistakes that could lead to misidentification can't be made.

Naming lottery winners

The National Lottery has captured the interest of the nation. Many people want to know more about those who win millions of pounds on the lottery, and newspapers often pursue lottery winners in order to satisfy their readers' curiosity.

Case study 10.1 Winning the lottery

The first rollover lottery jackpot was won on 10 December 1994 by a resident of Blackburn, Lancashire. The media's interest was intense, but the winner did not give permission for his name to be revealed. The organisers of the lottery, Camelot, said the winner had requested

▶

that quite detailed information be released to the media but that Camelot decided it would be more prudent to release only information about the region in which he lived, the size of his family, that he was a factory worker, what paper he read and that he watched satellite television.

Two national newspapers, the *Mirror* and *The Sun* (12 December 1994) offered £10,000 rewards for additional information. Camelot obtained a High Court injunction preventing the naming of the winner but this was challenged and overturned. The *Mirror* and *The Sun* then decided not to publish the name and made much about their decision in their papers. The editor of *The Sun* made it clear at the time that he had been influenced by the strength of feeling of readers. However, the *News of the World*, *Yorkshire on Sunday* and the *Sunday Mercury* all identified the winner the following Sunday.

Although the winner himself did not complain, his MP, Jack Straw, did and wrote to the PCC. Labour's media spokesperson, Chris Smith MP, also wrote, asking the Commission to adjudicate over the practice of offering money for information. There were also thirty-two letters from members of the public on the issue. The Commission asked editors for their views. *The Sun* responded that while they had decided to cease the practice of 'bounty money', they would certainly fight any move for a blanket restriction on naming lottery winners. The editor said he 'would have no hesitation in identifying winners such as the Queen, the prime minister, Myra Hindley or the Archbishop of Canterbury, irrespective of whether anonymity had been requested' (PCC, Report No. 29, 1995: 27).

The PCC condemned the decision of some newspapers to offer rewards and went on to draw up guidelines for the future (see Exhibit 10.2).

The media's treatment of lottery winners has been mixed, but there does seem to be a streak of invasive jealousy about much of the coverage. Mark Gardiner won the lottery on Saturday 10 June 1995. By 13 June, *The Sun* had branded him a 'Lotto Rat' and exposed his private life to the world. The newspaper claimed he was a heavy-drinking womaniser who had had three wives and two mistresses and was now living with someone else's wife. Another lottery winner was photographed on holiday at an exotic location with a group of friends. Allegations were made about the 'lively' behaviour.

Exhibit 10.2 The National Lottery: PCC guidance

- The press should generally respect the wishes of a winner of the National Lottery to remain anonymous if he or she so wishes.
- The press should not seek to obtain information about winners from the operator of the National Lottery in breach of any duty of confidentiality which the operator owes to winners under the terms of its licence.
- The press should not seek to obtain information about winners who have requested anonymity, from their family, friends or work colleagues through any form of harassment contrary to clause 8 of the Code of Practice (this refers to the old Code of Practice; for the new code, see Appendix 1).
- It may be permissible for the press to identify a winner of the National Lottery who has requested anonymity if such can be justified in the public interest under clause 18 of the [old] Code of Practice; the size of the win alone would not be sufficient justification for such disclosure.

> - The press should not offer rewards for information about the identity or private life of a lottery winner. Such offers can only be justified in extreme cases where there is prima facie evidence that a serious fraud or scandal is involved.
> - The Commission believes that the press cannot be expected to act as scapegoat in maintaining the anonymity of winners, irrespective of all circumstances, including the actions of Camelot or the winners themselves. Accordingly, this guidance will be applied by the Commission in the context of any future complaints after taking into account the circumstances of each particular case.
>
> (PCC, Report No. 29, 1995: 32)

Fair trials

One of the major human rights is the right to a fair trial. Together with the right to be presumed innocent, these have a direct bearing on what can be reported at a criminal trial. The law in the UK limits what can be written about a criminal event and the arrest of a person suspected of committing it until they come to trial. This is intended to prevent a would-be jury being adversely influenced by what is written before the trial. There is some debate as to whether there is any influential effect from publishing prior to a trial. Researchers in the USA, where pre-trial publicity is allowed, generally found in several research projects that there was very little evidence of influence in any prior publicity. Very few cases were of such public interest that they had very much pre-trial publicity and often where this did happen, research suggested, juries were more likely to be influenced to take a detached and neutral view rather than following whatever line was taken in the pre-trial publicity (Bruschke and Loges 2004: 135–7). UK law, however, limits what can be written until the trial itself and then a full and contemporaneous report can be given. One of the elements to be strongly considered is the amount of coverage. Coverage is unlikely to be fair if only the prosecution case is published, for instance. This could mean having to plan to cover a major trial over several days, or even weeks, in order to ensure fair coverage.

Other courts

The government has recently opened the family courts to wider reporting as it believes that the public should be able to see how evidence is weighed up and judgments made in the family courts. The names of the children and the family are still be kept confidential in order to protect the family's privacy (Harman 2006: 7). There has been a wide-ranging debate about the rights of expert witnesses to keep their names confidential but the government and the courts have made it clear this should only happen in very exceptional circumstances.

The government has also introduced a number of changes in the operation of coroners' courts through the Coroners and Justice Act 2009. The Act also introduces a new offence of prohibited images of children, allows for witness anonymity orders and abolishes the offences of blasphemous and seditious libel.

Issues for print

Newspapers and broadcasting are about more than gathering information: they are also concerned with how the information is presented. The target audience plays a major part in decisions made here. Should a newspaper choose a highly graphic approach suitable for an audience that is wary of too much printed word or should the emphasis be on presenting large blocks of text in a way that can be easily assimilated? Should broadcasters aim at a lively production with short takes and plenty of action or can the target audience appreciate longer, more static displays? The journalist also needs to consider such subjects as taste and decency. At what stage does an image become merely distasteful and no longer enlightening? In addition, there is the new opportunity to bias or slant the information that its presentation offers.

Presentation of material for print

Moral problems do not end when the text is written. Source-checking should continue throughout, but there is also a new range of problems. Once copy is written and presented to the editor or sub-editors, further decisions are made about its future. A decision will be taken about where the story is to be displayed. Other decisions will be taken about how it is to be displayed and how it is to be angled.

It may well be that the story already has the correct angle, but if not, it may well be rewritten. New angles are added for several reasons. The most important is the market approach of the product. If a newspaper sees its target audience as middle-aged women with middle-class traditional views, it will target the type of news it uses and the way it presents it to be attractive to that audience. Take a look at the *Daily Mail* to see how this works. A newspaper may also choose its news and the way it presents it in order to pursue a political or commercial agenda. The *Mirror*, for instance, likes copy that embarrasses the Conservative Party whereas the *Mail* prefers to attack the Labour Party.

During this editing process, inaccuracies or bias might well be introduced into copy that had been error-free. This might be accidental, in the attempt to make the story more lively. Often a reporter will have been ambiguous because it has not been possible to guarantee the accuracy of a particular fact, yet an editor might well rewrite the careful phrase into something more dramatic, but less accurate. Occasionally, in order to make a story 'stand up' or appear more dramatic or exciting, facts will be stretched and distorted. Stories are also presented in a different style. A single piece of copy might be split into several smaller articles, each with their own new introduction. Headings have to be written, along with other pieces of copy, that give the opportunity for further errors to creep in. Headline writing is a difficult art. They have to be bright and lively yet still reflect the story accurately. They must also be accurate in themselves – all this in just half a dozen words or less. Whether it is 'MPs in a new sleaze wheeze' or 'Minister in new sleaze claim' (to give two invented, but plausible, examples), the temptation to go over the top is high.

Finally, pictures are added. Choices here add a new dimension to the decision-making process. Pictures need to be closely linked with the story. Some will have been taken especially for the story and care needs to be taken to ensure that the picture is of who or what the journalist thinks it is and that the caption accurately conveys this. Often picture captions carry names that are spelt differently from the way they are in the story. Library pictures are also a danger area. It is all too easy to get a picture from a library of the wrong person. On 20 June 1996, *The Guardian* carried an obituary of Vivian Ellis, the writer of the song 'Spread a Little Happiness'. Unfortunately it used a picture of Vivienne Ellis. Wrong sex, wrong person. I did not get to see the correction carried later in the week, but I assume there was one. All very embarrassing and potentially libellous in some instances.

The choice of picture offers yet another opportunity for presenting the story in an untruthful way. Even a picture of a politician giving a speech can give very different slants to a story. The way the picture is cut, the gestures the politician is using or the facial expressions can all give a perception that is wrong or at least misleading. Politicians learn early on to take extreme care with facial gestures while sitting on platforms. A row of photographers is just waiting for that funny gesture, the drooping eyelids, the whispered aside or the signs of momentary boredom. Many politicians have woken to find their breakfast spoiled by a picture of themselves on the front of the newspapers apparently deeply upset, when all they actually did was briefly rub their eyes at the end of a long and tiring conference. Smiling for six hours solid in case your picture is being taken is hard work.

Hoaxes

There is also the problem of new material offered for publication which later turns out to be a hoax. There are several reasons why newspapers and broadcasters get their fair share of bogus stories or hoaxes. One of the major reasons is that good stories or pictures are worth money. Reductions of staff combined with a rise in contributions from the public, many of whom now regularly carry relatively high-quality digital cameras and videos built into their mobile phones, has meant that many pictures or film clips of newsworthy events are now routinely used by news media. This can lead the unscrupulous to send bogus pictures. *The Guardian* and Sky TV fell victim in March 2006 when they reported a heath fire in Dorset. They accompanied the story with a picture, which later turned out to be of a forest fire in the US state of Montana six years before. Explaining the hoax to readers the next week, *Guardian* readers' editor Ian Mayes explained that *The Guardian* had grabbed the picture from rolling news coverage on Sky TV, which had received the image from a viewer. Mr Mayes said:

> The Guardian report, addressing the picture, said: 'Wild animals, silhouetted by the bright orange inferno in a photograph taken by a local resident, were left to fend for themselves.' The wild animals in fact are elk, which, as one of my correspondents later that day put it, are rarely seen in Dorset. I can sympathise both with Sky and with the Guardian picture desk for running this picture in, so to speak, the heat of the moment. As the Guardian story made clear, the Dorset fire was a big one, residents in the area had to be evacuated to safety, and it took 170 firefighters from Dorset and neighbouring Hampshire to bring the fire under control. Sky showed the picture twice on Sunday evening. A spokesperson told me: 'It was one of several sent in by viewers. Once we had established it was a hoax, we pulled it immediately. We do all we can to ensure that email images sent in by viewers are genuine, but it's inevitable that in a fast-breaking news environment such photos occasionally slip past the checks and balances we put in place.' The discovery was too late to save the Guardian from also falling victim to the hoax.
>
> (http://www.guardian.co.uk/print/0,,329443399-103677,00.html accessed 5/06)

In fact the picture was taken on 6 August 2000, on the east fork of the Bitterroot River, Montana, and the photographer was John McColgan, a fire behaviour analyst from the Alaska Fire Service, according to one of Mr Mayes' correspondents.

Juxtaposition of material

Care needs to be taken when working in print about which items on a page go alongside other items. For instance, a story about bogus builders alongside an advert for a respectable local building firm, could certainly bring complaints. A prominent picture of a local person alongside a major headline about a criminal act also needs to ensure the two cannot be accidentally linked.

Image manipulation

Image manipulation has always been a possibility, but the modern computer software makes it very easy and very tempting to do for newspapers and magazines. This subject was covered from the ethical point of view in Chapter 5, but should be referred to here as a reminder that it would be unethical not just to manipulate the content of the picture, but also to squeeze or stretch a picture in order to make it fit a space. Making someone look fatter or thinner than they really are distorts the truth, and might also offend the subject of the picture.

Issues for broadcast

Broadcasting has a number of particular issues that do not apply to print. The use of video and sound make TV and radio a much more urgent media and their closer scrutiny by the law makes their need to be ethical that much stronger.

Presentation of material for broadcast

Broadcasting brings its own problems in terms of presentation of news packages. Just as newspapers need attention-grabbing headlines that scream drama and sensation, so broadcasters needs to grab the viewers' attention. The easiest and most attractive way of doing this for television is with good pictures. Desperate to provide interesting film to go with news reports, broadcast editors will often try to build up the drama that seems to exist in video footage, whether it actually does or not. Others are aware of this and can also manipulate it. Video from the House of Commons, for instance, often shows smiling, supportive politicians posing on either side of whoever is speaking. Often we find that the only people in the House are those crowded around the spokespeople on the front bench as this makes the shot look better for TV.

Covering disasters provides excellent picture coverage and the only ethical debate is about how to cover it. Often TV will show foreign news, not because it will particularly interest viewers as such, but because it offers great pictures. We seem to get extensive coverage of hurricanes when they hit the USA, for instance, because the US networks are there to take the pictures and the pictures make good TV. In other words, the pictures are available, cheap and are dramatic viewing. We rarely see pictures of such hurricanes as they rip through the Caribbean as this would require a film crew to be sent out especially, at high cost.

Providing good pictures is not so easy on an issue-based subject. Politicians have long realised this and try their hardest to produce photogenic ideas that reduce issues to images that can attract audiences both on TV and in still pictures. PR companies will always try to present ideas as photogenically as possible. This has the effect of reducing political debate to the level of jousting – plenty of action and drama but not much understanding of the underlying principles. Party conferences become places to attack the opposition rather than develop ideas because idea generation is represented in the media as political drama rather than political debate. Discussions become wrangles, debates become clashes and passionate exchanges of views become party splits. Television, forced by its regulators to be impartial, needs to present an often complex issue, give detailed information about it and present the two or three different viewpoints that surround it in a 30-second (or even 15-second) package that needs to be exciting and visually attractive. It may be accurate, but is it truthful? While such packages are usually relatively unbiased, they are rarely able to tell the whole story and all too often concentrate on the row, not the issue; the heat, not the light.

Live questioning

There are a number of issues with regard to interviewing somebody live. Where at all possible, any time available before the interview should be spent in research – have you got their name right, what is their title, why are you interviewing them? The journalist needs to be certain that informed consent has been given by the interviewee to take part in such an interview. As a professor of journalism, I'm occasionally asked to be interviewed and I am amazed at how often journalists do not bother to check on my precise credentials before being interviewed. In common with many people I sit on several committees and hold different titles, all of which concern journalism, but bring a different slant to my answers. The public deserves to know which hat I am wearing during a particular interview.

The journalist also needs to fill the interviewee in on the line of questioning that is to be followed. For a politician or someone else who is used to being interviewed in this way, just the broadest outline is acceptable, but for someone who may have no experience of the media at all, a more detailed description of the type of questions that will be asked gives them a chance to come up with a more focused answer.

John Sergeant, ITN's political editor from 2000, in his memoirs *Give Me Ten Seconds* tells of one woman who fainted away during questioning. He does not specify if this was a live interview, but it does show that the strain of a television appearance is high, particularly for those who are not used to it (Sergeant 2001: 241).

In another TV interview gaffe, Guy Goma, a graduate from the Congo, waiting for a job interview was accidentally called on to a live business programme on BBC News 24, instead of IT expert Guy Kewney. He then faced a two-minute grilling on the *Apple* v *Apple* court case. His shock at realising he was on TV and was being called by someone else's name is readily apparent on his face and is likely to be a staple ingredient of a whole future series of outtake-style TV shows. Indeed, for a short while after his appearance, he picked up a small fan club and made other TV appearances including the Jonathan Ross show. He even has a website (www.guygoma,com). Although he was asked his name by the producer, the mistake was not spotted until he was seated in the studio (http://news.bbc.co.uk/1/hi/entertainment/4774429.stm accessed 16/2/10). Broadcasters also need to check archive material to ensure that the picture being used to illustrate a story is of the right person, or the right building. Just because the file name is right doesn't mean it will be the right picture or video.

Two-ways

The BBC has taken a strong line on two-ways ever since the Hutton Report. Two-ways on contentious issues are now seen as potentially dangerous. A two-way is when the presenter in the studio interviews the station's own correspondent about the situation. It is used extensively in sport but also in news as a way of breaking up the image of the static talking head of the presenter. However, it was Andrew Gilligan's unscripted comments on the *Today* programme's 6.07 a.m. broadcast that led eventually to the death of Dr David Kelly and the resignation of senior BBC figures. The problem with talking, unscripted, about a highly contentious issue is that it is very easy to stray from the precise truth under the pressure. This can be particularly true if other factors are added, such as an early start or an interview following a long and gruelling trip to the news site.

Hidden cameras, hidden mics, etc.

Hidden cameras and microphones are problems that particularly affect TV and radio. Their use is clearly both intrusive and deceitful. Not only is the camera likely to be recording material taking place in a private area or at least at a time when the subject thinks they are in private (and if this is not the case, why use a hidden camera?) but also the person concerned is being deceived because they will behave with far less consideration than for their public persona. The very expression 'letting one's hair down' clearly illustrates that we all accept that our public persona may well be very different from the one we assume when we know we are out of the public gaze. Journalists therefore normally have a duty to make it clear to the subject of an interview that they will be appearing on camera or that their speech is being recorded. Failure to do this can only be justified by recording for a story that it is in the public interest and where the information required can only be gathered by using this method. This is a two-stage process. First the journalist must be certain that the only way to get further evidence for this story is by using hidden cameras and then the decision must be taken about whether the story is in the public interest. Only if both these questions can be affirmed should the journalist proceed. In the case of the BBC, permission also needs to be granted by the journalist's editor.

CCTV and webcams are not strictly speaking hidden cameras, but they may well be recording people without their knowledge and consent. Checks should be made about copyright and permission before a clip from a CCTV camera is used. The same is true about pictures lifted from websites or social network sites. The PCC does not see this as unethical if there is a good public interest defence, but both Ofcom and the PCC include electronic communication within their privacy limitations and so pictures sent by e-mail from home addresses could breach the codes although the PCC at least accepts that pictures sent by e-mail from a work address are not in the private domain. These issues can also arise during what are known as 'tag-along raids', exercises by police or security services at which a journalist and camera crew attend. Often these lead to arrests where identity might well be a problem and so filming needs to be handled with care. The PCC has upheld two or three complaints following such raids. A complaint was upheld against the *Barking and Dagenham Recorder* after a 17-year-old was pictured in his room during such a raid, even though the picture was pixellated to hide his identity. The PCC said there was no public interest defence for such a serious intrusion. In another case involving the *Scarborough Evening News*, a drugs raid was filmed which showed the complainant's son's bedroom. This complaint was also upheld, with the PCC saying:

> Showing a video and publishing a picture of the interior of the complainant's house, without her consent, was clearly highly intrusive ... There were two strands to the public interest defence. The first was that the footage showed an important part of local policing in operation. The second was that it allegedly exposed a specific criminal offence.

> The Commission considered that, while it may have been in the public interest to illustrate the police campaign against drugs, insufficient regard had been paid to the complainant's right to privacy in this case.
>
> > (http://www.pcc.org.uk/cases/adjudicated.html?article=NTE0OQ== accessed 1/6/09)

Suicide

Ofcom and the PCC have both put clear rules into their codes about broadcasting or publishing unnecessary detail about methods of suicide and harm (see Chapter 11 for full details). It also warns about the dangers of showing demonstrations of exorcism, the occult, the paranormal and divination that purport to be real and warns that they must be treated with due objectivity.

Simulated news or reconstructions need to be handled with considerable care. They should always be clearly labelled as being reconstructions so that no viewer can be under the illusion that they are real. It is also wise to make sure that library archive material is clearly labelled as such.

Choice of location

The choice of location for a broadcast journalist is also important from both a professional and an ethical and legal viewpoint. The background and scene chosen become part of the story and need to be considered carefully. It is possible to defame someone by choosing your background badly. Since the background supports what is being said, it can affect the truth of the report. The same is true of any props or costumes that might be used. Fans of *Drop the Dead Donkey*, the realistic Channel 4 sitcom set in a TV newsroom, will have seen several episodes wrapped around the dubious antics of ambitious tabloid TV reporter Damian Day as he attempts to spice up his reports. In one memorable incident, his news editor accuses him of using an apparently abandoned teddy bear as a symbol of pathos in a number of packages from disasters around the world only to find that Damian has the teddy bear in his bag, ready for the next assignment. Yet the news editor feels unable to sack him for this unethical approach. As the station's most popular reporter, Damian is looked on with favour by managers with both eyes firmly on the viewing figures.

It is this twisting of the story by the sly use of props, backgrounds or costumes that should be avoided. Try to set people in their natural habitats; if the story is about a person's work, try to film it in their workplace; if it is about their family, then the home would be appropriate.

Background sounds and sound effects

In addition to the straight interview, the reporter can add sound effects or even background music to a report. These need to be considered carefully. The insertion of inappropriate sound effects or library video clips can give the incorrect impression, slanting an interview one way or the other. In extreme cases, playing 'evil' music whenever the 'baddy' appears could turn a report into pantomime, but care should be taken that more subtle effects don't have a similar result. On the other hand, some level of realism might be required. Taping a radio interview about the closing of a swimming pool from the busy pool itself might be difficult. The noise might prevent us hearing the subject. But playing a recording of the baths in the background and adding a little echo to the interview might restore reality. Birdsong and the laughter of children added to a human-interest piece about the coming of summer might brighten things up, but other sound effects might give completely the wrong impression.

Archive material of sound and video needs to be clearly identified as such. We should be certain that material we may be seeing on the screen is not happening live, but is rooted in the past. A simple caption describing it as library material is sufficient.

Watershed

Broadcasters need to be aware that there is a range of material that is considered to be unsuitable for broadcast and Ofcom identifies this as any material that might seriously impair the physical, mental or moral development of people under 18. Children (that is anyone under 15) must also be protected by appropriate scheduling from material that is unsuitable for them. This includes bad language, sex, nudity, misuse of drugs, dangerous behaviour, exorcism, the occult, the paranormal and violence. Ofcom advises that appropriate scheduling should be judged according to the nature of the material, the likely number of children, the start and finish time of the programme, and the expectations of the audience. However, the major tool is the watershed; a limitation on broadcast time, which means programmes shown between 0530 and 2100 should be entirely suitable for children. After the watershed, material can become increasingly adult, bearing in mind the audience and likelihood of children watching. While the watershed as identified by Ofcom only applies to television, radio also needs to pay regard to times when children may be particularly likely to be listening. There is no watershed on premium subscription film services. Ofcom warns that the switch to adult material at 2100 should not be unduly abrupt and a clear context should be given.

When programmes are made specifically for children, they should not feature the use of illegal drugs, the abuse of drugs, smoking or alcohol unless there is a strong editorial justification (http://www. ofcom.org.uk/tv/ifi/codes/bcode/protectingu18/ accessed 15/2/10). Violence and its after-effects must be appropriately limited. Care should be taken with language, and the most offensive language should not be broadcast before the watershed. This is a constant source of complaints to Ofcom and a major proportion of the complaints made concern bad language for material that is unsuitable for children.

Issues for websites

Online journalism is relatively new, but is already building up issues of its own despite those who prefer to see this as virgin territory; a clean, new frontier where anything goes and there are no rules. Weblogs, citizen journalism and interactivity are key elements of online news and these bring particular problems for those dealing with news websites. Moderators will need to ensure material submitted interactively is suitable before it is published, in the same way as readers' letters.

Another key issue for websites is the hyperlinks that take readers to other sites. Direct links to other sites can provide additional content for the browser and improve their experience. Such links can give much fuller information than the home website. A news report on a new government initiative linking the reader to the government's own report and the opposition's attacks on it can add much more depth than the straight news report. It may even be more than the reader wants, but it gives them a choice. However, links to sites that might sit outside the news provider's usual policy need to be handled with care. A story about neo-Nazis that takes the reader on to a neo-Nazi site, for instance, may well be a hyperlink too far. Decisions need to be taken before the link is made, according to predetermined site policy.

A new issue that is facing traditional newspapers and online news sites is the risk of jigsaw identification in defamation cases. One of the things a defamation complainant must prove is that people would believe the article published is about them. This is easy if a name or clear identity is published. Footballer Ashley Cole sued *The Sun* and the *News of the World* for defamation following their use of a picture of two men, with their faces pixelated to hide their identity, who, the papers claimed, were involved in a gay sex orgy. The footballer's lawyer said they would produce witnesses who believed that the person in the picture was Ashley Cole after searching the internet and finding a copy of that picture, unpixelated. Cole's lawyer, Graham Shear told the *Press Gazette*: 'I think the warning to journalists from this is that the internet is a powerful tool which means that you can't be suggestive unless absolutely certain of your facts. In this case they weren't sure of their facts and their facts were wrong.' The newspaper agreed to settle for a large sum of damages (Ponsford 2006: 1).

Further reading and support material

The production process for print and broadcast needs to be understood in order to fully understand the ethical issues that arise and so good books about production will help. Print design and editing practice is covered in my book, Chris Frost (2003) *Designing for Newspaper and Magazines* (Routledge, Abingdon). Broadcast production is covered by a number of books but one of the most up to date is Gary Hudson and Sarah Rowlands (2007) *The Broadcast Journalism Handbook* (Pearson, Harlow).

Chapter 11

Harm and offence

This chapter discusses the complex issue of harm and offence, explaining:

■ What causes offence

■ The difference between harm and offence

■ How we can identify the moral issues involved in offence-giving

■ The importance of audience when considering offence

■ Issues of taste and decency

Freedom of expression is one of the basic rights and one that allows us to say what we like. However, there may be limits that should be placed in this freedom of expression and I have already looked at some of them. The reputation of a person may need to limit what we say; our desire to tell the truth may be another limitation. After all, if we have freedom of expression, then we have the right to lie, but lying will not lead to consumers trusting what journalists write and so it must be a limitation.

Another major limitation on freedom of speech involves issues that may cause harm or offence. Harm and offence was identified as a matter of concern in the UK's Communications Act 2003, and covers issues of taste and decency such as nudity, sex, violence and bad language but also covers issues of harm and offence such as suicide, depiction of drug-taking, exorcism and discrimination and is of particular concern to broadcasters although that does not mean that newspapers, websites and magazines need not concern themselves about this issue at all. The Communications Act requires Ofcom to review broadcasters' compliance with *the standards objectives* and so ensure that 'generally accepted standards are applied to the contents of television and radio services so as to provide adequate protection for members of the public from the inclusion in such services of offensive and harmful material' (Communications Act 2003 http://www.opsi.gov.uk/acts/acts2003/ukpga_20030021_en_29#pt3-ch4-pb16-l1g319 accessed 4/3/10).

The vast majority of complaints received by broadcasters concerning offensive material are about drama or other entertainment programmes, but the news and factual media still needs to take care about depictions of violence, whether from a war zone or a road accident, and about nudity and bad language and we also need to understand why these issues may place a limitation on the artist's right to freedom of expression in other types of programming.

Images are often the most likely to cause offence. Pictures, whether for print, website or broadcast, carry more potential for upsetting readers or viewers than is normally the case for text. Many good pictures can be offensive. Several of the award-winning pictures from the Vietnam War contained stark and disturbing images that many will have found upsetting and offensive. A police chief's street execution and a naked young girl fleeing a napalm raid are images that were widely used at the time and since, and stick firmly in the minds of those who saw them. They are offensive in the way that any picture of violence and destruction is offensive, but they say more about the war and what it meant than even the best of writers could have managed and it is probably these images rather than any text that turned the US public against the war and brought about its early end.

The whole topic of harm and offence is one of constant controversy. Free expression, as we have seen, must include the right to offend, but does it include the right to harm, and when does offence turn to harm? Even more complicated is when offence becomes solely a matter of taste and decency. One person's distasteful picture is another's 'bit of a laugh' and taste can vary widely within the normal parameters of a well-balanced society. The law has some say here and it is tempting to suggest some level of censorship. After all, if it is permissible for editors and producers to decide against using this image or that quote, why is it wrong for governments to do the same thing? Judith Andre has some help here: '"No one else has the right to decide what I can read" may work against governmental censorship; it will not work in areas where others are already and necessarily deciding among competitors for limited space' (1992: 78).

So Andre explains to us that it is right for us to oppose government censorship because, when we get into making choices about what we may see, then it is more appropriate that this applies in areas where we can have a direct and significant say in the limitations in a way that government can never allow, no matter how democratic.

Anyone can set up their own publication and make their own decisions about what is or is not published in it – in theory at least. Although there is no censorship in the UK, though, there are a number of laws that limit what may or may not be published in the area of taste and offence in the UK. The Obscene Publications Acts 1959 and 1964, Race Relations Act 1976, Broadcasting Acts 1990 and 1996, Public Order Act 1986, Terrorism Act 2000, Terrorism Act 2006 and the Coroners and Justice Act 2009 are just some of the laws which limit what may be published or broadcast in an attempt to avoid causing offence (see any good media law book for further details such as Frances Quinn's *Law for Journalists*, 2nd edn). Sexually explicit pictures and text are frequently edited in Britain because they are likely to offend. Pictures of death and violence are also handled with care for fear of upsetting consumers. However, people can be just as offended by religious images or the ideas some politicians put forward, so should these ideas also be edited to protect people? If not, why should there be protection from emotional offence but not religious or intellectual offence?

Issues of taste and decency can be put under a number of headings: obscenity, sedition, blasphemy, violence, bad language, sex, explicit pictorial or video images (e.g. of death), bigotry, nudity. In all the above areas, decision making is tough for journalists, and often even more so for others in the arts and media. The Viewers and Listeners Association, a group led throughout the 1970s and 1980s by the vociferous Mrs Mary Whitehouse, believed that no images, pictorial or textual, that might offend their very traditional sensibilities should be used. They wanted to see tougher laws brought into force to allow government to censor such images. Some of their opponents take the ethical standpoint that all censorship is wrong and that all people should have full access to all information. Many pro-censorship moralists use religion as their ethic and the traditional view of family life inherent in the ethos of many religions explains their viewpoint.

Inevitably, there is another group of people who see things differently. They take a consequential approach and tend to be for or against censorship depending on whether they believe that images of a sexually explicit or violent nature are likely to corrupt and cause more crime or violence or the break-up of the family; in other words a real harm, as identified in the Communications Act. They do not believe that using such images is either right or wrong, only the pragmatic effect should be considered. According to Rajeev Dhavan and Christie Davies (1978), the intention of the journalist is irrelevant. They are only concerned with whether the article is likely to cause a bad effect. On the other hand, motivists are concerned with the author's intention because this could have a direct effect on whether the image is presented for morally sound reasons.

While a motivist standpoint that there should be a law ruling out all images that are likely to offend is debatable, the vast majority of people in Britain tend to believe that there can be arguments made for using explicit images on occasion. This makes it almost impossible to work out a code of conduct for the use of nudity, describing or showing sexual practice, violence or death. Ofcom has drawn up a section of its Broadcasting Code concerning harm and offence:

> To ensure that generally accepted standards are applied to the content of television and radio services so as to provide adequate protection for members of the public from the inclusion in such services of harmful and/or offensive material.
>
> (http://www.ofcom.org.uk/tv/ifi/codes/bcode/harmoffence/ accessed 17/2/10)

This is a very broad principle that requires its interpreters to understand what generally accepted standards are. What might be acceptable on late-night television, if handled sensitively, might not be considered at all acceptable in the early evening. A pin-up nude picture of the sort carried by *The Sun* newspaper is considered by many Britons to be acceptable in a family newspaper, but carrying the same picture on a television commercial at 7.00 p.m. would provoke outrage – and not just from the moralist minority. Furthermore, material that can be published without comment in the West would spark storms of protest in a Muslim country. The highly controversial Danish cartoons depicting Muhammad, published in late 2005 and again in January 2006 are evidence of this, with riots in a number of Muslim countries leading to the sacking of several Danish embassies and the deaths of a number of people. Conversely, papers in many Muslim countries regularly carry pictures of road accidents and the like containing scenes of death and injury that would be unacceptable in the UK.

One way of measuring whether the consumer is happy is by using sales figures, therefore, many journalists start to equate the two. Higher sales figures show the consumer is satisfied, therefore the decision to print, or not to print, was right both ethically and financially. Under the circumstances, journalists will often cease considering such problems as ethical tests, and take each image, both pictorial and descriptive, on its merits, weighing it against the possible reaction of the consumer and any regulatory authority. Is the consumer going to feel better informed because of this image, offensive though it may be, or are they going to stop buying the newspaper? Is the regulatory authority likely to take action against the newspaper, or can they be persuaded that this story or image is part of an important truth-telling exercise? While hardly anyone wants journalism to be simply a bland consideration of only those things with which we feel comfortable, this pragmatic approach to the use of image and text that might offend is fraught with difficulty. While mainstream media outlets might well be taking sensible and balanced decisions, smaller circulation newspapers and magazines may not, as Case study 11.1 illustrates.

Bigotry, in the form of racism, sexism and religious intolerance, can also cause offence and needs to be considered in the same way. It is important to remember that it is bigotry we should be concerned about and not the presentation of views that are opposed to our own and on which we may feel strongly. John Stuart Mill wrote about challenging true received opinion:

> Unless it is suffered to be, and actually is, vigorously and earnestly contested, it will, by most of those who receive it, be held in the manner of a prejudice, with little comprehension or feeling for its rational grounds. And not only this, but ... the meaning of the doctrine itself will be in danger of being lost or enfeebled, and deprived of its vital effect on the character and conduct.
>
> (Mill 1991: 59)

Case study 11.1 Taste and decency

The *Daily Sport* and *Sunday Sport* newspapers constantly use photographs of naked or semi-naked women in a way that many find offensive. Of course regular readers of these papers do not, and indeed they buy them precisely because they include such photographs. Therefore, if one considers providing such material to be their duty to the consumer and proprietor, journalists working on the *Sport* and *Sunday Sport* are ethically pure.

In contrast, compare the reaction to the women's magazine *Company* which ran a feature in 1995 about the pornography industry in the suburbs (*Company*, January 1995). This reasonably well-written, certainly unsalacious, article about suburban housewives who acted in pornographic videos for fun and profit was illustrated with explicit stills from the videos, with faces blanked out. It would have been possible to use photographs which showed the set-up just as well without being explicit but presumably the decision was taken to use pictures which would send the circulation soaring. The reaction was mixed. Sales soared but the main retailers, newsagents John Menzies and W.H. Smith, refused to stock the magazine that month.

What we have to recognise is that morality in any society is controlled by the whole society and not just sections within it. The *Sport* is well outside the norm that is acceptable to society as a whole and, while it is probably acceptable to allow some small deviation from the norm to specialist reader groups, the *Sport* probably falls too far outside this definition to be considered morally acceptable for its decision making about the type of stories and pictures it uses. However, it is not just this area of the publication market that has problems. During the first Gulf War, *The Observer* (3 March 1991: 9) used a picture (taken by Kenneth Jarecke) of a dead soldier in the turret of his burnt-out tank. As an image it was upsetting and offensive, but it said much about the horror and brutality of war. There was much discussion before the picture was used. Only a broadsheet decided that its audience could handle the complex mixed messages contained in the image. No tabloid took the risk of upsetting a readership that was considered by them to be intellectually unable to deal with the image. The tank commander was Iraqi. It is unlikely that even the broadsheets would have risked using an image as offensive as the charred corpse of a British officer. According to John Taylor, no US paper used the picture either: 'The newspaper pushed an accusatory photograph of a burned man in its readers' faces. Yet forcing viewers to look at such a horrific picture, closing the gap between a distant action and its effect, is not enough to ensure its moral meaning' (Taylor 1999: 182).

The teenage girl magazine market also came under fire in 1996 when Peter Luff MP proposed a private member's bill which attempted to limit what he saw as unnecessary sexual material appearing in magazines aimed at teenagers and young girls. It led to the setting up of the Teenage Magazine Arbitration Panel by the Periodical Publishers Association. This has issued guidelines for magazines to follow. The TMAP has not advertised itself widely and is seen by at least one researcher as ineffective: 'I have yet to meet a teacher or parent or journalist who has heard of it, even though it has now been in existence for almost three years' (McKay 1999: 23). If anything, its profile is even lower now with the general public and it dealt with only one complaint in 2005.

The complication follows from the publication of things that cause offence if the purpose was to offend. Religion is a particular case in point. Many Christians condemned the broadcasting by BBC 2 of *Jerry Springer the Opera* in 2005. The BBC was contacted by at least 55,000 people, mainly to complain about swearing and religious themes. Director General Mark Thompson, himself a practising Christian, defended the decision to run the programme, saying he believed there was nothing blasphemous in the production and that it was being shown after the watershed with 'very, very clear' warnings about strong language. Vice-president of the national secular society, Terry Sanderson, said: 'This organised attack is the latest of a series of attempts by religious interests to control what we can see or say in this country' (http://news.bbc.co.uk/1/hi/entertainment/tv_and_radio/4154071.stm accessed 20/6/06).

> The BBC's Governors' Programme Complaints Committee decided by a majority of four to one not to uphold complaints made about the decision to broadcast the show. Key to their decision was the BBC's commitment to freedom of expression linked to their 'reasonable and comprehensive attempts to minimize offence through appropriate scheduling, clear warnings and use of other programmes prior to the broadcast to set the piece in context.
> (http://www.bbc.co.uk/pressoffice/pressreleases/stories/2005/03_march/30/springer.shtml
> accessed 20/6/06)

The BBC faces the problems associated with the issues of harm and offence more than most. As a public broadcaster it has to take the broadest possible view of its consumers and is therefore more likely to offend than almost any other medium. This is not because the BBC is careless or unthinking, but because more people are likely to be watching who will find they are offended by something. The BBC is required in the agreement associated with its charter to observe relevant Programme Code Standards as outlined in the Communications Act 2003, particularly the section on 'application of generally accepted standards so as to provide adequate protection for members of the public from the inclusion of offensive and harmful material' (http://www.bbc.co.uk/bbctrust/assets/files/pdf/about/how_we_govern/agreement.pdf accessed 17/2/10). The BBC says:

> The BBC aims to reflect the world as it is, including all aspects of the human experience and the realities of the natural world. In doing so, we balance our right to broadcast innovative and challenging content... with our responsibility to protect the vulnerable and avoid unjustifiable offence.
>
> http://www.bbc.co.uk/guidelines/editorialguidelines/page/guidelines-harm-introduction/
> accessed 14/10/10)

Newspaper codes in Britain don't mention harm and offence as such, although there are clauses in the PCC code about not intruding into private grief and distress, and another clause about the care to be taken in reporting suicide. It is otherwise left to the discretion of the newspaper or magazine. The Press Council used to entertain complaints about bad taste and found against the newspapers in question on several occasions. Importantly, nearly all of the complaints appear to be cases where the journalists involved had not thought through the full details and consequences of the material they were writing.

Causing offence

A journalist should always be aware of the risk of causing offence, whether it is through poor choice of language or sentence construction, or too detailed an approach to the subject. Some subjects are, by their very nature, likely to cause offence and journalists should not shy away from that. For instance, trying to alert readers to the horrors of war by printing horrific, shocking photographs could cause offence and the journalist needs to be sure that the offence caused is not an end in itself.

What upsets consumers will, of course, vary from media outlet to media outlet. What is acceptable in the *Daily Telegraph* would not be acceptable transmitted on the BBC six o'clock news. The *Telegraph*'s readership is generally intelligent, mature and well-informed. It would not be so easily shocked by detailed descriptions of offensive material, provided it was dealt with unsensationally. The mixed audience of all age groups watching the six o'clock news on television needs to be handled more delicately. For example, in 1995 Rosemary West stood trial for torturing and murdering a number of young women, including her own daughter. The details were so shocking and horrific that the jury, court officers and many reporters required counselling to get over it. The details of the case were not reported extensively on the television news. Even the tabloids carried little detailed evidence of the trial. However, the *Daily Telegraph* carried a considerable amount, certainly enough to give readers a flavour of the true horrors: for example see issues for 11 October 1995; 31 October 1995; 22 November 1995. News editors had to spend a lot of time deciding just how much detail to carry about the trial to give a true picture of the horrors without offending consumers.

Television and radio tend to carry the least detail about stories that are likely to offend because it is more difficult for people to control what is let into their home through these media. National newspapers have to be purchased by the consumer, but even so the tabloids tend to carry little detail because their audiences are a much wider spread of society and therefore more open to being offended. The broadsheets take a different attitude, but even they rarely put stories such as the West trial on the front page. If they do, it is to use a sanitised version pointing to a fuller report inside. Free newspapers have a similar responsibility to television's, since they are delivered to the home without the reader having any choice in the matter.

Case study 11.2 The publication of offensive material

A case that was taken to the Press Council in 1984 illustrates the point perfectly. The *East Grinstead Observer* carried a front-page report of a court case about a man who had indecently assaulted his seven-year-old step-daughter. A complaint was lodged that the paper had included unnecessarily explicit detail about the case, rendering it offensive. The complainant was particularly upset as the newspaper was a free paper delivered 'unrequested, through his door'. The Press Council agreed that the report was offensive and upheld the complaint: 'In the Council's view, it is immaterial in this case whether the report appeared in a free or in a paid for newspaper. The Council agrees that the report published prominently as the paper's front page lead included unnecessarily explicit detail of an indecent assault. The publication was particularly offensive as the victim of the assault was a seven-year-old child' (Press Council 1984: 167) (see Appendix 1, clause 7).

No one has the right to be protected from offence, because what might offend one person would not offend another. The young male reader of *Bizarre*, a magazine specialising in presenting stories and pictures designed to offend, is not going to be offended by the same material as his grandmother, but that is not to suggest that there is nothing that would offend him. If there is no human right not to be offended and there is a human right to freedom of expression, it would seem that the right to freedom of expression will allow offensive material to be published every time. However, things are not that simple. Some material that offends breaches or potentially breaches other rights. Material designed to incite violence or hatred could be prevented on the grounds that it would potentially interfere with someone's right to life and to security. The Race hatred laws are drawn up on this basis and it is possible to argue that obscenity laws work by preventing the corruption of some sections of society to the detriment of their or others' lives and liberty. Cohen-Almagor poses what he calls the 'offence to sensibilities' argument. This is when 'the content or manner of expression is designed to cause severe psychological offense against a target group, and the objective circumstances make that group inescapably exposed to that offense'. In those circumstances, he says, freedom of expression should be restricted (Cohen-Almagor 2006: 107). Generally, that sort of circumstance may well be found in the media which could well 'inescapably' expose a sub-group to that offence. There can certainly be an argument that where offence is indulged in by a powerful body such as a national newspaper, its freedom of expression should be more limited because the people offended will not be in a position to answer back in a true debate and so will be inescapably exposed to harm. One of the reasons that many campaigners have attacked the coverage of asylum seekers by some newspapers is for exactly this reason: the offence caused (compounded often by inaccurate reporting) was disproportionate and, in any case, inescapably exposed refugees, whatever their status, to potential harm in terms of discrimination, contempt and violence. Had the refugees been a powerful group in society, then the offence might not have been harmful and the full freedom of expression could have been used. Any newspaper, for instance, can say what it likes about members of any of the political parties; these people are members of a group in society that has sufficient power to ensure a more balanced debate and while they might well be offended, they are not inescapably exposed to harm and have plenty of options concerning their response.

In the same way, according to Cohen-Almagor, 'it is one thing to allow the publication of *The Satanic Verses* and quite another to grant Salman Rushdie permission to promote his book in the religious Pakistani neighbourhood in Bradford, northern England, should he wish to do' (2006: 116). He believes the offence caused by this book to this neighbourhood is so great as to override Rushdie's right to freedom of speech.

So dealing with harm and offence, whether in newspapers or broadcast, involves us in looking at audience and consequence. This makes it a different type of moral problem to most of those we face. Most code of conduct issues are motive decisions. Journalists have a moral duty to follow a certain path as identified in the code clause and if they do this, then they will have behaved morally. But in harm and offence, we cannot draw up a universal law that guides us to the right course. We must look at a number of issues including the consequences.

Ofcom identifies 'offensive language, violence, sex, sexual violence, humiliation, distress, violation of human dignity, discriminatory treatment or language (for example on the grounds of age, disability, gender, race, religion, beliefs and sexual orientation)' as being potentially offensive and that broadcasters must ensure such material is justified by the context. Appropriate information should also be broadcast where it would assist in avoiding or minimising offence. The context would be affected by:

- the editorial content of the programme, programmes or series;
- the service on which the material is broadcast;
- the time of broadcast;
- what other programmes are scheduled before and after the programme or programmes concerned;
- the degree of harm or offence likely to be caused by the inclusion of any particular sort of material in programmes generally or programmes of a particular description;
- the likely size and composition of the potential audience and likely expectations of the audience;
- the extent to which the nature of the content can be brought to the attention of the potential audience for example by giving information; and
- the effect of the material on viewers or listeners who may come across it unawares.

(http://www.ofcom.org.uk/tv/ifi/codes/bcode/harmoffence/ accessed 17/2/10)

Most of these directly refer to the audience and the degree of inescapable offence. In the *Jerry Springer the Opera* example given earlier, the programme was put out late, on BBC 2 (a more specialist channel), had plenty of warnings and was surrounded by contextualising programmes. The likely audience was seen as adult, mature, educated, inquisitive and capable of forming their own judgements. Therefore the risk of inescapable harm or offence was small and so the imperative of freedom of speech won out, as the consequences of broadcasting should have meant that an educated audience had the intellectual freedom to see the play for themselves and make up their own minds about its merits or demerits, while those who knew they would be offended or were too young to make such a decision received sufficient information to ensure they did not watch or that their parents could prevent them watching.

News reports require more difficult judgements. These are not able to be flagged so obviously, although occasionally news reports of disasters, famines and the like are preceded by clear information to allow those who may be offended to switch off or over. Bulletins are also transmitted at different times, so what may well be acceptable for broadcast on *Newsnight* may be unacceptable in the six o'clock news, when children might be watching. Equally, the *Daily Telegraph* with its older, more educated audience can take a more adult view of the news than most of the tabloids. While news is fast changing and the potential for offence always there, a journalist who is aware of this and the target audience, and their ability to ensure it can escape harm by turning off, or not reading following a suitable warning, will be able to deal fairly with the consumer.

Many of the elements of harm and offence identified by Ofcom in its code concern minority groupings of one sort or another who are particularly at risk from the kind of psychological offence outlined above by Cohen-Almagor. Ethnic minorities, people with disabilities and the transgendered, among others, are groups who are particularly vulnerable to offence and I deal with them in Chapter 9. However, bad language is something that causes immense offence to a number of people from all sorts of sections of society.

Intrusion into grief and shock

There is one area where the PCC does examine harm and offence and that is under clause 5 of its code: in many cases these concern straightforward, but unacceptable, intrusions into the grieving process. For instance, a Mrs Hazel Cattermole complained about the coverage of her son's funeral by the *Bristol Evening Post*. Her son had taken his own life and on the day of the funeral a photographer was seen hiding in bushes outside the crematorium. He was asked to leave by the undertaker on behalf of the family. The subsequent article included photographs of the mourners as well as details from the order of service and from messages left on flowers outside the crematorium. The PCC upheld the complaint (http://www.pcc.org.uk/cases/adjudicated.html?article=NjA3Ng== accessed 18/2/10). However, sometimes the intrusion is less about invading privacy and more about causing offence or offending taste and decency.

For instance, a Jan Moir column about the death of Boyzone singer Stephen Gately in the *Daily Mail* in October 2009 raised some questions about his death in a way that upset a number of his fans and launched a Twitter campaign that brought more than 25,000 complaints to the PCC, deluging the complaints body with its biggest ever postbag. The article is still available at http://www.dailymail.co.uk/debate/article-1220756/A-strange-lonely-troubling-death--.html (accessed 18/2/10) but it is the suggestion that his death was not a natural one that has upset most complainants. However, the PCC does not take complaints from third parties, so they were left in a quandary; what to do about the single biggest item of concern to readers in its history? Eventually Gately's partner Andrew Cowles rode to their rescue by putting in a complaint and in February 2010, the PCC repaid him by not upholding it. To be fair there was never very much chance that they would. The complaint was made under three clauses. The first was accuracy, which was easily dismissed. Second was discrimination, which was not seen to be an issue here:

> The Commission made clear that this part of the Code was not designed to prevent discussion of certain lifestyles or broad issues relating to race, religion or sexuality. There was a distinction between critical innuendo – which, though perhaps distasteful, was permissible in a free society – and discriminatory description of individuals, and the Code was designed to constrain the latter rather than the former. The Commission may have been uncomfortable with the tenor of the columnist's remarks on the topic; it did not consider, however, that the column had crossed the line on this occasion such as to raise a breach of the Code.
>
> (http://www.pcc.org.uk/cases/adjudicated.html?article=NjIyOA== accessed 18/2/10)

The final one and the one of most concern to this chapter was intrusion. The PCC considered that 'the context of its publication was paramount' and that therefore Gately's fame and the interest surrounding his death were significant.

In concluding that the paper did not intrude, the PCC identified a number of important points:

- It is not inherently wrong for newspapers to 'publish items that present a negative slant on a person's death.'
- The article had questioned the death but had not sought to do so in a flippant manner.
- It had not presented gratuitous detail about the death.
- To prevent publication of such opinions on events that are a matter of public discussion would be a slide towards censorship.

It did, however, join the more general condemnation, saying that the timing of the piece was questionable and that the newspaper's editorial judgement on this subject could be subject to legitimate criticism (ibid.).

Winding up its verdict the PCC said:

the Commission considered that it should be slow to prevent columnists from expressing their views, however controversial they may be. The price of freedom of expression is that commentators and columnists say things with which other people may not agree, may find offensive or may consider to be inappropriate. Robust opinion sparks vigorous debate; it can anger and upset. This is not of itself a bad thing. Argument and debate are working parts of an active society and should not be constrained unnecessarily.

(ibid.)

This article was an excellent example of material that caused offence, but not inescapable offence or harm in the way described by Cohen-Almagor as there were plenty of opportunities for people to join in the debate and respond to the comments. The number of complaints it drew is some evidence of that and the use of Twitter to build the campaign against the column just one of the methods available.

Coverage of suicide

Both Ofcom and the PCC have detailed clauses in their codes covering suicide. These are designed to prevent detailed coverage of methods. This is quite a sweeping clause covering everything from the method to the location of the suicide.

The number of pain-killers a suicide took, for instance, could well give guidance to someone else seeking to take their life. The location of places such as bridges or high buildings that have been the location of successful suicides could also breach this section of the code. At the time of writing, no complaint has been upheld against a broadcaster in this category, but several complaints dealt with by the PCC have been upheld.

In one of the most spectacular, complaints against the *Crawley Observer Online*, *The Independent Online*, *Daily Mirror*, *Daily Record Online*, *Mail Online*, *The Sun*, *The Sun Online*, *The Daily Telegraph Online*, *Daily Star* and *Metro Online* were all upheld. All of them had published a story about a man who had committed suicide using a chainsaw after a long battle with developers. The PCC says in its report that:

The article contained a long and graphic reference to the method of suicide. It set out the precise apparatus that had been constructed by the individual to enable his death.
http://www.pcc.org.uk/cases/adjudicated.html?article=NTQ1MA== accessed 17/2/10)

Unusually, the PCC had launched the complaints itself and generally found that, while there had been some differences in approach, all the newspapers and website articles 'contained far too much detail and had not been sufficiently edited. It was a matter of concern that the newspaper had allowed the material to be published'. The Commission went on to welcome the fast response to the majority of websites that either removed the material or substantially edited it.

In another adjudication, the PCC criticised an 'entirely gratuitous guide to where individuals have killed themselves' that was published in *The Sport* (http://www.pcc.org.uk/cases/adjudicated. html?article=NTIOMA== accessed 8/3/10).

Violence, dangerous behaviour

The PCC is less concerned about depictions of violence as this sits outside its code of practice, but Ofcom warns that programmes must not include material that condones or glamorises violent, dangerous or anti-social behaviour. It is also an offence under the Terrorism Act 2006 to glamorise or encourage terrorism.

An interesting case arose in May 2010 when *Zoo* magazine was forced to apologise after its agony uncle – actor Danny Dyer – advised a reader to: 'cut your ex's face, and then no one will want her.' His comment sparked widespread outrage and the magazine rushed out an immediate apology blaming a 'production error'. The magazine later ended the column. A magazine spokesman said: 'As an immediate result of an ongoing internal inquiry following an indefensible comment published in this week's issue, *Zoo* has decided to bring the Danny Dyer column to an end.' The column was dictated to the magazine over the phone, a common practice with such columns and at the time Danny Dyer strongly denied making the comments, saying he was misquoted and was devastated by the incident. He said: 'this is not advice I would give to any member of the public. I do not condone violence against women.' Of course this was not an incident about which a complaint could be sent to the PCC, partly because there was no subject of the story and partly because it concerned taste and decency.

Bad language

Bad language is a constant source of concern to TV viewers and radio listeners and makes up a substantial number of the complaints sent to Ofcom every year. Newspapers and magazines have less of a problem. Bad language is only normally used in print if there is a good reason, otherwise it is easy to replace some of the letters in the word with asterisks in quotes containing bad language.

Broadcasters can edit out such words, kill the audio or bleep over the word if it is thought inappropriate and if there is time. This requires some forethought for programmes that are broadcast live and require a short time delay to give the producer a chance to bleep over the word. Approximately one-quarter of complaints to Ofcom concern harm and offence, many of the complaints about bad language. Similarly, about a quarter concern children and many of these also concern bad language since Ofcom's code effectively offers two chances to complain about bad language, the first concerning using such language before the watershed, or at an inappropriate time for radio which breaches the section of the code designed to protect children. But it is also possible to use bad language after the watershed, causing harm and offence. Ofcom identifies a range of contextual issues that will help determine whether such language (and indeed other issues of harm and offence) is appropriate in a particular programme (see above).

Sex and nudity

Sex and depiction of sexual acts is rarely troublesome for journalists, but it can be for other programme makers. Ofcom's rules cover sex and nudity in the same way as they cover bad language. The PCC has no rules of this sort as its code does not cover these issues.

Humiliation and distress

Humiliation, distress and violation of human dignity are definitely issues for journalists though. Covering disasters, for instance, can often tempt journalists to film or photograph people in distress; it is a way of illustrating the extent of the disaster. This needs to be considered from the point of view of the effect on the audience but also from the point of view of the victim and the potential harm it may cause.

Both Ofcom and the PCC have had things to say about published pictures showing people being stretchered away from road accidents. While the PCC has not yet upheld such a complaint, it reminded editors that 'the code requires newspapers to handle publication sensitively' (PCC.org. uk/cases/adjudicated.html?article=NTA4Nw== accessed 18/5/09).

Exorcism, the occult and the paranormal

Although unlikely to be used in news bulletins, Ofcom does warn that exorcisms, the occult and the paranormal must be presented with due objectivity, and must not contain life-changing advice directed at individuals.

Photosensitive epilepsy

Ofcom specifically identifies a variety of techniques as being potentially harmful. These include flashing lights, such as those often seen at media events such as award ceremonies. The uncontrolled explosion of flashguns from still photographers can trigger photosensitive epilepsy and Ofcom insists that appropriate warning is given at the start of such reports to give viewers a reasonable warning. Similarly, it warns against simulated news bulletins as used in dramas and hypnotic and other techniques.

Further reading and support material

Helpful texts covering the issue of harm and offence from different sources include Raphael Cohen-Almagor (2006) *The Scope of Tolerance: Studies on the Costs of Free Expression and the Freedom of the Press* (Routledge, London) which looks in depth at the concept of judging offence by the ability of those likely to be offended to minimise harm.

John Taylor (1999) *Body Horror* (Manchester University Press, Manchester) concentrates particularly on pictures and film in the news and the issues of war and violence.

One of the leading researchers into harm and offence in broadcasting is Andrea Millwood Hargrave, who as head of research for the Broadcasting Standards Commission did a lot of research into the issues of harm and offence and bad language on TV. Her report: Andrea Millwood Hargrave (1991) *Taste and Decency in Broadcasting* (BSC, London) is not easy to get hold of, but should be in most university libraries. She has recently published *Harm and Offence in Media Content: A Review of the Evidence*, 2nd edn, Chicago: Chicago University Press, which would also be worth a look.

Chapter 12

Professional practice

This chapter concentrates on professional issues of a general nature not covered in other chapters, in particular:

■ The importance of sensitivity

■ Issues involved in interviewing

■ Issues involved in dealings with sources and contacts

There are some basic patterns of working that underpin ethical journalism. They are not about the big issues, such as invasion of privacy, or truth, but more about fair professional practice. Good journalists will be aware of these aspects of their work and will understand the implications of how they deal with them.

Dealing with people

Much of a journalist's life is spent dealing with people, either extracting research information from them in order to back up a story or interviewing them to provide credible witnesses and sources for the story.

Sensitivity

A journalist needs to be sensitive both when gathering stories and when writing them up for publication and the journalist who is anxious to avoid unwitting offence will generally perform better as a journalist than one who is not. Dealing sensitively with those who have been bereaved, voted out of office, sacked or made bankrupt is an important professional skill and therefore one that a good journalist has a moral duty to acquire. However, a journalist will sometimes use the appearance of false sensitivity as a technique to ingratiate him or herself in a way that is itself dishonest and therefore morally dubious.

Intruding into private grief is covered in the chapter on privacy but the PCC and Ofcom have both made it clear that journalists who are asked to leave the recently bereaved alone should not continue to harass them.

Meeting people

Most journalists work hard at being personable. They discover early on that being liked is an important part of gaining people's trust and getting them to talk openly. Journalists in television dramas are often portrayed as blatantly nasty, untrustworthy characters. This is far from reality. Who would talk to such a person? Even the rottenest journalists, provided they have any professional ability at all, can produce a veneer of friendliness, and many of the best have considerable charm. It is usually their interest in people that has drawn them to this career in the first place. The gap between fact and fiction works in the journalist's favour here. Those who do not deal often with the media get their experience of journalists from soap operas and the movies and so expect a journalist to be sly and seedy and are pleasantly surprised by the personable character they meet and find it difficult not to say more than they intend. Journalists are trained to be friendly, to put people at their ease – it is an important professional skill.

Interviews

Interviews always require a professional approach. As stated earlier, a journalist has a loyalty to contacts and must treat them fairly. The only exceptions to this that might arise are when subterfuge or deception are the *only* way of getting a story which is in the public interest. The PCC dealt with such a case in 2008. A woman complained about footage on *The Sun*'s website that showed her son working in a supermarket. Her son had been convicted in 2007 for possession of internet pornography, although he had not been put on the sex offenders register. The journalist had filmed him secretly in the supermarket and took pictures of him making a delivery to a nursery school. Although the PCC agree with the newspaper that there was a public interest in the story, there was not, they said, a public interest in anything other than the delivery to the nursery school and it upheld the complaint. (http://www.pcc.org.uk/cases/adjudicated.html?article=NTE5Ng== accessed 18/2/10).

In another case in 2007, Cornwall County Council complained after *The Falmouth Packet* published a story about a 15-year-old boy used by trading standards officers to visit stores to see if staff would sell him alcohol. It is illegal to sell alcohol to people under 18 in the UK. The newspaper published a picture of the boy taken by a security camera in a store that had sold alcohol. The owner of the store had sent the tape to the newspaper to support his view that the boy looked to be older than 18. The newspaper claimed that the transaction took place in public so this was not a privacy issue and was a matter of public interest as it was a 'sting' operation carried out by council officers. The Commission dismissed all elements of the complaint including the part about the use of hidden cameras:

> The Commission noted that the article used footage taken from a CCTV camera in the shop. It made clear that it did not consider such a camera to be 'hidden' under the terms of Clause 10 of the Code.
>
> (http://www.pcc.org.uk/cases/adjudicated.html?article=NDMzNg== accessed 18/2/10)

In a majority of cases a journalist should be both fair and honest with interviewees. Most people are not used to being interviewed whereas most journalists are skilled and experienced at interviewing. There are, however, some people, politicians for instance, who are experienced at being interviewed and have a few tricks of their own. An inexperienced, local reporter interviewing a Cabinet minister could use every trick he or she had learned without being able to take unfair advantage of the politician. However, since a local paper is likely to support the status quo, there probably wouldn't be much point in hammering the minister anyway – the paper would be seeking an interview with a celebrity visitor rather than the grilling of a Cabinet minister. Only if there were a local campaign under way about a major issue would a local reporter normally take a minister to task, and then most street-wise politicians steer well clear of such situations until the campaign is over. For instance, a town that is reeling from the closure of a defence establishment with the loss of hundreds of jobs is unlikely to receive a visit from any Cabinet minister, never mind the ministers for Defence or Employment, for some time after the announcement.

Behaving fairly to interviewees requires journalists to make it clear from the start who they are, who they represent and their reasons for quizzing the interviewees. Good professional practice will mean putting interviewees at their ease, talking them through the situation and making it clear that notes or a tape recording will be taken and seeking their approval for this. For a broadcast interview this is a two-stage process. First, talking through the issue with the interviewee, collecting the facts and deciding on what line to take for the recorded interview and preparing the interviewee. The second stage is recording the interview. Even audio-taping an interview can be an ordeal for the inexperienced, but a television interview with a camera operator, sound technician and interviewer can be a real trial. Good professionals will do all they can to put interviewees at their ease and thus allow them to put their case in the way they want.

One of the huge advantages that broadcasting has as a news medium is the ability not just to transmit people's words, but also their demeanour and, to a certain extent, their personality. It is a matter of professional morality to ensure that the interviewees are given the opportunity to present themselves in an accurate light. This does not mean that the reporter needs to alter the image in an attempt to improve it. If, for instance, the interview is with a farmer about farming issues, then interviewing the farmer in his working clothes out in the field or farmyard would be accurate and give the viewer a rounder picture. But to interview the same man in the same position just after he has been elected president of the area Rotary Club would be to give a different impression and it would be important to give him the opportunity to change clothes and setting if he wishes. Only by taking care over these matters can a journalist be sure that he or she is being as truthful as possible with the audience. For a newspaper journalist, this is not so important as the interviewee is not seen. But if pictures are taken, then the same thing would apply.

It can be reasonably assumed, provided all this is done, that the interviewees are happy to see their names and what they say in print or broadcast. There is no need to confirm that they are prepared to go 'on the record' (see below). Provided a reporter has correctly identified him or herself and the reason for the interview (publication or broadcast), it can be assumed that the interviewees realise that they could end up in the newspaper. Occasionally, however, a reporter may be aware that there are good reasons why interviewees might wish to remain anonymous. Perhaps they are talking about drug dealers setting up in their neighbourhood or perhaps they have committed a crime themselves. In these circumstances, in order to be fair to the interviewees, the journalist should specifically check that the interviewees are happy to have their names used in any published piece.

Sometimes interviews are only given under certain terms and conditions. These place the journalists under a moral obligation to use the information they have gathered only in the way the interviewee has stipulated.

On the record

This means that the interview is open and that anything said can be used with the name of the person who said it. It does not mean that quotes can be adjusted to suit the journalist, or that they can be made up. It does mean that things said can be used verbatim or edited to suit the length and style of an article. A journalist is not obliged to use full utterances, but the chosen extracts should be a fair representation of what was said and what was meant and presented in the order that it was said. Often in an interview, people are nervous and their tongues play tricks on them that their brains did not mean. If an interviewee, for instance a politician, were to say something that seemed to support an opposite viewpoint, then it is important that the journalist should check that that is what he or she really meant in order to play fair with the interviewee and be honest with the consumers. It would also be wrong to mislead the interviewee about the journalistic status of the interviewer unless there were some overriding reason of public concern involved. A journalist keeping his or her identity secret in an interview can rarely be justified.

Off the record

Off the record is an increasingly popular way for those in official or semi-official positions to communicate with the media. Many public servants in such areas as health, education or social services are concerned about developments in their fields and wish to speak out. But they may be afraid to do so because they fear losing their jobs, or making things difficult for themselves. By speaking off the record they can alert reporters to a situation without specific quotes being used or without them being named. Reporters do not have to agree to an off-the-record interview. Often the information is already in the public domain and reporters are only after confirmation and comment. However, sometimes the information cannot be obtained from another source. In such cases journalists should only agree to an off-the-record interview if they are confident they can keep to their side of the bargain, that is, promise not to reveal the interviewee's name in print or a broadcast. Of course, if reporters say no to off-the-record interviews, then it is up to the interviewees whether they give any further information, and up to the reporters whether they continue to seek information from the interviewees. Sometimes interviewees will say at the end of an ordinary interview: 'Oh, that was off the record of course.' Clearly it is not right for interviewees to introduce different terms to the way the interviews are being handled *after* the interviews have taken place and the journalists can be morally justified in saying: 'Tough, I'm using it.' However, since this would mean upsetting contacts, the journalists may well need to take a more sanguine view and pick up the interviewees' requests or at least negotiate a compromise. Morally, the reporters are not bound by the late request. Practically, of course, they may find it politic to oblige.

Sometimes, though, journalists interview people who are unused to dealing with the media and may not fully understand the difference between on and off the record. This needs to be explained to the contact so that if it is clear they are intending that their comments be off the record, then that is what will happen. The PCC has made it clear that it will accept complaints from the public about breaching off the record under clause 15 or under the general spirit of the code. Ofcom would also take such a complaint under the fairness section of its code.

Non-attributable

This is slightly different to off-the-record statements and is used a lot by politicians and royalty. It leads to such tags as: 'A Whitehall spokesman said ...' 'A close friend of the princess said ...' 'An influential member of the Party said ...' What the interviewees said can be used in full, but their names must be kept secret.

In the House of Commons lobby, this method allows politicians to talk to journalists without risking their political careers. They can leak information without it necessarily being blamed on them. The main lobby is the twice-daily briefing by the Prime Minister's Office at 10 Downing Street, although other departments and ministers also use the lobby on occasion. Only accredited journalists who are prepared to accept the tight conditions laid down by the Downing Street Press Office are allowed to attend these briefings. The system is controversial and has its detractors, who claim that journalists taking part become part of the system they should be criticising. Supporters say it allows them access to information and opinion from important sources they would otherwise be denied. The government finds these lobby briefings useful as it allows ministers to 'fly flags'. This means the minister can suggest that government intends to do something without the source of the information being known. The politicians can then gauge reactions to the idea before deciding whether to make the plan public or to deny it altogether. The lobby can also be used to attack politicians on both sides of the House. Sir Richard Wilson, the then Cabinet Secretary, took the unusual step in June 1998 of revealing that he had warned Tony Blair's Press Secretary, Alistair Campbell, to tone down political activity in the lead up to the local elections that year in order to prevent civil servants being dragged into a slanging match with the opposition.

> Sir Richard described Mr Campbell as a 'free bird' who was able to present Government policy in a party political context, unlike civil servants who are constrained by the traditional Whitehall code of impartiality.
>
> Having monitored the notes of twice-daily lobby briefings for parliamentary journalists, he believed none of the material suggested that Mr Campbell 'comes anywhere near attacking the opposition'.
>
> (*Daily Telegraph*, 17 June 1998: 1)

The lobby system has at various times been condemned by journalists and politicians. It can lead to a lack of responsibility on the part of politicians. A politician can leak a story, gauge the reaction and then confirm or deny the story's truth later. This is a useful tool for governments, particularly those with slim majorities. It is also useful to unscrupulous journalists who can provide quotes without having to justify them and without anyone being able to complain of being misquoted.

At its worst it allows journalists to take a story and use it uncritically because it is difficult to follow through a story that is not attributed to a source. Such stories can be difficult to attack or defend, prove or disprove. Several attempts have been made over the years to end the lobby system. *The Independent* refused to join when it was first launched but had to review its position later. Although most people agree that the lobby system is far from ideal, no one has yet come up with an alternative which is able to offer all the benefits to both sides afforded by the present system.

Quotes

The quotes the journalist uses to support a story are the only true record of an interview or report. Watched on television or listened to on the radio, the consumer can be confident that what is heard (supported by voice intonation and facial expression in the case of television) gives them accurate information. A newspaper or magazine is at a disadvantage (in the confidence stakes) because it cannot show, in the same way, that its reporting of the person's words is accurate. For this reason, as well as all the moral arguments about truth-telling, it is important that quotes are dealt with scrupulously. This does not mean that the whole of a twenty-minute interview must be transcribed (although it is a technique used occasionally in magazines); almost everyone benefits from a little editing. What is important is that quotes are used accurately, appropriately and in correct chronological order. Mixing and matching what someone has said to put words in a different order, or to cut qualifying phrases away from the main sentence, is to cheat the interviewee. For instance, a union leader who says 'I will have to consult the membership but I believe we will be on strike from next week' is entitled to be angry if he is quoted as saying 'We will be on strike from next week'.

Editing and chronological order are as important as accurate reporting. However, that does not mean that we should not improve people's grammar. What is said in a heated and emotionally-charged situation might sound fine but would look terrible in print. For example, 'The copper just stood there and didn't do nothing to save him' is just the kind of phrase a witness might use, but it could be transcribed to 'The copper just stood there and didn't do anything to save him'. Exchanging the 'nothing' for 'anything' corrects a common grammatical mistake which is barely noticed in conversation but in print makes the speaker seem ill-educated. Changing the 'copper' would, I think, be taking it too far. This word is widely used, so there is no problem about comprehension, yet its choice by the witness says something about the witness's views of the police, and his or her position in society. It helps us gain a better picture of what is going on. A reason for using direct quotations from witnesses is that an accurate report often says much more than they had intended to tell us. Their choice of language and phrasing can help us decide how much we believe them.

Journalists often use the trick of saying: 'Well, would you say that . . .' and then, if the interviewee agrees with what they have said, go on to use it as an original quote. Providing that journalists are aware that putting the interviewees' views into their own words sacrifices accuracy for a sharper soundbite, then it may be a fair exchange. It is a judgement only journalists who are faced with an inarticulate witness can make.

Photos and video

In an age when everyone armed with a mobile phone is a photographer, what rights do journalists have to take pictures or video in the street? It became a matter of controversy through 2009 with police officers preventing people, journalists and tourists alike, from taking pictures of landmarks or at demonstrations under the terrorism legislation.

TV viewers of the 2009 G20 protests in London saw protesters surrounded by much larger crowds of photographers, mostly mobile-phone-camera wannabes, all hoping something exciting would happen. So where do they all stand with regard to permission to take photographs? Can they use any of the pictures, either for sale or personal use or do they need permission from everyone involved?

The first thing to check when taking pictures is whether you are on public or private ground. If the land where you are standing is public ground then you have reasonable freedom to take the pictures. Second, is the subject on public or private land? If it is public, then no problem, but if the subject is on private land – their home, a hotel or restaurant – they may have a reasonable expectation of privacy and the Press Complaints Commission or the courts might well be supportive towards such a complainant. More detail is given in the chapter on privacy.

Taking pictures of children is not in itself illegal, although possession of a prohibited image is illegal under the new Coroners and Justice Act 2009. It is unlikely that any newspaper or magazine would want to publish such a picture but as the law is new, it's difficult to know precisely where the boundary will be drawn. The Act identifies a prohibited image as one that is:

- pornographic (that is that it has been taken solely or principally for the purpose of sexual arousal);
- focuses solely on a child's genital or anal region or portrays sexual acts with children; or is
- grossly offensive, disgusting or otherwise of an obscene character.

In the more likely case of a picture of a child at school or at play the PCC and Ofcom would expect you to have parental or school permission or a very good public interest defence if any particular child is featured. Taking pictures of children at a school sports day or at a school play would need permission from the school, and the Information Commissioner's Office says that provided such permission is granted and the children and/or their guardians are aware that photographs might appear in the newspaper, there are no Data Protection Act issues. Taking pictures of kids in a park, on the street or at the beach are legitimate although if the shots feature one or more children it might be safest to get permission. Taking photographs in these circumstances has sparked the concern of park wardens, police officers or occasionally parents in the past so it is important to ensure you have your press pass.

Taking pictures of adults is fine so long as you are not harassing them by following them or thrusting a lens in their face. Of course it may well be sensible to move on or stop taking pictures if asked to do so, particularly if such requests are accompanied by threats. However, if you are intending to sell such pictures to an agency, you must remember that their use will be limited to the UK because the law is different elsewhere and may well require signed permission. If you want to sell such pictures to a potential international audience, then get the subjects to sign a model release form. It would also be sensible to do this if a person you have filmed was not aware you were filming them and you intend to broadcast the video. A face to face interview implies permission to broadcast, but anything else would need a release form.There is also a risk that pictures or video taken in the street without permission will be subject to the Data Protection Act as it could be conceived as processing personal data, although no such case has yet been brought. The ICO's position on this is unclear at the time of writing and while it is unlikely that pictures taken for news use could face DPA problems, it does explain why Google's street view pictures automatically pixelate people's faces.

Security and terrorism are probably the biggest problem facing journalists taking pictures or video these days. First, there is the long list of places where it is prohibited to take pictures that might be of use to an enemy or for purposes of terrorism: defence establishments, airports and munitions stores are top of the list but the siting of CCTV cameras and the entrances to railway stations are less obvious areas that have figured in successful prosecutions.

The Criminal Justice and Public Order Act 1994, Terrorism Act 2000, Terrorism Act 2006 and the Counter Terrorism Act 2008 are now perhaps the most widely used legislation to attempt to prevent photographers from taking pictures. The Public Order Act allows police to stop and search people they suspect of criminal activity or carrying illegal weapons. The Terrorism Act 2000 section 43 allows police to stop and search people they suspect of terrorist activity. This could of course include taking photographs of targets, but the law does not specifically allow the confiscation of equipment unless the officer believes it to be evidence of an offence. Section 44 of the same act allows police to stop and search anyone for no reason whatsoever, provided there is an authorisation from a senior officer. These seem to be issued reasonably routinely for areas that are likely to be terrorist targets. Complaints about the use of section 44 to prevent photographers taking pictures were made in a 2009 parliamentary debate. Home Office junior minister Shahid Malik said: 'I would like to make it clear that section 44 does not prohibit the taking of photographs ... The police may stop and search someone who is taking photographs in an authorised area, just as they may stop and search any member of the public, but the powers should not be targeted on photographers.' Following a number of complaints, the Home Office recently issued new guidance to police. The Counter Terrorism Act 2008 section 76 amends the Terrorism Act 2000 to make it an offence to elicit and publish information about a member of the armed forces, a member of any intelligence service or a police constable 'which is of a kind likely to be useful to a person committing or preparing an act of terrorism', and, certainly in the early days following the introduction of the Act, some papers blanked out pictures of police officers, just in case. Mr Malik said: 'A photograph of a police officer may fall within the scope of the offence, but would do so in only limited circumstances. The important thing is that the photographs would have to be of a kind likely to provide practical assistance to terrorists, and the person taking or providing the photograph would have to have no reasonable excuse, such as responsible journalism, for taking it. I want to be clear about this: the offence does not capture an innocent tourist taking a photograph of a police officer, or a journalist photographing police officers as part of his or her job.'

As is always the case, however, the problem for the photographer is not the interpretation of the minister, or even the courts, but of the police officer on the ground who would simply prefer the journalist wasn't there.

Research and cuttings

The pressures on journalists to be more efficient and cut costs has led to an increase in the use of telephone interviews, instead of talking face to face, and the more extensive use of press-cuttings libraries for research. Although these methods can be useful to overworked journalists working to tight deadlines, the PCC felt it necessary to include a warning about them in its March 1992 report. In relation to cuttings it said:

> Cuttings are an essential part of newspaper research but too many journalists now seem to act in the belief that to copy from 10 old stories is better than to write a new one with confirmation by proper fresh enquiry. In one instance ... a magazine admitted that because it had been unable to contact a woman who had been attacked by her husband some months previously, it wrote up the story on the basis of newspaper reports, inventing dialogue to put the story into the magazine's style. The result was an article that contained serious inaccuracies and was to a degree fictitious.
>
> (PCC 1992: 2)

In relation to telephone interviews it warned:

In one article the reporter said of the interviewee: 'Watching her, sitting up in bed ...' when in fact the reporter had never visited the house. This led the reader to understand that the reporter had been invited into the person's house when in fact what really happened was that a short and somewhat reluctant telephone interview had been given.

(PCC 1992: 3)

The PCC editorial went on to say that such practices could give rise to complaints under clause 1 of the Code that requires newspapers not to publish inaccurate or misleading material.

Use of language

Journalists have a professional and moral duty to ensure they use language precisely and carefully. It is very easy to offend people or distort the truth by the poor use of language. The wrong word or an ill-chosen phrase can put a slant on something that might not be intended. Journalists can never use the excuse that they did not mean what was written; their tools are words and they must ensure they use them well. Although the PCC doesn't tend to accept complaints about the use of specific words, there are numerous examples of the use of offensive language in the Press Council's annals. The Press Council, for instance, made it a rule that the word 'poof' was offensive and should not be used (Press Council 1990: 189). In another judgment they ruled that the word 'chinky', as a reference to people of Chinese origin, was offensive and should not be used in newspapers (Press Council 1990: 193). The then editor of the *Star* (which had used the word in a headline), Brian Hitchin, argued that most people thought the headline was very funny. However, the Press Council upheld the complaint: 'The *Daily Star*'s headline was superficially an amusing play on words and rhyme but its use of the derogatory term "chinky" was offensive and is happily outmoded. The temptation to use it should have been resisted' (Press Council 1990: 193).

Case study 12.1 Journalistic methods and bad practice

Many of the issues discussed above are raised in the 1989 annual report of the Press Council which contains several examples of bad practice. One case concerned the *Daily Mail*. In trying to find information about a reported murder, journalists resorted to telephoning houses near the village murder site at random. Since the call to the complainant came at 1.40 a.m., he was understandably upset, particularly as there was no reason to suppose he knew any more about it than anyone else. The Press Council adjudication said: 'There are rare occasions when a newspaper may be justified in disturbing someone by telephone in the early hours with a request for comment or information. This was not one of them. Such conduct is tolerable when a story is important and urgent, and when the person telephoned is known to be directly connected with the story being covered or, say, an official spokesman. There is no such justification in this case' (Press Council 1989: 205). In this instance the paper apologised to the complainant.

In another case, a former borough councillor, who had written to a paper, found his letter used as though it were an interview. No contact had been made with the complainant, although the *Milton Keynes Citizen* said it had tried. The Press Council agreed that it was wrong to use statements from the letter without further reference to the writer, giving the misleading impression that he had been interviewed. If the report had made it clear the comments were made in a letter, the readers would not have been misled and there would have been no breach of ethics (Press Council 1989: 204).

▶

A more recent case of the misuse of an interview occurred in 1998 when the *Sun* newspaper went one step further in misleading the reader. In January 1998, it published a piece about a mother who gave birth at the age of sixty and described it as written by Lord Winston, the eminent Professor of Fertility Studies (*The Sun*, 23 January 1998). The following week the paper published an apology in which it admitted that a reporter had spoken to Lord Winston but the article was not written by him (*The Sun*, 29 January 1998: 2). To attribute the article to Lord Winston was clearly unprofessional and highly unethical.

Many words of this sort are offensive to different groups in society and the good journalist needs to be aware of this. To use such words in a deliberate attempt to offend or be provocative is one thing, but to use such a word without thought and be offensive by accident is unprofessional. There are a wide range of words and phrases that require care. Racist and sexist language, religious niceties, slang, bad language, sexual and anatomical words should all be thought about before use (see Appendices 1 and 2). How would readers feel about the use of such language? It may be fine to use bad language in a magazine aimed at a readership that expects it (for example, a magazine aimed at young men, such as *Loaded*) but probably not in a local newspaper where readers do not expect to read such language. The BBC issued new guidelines to employees when separate legislatures were introduced for Scotland and Wales. It was concerned with the detail of language surrounding nationhood and its likelihood to cause offence. It warned: 'Words like "nation", "country" and "capital" can be interpreted differently by different audiences … It is better that programmes which are broadcast throughout the United Kingdom talk about things happening "across the United Kingdom" or "UK-wide" when that is what they mean' (BBC 1999: 5). The guidelines go on to warn against using England and Britain interchangeably.

Pronunciation is as important as language use for broadcasters and can cause offence just as easily. It is important to check you have the right pronunciation.

Making promises

A journalist should be aware that making a promise binds him or her to a course of action. However, the temptation is often there to agree to do something in order to make life easier. For instance, an interviewee will often ask to be sent a copy of the newspaper in which the interview appears, and the easy course is to agree. However, keeping a check on when a particular article appears and sending it on can be more irksome than it sounds and so a journalist would be well advised to refuse to promise to send a paper.

Vetting copy

Reporters are sometimes asked by interviewees to provide them with a copy of the report for checking.

If a reporter agrees to telephone someone and read back the copy, or put a photocopy in the post, that reporter has abrogated editing responsibility to the interviewee. No matter how firmly the journalist tells the interviewee that he or she cannot change a word, inevitably there will be words that the interviewee insists should be changed – the interviewee may claim they are wrong or give a bad impression. The journalist may say that the piece was only offered for checking, but can hardly complain when alterations are offered. In any case, checking is the journalist's job and he or she cannot pretend that a piece is accurate and fair if the piece is to be shown to one or more of the people interviewed before publication.

Covering stories

Promises are often sought about the use of stories. Court cases are a good example where journalists are often approached by people accused of committing a crime, or their relatives, and asked to keep a certain story quiet. However, journalists' loyalty is not to the accused but to the editor, the reader and society in general. Therefore, any approach made to a journalist about a story should be referred to the editor and it should be the editor's decision whether copy is used or not. This is doubly true if a bribe is offered, threats are made or the journalist is somehow personally involved. To allow these considerations to influence whether or not to submit a story would be highly unprofessional. Some editors are so concerned about undue pressure being brought to bear that they will automatically use such a story even if they wouldn't normally have bothered. Because this is the case, many experienced reporters will advise distressed relatives not to contemplate suppression; that they should contact the editor if they feel they must but that their chances of non-publication would be much better by leaving the matter to the lottery of space and news values. I see nothing wrong with journalists using their knowledge and experience of the system to advise those in distress, provided the reporters then go on to write up the story as though nothing had happened and file it in the normal way. Failing to file the copy would be unethical, unprofessional and could well be a disciplinary offence if discovered.

Embargoes

Organisations sometimes place restrictions on the publication of their press releases. For instance, government departments often release lengthy documents to the media before the official publication date to give them a chance to read and digest the contents. In return, journalists are expected not to use the material until the date given on the embargo. For instance, the New Year's Honours List is published at the start of the new year, but the list is issued to the media around 20 December. This allows journalists to contact the people on the list for interviews and pictures before the Christmas holiday break – a time when many of the award recipients will be unavailable and when many journalists are also on holiday, leaving skeleton newsrooms to do the work. The embargo lets the newsrooms do the work when both the reporters and recipients of the award are available.

Neither the PCC (which embargoes its own quarterly reports) nor the NUJ has specific clauses on embargoes but both have clauses specifying that journalists have a duty to maintain the highest professional and ethical standards. It is unlikely that an embargo complaint would be considered by the PCC but one was dealt with by the Press Council in 1989 when the *Gateshead Post* and *The Times* (24 April 1989) broke an embargo by publishing the news that a local firm had won the Queen's Award to Industry. The company told the Press Council that it had not been allowed to tell its workforce of the award and the publication of information in a press release a day early was not good for worker morale. The company had intended to break the good news to its workers on the day agreed. The newspapers said that the embargo was inadvertently missed, but the managing director of the company said he did not believe that because it was printed plainly at the start and end of the press release. The Press Council upheld the complaint (Press Council 1989: 214).

Breaching embargoes can also raise copyright issues. The issuer of a press release has moral rights over the text of a press release under UK copyright law. This means they can say under what circumstances the press release can be used. This is probably not appropriate protection if the copyright holder wants to prevent publication of details of an event such as date or place, but it can prevent use of the text of a release. This was the issue in a case involving the Queen. She sued *The Sun* for publishing details of her Christmas broadcast speech in 1992. The newspaper had been sent a copy of the speech in time for it to write the news story, but decided to publish two days early on 23 December. The Queen threatened to sue and the newspaper settled, paying £200,000 to charity.

All press releases should be checked for embargoes and any decision to breach them should be considered very seriously. A paper or broadcast station that continually ignores embargoes risks not receiving press releases in advance. Since this facility is often to the advantage of the media, common sense suggests that embargoes should be adhered to unless there are good reasons not to, such as an embargo being used to prevent publication of information already widely known.

Plagiarism

Plagiarism involves passing off someone else's writing as your own. The most obvious use of plagiarism is when another media outlet has a story that a journalist wants to use. It is very tempting – bearing in mind the pressures of time journalists are often under to meet copy deadlines – to use that story, perhaps rewriting it in order not to breach copyright and to avoid detection. However, the problems with this are threefold:

1   The story, or elements of it, may well be copyright.
2   It is deceitful to take someone else's work and pass it off as your own, perhaps depriving the original journalist of fees that are rightfully his or hers.
3   What if the original story is wrong? A journalist who copies a story risks repeating any error contained within it. Furthermore, he or she may bow to the temptation to firm up elements left deliberately vague in the original, thus increasing the number of errors. Often sub-editors who have rewritten a reporter's copy to make it 'brighter' have been forced to return to something closer to the original because the copy says more than the reporter is able to support and is straying into the area of defamation or sensationalism.

The courts generally accept, following *Express Newspapers* v *News Ltd* (1990) that news cannot be copyright; facts are available to everyone. However, you could well breach another paper's copyright if you copy quotes gathered by another reporter. The courts have held that the skill and labour of a reporter in getting quotes during an interview can be copyright.

This is not to say that we should not use other media to alert us to stories. Sometimes a newspaper will carry a story that is of such importance that rivals are duty-bound to follow it up and provided you only retell the facts, which you should check, and get your own quotes to support them there should be no problem. Because of this, national tabloids will often hold a superb story until after the first edition has been printed and then publish the story in the second edition when the time available for the rivals to pick up the story is greatly reduced. All news desks use television and radio news to alert them to a breaking story. Listening to local radio stations can alert local newspaper journalists to any serious accident or fire in plenty of time for them to ring the appropriate service, get the details and go out and get the story. The television and radio can be extremely useful in providing us with eye-witness information on events such as royal weddings and sporting occasions.

Bribes, threats, influence and corruption

No journalist should take a bribe or inducement to write a story a certain way or to prevent publication of a story. This would include commercial pressure from advertisers or proprietors to distort or spike a story, and possibly any other gift or freebie. The NUJ Code of Conduct says: 'A journalist resists threats or any other inducements to influence, distort or suppress information' (http://www.nuj.org.uk/innerPagenuj.html?docid=174 accessed 8/2/2010). The British PCC's Code has nothing to say on the subject but does talk about the inadvisability of journalists who work in the financial sphere cashing in on their own advice by taking early advantage of confidential information. The most significant case in this area concerned the *Mirror* when its editor Piers Morgan and the *City Slickers* columnists Anil Bhoyrul and James Hipwell were accused of multiple breaches of the PCC Code over a sustained period of time. The *City Slickers* advised readers to buy shares in Viglen computers in January 2000. *Mirror* editor Piers Morgan told the PCC he had bought £20,000 worth, but later, after adverse publicity about the shares, sold them and donated the profit to charity. During Bhoyrul and Hipwell's trial in February 2006, however, it was alleged he had bought £67,000 worth of shares. Bhoyrul pleaded guilty to manipulating the stock market and was sentenced to 180 hours of community service, Hipwell was found guilty at trial and sentenced to six months in prison, three of them suspended.

It is important that journalists should be seen as providing truthful information. To alter the balance of a story for financial gain would be to make void that essential pact with the reader. Whether untruthfulness is caused by laziness or incompetence, or by a more reprehensible desire for financial reward, doesn't really matter that much. The effect is that the reader can no longer trust the report and the publication's purpose is no longer served. So although the PCC does not have clauses on bribery, its clause on accuracy is sufficient to deal with the problem, should it arise, because the offending material should not be published.

The pressures from advertisers tend to be not so much on what is written, but whether it is written at all. The Royal Commission on the Press (1949) said: 'We have had evidence ... that the direct influence of advertisers on the policy of newspapers is negligible.' While there may be even today little evidence of *direct* influence on *policy* there is plenty of anecdotal evidence of indirect influence on the type of stories used and the way they are handled.

It is worth reminding ourselves that taking a bribe in order to use or suppress a story would be immoral unless of course the reporter is totally honest with the reader about it, in which case it is arguable that it is a bribe. What may not be so clear to those outside the industry is the range of 'bribes' on offer to journalists and the difficulty many have with dealing with them.

Being slipped a £50 note in order to suppress a story is extremely rare these days, although a hundred years ago it was standard practice for some of the more unsavoury press. It was in answer to a request for a 'suppression' fee that the Duke of Wellington made his famous statement, 'Publish and be damned.' But being offered 'freebies', from a bottle of Scotch at Christmas to sunshine holidays, or free dinners, theatre tickets, books, records, CDs or loans of cars is common. Many new products are launched at lavish receptions with free food and drink to put the journalists in a receptive frame of mind.

Dealing with these freebies is difficult. Many media outlets would not review books, CDs, restaurants or holidays at all if the product was not provided free – they would not (so it is claimed) be able to afford it. Even if they could or did, the journalists themselves would not be paying so it would still be a benefit.

The freebie is a vexed question that has bothered some journalists for years. Some see no problem in accepting hospitality, claiming that it does not alter what they would have written without it. Others argue that journalists should be squeaky clean and that all freebies are tainted. Some American and Scandinavian papers refuse to have anything to do with freebies.

Of course, the difficulty is deciding whether a freebie alters a journalist's view of the product. Some financial institutions are legendary for the lavish scale of their trips, which their PR departments claim are to allow journalists and company personnel to get to know each other. One cannot help thinking that this could be done just as easily over a glass of wine at home.

The real danger of freebies is that the journalist is unable to bring the full range of sceptical faculties to bear, which is why companies are so generous. As a young editor on a cash-strapped weekly, the records that companies happily sent me each month meant I was able to run record reviews. I enjoyed listening to the music and writing the reviews, but would I have been more critical if the records had been paid for out of my own personal resources? And what about the record company? As far as the records went, I was never aware of pressure to write positive reviews. Presumably, they took the view that merely advertising the existence of a new record was enough to entice fans to buy it; my opinion probably did not count for much.

But there have been more serious suggestions of companies trying to bring pressure to bear for good write-ups. Football clubs have banned reporters from the press stand, forcing them either to buy a ticket or not attend, because of a report the football club disliked. The same has been known to happen at press premières of films. There are those who say that the only way to do reviews of things like cars is to accept loans of cars. Because all the cars tested are on loan, they are all measured to the same standard and the fact that no payment is made does not become an issue. An interview with former BBC 2 *Top Gear* front-man, Jeremy Clarkson, reported in *Private Eye*, gave an insight into the perks and problems of free loans:

> Clarkson tells the *Eye* that he has not one Jaguar but four on indefinite loan. 'I've got lots of cars on free loans,' he cheerfully admitted to the *Eye*. 'If they're really good I just don't give them back. Everybody does it. We've all got Jags.' But he insists this would never influence his judgement. 'I'm quite straight. You don't last very long in this business if you start taking corporate backhanders.
>
> (*Private Eye*, 19 March 1999: 7)

The BBC's *Editorial Guidelines* takes a robust view of bribes and influence (http://www.bbc. co.uk/guidelines/editorialguidelines/page/guidelines-editorial-integrity-product-prominence/ accessed 14/10/10) – '… we must avoid any undue prominence which gives the impression that we are promoting or endorsing products, organisations or services. To achieve this we must:

- not accept free or reduced cost products or services in return for on-air or online credits, links or off-air marketing.'

However, even the BBC accepts that in order to use the licence-payers' money wisely, there may be occasions when products or services can be used free or at reduced prices. Consumer programmes reviewing products may accept freebies, provided it is made clear that this does not allow a right of preview or guarantee a favourable mention. The BBC makes it clear that staff should not accept personal benefits under any circumstances. The PCC makes no mention of bribes in its Code, but this is because it is a code aimed at publishers, not news-gatherers.

A freebie is not the only way that journalists can be influenced. Threats, either direct ('You write up that report about my brother and I'll come round and sort you out!') or indirect, can have a similar effect. Pressure from advertisers, real or potential, is one of the major sources of undue influence. Often editors worry that writing up a story which is likely to show an advertiser in a bad light will cause the advertiser to withdraw the advertising, so consequently the story is dropped. The Royal Commission on the Press (1947–49) spent some time examining this area. It came to the conclusion that attempts to influence by individual advertisers were infrequent and unsuccessful. The Commission had no evidence of concerted pressure by advertisers for a particular policy but noted that: 'So long as newspapers do not pay without advertising revenue, a newspaper may well think twice before it adopts any policy which is likely to reduce advertisers' demand for its space' (Royal Commission 1949: 143). Finding proof in this area is almost impossible, but going purely on intuition and anecdotal evidence, it seems to me that things have worsened since the 1949 Royal Commission and that editors and proprietors are now much more likely to allow pressure from advertisers, either real or anticipated, to influence editorial decisions. I can certainly recall a case that happened to me. Writing an advertising feature about a chain of shops, I was rung by one of their managers asking to read the copy. I refused and was told that if I didn't read it to them, they would pull their advertisements in the paper. I refused again and reported the incident to my editor who, to his credit, supported my stand. The advertisements were not used, but I am always glad it was the editor who had to face a fuming advertising department and not me.

Sometimes, of course, reverse influence is the case. A paper may want to show an advertiser (or a linked business) in a good light. *The Sun*, for instance, so regularly puffs BSkyB, its sister satellite TV station, that *Private Eye* started a special column to mock better (or should that be worse?) examples.

Conflicts of interest

Just how impartial should journalists be in their personal lives? This is a subject that is not often talked about among journalists. It tends to be accepted automatically, for instance, that although a journalist may belong to a political party, he or she will write fairly about a range of political issues.

Personal lives

Many people believe that journalists should be impartial (see Chapter 3). At its most extreme, this view proposes that journalists should not have any personal political views, that they should be aloof from society and act as pure observers. However, journalists do need to be concerned about the society on which they are reporting and commenting. If they are not concerned about it, not involved in it, then they will probably be very poor journalists. Journalism is about people and journalists should be gregarious, and interested in the people and the issues on which they are reporting. This means that many reporters have political ideals and are politically active (though many have also seen far too many politicians to be anything other than cynical about politicians and politics). Furthermore, some journalists have other outside interests and are involved in various clubs and societies, although others find their hours of work militate against joining such groups. Because of this, journalists, more than many professional groups, enjoy each other's company.

In order to keep their personal and social lives clear of professional conflicts of interest, it is important that a journalist should inform the news desk if any story on which he or she is working is likely to produce such a conflict. Having said that, most journalists should be professional enough to avoid the obvious traps. If, for instance, a Labour-supporting journalist cannot interview a Conservative MP and produce a fair and balanced piece, then maybe that journalist should reconsider his or her career. That is not to say that the piece would be necessarily completely impartial. There are bound to be issues on which the Conservative record was not perfect and these should be picked up by any journalist, no matter what his or her political views. Indeed, it is often more difficult for journalists to be certain they have left their personal views on hold if they are supporters of the person being interviewed, rather than generally disagreeing with the interviewee. There is the constant fear that one is being too soft, not going for the main issue.

Some personal links are, however, more difficult to deal with. For example, it would not be easy for a journalist to investigate a company whose environmental record is poor if his or her partner worked for the company. Furthermore, if the partner's job was potentially at risk, the investigation might well become too stressful. In a case like this the journalist should tell the news editor the problem and the news editor should then assign another reporter to the job.

Another area of concern would be when a journalist hits a problem and abuses his or her position to get special treatment. For instance, say you received poor service or a poor quality of goods while shopping. It might well be an abuse of position to produce a story or to threaten to produce a story about the incident. On the other hand, it may well be that you are confident that your experience mimics that of others and you can use the experiences of others to publicise the story to get justice for all. To flash your press card to get a better table at a restaurant would probably be an abuse, but to write a story about a botched package holiday when dozens of you had all been equally affected would be to just confirm you were simply in the right place at the right time to get a story.

Other conflicts of interest, apart from advertising and the misuse of information, can arise, particularly for broadcasting journalists where the need to be impartial is so important. Promotional activities, advertising and political activity can all be hurdles for the journalist, especially those in broadcasting. The NUJ Code of Conduct prevents journalists from endorsing material in advertising unless they are advertising the publication for which they work. The BBC also has much to say about advertising and promotional activity. It tells its staff that all such work is unacceptable when it might compromise public trust in the integrity of programmes. It might be possible for a journalist to support a worthy cause, but to support a commercial organisation would be putting impartiality at risk. The same applies to political parties. The BBC is also concerned about its staff training people on how best to use the media to promote themselves or their organisations, and this is also proscribed, presumably for fear of seeming to offer an unfair advantage.

Personal blogs and social networking

Another issue that is starting to become a problem for journalists is personal blogs or social network pages. Facebook pages are often seen as a private space, but it needs to be remembered they are in fact public spaces. They are more analogous to a group of friends in a pub. As the drinks flow, you are likely to become increasingly indiscreet, but it matters little as no one is likely to go to the effort of eavesdropping. However, they could and that could lead to embarrassment. The same is true of Facebook. People can easily eavesdrop and so a journalist should be cautious about what is published as it could affect his or her professional standing.

The same is true of a blog. While we are all fully aware that blogs are definitely public spaces, where we can take the opportunity to broadcast to the public, we should also be aware that there is a difference in our approach. The point of the blog is usually to be more opinionated than is normal in a mainstream news outlet. Our comments may well affect our dealings with the public, who normally read our output, and with our contacts. We can no longer claim impartiality if we have made it clear on our blog that we have definitive views. Some bloggers are seeking the possibility of some sort of kitemark and a code of standards. Others find the whole idea of such an approach to be repugnant. I suspect that the difference is marked by whether the blogger sees him or herself as a blogger or as a journalist who blogs. Again it adds to the difficulty of separating our personal and professional personas.

Safety of others

Although we have a moral obligation to ensure our own safety, we probably have an even greater obligation to be concerned about the safety of others. Keeping the identity of some sources confidential is a clear example of this as we might put them at risk if we said who they were.

However, we also need to be constantly aware that we might be endangering others, whether contacts, witnesses or co-workers. It is important to give full consideration of the likely affect our news-gathering activities might have on those with whom we have to work and who are most likely to be placed in the front line. But there may also be consequences for others that we could and should have considered before the story was published or broadcast.

Guidelines

The PCC issues guidelines on topical issues from time to time as did the Press Council before it. The old Press Council's reports on the coverage of major events such as the Strangeways riot (PC Booklet No. 8, January 1991) drew the media's attention to important lessons. It is a shame that the PCC does not carry out such full-scale enquiries.

The PCC guidelines (which are available at http://www.pcc.org.uk/advice/editorials-detail. html?article=NTc4Nw==) cover issues such as:

Editorial cooperation: this concerns an editor's obligation to deal with complaints promptly and make complainants aware of the existence of the PCC.

Lottery guidance note: This advises editors on how to handle lottery winners who have opted for anonymity.

Data Protection Act, journalism and the PCC Code: This gives guidance on the Data Protection Act and its application to journalism.

On the reporting of people accused of crime: This gives guidance on the area of presumption of innocence as well as advice on dealing with the relatives of those involved in criminal activity.

Refugees and asylum seekers: Advises on the terminology and approach to be taken to writing about asylum seekers and immigration.

The judiciary and harassment: This reminds editors that convention does not allow judges to comment on cases and that an approach for comment could be considered harassment.

Financial journalism best practice note 2005: This advises on best practice with regard to financial journalism and a journalist's duty not to benefit from prior knowledge.

On the reporting of cases involving paedophiles: This is the PCC's advice following the *News of the World*'s high-profile campaign against paedophiles.

Prince William and privacy: This advice was given in a speech by Lord Wakeham as Prince William reached 18 and was intending to go to university.

Reporting of international sporting events: A reminder to editors not to encourage supporters of national teams to behave in a violent manner at international sporting events.

Court reporting: This offers guidance on the three types of complaint the PCC regularly receives about court reports.

Patients detained in hospital under the Mental Health Act 1983: A detailed reminder about the terminology that should be used about patients held in hospital under the Mental Health Act 1983.

Briefing note on the reporting of suicide: This gives guidance on the coverage of suicides including advice on graphic images, the cumulative effect of repeated media inquiries and the glorification of suicide.

Paying parents for material about their children: The Alfie Patten case, where a 13-year-old boy claimed to be the father of a child only to find after publication that he was not, led to new guidance in that area.

The PCC also now issues *The Editor's Codebook*, a book of advice on issues drawn from the PCC's experience.

The NUJ also puts out guidelines on various issues from time to time. In 1984, in cooperation with the Health Education Council, they issued guidelines about HIV and AIDS, although this did not appear to affect the messages put across in much of the press coverage which represented AIDS and HIV as a 'gay plague' visited upon those who deserved it (Wellings and Field 1996: 251). Other guidelines include those on sexist language, racist reporting, reporting on disabled people and mental health (see Appendices). The BBC allows access to its guidelines and also to its College of Journalism (http://www.bbc.co.uk/journalism/) with a wealth of guidance material.

Chapter 13

Regulation

This chapter opens the second section of the book, moving from ethics to regulation.

- It identifies the purpose of regulation and accountability

- Identifies basic regulatory systems

- Explains the difference between restraints and constraints

Regulation is an inevitable part of ensuring standards in everyday modern life. Without regulation of the society with which we come into contact on a regular basis, life would become more dangerous and more uncomfortable. Regulation and its associated agents of enforcement ensure that our after-work pint is a full measure of un-watered beer, our purchase of petrol to take us home is of specific quality and a full litre and that the food we eat when we get home is relatively safe and free from excessive quantities of dangerous bacteria.

Many people over the years have condemned the ethical standards of newspaper journalism in the UK, claiming that newspapers are intrusive and often inaccurate, or worse. Only recently, the then Home Secretary, Charles Clarke, called for statutory regulation of the press:

> He urged a 'stronger regime' of press regulation and said: 'My own view is that the code of conduct operated through the Press Complaints Commission ought to be put on a statutory basis. We ought to move towards a regulated regime for the media, where the media regulates it, not the state, but the decisions are actually enforced.'
>
> (Smith 2006a: 1)

The media cannot be exempt from the need for regulation to ensure acceptable standards and so any debate about media regulation concerns the amount of regulation and how it should be enforced.

There are a number of issues to be considered by media regulation. First are the social and economic issues. Society needs to decide what controls, if any, it should place on the ownership of newspapers or broadcast stations. It also needs to consider whether there are any social limitations and how these should be enforced. Then the concept of content regulation needs to be considered. Should newspapers and broadcast stations have their content controlled or limited in some way?

Traditionally newspapers and broadcasting have always been treated differently in the UK. A limited amount of bandwidth on the transmission spectrums has always ensured a need for someone to choose who will be allocated the different channels. If selection is taking place, then some sort of criteria are required and this might as well be along the lines of who society thinks will best run a broadcast. The concept of only allowing broadcast stations into the hands of 'a fit and proper person' has grown up over the years and become enshrined in the various broadcasting Acts up to and including the Broadcasting Act 1996.

Newspapers, on the other hand, were not so limited. In theory, anyone could set up a newspaper and attempt to sell it. The only restriction is the amount of money required to launch a paper. Things are changing now, of course; with far more bandwidths available on the digital networks, not to mention streaming on internet broadband, scores of channels are springing up and it is probably now easier in real terms to launch a new TV channel than it is to launch a new national newspaper.

The move towards digital broadcasting and the technological moves towards convergence have made regulation of media an important debate around the world and the UK is no exception. Terrestrial broadcasting will soon become digital-only for the whole of the UK with large areas already switched over in a process due to finish in 2012.

The internet is another fast-developing medium and about 70 per cent of homes in the UK (18.31 million) have internet access, 90 per cent of them connected by broadband according to the Office of National Statistics in 2009. This is a number that is clearly set to grow as the statistics show that more young people use it than older people and the trend over the past few years has been for consistent growth.

Convergence of the internet and traditional television will lead to a blurring of understanding about which is which, with consumers happily downloading movies, music and television programmes from the internet and playing them as they now do with transmitted TV programmes.

This expansion means that TV will no longer be provided by a limited number of broadcasters using a scarce resource. Server-based technology, combined with hugely improved broadband bandwidth will mean that soon anyone can set up as a broadcaster, transmitting programmes from their server to anyone who cares to link up. The BBC and commercial channels already offer the chance to see or hear programmes that were missed, or to view the next episode before it is transmitted. All of this is leading inevitably to a relaxation of regulation rather than risk the kind of revolution that brought pirate radio to the UK in the 1960s.

However, although the social and economic control of franchise holders may be less important than before, it is unlikely that anyone will want a free-for-all when it comes to content, and some element of regulation is bound to continue.

The other major debate surrounding regulation concerns ownership and funding. Media can be publicly owned and funded from the public purse or privately owned and funded either by advertising, subscription or by pay-per-view. The first two methods of payment can fit a public service broadcasting model, where the funding is not dependent directly on the viewer. The programme is transmitted and can be received regardless of whether the viewer wants the programme or even turns on their set to receive it.

Public service broadcasting is an important principle that needs to be understood in the regulation debate. PSB has a long tradition in many countries, including the UK, allowing viewers to see programmes that inform, educate and entertain without having to decide whether to pay for that particular service at the point of delivery. The debate hinges around the purpose of broadcasting and media. Do we make programmes to acquire money, or acquire money in order to make programmes? Commercial broadcasters are there to make money to pay to shareholders as dividends in the same way that newspapers do. This means they must maximise audiences, either to maximise fees or subscriptions or to provide advertisers with the largest possible audience of suitable people, for which the advertisers will then pay; the bigger the potential audience, the more the advertisers will pay to reach it.

Public service broadcasting, though, should not be so directly concerned with large audiences. It has long been the view of many that broadcasting that is aimed solely at money-making will reduce the range and quality of broadcasting on offer. Programmes that are cheap to make but attract a relatively large audience will become the programmes of choice for commercial channels.

PSB has to fulfil eight principles. The first of these is that its output should be universally available. This requires a good distribution network to ensure that all citizens are able to receive programmes regardless of the geography or financial status. It also means there should be no payment on consumption. The cost should be carried in some other way, through taxation, perhaps, a licence system or some other method that might allow for those who cannot afford to pay to be provided with the service free or at reduced cost.

The second principle is universal appeal. The audience needs to be thought of as citizens, not as consumers. This is not a market group being drawn together to be sold products that are identified as being of particular interest to them. These audiences are citizens who should be informed, educated and entertained. To give a stark, but entirely random example: on the day this was written, peak-time evening viewing had BBC 1 showing *Masterchef*; BBC 2 was showing *Who Needs Fathers?* an examination of the experiences of parents in the family courts and Channel 4 was showing *Embarrassing Bodies: Charlotte's Story*, a one-off special of the medical series that attempts to educate about health in a populist way. On the commercial channels, Channel 3 was broadcasting football: Manchester United v Bayern Munich, while Channel 5 was showing *NCIS*, a crime drama series. The PSB offerings are educational and universal, but perhaps not a hugely popular choice. The football and the crime drama are both aimed at maximising the audience during peak time in order to provide a good platform for advertisers. Universal television needs to appeal to a lot of people a lot of the time, but has to understand that sometimes it must produce programmes that will only appeal to a minority. It should not always be aiming to attract big audiences. This is a difficult area with many critics of PSB claiming that it should not be running any programmes that are very popular. If programmes are popular, then surely people will pay for them. However, these critics then continue: if PSB is only putting out programmes for minorities, why is everyone having to fund the system?

The third principle of PSB is that minorities should be catered for. PSB should allow a nation to speak to itself. This includes minority groups and working in minority languages such as Welsh or Asian languages. Television should be educating and explaining the modern condition, and so serving the public sphere is the fourth principle. The commitment to educating the public is also an important part of PSB, making up the fifth principle. An important element of PSB is that it should be distant from all vested interests (the sixth principle). Government, big business, campaigning groups and NGOs should all be listened to and their views transmitted to the viewer, but they should not be in control of the broadcaster.

The seventh principle is that PSB should be structured to ensure that the competition is for good programmes, not for audiences. PSB should be providing good programmes that draw big audiences because those people want to watch something worthwhile; the aim should not be to attract as many viewers as possible by only broadcasting populist themes. For instance, the *Big Brother* programmes attract big audiences, but no one would call them worthy. However, it is possible to have worthy dramas that are so good that they pull big audiences. Finally the role of broadcasting should be to liberate the programme maker, not to restrict them to doing things that are known to be popular and therefore to make money.

The BBC has provided PSB in the UK since TV first started in the 1930s. It has a good international reputation and by and large produces high-quality TV. However, many critics believe that programmes should only be funded by people making direct choices about what they want to watch. They should be able to view what they want, and pay for it, rather than watch what is good for them and is paid from the public purse, by their licence fee.

The BBC's Royal Charter, which allows it to transmit, was renewed in 2006 and is due to run until 2016 and there has been a long debate about its future and the future of broadcasting in a digital age. The coalition government has said it will maintain the independence of the BBC.

Accountability systems

Regulation involves every aspect of controlling the media including:

Technical: limiting access to airwaves, distribution and so on;
Economic: controlling ownership; ensuring access to the market; ensuring plurality, profitability.
Political: controlling content for political and social reasons; protecting citizens from intrusion, harm and offence.

My major concern in this book, though, is the regulation of content, particularly with regards to journalism. This means regulating the content of programmes and publications. There are a number of accountability systems that assist in regulating. Bertrand identifies scores of different MAS – media accountability systems – covering everything from press councils to readers' letters to journalism courses and professional bodies. All of these regulate the media by restraining or constraining its right to free expression and they do it in different ways to different effect for different purposes.

Restraints and constraints

As I have already explained in earlier chapters, the media's right to free expression needs to be curtailed in certain circumstances in order to protect the rights and sensibilities of others. This may mean attempting to prevent the media behaving irresponsibly or it may simply mean trying to ensure that we have a media that behaves in the way that the majority of people think is appropriate. This presumably means it should behave in line with general views on human rights, using its right to freely express itself responsibly, to carry information to its consumers, while ensuring no undue damage to the human rights of those it writes about or overwhelming offence to those for whom it is writing or broadcasting.

Claude-Jean Bertrand (2001) identifies four reasons for the need to regulate journalism in order to ensure it behaves responsibly:

- commercialisation;
- concentration of ownership;
- decline of news; and
- silence about inconvenient stories.

Some of these inevitably overlap. Ownership is often concentrated because it operates in a commercial marketplace, so not only is the journalism becoming more commercialised in order to maximise profit, but also ownership becomes concentrated as a way of ensuring the major players are making a profit because there is little competition. If there are only a handful of newspaper owners, as is the case in the UK and many other countries, again it can hardly be surprising if those outlets tend to concentrate on the same type of stories – ones they are confident will maximise audience, and are in the interests of the owners of the media outlets. This leads to a decline in news, as all providers play it safe, working to a news agenda they know will attract the audience, and silence news that is inconvenient because it plays to a social or political agenda that is inconvenient to the corporate ownership of the media.

Restraints

Restraints are limitations placed on the media from external sources – usually the law. Restraints can include civil and criminal law and cover a wide range of issues such as protection of reputation, guaranteeing a fair trial, obscenity, matters involving specially vulnerable groups, such as children or the victims of sexual assaults, and security matters. In all these cases there are legal restrictions that limit what journalists may write. These restrictions are part of the criminal law, so a journalist breaching the law could find him or herself before the courts, charged with a serious offence. There are also civil offences, matters which are considered torts (wrongs) by the courts for which the complainant can seek redress. Normally this will be financial redress with the journalist or his/her employer forced to make a payment, often quite substantial, in addition to any legal fees involved, but it can also involve the court ordering an injunction, an order to prevent a paper from publishing a certain story. This would cover such matters as protecting intellectual property (copyright), protection of reputation, invasion of privacy or breach of confidence.

Constraints

Constraints are restrictions in which we play a role. These are often self-restrictions, or consensual restrictions. This involves the industry, or parts of it, looking at how it goes about its business; how it can ensure that it behaves responsibly and fairly, offering its audience what they need, to standards that they can understand and support.

Constraints will include self-regulatory bodies, professional associations, in-company schemes and codes of conduct.

Law versus ethics

There is a close relationship between the law and ethics as both are attempting to restrain or constrain the media to behave responsibly, but the purpose of the law is always to set the limits of behaviour, to identify those things we must do (or, more often, must not do). Ethics set out those things that we ought to do or not do. Think of a hen's egg – the hard outer shell represents the law – an easy-to-detect boundary that marks the limits of responsibility. But the inner boundary between the white and the yolk is a much softer boundary, and although it is obliged to stay within the hard shell of the law, it can easily be pushed in one direction or another, depending upon our desire and beliefs.

The law has a more powerful effect on people than a code of conduct. A person's own moral code may supersede the law every time, but a professional code can only be for guidance. This means that when there are conflicts between the law and professional practice, the law will almost always take precedence.

However, there can be a major warping effect introduced by laws affecting the media. There are a number of elements in UK law that override potential clauses in a code of conduct, clauses which are often included in codes used in other countries. Particular examples in the UK are protection of personal honour and presumption of innocence, although there are other areas where the law cuts across codes of practice to their detriment. Because this hard shell of the law cuts close to the softer yolk/white boundary, it is often difficult to remember that that softer boundary exists, and journalists often concentrate only on the hard shell of the law and how to get around it without breaking it, and forget they also need to consider the ethical elements of what they ought to do.

Media regulation in the UK, for instance, is strong in the area of presumption of innocence. The British have traditionally believed in fair trials and have gone to some lengths to protect the fairness and impartiality of the justice system. This is particularly concerned with protecting the jury and being scrupulous about giving the accused a fair trial. The right to be presumed innocent is protected by law, preventing a journalist from talking about a case after an arrest has been made until the trial starts. Because it is so firmly protected, and the British journalist generally believes in the maxim innocent until proven guilty, he or she does not think of it as an ethical issue, only a legal one. After arrest and charge, the accused is protected by various Acts of Parliament that make it an offence for the media to publish anything other than legally limited facts about the accused and the alleged crime. Before arrest (and indeed after the verdict) the accused has some protection under the libel laws.

The protection of personal honour is also something the British feel strongly about. No one likes the idea of his or her reputation being wrongly impugned (as Case study 13.1 illustrates). The laws of defamation seek to ensure legal redress for those so accused. Unfortunately, this means that any moral view on protection of personal honour has been subsumed by the legal requirement.

The same is true about reporting on minors. This is not too surprising if British society believes, as it seems to do if the law is any guide, that children are not fully responsible for their actions until the age of 18. They continue going through a learning process which means that they are not always fully responsible for their actions and that their behaviour and relationship with society are redeemable. Although in discussion many journalists might accept this argument, that does not mean they automatically consider not naming the child when faced with a story about children.

To give an example of a PCC adjudication, the *Reading Evening Post* named an 11-year-old child who had been admitted to hospital with meningitis:

while the Commission had sympathy with the newspaper's wish to keep its readers properly informed, it nevertheless considered that in the light of the action taken by the school, publication of the boy's name was not essential for the protection of public health. In reaching its conclusion the Commission took into account that the school was named and that concerned parents unconnected with the school could have made further enquiries. The complaint is therefore upheld, but in view of the sensitive handling of the matter, the Commission decide on this occasion not to censure the paper.

(PCC, Report No. 37, 1997: 26)

It is unlikely that this was a deliberate attempt on behalf of the *Reading Evening Post* to stretch the limits of the PCC Code. It was trying to keep readers informed and the idea that the child should not have been named simply did not occur to anyone. Naming youngsters is not an issue of major ethical debate for most UK journalists although there is clear evidence that the strong line the PCC has taken over the coverage of children has changed the approach of many newspapers in this area (see Frost, 2004). While most journalists accept the sense in the law preventing identification, they see it as a restrictive area of law to be worked around, not as the first step in an ethical tussle which pits the rights of young people against the right of the public to be informed.

Since the cost of legal action can scare publishers from telling the damaging truth it has until recently meant they are more likely to write about the less rich, secure in the knowledge that they could not afford to sue. However, lawyers now increasingly take cases on a conditional fee agreement (CFA) (also called 'no win, no fee'), where the solicitor takes the case on the basis that the client need only pay a fee if the case is won. This means that the client would not have to pay his or her lawyers if the case is lost and the lawyers will claim their fee for winning from the defendant should their client win. This often means fees are punitively high in order to cover the additional risk the lawyer takes in pursuing the case. Many people believe this is having a chilling effect on newspapers, making them far less likely to publish stories that could put them at risk of a law suit. This has become such a problem recently that the UK Parliament's Culture, Media and Sport Select Committee said in its 2010 report *Press Standards, Privacy and Libel* that since the vast majority of CFA cases are won, they saw: 'no justification for lawyers to continue to demand 100% success fees which are chargeable to the losing party. We recommend that the recovery of success fees from the losing party should be limited to no more than 10%' (House of Commons 2010: Vol. 1: 7). Following this, the government attempted to introduce a statutory instrument in April 2010 limiting the amount lawyers could claim to 10 per cent, but a Labour rebellion by four MPs on the Delegated Legislation Committee in the Commons meant the law was not introduced before the 2010 general election.

Possibly because of this extra cost burden, more and more tabloid newspapers are invading the privacy of ordinary citizens who do not have the money or inclination to fight privacy actions, rather than celebrities who do. The *Star* (12 February 1996) told the story of a 'do-gooder' who ran off with the wife of his rugby coach friend. The story was based entirely on the comments of a cuckolded and presumably embittered and vengeful husband whose wife of twenty-one years had ended her marriage to be with her lover, who had also left his wife. The abandoned wife did not want to be involved and told the *Star* she did not wish to comment. There were no quotes from the other parties. What possible public interest could there be in this story? Yet the *Star* ran it across two pages. All the parties involved had their names used, their privacy invaded and their personal honour dragged through the mud. There was nothing defamatory published, provided it was true, but it was an unnecessary and unsavoury report.

Case study 13.1 Libel suits and the press

For most British editors, it is not a debate about the morality of exposing someone's private doings that is the major deciding factor about whether to publish, but whether the person is likely to sue. The debate has all too often become 'will they sue?' not 'are we right, and can we prove it?' As the following examples show, things do not always work out for those seeking to protect their reputation by suing the media, and there have been some very expensive failed actions by the those in the public eye.

Gillian Taylforth, an actress in the BBC soap opera *EastEnders*, sued *The Sun* newspaper in 1994 after it repeated a police allegation that she and her boyfriend had committed an indecent act in a Range Rover on a slip road off the A1 in June 1992. She lost in the High Court and was ordered to pay £500,000 costs.

Sonia Sutcliffe, the wife of Yorkshire Ripper Peter Sutcliffe, lost an action against the *News of the World* at a cost of £200,000, and Janie Allen, a South African journalist, lost an action against Channel 4 at a reputed cost of £300,000. These examples have shown newspapers measuring a potential victim's purse rather than their reputation.

The spectacular collapse of the then MP Neil Hamilton's action against *The Guardian* was blamed by him on the exorbitant cost of such actions, although Alan Rusbridger, *The Guardian*'s editor, said that research carried out as part of the paper's defence showed its original allegations were 'just the tip of the iceberg'. He added: 'This research, together with documents which were disclosed to us by 10 Downing Street as part of the legal process, made it apparent that [Mr Hamilton and Mr Greer] didn't have a leg to stand on' (*Electronic Telegraph*, 'Tory drops libel fight over sleaze', 1 October 1996). *The Guardian* went on to publish further and far more detailed allegations in the days following the collapse of the case. Hamilton continued to protest his innocence but lost his parliamentary seat in the 1997 general election to the independent candidate Martin Bell, a former BBC journalist standing on an anti-corruption ticket.

Another Tory MP, Jonathan Aitken, the former Cabinet minister, faced legal costs of £2 million after abandoning his action against *The Guardian* and Granada TV. *The Guardian* produced documents which allegedly showed he lied under oath over details of a weekend spent at the Ritz Hotel in Paris. He agreed to pay 80 per cent of the defendants' costs. The *Daily Telegraph* reported:

No reason was given for his decision to abandon the action.

Afterwards, Alan Rusbridger, editor of *The Guardian*, said: 'For three years he has lied to newspapers, lied to the Cabinet Secretary, lied to the Prime Minister and lied to his colleagues. Now he has made his fatal mistake by lying on oath to the High Court.'
(*Electronic Telegraph*: 'Aitken faces £2m bill in libel defeat', 21 June 1997).

Aitken and his daughter were afterwards investigated by the police over allegations of perjury. He resigned from the Privy Council, was found guilty of perjury and was sentenced to a term of imprisonment.

Most recently, in 2009 Express Newspapers owner Richard Desmond sued author and journalist Tom Bower, claiming he was defamed in a biography of former *Telegraph* owner Conrad Black. Bower claimed Desmond ordered journalists at the *Sunday Express* to run stories critical of Black and then authorised an apology to be published. However, a jury rejected Desmond's claim by a majority verdict, leaving a legal bill for the trial believed to be £1.25 million.

What may be restrained?

The law can be used to restrain a number of issues involved in the business of the media. First is ownership. This can include selecting who may be an appropriate person to own a particular channel or newspaper. It could involve licensing or obliging the registration of newspapers or broadcast stations. This is a method that is used by many countries or governments as a way of limiting criticism from the media. Only media which is supportive of the government receives a licence or permission to broadcast or publish. For this reason, registration is not normally used as a control method in Western-style democracies. However, there has to be somebody to allocate frequencies to broadcasters and some method of deciding who gets them. In the UK at the moment, this is done by Ofcom, the Office of Communications, on the basis of competitive bids allowing the market to play an important part in selection alongside some other significant criteria.

The method of publication or broadcast can also be state controlled. For instance, if the only presses or broadcast equipment is stated owned, then there are automatic limits on who may print or broadcast.

The cost of distribution or production can also be controlled as a method of restraint. This could be through taxation – newspapers in the UK used to be obliged to attach a stamp duty, a small payment per newspaper that often significantly increased the cover price and made it more likely that people would not buy the paper. On the other hand, some Scandinavian newspapers have their production methods subsidised, while there is a state subsidy on newspaper distribution. Both methods ensure that there is a wider distribution of newspapers than would otherwise be the case, ensuring a wider participation in the democratic process by readers.

Moving on to the content of a newspaper or broadcast news bulletin, there can be control over what matters are investigated or reported and who can investigate them. It is also possible to license journalists so that only licensed practitioners can work for newspapers or broadcast stations. These journalists could then face a disciplinary hearing if they did not behave responsibly, and have their licence to practise removed. Governments can also limit what can be reported with specific statutes. These might cover anything from security matters to personal details. The UK has a number of laws preventing reporting in the areas of security, defence, inciting hatred and the presumption of innocence.

What may be constrained?

Not surprisingly exactly the same range of limitations or assistances can be achieved by constraints. This is particularly true in the area of responsible reporting where constraints such as codes of conduct have a major role to play in determining how reporters and other journalists should behave.

Accountability

Claude-Jean Bertrand identifies three types of media accountability systems – systems that can help the constraint process (Bertrand 2001). The first of these is *documents*. These can be anything from a written code of ethics to a letters page, a memo of guidance or a style book. The second type is *people*. This would include an ethics council or an ombudsman or a readers' editor. The third type is *processes*. This would include education, research or questionnaires.

There are now four main constraint or restraint organisations in the UK. The Press Complaints Commission is a self-regulatory body that regulates publications in the UK. The Office of

Communications, Ofcom, is a statutory regulatory body that regulates the broadcasting industry. It was set up under the Office of Communications Act 2002 to administer the Communications Act 2003. It licenses broadcasters and the telecommunications industries and monitors their performance.

The British Broadcasting Corporation, the BBC, is a Public Service Broadcaster run under a Royal Charter. It also regulates itself, although Ofcom has some responsibility for some of its actions.

The National Union of Journalists has a code of conduct and an Ethics Council charged with upholding it. The union has 40,000 members who are obliged to uphold that code of conduct.

Regulatory systems

There are a several different types of regulatory systems, each with its own characteristics of advantage and disadvantage.

Individual regulation

Individual regulation covers regulation by the individual or by a company or in-house scheme. This system could be run by a single person and would cover the kind of ethics that that person sees as important. Equally, it could be a company scheme. The Guardian Media Group for instance, has its own regulatory system, through its style book and its own press ombudsmen, one for the *Guardian* and one for the *Observer*. The BBC also has a detailed in-house regulatory system. Such a scheme can have quite strong internal policing and enforcement. A scheme run by an employer can have employment discipline to enforce compliance: breach the code, and you could be sacked. However, its public relations value is limited. An individual or a company can tell readers or viewers about their code and methods of policing it, but they may not be convinced. Nor is it that easy to discipline someone for a breach of the company's code. Standards also tend to be variable across the industry. One newspaper might have very high standards while another might have much lower. An individual system of regulation does not allow customers to understand what the industry standard is. Standards may also be arbitrary, picking up particular foibles from this editor or another. An individual system does not allow for significant debate about the required standards. Finally, there is no real appeal. If a journalist is accused of breaking the code or not behaving to the required standard, it may not be possible to appeal against the decision.

Self-regulatory authorities

A self-regulatory body is one that is set up by the industry to control standards in that industry. Such systems are often set up by an industry that is facing sustained criticism over its performance and that wants to convince customers and the general public at large that it is doing a good job to high standards. The self-regulatory body is funded by the industry itself in some way – often by a levy on those who become members. In the case of the Press Complaints Commission, the money is raised by the Press Standards Board of Finance and comes from the whole industry. A self-regulatory body is able to present itself as a way of protecting standards in the industry and so offers good public relations for the industry, helping to convince consumers that the industry is doing the best that it can to raise or maintain standards. It also often builds its enforcement programme around a code of conduct and this is good for allowing debate about standards and what should be in the code. This is a system that can work fairly well for some sections of the industry. The travel industry, for instance, has ABTA – the Travel Association. This Association represents travel agents and helps holidaymakers by 'working to high professional standards and offering choice, value and quality' (www.abta.com). Members of ABTA are obliged to adhere to the Association's code of conduct and can presumably be removed from membership if they fail to live up to the standards required. Since there are considerable advantages to membership, it is worth the agent adhering to the code for the benefits achieved for themselves and their customers.

However, when it comes to the media such a body has a limited ability to enforce regulation. Since the media industry requires that all publishers join the regulatory body, it has to set its standards to the lowest common denominator. A self-regulatory body that only took complaints about a limited number of papers would be largely pointless as newspapers would be unlikely to join if there was no real advantage to joining and some other publications were outside membership. The lowest common denominator of standard would apply because if a newspaper or magazine was continually criticised it might soon withdraw, again leaving the regulatory body with a serious credibility problem. The PCC could not operate if several of the country's major newspapers were not members, and adhered to different standards or espoused no standards at all. For this reason, enforcement can often be a problem. For a commercial group of professionals requiring regulation, such as plumbers, travel agents or double glazing firms, such a regulatory body can maintain high standards, since it is in the consumer's interests to be able to access a firm that is a member and so the authority can expel members without worrying about the effect that will have on the total industry. Such a scheme would not work in the media, however. If a body such as the Press Complaints Commission is to carry any weight, all publishers must be members. That means enforcement is limited because it is in the interests of such an authority to limit upheld complaints; punishments are mild as serious punishments would be difficult to enforce, and would likely lead companies to quit. Large fines, for instance, might not be paid, with the authority unable to enforce them. Closures or other strong penalties would equally be unenforceable. There is also nowhere to go to for appeal, either for the paper or for the complainant. Although there have been some court cases attempting to show that the PCC has not upheld its own code of conduct, none have yet forced a change in a PCC decision.

Statutory body

A statutory body is one that is defined by the government under legislation and is supported by legislation. This means that a government minister appoints the members of the authority and the authority has powers identified by statute. This gets over many of the disadvantages of the self-regulatory authority. There can be a varied range of penalties, including fines, or suspension from broadcast or publication. It is good for public credibility, as clearly there is a body, set up under law, whose role is to police the conduct of that industry. There can be a full ability to appeal such decisions to the High Court. However, there can be concerns about government interference. Again, were this any other industry, that would not be a huge problem. The financial sector has a number of statutory regulatory authorities and these are supposed to ensure that the world of banking, investments and insurance maintain constant high standards. One of the major rows over the credit crunch was whether there was sufficient such regulation and why it failed to protect consumers when things went wrong. However, in the media, the idea of government influence and ability to silence the media through a statutory body makes statutory regulation in this area much more controversial. Many people would be very concerned about having statutory control of newspapers and magazines. However, this does not seem so problematic in broadcasting, for some reason. The various regulatory authorities for broadcasting have always been statutory, without there being much concern about this.

The main broadcasting authority, Ofcom (the Office of Communications) was set up under the Office of Communications Act 2002 to enforce the Communications Act 2003. There had been a plan to make the Press Complaints Commission a statutory body. Sir David Calcutt, in his second report, concluded that this was the only way to deal with the press: 'I recommend that the government should now introduce a statutory regime' (1993: para 9, p. xii). He went on to describe in detail a tribunal composed of three judges which would have had the power to require the printing of adjudications and apologies, to impose fines and award costs. The Heritage Committee also recommended a statutory tribunal although theirs was much more like the PCC but with the backing of the courts.

The law

A statutory body is often a much better choice for a government than having a range of laws enforcing ethics. Laws covering all the elements of a journalistic code of conduct would be very difficult to word and enforce. There is also the point that the law says what we must not do – it sets limits – so often journalists would try to push those limits to see how far they could be extended. However, with ethics, we are advised what we ought to do and therefore journalists would be more guided than prevented. Having a regulatory body that attempts to offer guidance, rather than a law that merely sets the limits, should provide a better chance of raising standards within journalism. The law in the UK is used to set standards for protection of reputation, fair trials, presumption of innocence and discrimination. These are better adhered to at the limits, but it is in the grey areas where the law becomes useless that there needs to be more guidance for journalists. As has been explained, when societies become particularly concerned about an ethical issue, they often include the principle in their law. This has the advantage of short-circuiting any debate about the issue.

A statutory body is much more manageable. It would not be too difficult to persuade a public, which is often disgusted by the antics of the tabloid press, that this was just a way of giving the Press Complaints Commission teeth. The public is now used to the Press Complaints Commission and accepts that it has industry support. Despite the industry's claims about the 'horrors' of statutory bodies, it is very difficult to portray such bodies as unacceptable when self-regulatory bodies doing the same thing are claimed to be fine. The argument then seems to be that it is all right to have a controlling body only if it is run by the industry it is set up to control. Not making the body statutory would be a difficult case to make, particularly when broadcasters are already under the aegis of statutory bodies, begging the obvious question: what is wrong with statutory regulation for the press if it is all right for broadcasters?

A statutory body would have many of the advantages of the present system with the force of law to back up its decisions. Crucially, it would also offer journalists a right of appeal with a recourse to judicial review of the Commission's judgments.

Regulatory councils

Newspaper proprietors have made it clear they dislike, and even fear, the idea of a press regulated by law, and that any government considering it should be wary. What proprietors and editors are prepared to accept is some form of code of practice and an accompanying regulatory authority. There are three types of enforcing body for codes of conduct and ethical issues in newspapers and broadcasting that can be set up, each with their own unique advantages (see Exhibit 13.1).

Exhibit 13.1 Regulatory bodies and their powers

A voluntary regulatory body: This is usually set up by the industry to consider complaints. It may also be a lobbying body for the industry and have other functions such as training, standards and promotion. Such industry bodies have been formed in many countries, sometimes following pressure from the government. One of the first was Sweden. There is a wide variety of industry-appointed regulatory bodies. Some, such as Sweden's, are true cross-industry bodies with representatives of editors, journalists and proprietors. Some, such as Britain's PCC, are set up only by proprietors. The only power these bodies have is to ask newspapers or broadcasters to publish their adjudications so that newspapers would be obliged to publish any criticism within their columns. Many councils contain members of the public to balance the self-interest of the industry and to add a perspective that only interested but non-expert members of the public can bring.

Voluntary regulatory bodies with statutory powers: These councils are similar to voluntary regulatory bodies but have statutory authority to fine or punish transgressors in other ways. Bodies of this type exist in a few countries, for example India and Sweden, and it was proposed for Britain by the Heritage Select Committee in 1993. Neither the then Conservative government nor the later Labour administration wanted to move away from the present system of press self-regulation.

These bodies are still voluntary, although they may be funded by public money, and various schemes can be suggested to determine the constitution. The one suggested by the Heritage Committee required lay and professional members. The code of conduct in these circumstances has the support of law and some section of the judiciary is usually used as a court of appeal. Fines, or strict instructions about how and where in a publication the council's findings should be used, are standard punishments. The punishment element and right of appeal against a decision of the regulatory body by a journalist or publication adds a strength to this system that does not exist in the solely voluntary bodies.

Statutory regulatory bodies: These councils are constituted under statute and have legal obligations and powers, but are not part of the judiciary. They are funded by public money or by money collected for licences (as is Ofcom) or fines. The code of conduct in these circumstances is supported by statute and so there is a right of appeal. Fines, licence suspensions or withdrawals are often used to punish infractions of the code. The punishment element and right of appeal against a decision of the regulatory body by a journalist or publication adds a strength to this system that does not exist in the voluntary bodies.

A statutory tribunal: Such a body was recommended by Sir David Calcutt QC (Calcutt, 1993) in his review of press regulation. It would have statutory powers to investigate and punish. Such tribunals would have contained at least one judge and would have been closer to courts of law than the arbiters of professional morals that the voluntary or even statutory bodies can claim to be. Sir David Calcutt, in his 1993 review, found that the Press Complaints Commission was not working and wanted to set up a Press Complaints Tribunal. This would have had three members and would have heard complaints on an adversarial basis and been entitled to punish newspapers and magazines by instructing them how to present adjudications in the paper or magazine, or have the power to fine transgressors.

Ofcom is a body constituted under statute with powers to punish – either with fines or the withdrawal of the licence if necessary – broadcasting companies that break the rules. The BBC is awarded its charter under statute and has obligations for the standards of its broadcasts. The decisions of all these bodies can be challenged in the courts and they must all report annually on their activities to the Secretary of State for Culture, Media and Sport.

Working with different styles of media council

Media councils (as opposed to press or broadcasting councils) work in different ways. Those which are true cross-industry bodies tend to have codes of conduct that represent that broad church of views. Codes, such as those in Sweden, often contain more matters of concern about the gathering of news material while Britain's press code, drawn up by editors and publishers, is much more about what may be published. Only intense public pressure, particularly after the death of the Princess of Wales, has forced the Press Complaints Commission in Britain to include additional clauses covering news-gathering on private land and the use of long telephoto camera lenses. Before 1998 we would have to look to the National Union of Journalists' Code of Conduct to see clauses which emphasised the moral aspects of how stories are gathered, rather than worrying solely about whether they are published (see Appendix 2). The PCC's new code (PCC, 2010) contains much stronger clauses on harassment and privacy.

Often countries have separate bodies for dealing with press and broadcasting and this may even mean different codes. Britain, as we have seen, has press and broadcast regulatory bodies, one statutory and one voluntary. Sweden has one code upheld by both broadcasters and print journalists. This is partly, at least, because the code's historical roots lie in the development of print journalism, with any additional clauses required for broadcasting being added as necessary. Britain and many other European countries developed press and broadcasting councils at different times and for different reasons. This means that their codes of conduct are often different as well. It is certainly true that Britain's press code and broadcast code are both posited from the position of a publisher or editor, yet many of the really interesting ethical issues occur whether or not the material is published, as Case study 13.2 illustrates.

Enforcing ethical standards

Statutory enforcement of ethical standards

State control of ethical standards is usually enforced either by the law or a statutory regulatory body or a mixture of both. Regulation is either by a practitioners' body, such as the Ordine dei Giornalisti in Italy, which registers practitioners and can prevent people practising if they are found to be in breach of the code, or it is a statutory industry council made up of a mix of proprietors, editors, practitioners and lay people which is able to condemn bad practice and in some cases level a penalty against the offender. Usually this is a fine. Systems such as this operate in a number of Western European countries and elsewhere. South Africa, Australia and India all have press councils. As explained, nearly every culture finds it necessary to enforce some issue of press ethics by introducing legislation. Most Western-style democracies have developed a cultural ethic for journalists that covers in some way most or all of the issues of truth, privacy, harassment and fairness. In some cases the society concerned will enforce that ethic by legislation and it is one of the more interesting and revealing areas of study for those seeking difference in national cultures and identities.

Swedes and the Dutch, for instance, are generally seen as liberal and free-thinking and have very little legislative control of media ethics. Their codes of conduct are controlled by media councils. Yet their journalists stick to the codes of ethics more strongly than journalists do in Britain, and journalists in Sweden and Holland are often shocked by the lengths to which journalists in Britain will go to get a story.

In Britain we have a much more rigid approach to such things. 'There should be a law against it' is our first thought when something displeases us. The only trouble is that when we produce a law against something, we then spend much of our time complaining about excessive regulation and trying to find a way around it.

Case study 13.2 Journalists' v Publishers' codes

Codes have different purposes, depending on who decides them. Broadcast codes are different to publishers' codes which differ from journalists' codes. For example, I came across a case of a freelance photographer working in England who would dress as a paramedic to attend the scenes of accidents to allow him closer access to the victim. In one incident, an 11-year-old boy was dragged from a canal and resuscitated. He had been dried, as he was suffering from hypothermia. The photographer splashed him with water again in order to get a more 'dramatic' picture. This sort of behaviour is reprehensible and would be accepted by very few people, journalists and public alike. However, there is no way to censure it. The Press Complaints Commission cannot handle it – it can only censure the newspaper responsible for publication and in this case there isn't one as the photographer was freelance. Even if there were a newspaper involved, it is very possible that it would not be aware of, or condone, this person's practice. If the photographer were a member of the NUJ, then that might accept a complaint.

Voice or video recordings made in secret are subject to the same ethical problems. Once a recording has been made, it is too late to decide whether it was ethical to make the recording: we can only debate whether it should have been broadcast or published as a transcript. Does this matter in practice? Can one imagine circumstances when the recording is unethical but the broadcasting or publication is not? Imagine a tape recording of a telephone call by a Cabinet minister, which exposed him as corrupt. Invading the minister's privacy by listening to the call is difficult to justify, but publishing a story that the minister is corrupt, backed by transcripts of phone calls, is an entirely different matter. The journalist could then justify the invasion of privacy as being in the public interest. Of course in the broadcast area, secret recording is something the Broadcasting Standards Commission is specifically charged to consider. Ofcom considers complaints about intrusion at both the reporting and broadcast stage.

Many people still blame the paparazzi for the death of the Princess of Wales. Had they not been following her car in order to take pictures, some say, the accident might not have happened. Leaving aside the what-ifs, there is certainly little question that following the crash, a number of photographers (approximately ten although witnesses differ in their accounts) were at the scene taking pictures before the ambulance and police arrived. This was generally considered so shocking that no British publication or broadcast used any of the many pictures that must have been taken of the crash site and the rescue. Yet pictures and videos of this sort are commonly used in news reports, from the assassination of President Kennedy to numerous train and plane crashes here and abroad. Even the

▶

many documentaries that have since been broadcast, speculating on the cause of the car accident, have not been prepared to risk attack by using photographs of the scene.

Few examples show as starkly the difference in ethical approach of the journalist and the public. Few journalists (I have not spoken to one) would find it acceptable for a photographer at the scene of such an incident to report to their news desk that they had not bothered to take pictures because they did not think it was quite right. The photographer's job is to take pictures of news events and that is what he or she should do. That does not mean that common humanity goes out of the window. Of course, the ever-present mobile phones should have been used to call an ambulance and of course basic first aid or rescue should have been carried out to the best of the photographer's ability. But taking photographs only takes a short time.

Further reading and support material

There are a number of books about regulation that are worth reading and these include: Claude-Jean Bertrand (2001) *M*A*S* (Transaction Publishers, New Brunswick) and Claude-Jean Bertrand (2003) *An Arsenal for Democracy* (Hampton Press Inc., Cresskill, NJ).

Mediawise, a charity, carries details of a lot of media codes from around the world on its website, www.mediawise.org.uk.

Chapter 14

History of print regulation

This chapter examines the history and development of regulation in print journalism and covers:

■ The development of regulatory concerns through the early part of the twentieth century

■ The founding and development of the Press Council (PC)

■ Its replacement by the Press Complaints Commission (PCC)

Press regulation first became an issue abroad. Sweden has had a press council from the beginning of the twentieth century: 'The Publicists Club [of Sweden], which was formed in 1874 with journalists, newspaper editors and other publishers as its members, had, on a number of occasions in the beginning of the 1900s, served as a self-appointed tribunal to hear complaints against newspapers' (Nordlund 1991: 1). Even before this, the Swedes had been adjudicating on complaints in an informal way. It also developed the first journalistic code in 1900, although this was not widely adopted. The French were next, with the Syndicat National des Journalistes (the French trade union) publishing a charter of conduct in 1918 (PC 1990: 285). Other European countries had also considered the subject and some had rudimentary laws by the middle of the 1800s. In the USA, journalism college teachers were discussing ethics and the need for journalists to set their own standards at least as early as 1913 (Bleyer 1913: 357).

In the UK, an indication of journalistic thinking on ethics around this time could be found in a small handbook for journalists, published in 1873 (possibly the first UK book designed to teach journalism), which included a chapter about 'Reporting Etiquette'. This identified an early need to improve the behaviour of journalists (Reed 1876). It is interesting to note that this chapter was only inserted in the second edition and nothing like it was in the first edition published ten years previously.

This etiquette was more about what the NUJ today describes in its rule book as 'Membership responsibilities' (NUJ, 2009) than about professional ethics. The book's main concerns were about the job (salaries, qualifications and working practices), libel, the duties of the reporter and note-taking (shorthand, by which it set great store, and transcribing the notes). The author was concerned about taking an accurate note and transcribing that accurately for publication, but he did not mention other ethical issues. Discussing reporting meetings, for instance, he says: 'In taking notes of a meeting, care should be taken to distinguish the speakers with accuracy' (Reed, 1876: 57). This also applies to speakers' names which, Reed advised, require special care (ibid.: 58).

He also advised that a reporter should not misrepresent a view antithetical to those of his paper:

Few papers report both sides at equal length and with absolute impartiality; and the reporter must be in a measure guided by the known sympathies of his journal, in selecting the speakers to be most fully reported.

(ibid.: 59)

However, Reed had nothing to say about the ethics of reporting methods or about intrusion into privacy. Another early writer about the craft of journalism also had little to say about such issues as intrusion, straightforward means of reporting, or harassment. Pendleton warned of the dangers of inaccuracy with examples of 'mirth-provoking errors' such as: 'Helen of Troy' described as 'Ellen of Troy', and the orator who quoted 'O come, thou goddess fair and free. In heaven yclept Euphrosyne', only to find it transcribed in press as 'O come, thou goddess fair and free; in heaven she crept and froze her knee' (Pendleton 1890: 173–4). Again, nothing was said about such issues as intrusion, or straightforward means of reporting. This is not because the types of stories covered are in some way more ethical in themselves. Pendleton lists an average day's news diary with such stories as: Steam tram accident at Bradford; Wife murder; Colliery explosion; Lord Salisbury in Nottingham; Double execution at Armley; and a Mill fire (Pendleton 1890: 154).

It might be light on celebrity compared to today but there are plenty of sensational stories and sensationalism in pursuit of readership, and therefore profits, is a technique as old as mass readership. Ever since universal education opened the media up to a mass audience, the media has been pursuing readers. Talk of golden ages of the press when everything was done by the book and ethics were the first consideration is just that – talk. As Raymond Snoddy says in *The Good*, *the Bad and the Unacceptable* (1993: 19): 'When you get down to the fundamentals of questionable journalism – sex, violence, sensationalism, bias, inaccuracy and forgery – it is remarkable how little has changed.' He illustrates this with a story taken from the first issue of the *News of the World* in 1843, telling of the trial of Edward Morse, a chemist who drugged a young girl before violating her and dumping her in a canal. Not that the *News of the World* was the first newspaper to realise that sex and violence sell newspapers. Throughout the eighteenth and nineteenth centuries, the press suffered many of the same complaints to which it is prey today. Yet as more and more people learned to read, newspapers became more and more popular.

Similar claims to falling standards and golden ages had been identified in the 1930s. The NUJ was particularly concerned about the issue of the responsibility of press freedom. Plans to beat what were perceived as falling standards included a law to prevent multi-ownership; a well-organised workforce; a well-paid workforce and a conscience clause, allowing journalists to make ethical decisions about their work without fear of losing their job (campaigns which the union continues to pursue to this day) (Mansfield 1935).

Large newspaper groups or the 'gramophone press' were seen as anathema to good journalism. Despite claims about falling standards and sensationalism, there were those who failed to see the past as a golden era of quality journalism and they pointed out that sixteenth-century journalists were adept at yellow journalism [sensationalism] (Mansfield 1943: 523). However, Mansfield was concerned that sensational journalism had recently become 'invested with a sinister significance'.

The question [of sensational journalism] has become so acute in recent times that newspaper organisations have been compelled to give serious attention on grounds of safety as well as morality.

(ibid.: 524)

The Newspaper Society was also concerned about the problem and condemned one incident as 'an unusual and unfortunate example of a tendency created by severe competition between popular newspapers'. It went on to say that it was impossible to lay down a code for reporters and photographers and that the only possible remedy was to stimulate the strong feeling already existing in the industry (ibid.: 525–6).

There should be no surprise about the importance of the press during the early part of the century. Until the late 1930s, the press was unchallenged in terms of its ability to bring up-to-date news to its readers. During and after the war, radio and then television were allowed to develop freely. The war had seen a halt of television development, but radio had become extremely important as a way of bringing news to people during a period of considerable national anxiety. Many serious threats existed: the potential for invasion; the risks to troops fighting abroad, many of whom were the loved ones of those at home; and then the day-to-day weariness of living under a war economy.

Paper rationing meant that newspapers were not able to continue publishing large numbers of editions, while the fast-growing BBC was able to bring people news of the war as and when it happened. Radio's power as an alerting medium is unsurpassable by print and it can be no surprise that by the end of the war many households were using the radio as a major source of immediate news as well as entertainment.

This put the press under considerable pressure. Publishers were used to competing with each other to get the story first. Trying to use this method of fighting back against radio, and later television, was doomed to failure. Even with limits placed on the times early television could broadcast, fixed newspaper edition times meant the press could not compete with regular bulletins and news flashes. The press had to move from being an alerting medium to become more of a reflective medium.

Newspapers were soon trying other methods of holding readers' attention. For the quality papers this was the in-depth analysis of the headlines provided by the radio. It was a successful system for their educated readership, who wanted up-to-date and accurate information and who were keen to find out the full background. The majority, however, were unwilling to spend the time and effort learning the background, or were not interested. The papers which aimed at this mass market took a different approach. The selling power of gossip, titillation and sensationalism had always been appreciated and used to sell papers, but now the differentiation between people-orientated papers and issue-orientated papers became even starker. It is difficult to tell whether the gossip about members of the royal family and celebrities led to the personality-orientated culture that boomed during the 1950s and 1960s or whether this culture reinforced and made popular what the popular papers had started. Either way, it ensured that papers stayed far more popular than many in the industry had feared during this difficult transition to an electronic media age. The circulation figures of both tabloid and broadsheet rose during the 1940s and although they fell back during the 1960s and 1970s, in a slump which continues to this day, the decay in circulation was considerably slower than many predicted.

Many of the first codes of ethical practice were drafted in America in the early 1920s with quite a number being produced in the period 1921–23. Nelson Antrim Crawford published a number of them in his book, *The Ethics of Journalism* (1924), one of the first books published in the field. European countries followed with codes of conduct in the 1920s and 1930s.

The first signs of a determination to do something about journalistic ethics in the UK came in the 1930s. The National Union of Journalists (NUJ) decided at its annual conference in 1936 to introduce a code of conduct. There had been talk of such a code for a couple of years, from a number of sources.

At the time, this was seen as a controversial issue and many NUJ members were opposed to the idea. They felt that a code would lead to control of professional issues being held centrally, and that ethics should be an individual matter of conscience (*The Journalist*, March 1936). The final document, agreed at the union's annual conference, was a mixed offering describing working practices, of the sort identified by Reed in his 'Reporting Etiquette' (1876: 103–9), alongside broader moral concerns of the sort we would recognise today as being appropriate for a code of conduct. There were thirteen clauses, starting with a general call for a member to 'do nothing that would bring discredit on himself, his Union, his newspaper, or his profession'. The clauses broke down into three classes:

- Behaviour to other union members and colleagues.
- Behaviour towards an employer.
- Professional standards.

The professional standards section of the code covered issues of concern to the media, the public in general and the reporter in five clauses, identifying the areas of fair and honest collection of truthful news facts, the freedom of the press to publish them, along with comment and criticism and warnings to journalists to protect confidential sources and that it was wrong to falsify information. They were reminded of the risks of libel and that there should be fair play in reporting court stories.

The clauses that would be identified as being ethical clauses now are:

9. Freedom in the honest collection and publication of news facts, and the rights of fair comment and criticism, are principles which every journalist should defend.
10. A journalist should fully realise his personal responsibility for everything he sends to his paper or agency. He should keep Union and professional secrets, and respect all

necessary confidences regarding sources of information and private documents. He should not falsify information or documents, or distort or misrepresent facts.

11. In obtaining news or pictures, reporters and press photographers should do nothing that will cause pain or humiliation to innocent, bereaved, or otherwise distressed persons. News, pictures, and documents should be acquired by honest methods only.

12. Every journalist should keep in mind the dangers in the laws of libel, contempt of court, and copyright. In reports of law court proceedings it is necessary to observe and practise the rule of fair play to all parties.

13. Whether for publication or suppression, the acceptance of a bribe by a journalist is one of the gravest professional offence.

(Mansfield 1943: 527)

All of these were about how the stories were gathered and used. The only clause that looked at the effect a journalist's work had on people was the request to journalists to do nothing to cause pain or humiliation to innocent, bereaved or otherwise distressed persons. This had only recently been seen as an issue of concern: both proprietors' and journalists' organisations passed motions in 1937 that condemned methods of news-gathering that caused distress to private persons. The NUJ's National Executive Council agreed that:

reporters should not be permitted to intrude into the private lives of private people; that they should not usurp the functions of official or private detectives, and that they should confine their activities to the reporting of, and commenting on, facts.

(ibid.: 525)

However, despite this concern about privacy, no clause was put in the code of conduct, an issue that was later raised by the Committee on the Law of Defamation meeting ten years later. There is also no mention in this NUJ code about dealing with various vulnerable groups, a matter of considerable concern to the modern NUJ and the Press Complaints Commission. The PCC in particular sees one of its major roles as being the protection of vulnerable people (PCC 2002: 1).

The Institute of Journalists (IoJ), a rival trade union at that time, wanted to go even further and agitated within the industry and Parliament for a State Register of Journalists. This would have meant that anyone calling him- or herself a journalist would have had to be registered and qualified by diploma. The NUJ strongly opposed this move and when a parliamentary bill was drafted by the IoJ, the NUJ at its 1937 conference decided to oppose the creation of a statutory body for journalism. The motion to oppose 'was carried amid cheers and without a single vote being recorded against it' (Bundock 1957: 150).

The NUJ felt that licensing would limit the wide and theoretically free access to the media. The war ended this element of debate and licensing has not been an issue in Britain since then, although the NUJ did debate and dismiss the idea at its annual conference in 2005. While some European countries do license journalists, it is generally viewed in this country as a gross interference with the freedom of the Press. Journalists in the UK are not generally considered to be professionals as journalism is 'the exercise by occupation of the right to free expression available to every citizen' (Robertson 1983: 3).

Towards regulation

The 1947–49 Royal Commission on the Press was set up by the government with the object of 'furthering free expression of opinion through the Press and offering the greatest practicable accuracy in the presentation of news, to inquire into the control, management and ownership of the newspaper and periodical press and the news agencies, including the financial structure and the monopolistic tendencies in control, and to make recommendations thereon'. The Commission was initiated by the NUJ. Two MPs, both journalists, moved a motion in the House of Commons on 29 October 1946 calling for a Commission to investigate the press, having regard for the monopolistic tendencies in control of the press. The demand for an inquiry had been developing throughout the union for the previous two years, as Maurice Webb, a member of the NUJ's National Executive Council explained to the House.

The 1947–49 Royal Commission was chaired by Sir William David Ross, and reported its findings to the government in 1949. The Commission made a number of recommendations, including the idea of setting up a General Council of the Press to represent the common interests of the press as a whole, in particular 'the problem of recruitment and training, and the problem of formulating and making effective high standards of professional conduct'. In its report, the Commission said:

> It is remarkable that although a number of organisations exist to represent sectional interests within the Press, there is none representing the Press as a whole. It is not that those engaged in newspaper production are unaware of the Press as an entity: they are on the contrary acutely aware of it and jealous for its independence and its reputation. It is the more surprising that there is no one body concerned to maintain either the freedom of the Press or the integrity on which its reputation depends: no single organisation expresses the common interest in these things of the men who share responsibility for the character of the Press; and there is no means, other than *ad hoc* machinery created to deal with particular problems, by which this common interest can be translated into action. Indeed, the Press has taken fewer steps to safeguard its standards of performance than perhaps any other institution of comparable importance.
>
> (Royal Commission on the Press 1949: 165)

The Commission went on to recommend that the General Council of the Press, by 'censuring undesirable types of journalistic conduct should build up a code of conduct in accordance with the highest professional standards' (ibid.: 170). The report then listed objects later adopted by the Council:

1 To preserve the established freedom of the British Press.
2 To maintain the character of the British Press in accordance with the highest professional and commercial standards.
3 To consider complaints about the conduct of the Press or the conduct of persons and organisations toward the Press, to deal with these complaints in whatever manner might seem practical and appropriate and record resultant action.
4 To keep under review developments likely to restrict the supply of information of public interest and importance.
5 To report publicly on developments that may tend towards greater concentration or monopoly in the Press (including changes in ownership, control and growth of press undertakings) and to publish statistical information relating thereto.
6 To make representations on appropriate occasions to the Government, organs of the United Nations and to press organisations abroad.
7 To publish periodical reports recording the council's work and to review, from time to time, developments in the Press and factors affecting them.

(ibid.: 174)

The 1947–49 Commission wanted a general council to encourage 'the growth of the sense of public responsibility and public service amongst all those engaged in the profession of journalism whether as directors, editors or journalists and of furthering the efficiency of the profession and the well being of those who practised it' (ibid.). Although the Press Council was proposed in the 1949 Commission report, nothing was done immediately. By 1951, the two main newspaper proprietor organisations, the National Publishers' Association (NPA) and the Newspaper Society (NS) had prepared draft proposals. These provided for voluntary organisations with twelve editorial members and twelve managerial members charged with preserving the established freedom of the British press. The inclusion of lay members on the Council (20 per cent was proposed by the Commission) was opposed by all the proprietorial bodies and their views were endorsed by a majority of non-proprietorial bodies. The organisations involved in the talks were:

- NPA (Newspaper Publishers' Association)
- NS (Newspaper Society)
- SDNS (Scottish Daily Newspaper Society)
- SNPA (Scottish Newspaper Publishers' Association)
- NUJ (National Union of Journalists)
- IoJ (Institute of Journalists)
- GBNE (Guild of British Newspaper Editors)

As the talks continued, a private member's bill proposing a general council for the press was presented in the House of Commons by Mr C.J. Simmons and had its second reading on 28 November 1952. The debate was adjourned, but sparked considerable interest, and in February 1953 an agreed draft for a council emerged. Lay members were excluded and there was no independent chair. The Council held its first meeting on 21 July 1953. The objectives of the new Press Council are shown in Exhibit 14.1.

The new Council's objectives excluded the Commission's proposals for the Council to deal with complaints. It also ignored proposals for an independent chair and some lay membership. The Commission had wanted the Council to censure undesirable conduct by journalists and build up a code based on the highest professional standards, detailing its work in an annual report. The Council did, however, accept in its procedures that people might complain: 'provided that in dealing with representations which it may receive about the conduct of the Press or of any person towards the Press, the Council shall be required to consider only those from complainants actually affected and shall deal with such in whatever manner may seem to it (the Council) practical and appropriate' (ibid.: 33). The Commission had also suggested that the Council should examine the practicability of a comprehensive pension scheme, to promote the establishment of common services and to act as a representative of the press to government and intergovernmental bodies. The new Council ignored these recommendations.

Exhibit 14.1 The objects of the new Council

1 To preserve the established freedom of the British Press.
2 To maintain the character of the British Press in accordance with the highest professional and commercial standards.
3 To keep under review any developments likely to restrict the supply of information of public interest and importance.
4 To promote and encourage methods of recruitment, education and training for journalists.
5 To promote a proper functional relation among all sections of the profession.

▶

6 To promote technical and other research.

7 To study developments in the Press which may tend towards greater concentration or monopoly.

8. To publish periodical reports recording its own work and reviewing from time to time the various developments in the Press and the factors affecting them.

(General Council of the Press 1954: 32)

The new body was made up of the fifteen editorial representatives and ten managerial representatives from the following groups: national newspaper editors (NPA), provincial newspaper editors (NS and GBNE), Scottish newspaper editors (SNPA and SDNS), the NUJ and the IoJ. It was funded by a levy of one twenty-fifth of the Council's expenditure for every seat. Colonel the Hon J.J. Astor of *The Times* was elected the first chairman and Sir Linton Andrews of the *Yorkshire Post* the vice-chairman.

The first Council came across many of the same problems that tax the PCC today. Crime, sex and scandal were all there to be reported. In addition, there were some problems we no longer face.

Reports of proceedings against homosexual suspects caused some public protests. In the view of the Council, such reports, carefully sub-edited in accordance with the law against indecent mention of physiological details, did a useful public service. If a great evil is rife in our midst, the facts should be made known in order that a search for the right means of reform might be encouraged.

(ibid.: 9)

The determination of what is right and wrong has certainly changed even if the self-righteous and pompous justification of its exposure in the papers has not. A quick flip to the Press Council Report of 1990 shows how things have changed with a judgment headed: 'Poof and Poofter offensive'. 'Although the words "poof" and "poofter" are in common parlance, they are so offensive to male homosexuals that publishing them is not a matter of taste or opinion within a newspaper editor's discretion', the Council said (Press Council, 1990: 189). What a difference thirty-six years makes.

One of the first privacy cases dealt with by the new Council was the publishing of a series of articles by John Dean, the ex-valet of the Duke of Edinburgh. The editor of the *Sunday Pictorial* justified publication, saying he was satisfied with their authenticity and that there was nothing derogatory in them (General Council of the Press 1954: 37).

In April 1955, Colonel Astor resigned from the Council because of ill-health and Sir Linton Andrews took over the chair. With the Council less than two years old, the Prime Minister was asked in the House of Commons (on 13 July 1955) whether he intended to take steps to establish a press council with statutory powers to deal with complaints. Sir Anthony Eden replied that he found it very hard to see how statutory powers could be effectively arranged. The Council had hit trouble with its first report. Attacking the use of the phrase 'private and confidential' by 'many a fussy little jack-in-office [who] would like to set up his own Official Secrets Act' (ibid.: 6) was seen by some as a doctrine allowing them the right to publish anything. In its second report, the Council went to some lengths to define the difference between arbitrarily labelling something 'private and confidential' and the times when the press might consider itself to be bound by such a description (General Council of the Press 1955: 7).

Four complaints were received on this question. First, a ballot by the Educational Institute of Scotland on the question of a strike fund was published despite the papers being clearly marked

'Private and Confidential. Not to be communicated to the Press.' The Council agreed that marking it 'Private and Confidential' did not prevent a newspaper publishing it if it considered the subject was one of general importance and interest. Second, the town clerk of Poole Council asked the Press Council if the *Poole and Dorset Herald* was justified in printing a document sent only to the members of the authority, and then refusing to disclose the identity of the person from whom the document was obtained. The Press Council agreed it was so justified. Third, the County Councils Association wrote to the Press Council asking if editors would feel themselves duty-bound to uphold the confidentiality of papers so marked that had been sent with other documents to the press. The Council pointed out that while embargoes should be upheld, any editor would weigh in the balance the public interest and would not feel bound to keep information marked 'confidential' private. Fourth, Llanelly Town Council ran into similar problems to Poole over the publication of a report on council house rents in the *Llanelly Star*. The town clerk received a similar reply.

The second report also raised concerns about the naming of children in court cases (ibid.: 29). Several complaints had been received by the General Council from readers. Editors by and large agreed with the complainants. Either a name was printed in error, or the editors felt obliged to print something they were not expressly forbidden to do. At this stage, the 1933 Children and Young Persons Act allowed the court to prevent identification and forbade the use of photographs. But if a judge forgot to direct the court in this matter, as often happened, the names could be and often were published. The General Council wrote to the then Home Secretary, Major Lloyd George, in December 1954. He wrote back in April 1955 without a final answer. He said he fully agreed with the Council and that he was intending to contact chiefs-of-police to seek their cooperation in ensuring the court's attention was drawn to suitable cases (ibid.: 34).

The General Council also came under attack from some editors. One editor took particular exception to the mild criticism meted out to him by the Press Council. Alastair Grant, Managing Editor of the *Highland Herald* sparked a row after Inverness magistrates complained to the Press Council when only one of three cases brought against coal merchants for selling underweight, dealt with by magistrates on the same day, was reported in the *Highland Herald*, something they felt was unfair. A copy of their letter, written by the Town Clerk, was sent to the *Highland Herald* by the Press Council. Mr Grant responded: 'Fortunately, town clerks or town councils have quite definitely not the right to instruct him [the editor] in the matter, nor, as you know, has the Press Council, and I resent this ill-advised attempt to do so.'

The Council expressed its regret over Mr Grant's attitude 'towards the council's efforts to investigate a complaint'. 'The Council looked on this attempt to brush aside the complaint without a word of explanation as high-handed, unworthy and a misuse of editorial power.' This brought an explosive response from the editor, who published a letter to his readers in the paper four days later describing the Council as 'a vague and powerless body' and accusing it of inaccurate reporting. The Council responded with a resolution regretting the publication of a 'totally misleading article about the recent complaint'. It went on: 'The paper now gives as its explanation the exigencies of space changing from week to week. The Press Council regrets it has needed so much effort to get this explanation. It deplores the offensive manner in which the editor has treated a proper request put by the Press Council in the interests of the Press as well as the public' (ibid.: 47).

By the third annual report, the Press Council had settled in. Sir Linton Andrews, the chairman, reported: 'Our first and second reports described the Press Council as an experiment. It has become an institution. No one expects it to give up. After three years of conscientious effort the Council is recognised by a large and increasing number of people as a professional court of honour, a safeguard of press freedom and press fairness' (General Council of the Press, 1956: 1).

The third report, published in the mid-1950s, makes fairly depressing reading. It seems some things never change. A long report on the difficulties between the Press and the royal family ended with three suggestions:

1 An improvement in quality and supply of news be sought from the palace press secretariat.
2 Newspapers refrain from offering large sums to former palace servants for their stories.
3 Royal news should be handled with discretion at all times.

(ibid.: 13)

In Parliament in 1956, the Earl of Selborne attempted to introduce a bill to set up a Press Authority which would supersede the Press Council and be 'empowered to receive complaints about the conduct of any newspaper or news agency' (ibid.: 36). This bill sought to set up a three-strong authority, with its members nominated by the Lord Chief Justice and the Lord President of the Court of Session, which would have the power to license newspapers and therefore control them. This was roundly condemned by the Press Council, which called it misguided and reactionary: 'This measure would not defend but abolish freedom of the Press, one of the proved historic safeguards of the British people' (ibid.). The Council felt the clauses were too widely drawn to be helpful and that therefore the right to appeal was not useful: 'The right to appeal to the High Court would be nullified because a verdict could be reversed only if it ran contrary to clauses of the bill so general and so far-reaching that the most outrageous decisions might be held to be justified under their authority' (ibid.).

A veto proposed by the Earl of Selborne on 'disrespect or discourtesy to the Royal Family' would see many of today's newspapers in the dock for revealing the affairs of 'descendants of Her late majesty Queen Victoria' and their 'spouses' (ibid.). The move was similar to one suggested by Sir David Calcutt in January 1993. He suggested nominations from the Lord Chancellor: three people sitting, selected from a panel. He did not, however, suggest licensing newspapers (Calcutt, 1993: xii).

The 1957 Council report tells of hard times in Romford. The *Romford Recorder* of 4 January carried a heading 'MPs too kind to themselves'. The House of Commons Committee of Privileges decided that the heading was a contempt of the House but not of such a nature as to make it necessary to take further action. The editor asked the Press Council to consider whether this was a danger to press freedom. The Press Council felt the House's 'leniency' explained the editor's concern that he had not been given a fair hearing but they felt his treatment was not unfair (General Council of the Press 1957: 33).

Mr George Murray took over the chairmanship of the Council following the resignation of Sir Linton Andrews in April 1959. During this period several matters had been vexing the press. Contempt of court had become a serious issue, with a number of papers running into difficulties with the courts. There was also concern about the right to be admitted to the meetings of public bodies. The 1959 printing dispute had led many local authorities to exclude journalists from meetings. A young and enthusiastic MP called Margaret Thatcher, the Conservative member for Finchley, won a good place in the private member's bill ballot and moved the second reading of the Public Bodies (Admission of the Press to Meetings) Bill in February 1960. Henry Brooke, the minister for Housing and Local Government, made it clear that he would not be content until all local authorities gave full facilities to the press and the bill passed into law in June 1961.

The 1960s started with a black year for the media. First the *Empire News* was absorbed into the *News of the World* in 1960, despite having a circulation of 2,100,000. It was closely followed by the *News Chronicle*, the *Star*, the *Sunday Graphic* and the *Sunday Dispatch*. The *Sunday Telegraph* was launched in February 1961.

Further afield, the recently formed International Federation of Journalists agreed a *Declaration of Principles on the Conduct of Journalists* at its World Congress in Bordeaux in 1954.

Despite needing to deal only with core issues in order to avoid upsetting any national sensibilities, this code covered much the same ground as the 18-year-old NUJ code. In eight short clauses, the journalists of the world agreed that journalists should:

respect the truth and for the right of the public to truth;
protect the freedom of the press;
not suppress essential information or falsify documents;
use only fair methods to obtain news, photographs and documents;
rectify harmfully inaccurate material;
observe professional secrecy regarding the source of information obtained in confidence;
be aware of the danger of discrimination being furthered by the media and shall avoid facilitating such discrimination on race, sex, sexual orientation, language, religion, political or other opinions and national or social origins;
see as grave professional offences the following: – plagiarism; malicious misrepresentation; calumny, slander, libel, unfounded accusations; the acceptance of a bribe.

(http://www.ifj.org/default.asp?Issue=ETHICS&Language=EN with 1986 amendments)

Another commission

In 1961, a second commission was set up. This was

to examine the economic and financial factors affecting the production and sale of newspapers, magazines and periodicals in the United Kingdom, including:

(a) Manufacturing, printing, distribution and other costs;
(b) The efficiency of production; and
(c) Advertising and other revenue, including any revenue derived from interests in television;

to consider whether these factors tend to diminish diversity of ownership and control or the number and variety of such publications having regard to the importance, in the public interest, of the accurate presentation of news and the free expression of opinion.

(Royal Commission on the Press 1962: 9)

The Commission was chaired by Baron Shawcross and it came to the conclusion that there was no acceptable legislative or fiscal method of controlling the economic forces to ensure diversification of newspapers. It also, in passing, pointed out that the General Council still had no lay element. It was critical of the industry's poor response to the recommendations of the 1947–49 Commission: 'Had they been carried out much of our own inquiry might have been unnecessary ...' (ibid.: 101). It went on to say that while it agreed with the previous commission that 'there are important advantages in a body of this kind resting upon a voluntary basis and deriving its authority not from statute but from the press itself', it felt that if the Council did not gain sufficient authority from the press, then the case for a statutory body was a clear one (ibid.: 102).

The Commission recommended that all parties reconsider the recommendations of the 1947–49 Commission urgently and reconfigure its constitution (ibid.: 117). The Commission said that: 'We recommend that the government should specify a time limit after which legislation would be introduced for the establishment of such a body (an authoritative general council with a lay element as recommended in 1949) if in the meantime it had not been set up voluntarily' (ibid.). The Commission also recommended that the General Council should act as 'a tribunal to hear complaints from journalists or editors about pressure from advertisers' (ibid.: 102). It suggested that it might be possible to extend this to complaints from editors and journalists who had been improperly obliged by their employers or superiors to suppress opinion, distort the truth or otherwise engage in unprofessional conduct (ibid.).

At the end of the day, very few of the Commission's recommendations were acted upon. The General Council changed its name to the Press Council in 1963 and allowed the appointment of five lay members out of twenty-five. Mr George Murray gave up the chairmanship and the first lay chairman was elected to serve from January 1964, together with the new lay members. Membership was now structured as follows: independent chairman (Rt Hon The Lord Devlin PC); five representatives from the NPA, three from the NS, one each from the SDNS and the SNPA, two each from the PPA and the GBNE, four from the NUJ, two from the IoJ and five lay members.

The year 1966 was a busy one for the Press Council with the 'Moors murders' trial. Ian Brady and Myra Hindley were both found guilty and sentenced to life imprisonment for murder. The chief witness for the prosecution said he had been in receipt of weekly payments from a newspaper under a contract to provide information. The judge, Mr Justice Fenton Atkinson, said in summing up that he did not think that the evidence had been substantially affected, but asked the then Attorney General, Sir Elwyn Jones (later Lord Elwyn-Jones), to consider the matter. He decided there was no evidence that any testimony was affected and that he would proceed no further. The Press Council, however, decided to issue a declaration of principle:

1 No payment or offer of payment should be made by a newspaper to any person known or reasonably expected to be a witness in criminal proceedings already begun in exchange for any story or information in connection with the proceedings until they have been concluded.
2 No witness in committal proceedings should be questioned on behalf of any newspaper about the subject matter of his evidence until the trial is concluded.
3 No payment should be made for feature articles to persons engaged in crime or other notorious misbehaviour where the public interest does not warrant it; as the Council has previously declared, it deplores publication of personal articles of an unsavoury nature by persons who have been concerned in criminal acts or vicious conduct.

In making this declaration the Press Council acknowledges the wide support given by editors to the broad principles set out.

The Council does not intend that the principles enunciated shall preclude reasonable contemporaneous inquiries in relation to commission of crime when these are carried out with due regard to the administration of justice. There may be occasions on which the activities of newspapers are affected by over-riding questions of public interest, such as the exposure of wrong-doing.

No code can cover every case. Satisfactory observance of the principles must depend upon the discretion and sense of responsibility of editors and newspaper proprietors.

(Press Council 1967: 9)

The Press Council decided to set up a complaints committee during this period. In the summer of 1967 the Press Council moved headquarters from Legatee House to 6 Salisbury Square, just five doors up from its present location at number 1, although it moved to 81 Farringdon Street in between.

The year 1967 saw a lot of parliamentary activity. Concerns over the commercial future of Fleet Street were raised in both Houses over the Economist Intelligence Unit report (Press Council 1967: 138), commissioned by the Joint Board of the Newspaper Industry. This report had predicted the failure of four national newspapers by 1970 if nothing was done. A huge row broke out in Parliament during February 1967 over the *Daily Express*'s alleged breach of a D-Notice. The editor of the *Daily Mirror*, Mr Lee Howard, resigned from the D-Notice Committee over the issue. This was also the year that introduced the Criminal Justice Act, which limits what reporters may write about committal proceedings. This was opposed fairly strongly by the press at the time although the then Home Secretary, the Rt Hon Roy Jenkins, reminded the House that the Tucker Committee, which had been set up by him to consider restrictions on the reporting of committal proceedings, had recommended no reporting at all.

A select committee report in 1968 recommended the rescinding of all resolutions prohibiting the reporting of parliamentary procedures, technically still illegal. Many resolutions had been passed by the House of Commons attempting to prevent publication of reports such as one in 1729 'to the effect that it was a violation of the house's privileges to publish reports of its proceedings and "that in future the offenders would be punished with the utmost severity"' (Pendleton 1890: 34). Pendleton goes on to give some superb descriptions of the work of pioneer parliamentary reporters such as Edward Cave and Dr Johnson who were obliged to write their reports from memory and often used various subterfuges such as not publishing the full names of speakers or 'publishing them in his magazine as "An appendix to Captain Lemuel Gulliver's Account of the Famous Empire of Lilliput under the heading Debates in the Senate of Lilliput"' (ibid.: 37).

Colonel Willie C. Clissitt OBE handed over the secretaryship of the Press Council to Noel S. Paul, a former features editor on the *Liverpool Daily Post*, in 1968 while Lord Devlin handed over the chairmanship to Rt Hon The Lord Pearce in September 1969. Back in Parliament, the Freedom of Publication (Protection) Bill was lost for the fourth time at its April 1970 revival by Mr Jasper More, MP for Ludlow.

In 1972, the government set up the Privacy Committee under the chairmanship of Kenneth Younger. This thoroughly investigated the desirability of introducing legislation on privacy but, on a majority decision, recommended against adding to existing laws. The Committee did, however, recommend that as far as technological surveillance devices were concerned, these should be generally restricted, such restrictions applying equally to the press and general citizens. The Committee also recommended a number of changes to the Press Council. It wanted the Council to increase its lay membership to half and introduce an independent element into the method of appointment of lay members. It felt it should do this at an early date. It also suggested that the Council should codify its declarations on privacy. The Committee also urged newspapers to give adjudications similar prominence as that given to the original article (Committee on Privacy 1972: 13). The Press Council decided in 1972 to double the number of lay members but allowed the other recommendations to lie on the table.

More changes at the Press Council

In 1973, the Press Council changed its constitution again. This time, a three-person body called the Press Council Appointments Commission, chaired by Lord Redcliffe-Maud, was set up to appoint lay members. The Council was now thirty-strong with ten lay members. The Complaints Committee was made up of six lay members and six professional members and was chaired by the chairman of the Press Council, now Lord Shawcross who replaced Lord Pearce in 1974.

In 1974, yet another Royal Commission was set up with Sir Morris Finer as chairman. Sir Morris Finer died in 1975 and was replaced by Professor Oliver McGregor (who as Lord McGregor of Durris became the first chairman of the Press Complaints Commission in 1991). The Commission investigated a wide range of press topics, but devoted a whole chapter (20) to the Press Council. It rejected the notion of a communications council set up under statute (Royal Commission on the Press 1977: 96). A communications council would have combined press and broadcast while the statutory suggestion would have removed the element of self-regulation.

The Commission reiterated its belief in self-regulation but again made it clear that the Press Council had to be seen to be working if legislation was to be avoided. It said that it believed the Press Council should show a determination to be independent of the press: 'The public will not believe that a council dominated by journalists and others from the Press can keep an effective watch on the standards of the Press or can deal satisfactorily with complaints by citizens' (ibid.). It continued the attack on the problem of too few lay members on the Council. It expressed its concern about the large number of criticisms it had received about the Council's self-satisfaction over the Press's alleged less than rigorous standards. It said that the Press Council's rejection of those criticisms and opposition to extending lay membership on the grounds that it was a voluntary, self-regulating body on which lay membership was unsuitable was inconsistent.

The Commission reported in 1977 with the following list of recommendations:

1 There should be equal numbers of lay to professional members on the Council with an independent chair.
2 The Appointments Commission chair should be the Press Council chairman.
3 There should be a right of reply.
4 There should be a fast-track conciliation service.
5 The legal waiver should be reconsidered.
6 There should be a code of conduct.
7 The Press Council should be provided with sufficient funds to advertise its services.
8 The publishers' organisations should be approached to agree that adjudications should be published in full on the front pages with a similar prominence to the original story.
9 The Press Council should undertake a wider review of the record of publications of journalists concerned in complaints.
10 The Press Council should undertake to investigate and monitor the press more often on its own initiative.
11 The Commission expressed its concern that there was no right of complaint over inaccuracy and that often opinion was based on inaccurate fact. It recommended that contentious opinion on the basis of fact should be grounds for censure.

(ibid.: 236)

In 1976 the Press Council decided to codify its adjudications to form a basis of precedence to their work on complaints and codes of practice.

The year also saw the launch of a new NUJ code of conduct. The final draft of the modern NUJ was produced at a meeting of the committee in August 1974. This modern code split ethical matters from working practices and the names Code of Professional Conduct and Working Practices were used to separate out the two issues. This new code, based on the International Federation of Journalists' code and a new code that had been developed for the proposed merger between the NUJ and the Institute of Journalists, was presented by the union's education officer, George Viner, as a whole document and was presumably discussed and finalised at that meeting.

At this stage it had ten clauses but there were several matters still outstanding that the committee felt should be discussed and the code was finally accepted with eleven clauses at the union's Annual Delegate Meeting 1975 in Cardiff.

The new code still mentioned little about privacy, or children. Concern about material gathered or published about vulnerable groups was an ethical dilemma that had still to seriously concern those involved in writing codes, but discrimination was now firmly on the agenda with a clause outlawing the originating of material which encouraged 'discrimination in the grounds of race, colour, creed, sex or sexual relations'. Disability was added to the list in the mid-eighties.

Intrusion into private lives was still giving the public and journalists alike considerable cause for concern. The growth of broadcasting as an alerting medium able to bring people the latest news had seen newspapers move more into either analysis or celebrity. The social changes that swept the country in the 1960s helped with this growth so that by the end of the period and into the 1970s there was a substantial appetite for news of the private lives of the rich and famous.

Codes up until then had talked about not causing pain or humiliation to the innocent or the bereaved, but not specifically about privacy. This was not the first time concerns about intrusion had been mentioned. The Committee on the Law of Defamation under the chairmanship of Lord Porter in the 1940s had heard evidence that representatives of certain organs of the press had been intruding 'upon those who have suffered bereavement, or cross-questioning those who are related to or otherwise incidentally connected with persons who have committed crimes or attained notoriety and of publishing in sensational form details of the private lives and affairs of such persons' (cited in Committee on Privacy 1972: 41). However, the concerns had, by the end of the 1960s, grown to involve widespread intrusion into the private lives of the celebrated.

There was something of a sea change at the Press Council in the year 1977, partly at least because of the Royal Commission. Kenneth Morgan, who as NUJ General Secretary had often attended Press Council meetings, became Deputy Director. The Secretary became the Director and in October 1978, Patrick Neill QC took over as chairman from Lord Shawcross. In May 1980, the NUJ quit the Press Council in exasperation over its refusal to consider many of the reforms suggested by the 1974–77 Commission, although the Press Council had increased its membership to thirty-six to allow equal lay representation. By now, Kenneth Morgan had taken over the directorship of the Press Council, a position he was to hold until is closure. He was also to become the first Director of the Press Complaints Commission. The Rt Hon Sir Zelman Cowen was appointed chairman in 1984; he handed over to Louis Blom-Cooper who took up the reins in January 1989.

All change

By the end of the 1980s, as Fleet Street publishers moved out to Wapping and Canary Wharf, criticism of press behaviour continued to mount and the Press Council was increasingly seen as weak and ineffectual. Its new chairman, Louis Blom-Cooper, set up a review body to consider the way forward. This recommended a new code of conduct (the Council had not had one until then) and the addition of a hotline for complaints. It had become clear, even to the most stubborn editor, that the writing was on the wall as far as press behaviour was concerned. The editors met in November 1989 at the Newspaper Publishers' Association in London and issued a communiqué which accepted the need to improve methods of self-regulation. They declared their unanimous commitment to the Press Council and to a five-point common code of practice (Press Council, 1989: 340). One of the main reasons for this was the avoidance of legal control rather than any real attempt to clean up their act. Nevertheless, a committee was set up under the chairmanship of Andreas Whittam-Smith, then editor of *The Independent*, which drew up a new code of conduct (the Editors' Code of Conduct). Many of the papers backed up the new code by appointing ombudsmen to 'represent their readers' to the paper. *The Sun* was one of several which made considerable play of appointing a 'readers' champion' to support the new Code of Conduct. By 1989, some of the Press Council reforms had been put in place, including a new code of practice, which was adopted by the Council on 13 March 1990. These improvements were an acceptable way forward for the NUJ, which rejoined the council in 1990 after gaining the approval of its Annual Delegate Meeting.

The government had also been concerned by the growing public anger about an over-sensationalist press and in 1989 had set up a committee under the chairmanship of David Calcutt QC (now Sir David) to investigate privacy and related matters. This concentrated entirely on the press. Broadcasting already had the BCC with its statutory duty to investigate privacy invasions.

Although the committee came up with helpful suggestions on dealing with minors in criminal cases, its recommendations on privacy were less welcome to the industry (Committee on Privacy and Related Matters, 1990). These were not a surprise, however, coming on the top of several royal scandal stories and the Gorden Kaye incident. The actor Gorden Kaye was seriously ill in hospital having suffered a severe head injury during a hurricane in London. On 13 February 1990 *Sunday Sport* reporters Gazza Thompson and Ray Levine managed to get into his hospital room, photographed him and even tried to interview him. The subsequent report provoked howls of protest around the country, which was not helped by the insensitive attitude of *Sunday Sport* editor Drew Robertson, who failed to accept a reprimand from the Press Council and printed a huge article condemning the Press Council as a waste of space in robust and, many felt, unnecessarily crude language. He was later sacked by the board of directors which was surprisingly sensitive to the dangers of the situation. This incident had almost led to immediate legislation and so it was no surprise when Calcutt published strong recommendations on privacy and called for the scrapping of the Press Council and its replacement with a Press Complaints Commission (ibid.). There was some bitterness in the Press Council about this move as most of the proposals for a PCC were included in the Press Council's own review body recommendations. The Press Council also felt that Calcutt's recommendation to remove the duty to defend press freedom from the PCC was ill-advised. Its other concerns about the proposed body were:

- It would not take third-party complaints.
- It was not allowed to investigate of its own cognisance.
- It was lacking in lay membership.

Although the new body was opposed by the Press Council, employer groups had already set up the Press Standards Board of Finance (Pressbof) to fund the development of a PCC with a new code of practice. Its constituent members were: the NPA, the NS, the PPA, the SNPA and the SDNS. The Press Council voted not to give up its jurisdiction, supported mainly by lay members and the trade unions. However, because of Pressbof, the new Press Complaints Committee was the body with the funding and the Press Council was forced, reluctantly, to close in December 1990, its officers and offices being taken over by the Press Complaints Commission.

Calcutt had recommended that this should be the industry's last chance to be self-regulatory and warned that if the media continued to misbehave then statutory regulation should be introduced. He suggested a probationary period of one year but no criteria were laid down about good behaviour.

The new PCC started work in January 1991. It was dominated by industry representatives, mostly editors, which did its new reputation little good. The Calcutt Committee had recommended removing the right of the constituent bodies to elect representatives in order that the Commission be seen as truly independent of the industry. It also recommended that the

Appointments Commission should have 'explicit freedom to appoint whoever it considers best qualified' (ibid.: 69). The Press Complaints Commission's constitution decided on a slightly larger committee than envisaged by Calcutt – sixteen rather than twelve – and also decided that the press representatives should be editors or senior journalists. To date, no press representative has ever been anything other than an editor. This was outside the spirit of Calcutt and angered many within the journalists' unions who saw this as a way of excluding trade union involvement with the new body. This is one reason for the NUJ's antipathy to the PCC.

Even the five lay members appointed to the first council were not seen as totally independent and were labelled 'toffs and profs' by Paul Foot. The Commission was chaired by Lord McGregor and he brought with him some of his team from the Advertising Standards Authority (ASA). They had considerable experience of dealing with complaints but things did not always run smoothly with the changeover to a new system. By the end of the year, the Director, Ken Morgan, the former Director at the Press Council, had left and his place had been taken by Mark Bolland from the ASA. There seems little doubt that Morgan was forced out, but neither side was prepared to talk about why.

The PCC's refusal, backed by Calcutt, to base its work on the precept of defending the freedom of the press was seen by many as unfortunate. How, they argued, could a journalist's conduct be measured if the freedom of the press was not seen as one of the goalposts? Surely the only defence for invasions of privacy was the freedom of the press to write of matters in the public interest? Nevertheless, a code of practice was drafted under the chairmanship of Patsie Chapman, then editor of the *News of the World*. This was to prove a later source of embarrassment to the Commission when the first complaint to be dealt with was against the *News of the World*. This code of practice did contain (as it obviously had to) a public interest defence against issues of intrusion and invasion. With royal scandal following royal scandal through the early 1990s, as well as a series of indiscretions by politicians, the debate about press excesses continued. The election of 1992 must have its part to play in explaining why these did not spark the introduction of laws on privacy.

Despite the claimed expertise of the former ASA staff, who spent some time rebuilding the complaints systems used by the PCC to follow the model used by the ASA, the PCC quickly showed itself to be ineffectual and self-serving and a few spectacular invasions of privacy by the tabloids led to further calls for legislation. Two major royal stories of 1992 in particular explain why David Calcutt was asked to prepare a second report on the press, and in particular the effectiveness of the Press Complaints Commission.

The first, the taking of photographs of the topless Duchess of York while on a private holiday, shortly after her formal separation from the Duke, showed how the public could both condemn and be titillated, self-righteous and hypocritical. Amidst widespread condemnation of the pictures, published first by the *Daily Mirror* (on a Wednesday) and then by *The Observer*, both papers sold out. The *Daily Mirror* went so far as to produce a new run on Thursday morning for the City. These also sold out. Stung by the attacks these publications drew, the papers were far more circumspect when tapes purporting to be of a telephone conversation between the Prince of Wales and Lady Camilla Parker Bowles were made available to the media after publication in an Australian newspaper (owned by Rupert Murdoch, the owner of News International, publisher of *The Sun*, *Today* and *The Times*). Most papers became terribly self-righteous about the story, condemning it on the one hand as an invasion of privacy while, on the other, giving a brief synopsis of its content: enough to tantalise without explaining what was in the conversation. Only the *Sport*, *The Observer* and a handful of provincial papers published the conversation in full, exposing it as childish and smutty. The Press Association (PA) refused to circulate the transcript generally and sent it only to papers that specifically asked for it. Most papers ignored the obvious story about where such a tape had come from in order to maximise the sordid nature of the conversation. In this incident, as in the abdication story of the 1930s, limited publication gave the story more impact than full publication would have done, with the added benefit of allowing the media to pretend that they were behaving responsibly.

The *Daily Mirror* followed a similar line when Budget papers were leaked to it in November 1996. Refusing to run the story, it returned the papers to the Chancellor amidst much smugness about its responsible stand. The next day it was stung badly enough by criticism of its news sense to crow that it had not run the leaked documents because they were not interesting enough. This was probably true. The story about handing back leaked documents was better than publishing the less than damaging leaks.

In its October 1992 report, the PCC spelt out some of the reasons why it felt it had been effective and was becoming more so. It contended that there was a lack of statistical evidence of serious criticism from readers. It also claimed that there was a scarcity of complaints about intrusion into privacy and few about harassment. The PCC submitted a 76-page dossier to Sir David Calcutt, including detailed statistics, to support its view that 'there is no case for statutory intervention in one of our greatest liberties – the freedom of the press' (PCC, Report No. 14, 1992: 5). This presented an interesting can of worms that Calcutt spent some time opening. The original Calcutt Report had quite specifically denied the Press Complaints Commission the chance to champion press freedom and indeed this was one of the reasons why many people opposed the changeover from Press Council to Press Complaints Commission. Yet in April 1991, by special resolution, the Press Complaints Commission added a clause to its objectives about press freedom. By June 1991, the Commission was including as its duties: 'The duty to promote generally established freedoms including freedom of expression and the public's right to know, and the defence of the Press against improper pressure from the Government and elsewhere' (PCC, Report No. 1, 1991: 4). Calcutt records in his report that Lord McGregor had assured him 'that it was not part of the Commission's responsibility to be a campaigning body' (Calcutt 1993: 16). This was followed by an article in UK *Press Gazette* headed: 'Calcutt test passed – now for Press Freedom' (ibid.), which contained an interview with Lord McGregor, allegedly taking a contrary view. Calcutt records his subsequent conversation with McGregor in which McGregor claims he was misrepresented in his views (Calcutt 1993: 17).

'Calcutt 2', as the new review was quickly called, sparked the PCC into a short burst of activity and the following month's report also contained an editorial, spelling out how the PCC was making its existence more widely known. It was certainly possible to complain that the Commission had not been good at making itself better known to the public. It now announced that it had produced a 'How to Complain' leaflet and information sheets about the Commission. One thousand copies of a small poster had been mailed to libraries, and newspapers were donating advertising space for the PCC. The Commission announced its intention to be listed in all the main UK telephone directories from the following year, something it does as a matter of course now. The Commission boasted about presentations explaining its role to MPs, editors, students and consumer groups, although anecdotal evidence suggests these were not as widely available as the PCC would like us to believe.

Sir David Calcutt was unconvinced by the Commission's case and reported in January 1993 that in his view the PCC should be wound up and a statutory body put in its place. He recommended that the only way forward was a statutory Press Complaints Tribunal, which would be able to carry out its own inquiries, draw up a code of practice, impose fines and costs, and award compensation, and to require a response to its inquiries. He also recommended criminal legislation for physical intrusion and a new tort of infringement of privacy, and called for tighter restrictions on the reporting of court cases involving minors (Calcutt 1993).

Shortly after the report was delivered, the Secretary of State for National Heritage, David Mellor, who had already warned the press about drinking in the 'last chance saloon', found he had been drinking there himself and he was forced to resign as allegation after allegation made his position untenable. This underlined the high-risk nature of being the Secretary of State responsible for trying to rein in the media. The National Heritage Committee on Privacy and Media Intrusion was set up in July 1992, running parallel with Calcutt's, and returned its conclusions to the House in March 1993. It was chaired by Mr Gerald Kaufman and came up with a number of recommendations concerning the future of the PCC and the basis of press self-regulation. It said that the approach should remain voluntary and that Calcutt was wrong to seek statutory control at this stage, but that he was right to want to ditch the PCC. The National Heritage Committee made forty-three recommendations including the following:

- Editors' and journalists' contracts of employment should include reference to the code of practice.
- Newspapers should appoint readers' representatives.
- A Protection of Privacy Bill should be introduced.
- A Press Commission should replace the PCC, with the power to impose fines and order compensation.
- A statutory Press Ombudsman should be appointed, with power to supervise the wording and position of retractions and apologies and impose fines and order the payment of compensation.

(National Heritage Committee 1993: xxiii–xxvi)

The government had promised in 1990 to bring in new laws on privacy, as recommended by Calcutt, but by the 1992 election these had still not been introduced. The government issued a consultation paper on the infringement of privacy at the end of July 1993 which had some fairly strong things to say about the issue but very little about the PCC. Lord Mackay, the Lord Chancellor, launched the paper with the view that it was time for a new right of privacy. This was supported by the National Heritage Committee. It was opposed, though, by various editors and was strongly attacked in the media. Surprisingly, the government announced an indefinite delay in the publication of the promised White Paper on privacy in March 1994.

The National Heritage Committee was not the only one trying to get involved with media ethics in 1993. The European Commission had also been becoming more concerned over the last few years and wanted to have its own code of ethics developed.

The PCC has spent most of its life trying frantically to change its processes in a bid to keep up with a constant stream of criticism. The ink on both the 'Calcutt 2' report and the National Heritage Committee report was barely dry before Pressbof issued a statement entitled *Strengthening Self-regulation* on 4 May 1993. This announced a series of measures designed to 'reinforce public confidence' in the authority of the PCC. The independent PCC quickly welcomed Pressbof's statement. First, it agreed to change the membership: 'Since it was set up in January 1991, the Commission have operated with complete independence. However, to meet any misconceptions regarding their independent status, the membership of the Commission will be altered to ensure a lay majority consisting of an independent chairman, eight non-press members and seven editors' (PCC, Report No. 17, 1993: 5).

Second, the PCC was offered, and agreed to accept, the final ratification of the Code of Practice. Despite consistently claiming that one of the strengths of the PCC was that the Code was drawn up for editors, by editors, the PCC now had the final say in ratifying the Code. By the end of 1998, the Commission had yet to use its power to veto a change publicly, but with substantial changes made in 1997, following the death of the Princess of Wales, it could be assumed that planned changes in the Code were notified to the Commission chairman before publication to ensure that the Commission would not be put in the embarrassing position of having to refuse publicly to ratify a Code change. Lord Wakeham had made it plain early on in his new role as chairman that he was unhappy with some elements of the Code and that a major rewrite was both needed and planned. His chance came with the death of the Princess of Wales and a new Code was introduced in January 1998. The next change was to set up a helpline for members of the public who felt the Code was about to be breached with regard to their affairs.

The Commission also boasted about the lengths it had gone to publicise itself. It claimed that £250,000 worth of advertising space had been donated and that 130,000 copies of the 'How to Complain' leaflet had been distributed in the previous twelve months. In addition, the Code Committee had tinkered almost endlessly with its definition of private property (June 1993, October 1993, February 1995). It had also taken to doing its own investigating and commenting on matters, although it was difficult to tell whether this was a deliberate policy or merely Lord McGregor taking any opportunity to gain publicity to show the effectiveness of the Commission.

Towards the end of 1994 the industry tired of McGregor's eccentric approach. When the Commission should have been calming public outrage under the guise of sober reflection and adjudication of the issue, McGregor was on the front steps of Salisbury Square addressing the TV cameras about the press 'dabbling their fingers in the stuff of other people's souls'. When it could and should have spoken out, McGregor was nowhere to be found. Those close to him during this time believe his illness had started to affect his judgement. He died in November 1997.

A carefully concealed, collective sigh of relief was uttered when McGregor's period of office ended in December 1994 and he was replaced by Lord Wakeham, the former Chief Whip for Margaret Thatcher, Secretary of State for Energy and Leader of first the Commons and then the Lords. He was undoubtedly seen by both government and the industry as a safe pair of hands to guide the PCC on the tightrope between the government and the press with diplomacy and states-manship. Acknowledged by all as a smooth and talented political operator, he was welcomed by an industry well aware that failure to walk this tightrope effectively would be certain to force the government, albeit unwillingly, to introduce press legislation.

Lord Wakeham set about a major, if subdued, shake-up of the PCC. He started by replacing some of the members of the Commission. His intention was to ensure that a majority of individual members of the PCC were independent of the press and that the whole of the Commission operated as such. He also reformed the method of appointing PCC members. The PCC's articles of association had been changed in 1993 to reflect the concerns of Sir David Calcutt over appoint-ments to the Commission. Unfortunately, the PCC had been operating in breach of those new articles ever since. As Lord Wakeham pointed out to the Secretary of State at the Department of National Heritage on 19 June 1995: 'If this is not open and independent, doubt will naturally be cast on the integrity of the appointments. I was therefore deeply dismayed to discover that the PCC's appointments system was operating in breach of its own articles of association' (Department of National Heritage 1995: 26). He immediately dealt with this.

Until Wakeham, the Appointments Commission had been appointed by Pressbof. Wakeham changed this so that he now appointed the Public Nominees – the three independent members of the Appointments Commission. He was the fourth commissioner and the chairman of Pressbof was the fifth. Several changes of Secretary of State at the Department of National Heritage had delayed the government's response to the National Heritage Committee's report but finally the Rt Hon Virginia Bottomley JP MP stayed long enough to produce, on 17 July 1995, a document setting out the government's policy on privacy. This made it clear that although the government had no objection to criminal legislation on invasions of privacy in principle, it felt it had 'not been able to construct legislation which is . . . workable in practice. Accordingly it has no immediate plans to legislate in this area' (ibid.: 9). Intriguingly, despite this inability to construct legislation in the criminal area, the consultative document had been able to include a hypothetical civil remedy, including a definition of privacy. In a far from subtly worded hint as to what awaited the industry, should it drag its heels over change, the report made the industry an offer it could not refuse: 'The industry has indicated that it wishes to adopt a tighter form of words on privacy in its code. The government welcomes this. It believes it may be helpful for the industry, in refining its code, to see what a hypothetical civil remedy might look like. Annex B accordingly sets out how legislation might have been framed …' (ibid.: 16).

The government's response to the National Heritage Committee's report deals with four main issues:

- Should regulation be voluntary or statutory? The government is in no doubt: 'It believes that, in principle, industry self-regulation is to be much preferred.' It also feels that this applies to the National Heritage Committee's plan for an ombudsman (ibid.: 5).
- Should criminal law be introduced? The government says it still believes in self-regulation and, in any case, legislation is too difficult to construct (ibid.: 13).
- Should a civil remedy be provided with a statutory right of privacy? The government feels not. Self-regulation should continue (ibid.: 16).
- Has the PCC gone far enough with its reforms? Certainly not. The government 'looks to it [the PCC] to make further improvements to ensure self-regulation can be made to work and to carry public confidence' (ibid.: 8).

The government was very clear about what it expected Lord Wakeham to deliver with his cleaned-up PCC. Chapter 2 of the government's response laid out a number of suggestions. Some of these had already been put into operation by Wakeham, but others were still undone:

Appointments: The government had welcomed Wakeham's change to the appointment system, allowing wider lay membership of the Appointments Committee and the move to a lay majority on the Commission itself.

Press hotline: This would allow editors to discuss sensitive stories with the PCC before publication. At the time of the government's response to the Heritage Committee this was still planned, but now seems to be working, at least on an *ad hoc* basis. Lord McGregor had opposed this as smacking of pre-publication censorship.

Improvements to procedures: The government welcomed Wakeham's plan to accept and investigate appropriate third-party complaints. It also called for the adoption of citizen's charter-style performance targets and the publication of fuller summaries of adjudications.

Code written into contracts: Wakeham reported that the code was gradually being incorporated into editors' contracts of employment and those of some journalists. This was welcomed by the government but they awaited further evidence of disciplinary sanctions. 'Sanctions are a crucial issue … Should not proprietors consider dismissal in appropriate cases, and the commission make recommendations to that effect?' (ibid.: 33).

Compensation fund: The government wished to see compensation paid to those whose privacy was unjustifiably infringed by the press. Wakeham did not mention this in his letter to Secretary of State Virginia Bottomley. Her letter said: 'The government is also attracted to the idea of a compensation fund … It would represent a form of insurance – there are no doubt ways in which contributions of the different papers could be equitably assessed' (ibid.). Newspapers disagreed. How, argued many proprietors, could a system be set up to build a compensation fund with contributions from papers as diverse as the *Stornaway Gazette* and the *News of the World*? How could you compare the extent of the invasion, the intent of the paper, and the damage done?

Contents of the Code of Practice: While accepting that Lord Wakeham was attempting to develop the Code, the government made it clear that a number of specific improvements were still needed. There was also a need to involve the public and the PCC in the framing of a code that at that time was wholly the preserve of the Code Committee – a body set up by Pressbof under the chairmanship of Sir David English of Associated News. This could have caused the PCC some problems. They made considerable play of the fact that the Code was drawn up by the industry. Although the Code Committee is, to all intents and purpose, self-selecting from among editors and therefore can be considered flawed, it does give the PCC a chance to stand away from the Code and say that it is not the PCC Code, but the Editors' Code. The PCC believes this ties the editors into the system much more closely.

In his introduction to the PCC's Annual Report of 1995 Lord Wakeham talks about what he sees as a momentous year for the PCC: 'We were finally taken off probation and given the green light to get on with working to provide a first-class complaints handling service to the public' (PCC 1995: 2). He explains that three things happened to convince him that self-regulation is the way forward:

1 The Commission renewed its independence from the industry that pays for it.
2 The PCC became far more consistent in its application of the Code of Practice.
3 There has been growing confidence in the system by the public.

(PCC 1995: 2)

Lord Wakeham pointed to an increase in complaints as evidence of rising public confidence. The number of complaints rose in 1995 by nearly 30 per cent on 1994 to a high of 2,508: 'Ordinary people won't waste time complaining to a toothless body' (PCC 1995: 2). The Press Council in 1995 received a record number of 1,588 complaints. Lord Wakeham was convinced the new high figure was entirely down to confidence in the PCC rather than falling standards sparking more complaints.

Although Lord Wakeham had made sweeping changes to the PCC, he was still fine-tuning the organisation. Mark Bolland, the youthful director who took over from Ken Morgan in 1992, had joined the Prince of Wales' press team and with a new director in place, Wakeham had virtually a completely fresh team. Rumours continued about tensions between Wakeham and Sir David English, then chair of Pressbof's Code of Practice Committee. This committee of editors had drawn up the Code of Practice used by the Commission. Lord Wakeham had expressed his determination to review the Code of Conduct and the way that it was drawn up. In his letter to the Secretary of State, Wakeham made it clear he was unhappy about a Code Committee composed solely of editors: 'It is arguable that the committee responsible for the initial framing of the Code should not be composed only of editors and convened under the aegis of Pressbof' (Department of National Heritage 1995: 28). Wakeham had been encouraging outside organisations to express their views on the Code of Conduct and was firm in his expressed determination only to accept a new Code that was completely satisfactory to the Commission. Sir David, on the other hand, while accepting that the Commission must ratify the Code, made much of the fact that it was a committee of editors who drew up the Code: 'The Code is, crucially, the industry's own Code. Although it must be ratified by the independent PCC to take effect, it is the fact that the Code is drafted *by* industry practitioners *for* the industry that ensures the unswerving commitment of all sectors of the newspaper and magazine publishing sector to self-regulation' (PCC 1995: 11). Sir David used the rest of his 1995 report to clarify the range and number of changes the Committee had made to the Code in the previous few years. His intention was to praise the Code Committee's flexibility, although he also succeeded in laying bare the inadequacies of the PCC's Code and its constant need to change in an effort to catch up with the latest breach.

At the end of October 1996, Lord Mackay of Clashfern, then the Lord Chancellor, announced, in reply to a question in the House of Lords, that the government intended publishing a consultation paper about a new law preventing the payment or offer of payment to a witness in a trial which is pending or imminent. Announcing the proposals and inviting comments, he condemned what he called 'widespread and flagrant breaches' of the PCC's Code. The consultation document released by the Lord Chancellor's department explained that as many as nineteen witnesses were believed to have accepted payments from the media in the Rosemary West trial. 'The existence or possibility of payment by the media does increase the danger of a witness's evidence being distorted ... The Government therefore considers that legislation is needed to deal with the threat which payments to witnesses pose to the proper administration of justice. Press self-regulation did not prevent the payments in the West case or others' (Lord Chancellor's Department 1996: 6). The consultation paper asked for comments on whether payments, offers of payment and requests for payment should be prohibited, and on specific questions relating to:

- Whether the prohibition should take the form of a contempt of court or a criminal offence.
- Whether a risk of prejudice to the proceedings needs to be proved.
- Whether an intention to interfere with the course of justice needs to be proved.
- At what stage the prohibition should begin.
- Whether the prohibition should cease at the end of the trial.
- Whether there should be any defences.

(ibid.)

Lord Mackay was concerned that witnesses might omit something from their evidence in court to leave something exclusive for a story in the media, or that witnesses might exaggerate evidence in order to make their stories more newsworthy. Witnesses might also become so committed to their particular accounts that they would be unwilling to examine points put to them in court.

Even where witnesses were not swayed by contracts, Lord Mackay believed it was likely that cross-examination would raise the existence of contracts, suggesting that their evidence might be flawed, sowing doubts in juries' minds. The Lord Chancellor said payments to witnesses risked damaging the integrity of the administration of justice. The government also noted that the PCC's Code of Practice did not apply to broadcasting journalists (Department of National Heritage, Press Release, 30 October 1996).

The NUJ National Executive Council, which discussed the consultative paper at its meeting in December 1996, agreed that there should be a strengthening of the law and that the contempt of court restrictions should be extended to cover this issue. The National Heritage Select Committee also agreed that there should be an extension, although they believed there should be a new law. The Bar Council also supported an extension of legislation on the payment of witnesses.

Several editors and the Press Complaints Commission itself opposed changes, saying that the Code was able to deal with the problem – despite the Rosemary West case suggesting that this was not the case. The bill was not to be, as the Labour Party came to government in June 1997 before the bill could be made law.

A change of government

A change of government in 1997 brought some fresh views to bear. The Labour government made it clear from the beginning that it felt self-regulation was the right approach and that it did not intend to introduce statutory control or privacy legislation. The death of the Princess of Wales and the subsequent anger of the public over what was, at the time, believed to be the involvement of the paparazzi gave a wobble to self-regulation, with many people calling for a new law on privacy. The full report on the crash, which blamed chauffeur Henri Paul for driving too fast while under the influence of alcohol, came two years later – too late to prevent the attacks on the media. Although the government had called for a period of 'calm reflection', both Media Secretary Chris Smith and Prime Minister Tony Blair made it clear they did not favour a privacy law. Earl Spencer, the Princess's brother, delivered a stinging attack on the tabloid press, accusing them of trying to bring down the Princess. Several newspapers responded by vowing not to use intrusive pictures of the Princes William and Harry and several agreed not to use paparazzo pictures at all. The Princess's death produced a new Code of Practice for the PCC but the other resolutions did not last long and papers were soon printing paparazzo pictures again. The introduction of the Human Rights Act 1998 was one of the new government's major pieces of legislation in terms of its effects on the media. The PCC came to a new deal with the Prince of Wales in early 1999 about coverage of his sons, the Princes William and Harry, following the publication of a series of intrusive pictures of them. The deal saw new guidelines issued to the press in return for the royal family being more open with the media.

One of the new government's election pledges was a Freedom of Information Bill and a draft was presented to Parliament in June 1999 to general condemnation as being too weak. This was eventually enacted in 2000 and took full effect in January 2005. Within a year the government was complaining that journalists were using the legislation so heavily that there might need to be changes to reduce access.

Lord Wakeham, who had agreed at the end of 1996 to a further period as chairman of the Press Complaints Commission, was obliged to resign in 2002 in order to defend his position in the Enron scandal where he was chairman of the Audit Committee. His place was initially filled by Professor Robert Pinker but in January 2003, Sir Christopher Meyer was appointed chair of the PCC. Sir Christopher had been the UK ambassador in Washington and was known to be close to the Labour government.

House of Commons privacy and media intrusion

Privacy continued to rumble on as one of the big ethical problems and the House of Commons Select Committee on Culture, Media and Sport held hearings on privacy and media intrusion through the spring and summer of 2003. They heard evidence from a range of sources about invasion of privacy and the behaviour of the media, particularly the press. Ofcom was running by this time, but had not fully taken over the reins as the Communications Act, which gives it its power, did not receive Royal Assent until July, and Ofcom did not take over its role fully until January of 2004.

The committee came up with more than thirty recommendations, some aimed at broadcasters and some at the press and the PCC. The most significant was the recommendation that there should be a law on privacy. This was immediately rejected by the government, as indeed were many of the other recommendations.

The Press Complaints Commission received a number of recommendations:

- The PCC should establish a procedure to allow people to refuse mediation and go for judgment.
- Journalists should be able to refuse an unethical assignment.
- The PCC should ban payments to police officers.
- Press members of the PCC with poor records should be barred from office with the PCC.
- The PCC should publish a league table of performance.

- There should be some form of punishment and compensation system.
- Registration fees should be linked to adverse judgments.
- There should be a front page 'taster' for adjudications published in newspapers.
- Press archives and libraries should be annotated as to their accuracy and sensitivity.

The timing of the SCCMS review was good for the PCC who had only recently appointed a new chairman. The committee's recommendations were also useful for the new chairman who seized upon some of them, at least, to introduce a number of reforms. Posts for lay members of the committee would in future be advertised and the selection would be more open. The first such advert, inserted at the insistence of Sir Christopher shortly after taking over the post of chairman, saw more than a thousand applicants for the single post. Other adverts followed. The PCC also decided to appoint a Charter Commisssioner and a charter compliance committee – a free-roving committee able to examine PCC decisions at will and make recommendations. This was not an appeals body, although complainants who felt that the PCC had breached their own rules or procedures could appeal to the charter commissioner. The panel and the commissioner were to report their findings at the end of each year and would expect the Commission to respond to these. The PCC also took to the road, visiting half a dozen provincial centres to explain their work and to face the questioning of local people.

The timing was also good for the government which quickly made it clear that it did not intend to introduce a new law on privacy but was able to quietly report that it was intending to leave all the other suggested changes for the PCC to consider with its new chairman.

Other more subtle, but perhaps more important changes started to happen at the PCC over the next couple of years. The meaning of third-party complaints became much more subtly refined. When the PCC first started, it had been determined not to take third-party complaints. Several active campaigners had kept the old Press Council very busy with their complaints. Bob Borzello, for instance, would send several complaints a month about racist coverage in the national press. The PCC was determined to end these: 'it would not follow the Council's practice of accepting "third-party" complaints. Thus would a heavy burden be lifted. About half the complaints dealt with by the Council were from people not directly concerned' (Shannon, 2001: 41).

This view was still going strong in 1996 when hundreds of complaints were sent in following the Euro 96 coverage, but 'both the Code Committee and the PCC persisted in the view that good procedure consists in not as a rule admitting third-party complaints, and that good policy consists in leaving collective racism outside the Code in a category of offences to taste and decency' (Shannon 2001: 257).

It is not clear precisely what caused the PCC to change its mind, but the definition of third-party complaints has changed significantly since Sir Christopher took over the chair with the PCC confirming in June 2006 that 'In cases that relate to named individuals, the PCC will generally require the co-operation of those individuals before investigating a complaint. This either will mean the complaint coming from the individual his or herself, or their authorisation for another person to complain on their behalf. In cases that relate to points of general fact – where there are no obvious first parties cited in the article, who might complain – the Commission will generally accept complaints under Clause 1 (Accuracy) of the Code from any concerned reader.'

The PCC also made some additions to the PCC Code. Payments to witnesses were generally outlawed in 2004 and transgendered people were added to the list of the vulnerable in 2005. More guidance was now generally being offered. A 'Code book' was written by Ian Beale, a former editor and secretary of the Editor's Code Committee and this was published by the PCC in February 2005. In 2006, a new clause was added warning newspapers to take particular care in reporting stories on suicide. This had been a growing area of concern over the past few years with some influential research showing that there could well be a link between suicides and how they were reported. Work by Professor Keith Hawthorne at the Research Centre for Suicide in Cambridge, sponsored by Befrienders International, identified several areas of influence. The new clause was designed to help prevent copycat suicides, and added a new sub-section to clause 5 that said: 'When reporting suicide, care should be taken to avoid excessive detail about the method used.' Code Committee chairman Les Hinton said:

> We have attempted to minimise that risk – while maintaining the public's right to know – by emphasising the need for care to avoid excessive detail, unless it is in the wider public interest to give the information. For example, while it might be perfectly proper to report that the suicide was caused by an overdose of Paracetamol, it would probably be excessive to state the number of tablets used. We have consulted with the industry on this and it has been accepted. The new rule, in effect, codifies a practice already currently followed by many editors.

Despite Sir Christopher Meyers calm words to the CMS Select Committee little changed at the PCC following the CMS report and so the CMS Select Committee decided to revisit self-regulation in 2007. This was driven by several press events that brought the industry into further disrepute. Chief among these were the Clive Goodman phone-tapping affair and the hounding of Kate Middleton, the then girlfriend of Prince William. The Committee took this as an opportunity to reaffirm its belief in self-regulation but made several proposals for change. First it found it extraordinary that the PCC had failed to question *News of the World* editor Andy Coulson as part of its investigation into the phone tapping. It also condemned the complacency of the industry to the Information Commissioner's evidence of widespread and illegal access to personal data by journalists.

The Committee reiterated its support for self-regulation and opposed the introduction of a privacy law as unworkable, but agreed that stiffer penalties were required under section 55 of the Data Protection Act 1998 to punish journalists who illegally obtain personal data. They felt there were sufficient safeguards for legitimate investigative journalism for this not to have a chilling effect.

They agreed that journalists required more safeguards against being obliged to use unethical news-gathering practices, but felt that the best way to achieve that was by inserting the PCC's Code of Practice into contracts of employment.

The Committee also agreed there should be more conciliation without the need to go to formal adjudication despite having been told that there were presently insufficient adjudications for good guidance to be given to journalists on the operation of the Code. While the Committee was minded to introduce a system of fines, they accepted that that would be anathema to the industry and would probably require statutory backing to enforce it. They called for a broader examination of the subject.

The Committee decided to look at the press again in 2009, examining the law on libel and reconsidering its view on privacy and press standards. During the process of its examination, the PCC appointed a new chairman, Baroness Peta Buscombe, a former deputy chair of the Conservative Party. She took up office in October of 2009 and the then director, Tim Toulmin, took the opportunity to step down, handing over the director's chair to Stephen Abell. Closely following Baroness Buscombe taking over the chair, the PCC was obliged to examine *The Guardian*'s claims that the PCC had been misled during its 2007 inquiry into the Clive Goodman phone-tapping affair and whether there was any evidence of continuing phone-message hacking. The PCC came to the conclusion that it could find no evidence for either claim, a finding that led *The Guardian* editor Alan Rusbridger to resign from the PCC's Code Committee in protest and brought strong criticism from the Culture, Media and Sport Select Committee:

We accept that in 2007 the PCC acted in good faith to follow up the implications of the convictions of Clive Goodman and Glenn Mulcaire. The *Guardian*'s fresh revelations in July 2009, however, provided good reason for the PCC to be more assertive in its enquiries, rather than accepting submissions from the *News of the World* once again at face value. This Committee has not done so and we find the conclusions in the PCC's November report simplistic and surprising. It has certainly not fully, or forensically, considered all the evidence to this inquiry.

(House of Commons 2010: 109).

The PCC were not the only ones to be criticised by the Committee over this affair. In recommending an amendment to section 1 of the Regulation of Investigatory Powers Act regarding the hacking of phone messages, the Committee criticised the Metropolitan Police decision not to investigate aspects of the case. 'The Metropolitan Police's reasons for not doing so seem to us to be inadequate' (ibid. 108) The *News of the World* also came in for criticism.

The whole sorry saga is summed up by the Select Committee on page 103 of its report:

We have seen no evidence that Andy Coulson knew that phone-hacking was taking place. However, that such hacking took place reveals a serious management failure for which as editor he bore ultimate responsibility, and we believe that he was correct to accept this and resign.

Evidence we have seen makes it inconceivable that no-one else at the *News of the World*, bar Clive Goodman, knew about the phone-hacking ... We cannot believe that the newspaper's newsroom was so out of control for this to be the case.

The idea that Clive Goodman was a 'rogue reporter' acting alone is also directly contradicted by the Judge who presided at the Goodman and Mulcaire trial. In his summing up, Mr Justice Gross, the presiding judge, said of Glenn Mulcaire: ' ... you had not dealt with Goodman but with others at News International'.

Despite this, there was no further investigation of who those 'others' might be and we are concerned at the readiness of all of those involved: News International, the police and the PCC to leave Mr Goodman as the sole scapegoat without carrying out a full investigation at the time. The newspaper's enquiries were far from 'full' or 'rigorous', as we – and the PCC – had been assured. Throughout our inquiry, too, we have been struck by the collective amnesia afflicting witnesses from the *News of the World*.

(ibid. 103)

CMS report

Whilst the CMS committee was critical of the PCC and vitriolic about News International it had a number of other matters to mention in its report, making almost 100 recommendations concerning key issues affecting media standards, such as injunctions, privacy, libel, the PCC and press standards.

While its condemnation of News International was important, most of its other recommendations are probably doomed to be ignored as the general election was announced just a scant couple of weeks after the report's publication.

Some of the key recommendations made were:

- The Ministry of Justice should seek to develop a fast-track appeal system for injunctions.
- The courts should gather data on injunctions.

- The law on privacy should continue to be determined according to common law.
- Pre-notification, in the form of an opportunity to comment, should be in the PCC Code.
- The PCC Code should be amended to include a clause making clear that headlines must accurately reflect the content of the article.
- The PCC should make better use of its power to launch an inquiry in the absence of a complaint.
- The Editors' Codebook should be amended to include a specific responsibility to moderate websites and take down offensive comments without the need for a prior complaint.
- Section 1 of the Regulation of Investigatory Powers Act should be amended to cover all hacking of phone messages.
- Our recommendation in our 2007 report that custodial sentences be used as a deterrent should be taken up as soon as possible.
- The Information Commissioner, the PCC and the industry should remain vigilant and take swift and firm action with regard to illegal practices.
- Self-regulation of the press is greatly preferable to statutory regulation, and should continue.
- The powers of the PCC must be enhanced, as it is toothless compared to other regulators.
- The membership of the PCC should be rebalanced to give the lay members a two-thirds majority.
- There should be lay members on the Code Committee, and that one of those lay members should be chairman of that Committee.
- In addition to editors of newspapers and magazines, practising journalists should be invited to serve on the PCC's committees.
- The Commission must be more proactive, issuing a public warning or initiating an inquiry.
- There must be some incentive for newspapers to subscribe to the self-regulatory system. The government should consider that proposals to reduce the cost burden in defamation cases should only be made available to those publications which provide an alternative route of redress through their membership of the PCC.
- The PCC should mandate the inclusion of a clause requiring respect for the Code in staff contracts of journalists of all subscribing publications.
- Corrections and apologies should be printed on either an earlier, or the same, page as that first reference, although they need not be the same size.
- The PCC should have the ability to impose a fine.
- The PCC should be more than a complaints body and should be renamed the Press Complaints and Standards Commission with a deputy director for standards.

Alongside the Select Committee report, several other major changes were being considered by the government. Libel had been receiving a thorough review, picking up on many of the points made to the Select Committee. Other areas attracting attention included the high cost of defending such actions, CFAs and after-the-event insurance, the growing trend for foreign applicants to bring cases to the London courts despite only a small part of the circulation of the publication appearing in the UK and the weakness of responsible journalism defence. Privacy was also under review, with the European courts expected to hand out judgment on the Mosley case. However, a general election and the election of a new coalition government means change is inevitable. The coalition has at the time of writing still to make it clear precisely where it is going in terms of journalism, the media and regulation, but it has already identified a few areas of policy. It intends to 'roll back state intrusion' and introduce a Freedom Bill as well as a Bill of Rights to extend and protect British liberties. The Conservatives had threatened to severely reduce the amount of broadcast regulation by axing or cutting back the broadcast regulator, Ofcom, but that is not mentioned in the coalition programme. They also promise to:

- Extend the Freedom of Information Act.
- Review libel laws to protect freedom of speech.
- Maintain the independence of the BBC but give the National Audit Office full access to its accounts.
- Enable partnerships between local radio, TV and newspapers to promote local media.

Further reading and support material

Two main books stand out when looking at regulation of the press in the UK. Tom O'Malley and Clive Soley (2000) *Regulating the Press* (Pluto, London) takes a critical look at the history of the Press Council and its replacement by the Press Complaints Commission.

Richard Shannon (2001) *A Press Free and Responsible* (John Murray, London) charts the founding and development of the Press Complaints Commission. This was commissioned by the PCC itself to mark its tenth anniversary and is consequently far less critical of the PCC than many commentators. However, it does have good access to PCC supporters, mainly editors and newspaper insiders.

Chapter 15

History of broadcast regulation

This chapter examines the history and development of regulation in broadcast journalism and covers:

- The development of the BBC radio news service in the 1930s

- The introduction of independent television and then the expansion of radio

- The development of digital broadcast services

- The changes and development in broadcast regulation

Journalism ethics were closely linked with the press in the early part of the twentieth century for the obvious reason that broadcasting did not start in earnest until the 1920s. Even then the tight control exercised over the BBC meant that there were not the kind of concerns about broadcast ethics that grew about the press.

Radio, like many technologies, was invented and developed by a number of people, but we can certainly identify radio being used commercially by 1900. At this stage, in the UK at least, the military was determined to keep it under its control as a method of strategic and tactical communication. This was not heavily resisted as the idea of using radio as a broadcast system, rather than as a two-way communication device, meant there was not much consideration of a public broadcast system; few (although not all) were prescient enough to see how the world would be swamped by broadcast entertainment in the future. After the Great War, the military were obliged to release their control a little and a ground-breaking transmission by the famous opera singer Dame Nellie Melba on 15 June 1920 (Crissell 1997: 10), heard across Europe and in America, showed what could be achieved; the British Broadcasting Company was set up in 1922 by the main manufacturers of radio sets, determined to increase their market by producing programmes the public might enjoy and would need to buy a radio set to hear. The new company was licensed by the Postmaster-General under the Wireless Telegraphy Act 1904 with funding coming from the licence fee and royalties from the sales of wireless sets. In 1927 the BBC was converted to a corporation, taking up the recommendations of the Crawford committee, which now saw clearly how important a public radio broadcast system could be. The new corporation was set up by the government, but was quasi autonomous with a board of governors and funding coming from the licence fee, a basic structure that has remained unchanged until 2007. The public took to radio and by 1939 there were 9 million radio licences and up to five times as many receivers. Because broadcasting was set up by government, controlled by a Royal Charter with governors appointed by the government of the day, the BBC was very much an establishment instrument, a criticism it has faced consistently throughout its history.

The one early disappointment in radio was a lack of news. Pressure by the Newspaper Proprietors' Assocation, owners of national newspapers, meant that the government forbade the corporation to carry news before 7 p.m. and even then the bulletin had to be provided by Reuters written with newspaper readers in mind (Crissell 1997: 15). For this reason, ethics in broadcasting was less of a problem than for newspapers, and although the National Union of Journalists (NUJ) decided at its annual conference in 1936 to introduce a code of conduct, there were very few, if any, members working in broadcast at this time. The BBC had a staff association and did not recognise other unions. In any case, with news being produced outside the BBC, there were few staff members eligible. This started to change with the introduction of radio news in 1938, and in 1942 there was the formation of the BBC chapel in Bush House – the European Service Chapel, joined shortly after by the Overseas Service Chapel. These became the London Radio Branch on their later merger. Although the Broadcast Report 1949 (1950) recommended that the BBC recognise appropriate unions, the NUJ wasn't finally recognised until 1 January 1955 (Bundock 1957: 192).

With the end of the Second World War, during which the BBC's news service had guaranteed it a place of trust with listeners, the BBC launched new services, offering its listeners more variety with the Light Programme, the Home Service and the Third Programme. The BBC also reintroduced its TV service, which it had started in 1936, but had suspended for the duration of the war. The Selsdon Committee in 1934 had recommended that the BBC should run a trial TV service. This should be provided on a transmission system using a minimum of 240 lines and in the event a 405-line service, using the EMI electronic system, soon proved itself to be the best. However, the system was closed in September 1939 because of the war. It was relaunched by the BBC in 1946 and was enthusiastically received by the public. The coronation in 1953 was a major event with many buying their first television set and inviting their neighbours to join them to watch the spectacle. This was the first of several major public events which have been pivotal in introducing major changes in technology, the latest being the introduction of high-definition TV for the World Cup in 2006 and 3D TV for the World Cup 2010.

Independent television

The Television Act 1954 set up commercial television. The Act, together with the reports that led to it, identified a number of issues of concern about television. These included regulation, standards of programming, hours of broadcast, ownership, advertising and sponsorship, and the broadcast watershed. The Act set up a regulatory authority, the Independent Television Authority, that had a duty to approve programmes before broadcast and so was able to prevent the broadcast of programmes it deemed unsuitable. Similarly, the Postmaster-General retained the right to instruct the banning of a programme or to insist on the broadcast of something particular.

The ITA was structured around a chairman, deputy chairman and eight other members. It had the power to provide television services in addition to those of the BBC and as a public service for information, education and entertainment. The programmes were to be provided by programme contractors rather than the authority itself, and those contractors would have the right to include advertisements. The programmes would not offend good taste and decency or incite crime or lead to disorder. The Act insisted there should be adequate news with due accuracy and impartiality. The authority was also obliged to draw up a code of practice for programmes covering such matters as children's viewing and watersheds. The ITA had the right to limit newspaper shareholdings in the new programme contractors and the government retained control over hours of broadcasting. The ITA was obliged to provide a news service for the new commercial station and set up Independent Television News in 1955. This provided national and international news for the new service. It took to television much more quickly than the BBC, according to Crissell. Its use of film clips from scene, and presenters with some authoritative analysis were welcomed by viewers and its reputation was quickly built up as being more populist than the BBC but certainly still an effective news-gatherer to be trusted.

BBC 2 launched in 1964 bringing with it the new upgraded transmission system. From now on, 625 lines would become the standard transmission quality, although it would be 1975 before the last 405-lines TV was built, and 1985 before transmissions in 405-lines were phased out. Colour, another innovation, was launched in 1967 on BBC 2, followed the year after on BBC 1.

By 1964 there were still only three UK radio stations, the BBC's Home, Light and Third services. These were very traditional and the fast-growing pop record industry that was building on airtime in the USA was attractive to young people who had been listening to American stars and home-grown offerings on Radio Luxembourg, which had been transmitting commercial radio since the war. This only transmitted at night though and its signal was not strong. Several pirate radio stations – Radio London and Radio Caroline were probably the best known – set up around this time to capitalise on this market, which had been fanned by a rise in disposable income for teenagers and the explosion of British pop from the Beatles' Merseysound and London groups such as the Rolling Stones, the Kinks and Manchester's the Hollies. The BBC's research found that despite there being large numbers of young people listening to the pirates, there was no significant change in Light Programme listening, suggesting there was a whole new market that had been previously ignored (Crissell 1997: 140). The government wanted to close down the pirates and instructed the BBC to change its radio policy. The BBC introduced Radio 1 to offer non-stop pop music together with Radio 2, 3 and 4 shortly after the government passed the Marine etc. Broadcast Offences Act 1967 in August of that year, which closed most of the pirates down. In November 1967 the first BBC local radio station opened in Leicester and within a few years, there were twenty local stations. The superior sound quality of FM was also introduced at about this time.

Up to this time it was generally accepted that broadcast news both on radio and TV were of a high standard – a view that largely holds good today. Any complaints that were made were investigated by complaints panels set up internally by the BBC (Programmes Complaints Commission) or the Independent Television Authority (Complaints Review Board for Independent TV). They would publish their findings in the *TV Times* or *The Listener*. The BBC's Complaints Commission in particular had been criticised for not having a broad enough base (Press Council 1972: 94) but there was not too much criticism of news and current affairs. This did not prevent much criticism from some sources that TV produced programmes that showed too much violence and bad language.

The passing of the Sound Broadcasting Act through Parliament in 1972, which allowed the setting up of a range of local commercial radio, coincided with the Younger Committee's recommendations on broadcasting that attempted to strengthen regulation in both the BBC and the ITA. It asked the BBC to extend the powers of the Complaints Commission to cover privacy and to amend some of its procedures. The Committee also asked the ITA's Review Board to publish its adjudications and extend its procedures to commercial radio, if and when the Authority took responsibility for the new services (Committee on Privacy 1972: 14).

In the Second Report from the Select Committee on the Nationalised Industries in April 1972, Tony Benn (who had earlier been Postmaster-General) said that the debate on broadcasting should move beyond who controls what to look at the broader question of broadcasting's role and status in society now it was the dominant medium. Some parliamentarians were becoming concerned that the controls of the Television Act and the BBC Charter might not be enough to prevent television overpowering Parliament itself.

Independent Broadcasting Authority

On 14 May 1970, John Stonehouse, the then Postmaster-General, announced that he had invited Lord Annan, Provost of University College London, to head an independent committee of inquiry, the Committee on the Future of Broadcasting, to look at the long-term future of broadcasting after the Television Act and the BBC Charter expired in 1976. Almost immediately, a general election was called which unexpectedly gave victory to the Conservative Party under Edward Heath. They decided not to rush into a new inquiry and instead the Sound Broadcasting Act (1972) introduced the possibility of local radio and changed the ITA to the Independent Broadcasting Authority, a move later confirmed by the Independent Broadcasting Authority Act 1973. This change also allowed the new Independent Broadcasting Authority to regulate the first independent radio stations.

The IBA consisted of a chairman, deputy chairman and eight other members. It was set up 'to provide the television and local sound broadcasting services as a public service for disseminating information, education and entertainment'. These services had to be of a high standard, particularly with reference to content and quality and a proper balance and wide range of subject matter (Independent Broadcasting Authority Act 1973, clause 19 section 2 subsection a).

These services were to be provided by programme contractors who would pay the authority for the privilege of making such programmes, but would be able to include advertisements within their programmes. This approach, mirroring what had happened with the old ITA meant that the authority was still responsible for programmes, giving it the power of prior restraint and making it, rather than the contractors, directly responsible for the standard and quality of programmes. This is an important point as it means that while there was definitely commercial television and radio being produced, it was still entirely controlled by a quango that was responsible to the government rather than being entirely independent. It also meant that the IBA could have set up its own studios if it wished, rather than relying on the programme contractors to do this for them. This meant that the IBA was responsible for TV scheduling and ensuring that programme contractors filled the spots designated to them. The Act laid down in detail what the IBA was supposed to provide in terms of programming. It was obliged to arrange for the provision of programmes needed in order to see a reasonable balance and to provide education broadcasting services and other public broadcasting services. This meant that the IBA had a specific duty to provide programmes that did not offend against good taste and decency, that there was sufficient time given to news output that was accurate and impartial, that there be a proper proportion of British material that suitably showcased British performance as well as providing programmes for minorities.

The dangers of subliminal advertising were mentioned and such adverts were banned. Also there was considerable concern about the detrimental effect on public morals that prizes on TV game shows might bring. Such programmes were not allowed to offer prizes of significant value, building up a viewer expectation that a pair of slippers was not only all you could expect for Christmas, but also all you could expect for winning a game show. The IBA was obliged to record all its output, and copyright legislation specifically ensures such recordings are exempt from infringing copyright. The IBA was also obliged to draw up a code of guidance on violence and other matters concerning standards.

January also saw the Minister for Posts and Telecommunications relax the rules on hours of broadcasting so that broadcasters could now broadcast when they wished, for the first time. This opened up programming, allowing lunchtime news reports on TV for the first time.

In February 1974 the Labour Party was returned to power and broadcasting was moved to the Home Office, following the abolition of the Ministry of Posts and Telecommunications. Roy Jenkins, Home Secretary, appointed the former journalist John Harris, now Lord Harris of Greenwich, to be Minister of State responsible for broadcasting. On 10 April 1974, Jenkins announced the revival of the Annan Committee to consider the future of the broadcasting services in the United Kingdom. New legislation was needed to extend the life of the Television Act and the Independent Broadcasting Authority Act which would otherwise have closed the IBA, and the services it was set up to provide, in July 1976. There was some concern in ITV circles about the sixteen members of the Annan Committee: 'Not a single one of the sixteen members was identifiable as what might be described as an ITV viewer and, to judge an industry with a multi-million pound turnover, fifteen out of sixteen had no first-hand experience of business' (Potter 1989: 225).

The Annan Committee presented its report to Parliament on 23 March 1977 and the government issued a White Paper shortly after in 1978. This recommended a number of new bodies: Local Broadcasting Authority (for local radio and cable), an Open Broadcasting Authority (for the new fourth channel), a Public Enquiry Board (to hold public meetings every seven years), a Telecommunications Advisory Committee and a Broadcasting Complaints Commission.

The Labour government lost the election in 1979 and the Conservatives took over, issuing a new broadcasting bill in February 1980 which received Royal Assent in November to become the Broadcasting Act 1980. It was followed by the Broadcasting Act 1981 that consolidated the 1973, 1974, 1978 and 1980 Acts. The Act did little to change the main structure of broadcasting regulation, but it did introduce a new body: the Broadcasting Complaints Commission, which had been strongly advocated by Lord Annan and which had received strong general support. It was set up to consider and adjudicate complaints of unjust or unfair treatment in television and radio programmes or of unwarranted infringement of privacy in, or in connection with, the obtaining of material included in programmes. Its first chairman was Lady Pike. Geoffrey Robertson said: 'its work since inception has been unimpressive' (1983: 163). He was far from being the only critic. The council was there to consider complaints about unfair or unjust treatment in sound or television programmes or unwarranted infringement of privacy. Having adjudicated on complaints, the Act gave the Commission the power to insist a broadcaster should broadcast the Commission's adjudication.

The Broadcasting Act 1981 also paved the way to Channel 4 and S4C and these channels launched in 1982. They were followed the next year by breakfast TV finally introducing what was virtually 24-hour TV.

A second regulatory council was set up in 1988 to keep a closer eye on the standards of broadcasters. It was seen very much as Mrs Thatcher's baby, her committee to reduce the amount of sex and violence on TV. Lord Rees Mogg, the former *Times* editor, was made its first chairman. The Broadcasting Standards Council was to monitor the portrayal of violence and sex and matters of taste and decency. This would include bad language and the treatment of disasters in radio and TV programmes or broadcast advertisements.

The Council was set up initially on a non-statutory basis pending legislation that arrived in the shape of the 1990 Broadcasting Act. The first director of the BSC was Colin Shaw, the former Director of TV at the Independent Broadcasting Authority and former Chief Secretary at the BBC where he had worked for almost twenty years.

At the end of the 1980s, the government introduced a media ban, directing the BBC, IBA and the Radio Authority to 'refrain from broadcasting any ... words spoken' by a person who represents an organisation proscribed by the Prevention of Terrorism Act seeking support from that organisation, including Sinn Fein, Republican Sinn Fein and the Ulster Defence Association. This was not lifted until the mid-1990s.

The market moves in

Broadcasting regulation underwent a major change during the early 1990s, following the signing of the Broadcasting Act 1990. This introduced a more flexible approach to broadcast regulation. The BBC continued under the control of the Board of Governors, but the Independent Broadcasting Authority (IBA) was replaced by the Independent Television Commission, the Welsh Authority, S4C, and the Radio Authority. These came into operation on 1 January 1993. The Broadcasting Complaints Commission was also retained, as was the Broadcasting Standards Council, now with statutory authority. Their responsibilities remained largely unchanged. They were charged with investigating complaints but could punish only by insisting on the transmission of findings.

One of the main changes of the Broadcasting Act was to remove from the ITC the control of programming that the old IBA had had. The ITC now awarded franchises to companies to transmit programmes in specific areas. This meant it was no longer able to vet programmes before they were shown; it could only deal with complaints made after they were broadcast. This was a major change in approach and finally opened the door to true independent commercial television, even though the Act still required franchise holders to follow public service rules designed to ensure the provision of news services, children's programmes, religious content and high standards of programmes and adverts. The new Act continued to ensure that newspaper owners were unable to invest heavily in broadcasting; ensuring that TV stations could not own significant shares in newspapers and vice versa was seen as an important part of limiting potential monopoly of the media.

The Broadcasting Act 1996 (first published on 15 December 1995 and receiving Royal Assent on 25 July 1996) brought in three main changes concerning regulation. One was to introduce changes in the way licences for existing broadcasting stations were granted. The requirement remained for licence holders to be fit and proper persons who had to follow a set of regulations, while the rules on cross-media ownership were significantly loosened, allowing big media groups to own far more. These rules came into effect on 1 November 1996 and allowed independent radio stations to own one AM, one FM and one other (AM or FM) service instead of a maximum of one FM and one AM service in overlapping areas. It allowed local newspapers to own local radio services in overlapping areas for the first time. Local newspapers with a circulation under 20 per cent were allowed to own one AM, one FM and one other service, like any other company. Papers with 20 to 50 per cent circulation in an area were allowed to own one AM and one FM service in that area, and those with more than 50 per cent were allowed to own one service in that area (provided there was more than one independent local radio service in the area). The Act also removed ownership controls on cable operators.

The second big change was to introduce digital TV and to offer the large number of digital multiplex channels to broadcasters. A multiplex is a frequency band on which several programme services and sometimes additional data services can be combined. The Department of National Heritage said six television and seven radio multiplexes were to be available initially and, with the exception of the BBC's television and national radio multiplexes, were to be licensed to multiplex providers by the Independent Television Commission and the Radio Authority. These multiplex operators in turn offered a range of programme services on each multiplex. Existing broadcasters were being offered half a multiplex for each existing channel. This gave the BBC full control of a multiplex. Channel 3 and Channel 4 share a multiplex, on which capacity is also reserved for the public teletext service. Channel 5 had half of the third multiplex and S4C were offered the other half of this multiplex in Wales. Terrestrial television broadcasters had to declare their intention to take up their guaranteed places on terrestrial digital multiplexes by 15 October 1996. Most did and digital services were launched in late 1997 and 1998. No fee is payable for the first of the twelve-year multiplex licences which were awarded to the applicants whose proposals were 'most likely to promote the development of digital terrestrial broadcasting. Companies must demonstrate a commitment to the "roll-out" of transmission and to promoting the take-up of receiving equipment. They must also be able to demonstrate that they intend to supply a variety of programming, that their plans are commercially viable and sustainable and that they will deal fairly with broadcasters' (Department of National Heritage, Press Release, July 1996).

The third change made by the Broadcasting Act was to alter the regulations and to amalgamate the BSC and the BCC into a new Broadcasting Standards Commission with a wider remit but similar powers. The amalgamation came into effect on 1 April 1997.

National Heritage Secretary Virginia Bottomley announced in July 1996 that Lady Howe of Aberavon would be the chairman of the new Broadcasting Standards Commission, with Lord Dubs as one deputy chairman and Jane Leighton as the other. Lady Howe had been appointed chairman of the old BSC from 1993 and so had continuity of experience.

Regulations on the requirement for regional programming were tightened up by the new Act, while provision was made for a list of major sporting events that could not become exclusive to pay-per-view or subscription television to be drawn up. The news service for Channel 3 would be provided by a company selected by the ITV companies from a field which met the ITC's quality threshold.

The Act also empowered the Independent Television Commission to regulate the BBC and S4C's commercial activities, and privatised the BBC's transmission network. From 13 August 1996, the Independent Television Commission and the Radio Authority were allowed to give decisions on the public interest test they intended to use on the common ownership and control of newspapers and broadcasters.

The Broadcasting Act 1996 had been set up to allow for convergence and to launch the new digital TV broadcasting. After the initial difficulties of setting up a digital service, the BBC and various commercial interests were able to produce a mixed service of free terrestrial broadcasting, paid-for cable services and satellite services that brought digital TV to people's homes. As the need for convergence became clearer, the new Labour government decided that broadcasting required a new, lighter-touch, streamlined regulator bringing together the convergence industries of broadcasting, internet and telephony.

Ofcom was launched after a short consultation period. So keen was the government to get Ofcom up and running that it launched the body with the Office of Communications Act in 2002 and only the year after followed with the Communications Act 2003 which said what Ofcom should be regulating.

The Communications Act facilitated the move to digital broadcasting and the new lighter-touch broadcasting regulation system. This allowed far more cross-media ownership than ever before. Gone were the strict quota systems. Ofcom is a long way from the old Independent Television Authority with its remit of providing commercial programming. Ofcom's light touch is designed to control a range of commercial broadcasters working in a variety of circumstances. They have an obligation to some public service broadcasting, but Ofcom does not have the power of prior restraint and merely allocates franchises to commercial bidders to use within the rules it lays down, rather than providing a service with the help of contract providers.

2003 – a year of drama

Three major events came together in 2003 to completely change the way broadcasting regulation works. First, the Communications Act made its progress through the House ready to give the fledgling Ofcom its power. Second, Lord Hutton reported on the David Kelly affair, exposing a range of weaknesses within the BBC that it rushed to seal. Finally, the House of Commons Select Committee into Privacy and Media Intrusion decided to look at complaints coming from a range of sources about invasion of privacy and the behaviour of the media. Although the committee was particularly concerned about the press, it also took the opportunity to look at broadcasting. The Committee met through the early part of 2003, announcing its findings in June. Ofcom was running by this time but had not fully taken over the reins, as the Communications Act, which gives it its power, did not receive Royal Assent until July and Ofcom did not take over its role fully until January of 2004.

The Select Committee came up with more than thirty recommendations, some aimed at broadcasters and some at the press and the PCC. The most significant was the recommendation that there should be a law on privacy. This was immediately rejected by the government, as indeed were many of the other recommendations. The fledgling Ofcom was told it must seize the opportunity to reconsider how complaints against broadcasters should be handled. It was also suggested it should debate with the industry how to handle media scrums. One of Ofcom's first concerns was to launch the debate about the future of public service broadcasting. The BBC's failings from earlier that year made this a particularly important debate and probably helps explain why the BBC was so quick to pick up the lessons from the Hutton Report concerning the death of Dr David Kelly. The BBC had come under sustained attack from the government after broadcasting a story claiming the government had lied about the existence of weapons of mass destruction in Iraq. This story had been based on evidence from a civil servant who later committed suicide following the pressure of the story. The BBC stood by its story until the Hutton Report finished its inquiry into the matter in early 2004, announcing that Andrew Gilligan's claim – that the government probably knew that the claim that WMDs could be launched by Iraq within 45 minutes was wrong or questionable before the dossier was published – was unfounded.

Hutton went on to announce that he believed the BBC's editorial system was defective in allowing such allegations to be broadcast without seeing a script of what was to be said and considering whether it should be approved. He also felt that Mr Gilligan's language was imprecise in that the term 'sexed up' used by Mr Gilligan in reference to the government's attempted changes to the document could have two meanings, one of which might be acceptable and one of which wasn't. Because of this, Lord Hutton considered that the allegation was unfounded because many who heard the broadcast would have taken the latter meaning. Lord Hutton was also concerned that there were two versions of Mr Gilligan's notes of his interview with David Kelly as this meant it was impossible to be sure what Dr Kelly had told Mr Gilligan. Because of this, Lord Hutton decided that Dr Kelly had not told Mr Gilligan that the government knew the 45-minute claim was wrong, or that he had told Mr Gilligan that the 45-minute claim was not included in the draft document because it only came from one source. Lord Hutton also wondered whether Dr Kelly had said more to Mr Gilligan than he had intended and that at the time of the meeting he had not realised the gravity of the situation which he was helping to create. It is entirely likely that neither Andrew Gilligan nor David Kelly were aware of how their breakfast meeting would end up rocking the nation, leading to the death of one of them and the resignation of the other and several other key personnel at the BBC.

In his conclusions, Lord Hutton said that the allegations made by Mr Gilligan about the government were unfounded, and that editors should have seen a script of what he intended to say and that the editorial systems were defective in not insisting on this. He was also critical of the BBC management system that had not picked up on criticisms of Andrew Gilligan's reporting style from Kevin Marsh, the editor of the *Today* programme (http://www.the-hutton-inquiry.org. uk/content/report/chapter12.htm#a90 accessed 17/7/06). The crushing criticisms of the BBC, its editorial systems, its management and its reporter led to the governors finally agreeing they should apologise, causing the resignation of the Director General, Greg Dyke (who still does not accept the Hutton criticisms), the reporter concerned, Andrew Gilligan, and the chairman of the governors, Sir Christopher Bland. The new acting Director General Mark Byford quickly set up a review committee chaired by the BBC's Director of News Ronald Neil. The Neil Report said the committee was satisfied that a proper core script had been produced and approved for the 29 May 2003 broadcast, but that that had not then been followed by Andrew Gilligan. The committee concluded that the BBC's report of 6.07 a.m. on 29 May 2003 'was inaccurate and that with hindsight it would have done a number of things differently' (http://www.bbc.co.uk/info/policies/pdf/neil_report.pdf accessed 17/7/06).

The committee also:

- identified the problem of only using one source for a story;
- found that the notes did not support the allegations made;
- agreed that the allegations were not put to Downing Street for comment;
- believed there was an issue of fairness in not being clear about the nature of the allegations which prevented a proper opportunity to respond;
- said that the broadcast should have been scripted (although the BBC insists a core script was prepared, but not followed); and
- advised that the rules about BBC journalists writing for the press should be tightened.

The committee went on to recommend to the BBC that:

- Names of sources should always be used if possible.
- Anonymity should never be granted casually or automatically.

- Single source stories could continue if they were in the public interest and proper procedures were followed.
- Good note taking was of paramount importance.
- Two-way interviews should not be used for stories containing serious or potentially defamatory allegations.
- BBC staff would not be allowed to write newspaper articles dealing with current affairs.
- More emphasis was required on training.
- It should firm-up its complaints procedures.

(http://www.bbc.co.uk/info/policies/pdf/neil_report.pdf accessed 18/7/06)

As the BBC rallied under its new chairman, Michael Grade, and its new Director General, Mark Thompson, putting into practice those recommendations, Ofcom was busy carrying out an extensive consultation process about the future of public service broadcasting. It issued several consultation documents and the debate raged on through 2004 and 2005. The government finally issued its White Paper on the future of broadcasting in March 2006, with Culture Secretary Tessa Jowell announcing that the BBC would continue to receive the bulk of the licence fee, but it would now be overseen by a new trust, separate from its management. This would replace the governors who had always been in a dual role: there to run the BBC but also to protect viewers. In the future, the White Paper proposed, the BBC would be run by an executive board and would be overseen by the trust which would be a unique organisation that would serve the public interest by ensuring the delivery of quality and value to licence-fee payers. Licences would be issued by the trust to the Executive Board for running each BBC service with a 'public-value test' to be applied to all new BBC services or significant changes to existing services. The market-impact assessment for the public-value tests would be carried out by Ofcom. The government started recruiting for the new trust in the summer of 2006, hoping to appoint up to seven new members to join Michael Grade, who was to be the first chairman, along with three other members of the existing board of governors, including the member designate for Scotland.

As part of the licence fee settlement, the government proposed new forms of assistance for Channel 4, such as asking the BBC to provide Channel 4 with financial help towards meeting its capital switch-over costs, and Channel 4's desire to secure a limited amount of additional digital terrestrial capacity from the BBC.

Advances in technology continue to be one of the major concerns for regulation. High-definition TV meant a new set of standards, but more important is the convergence of internet on broadband and TV and radio. The ability of broadband users to be able to access radio and TV services as well as HD television services and download them at times to suit themselves means that scheduling may soon be a thing of the past. Terrestrial scheduled broadcasts will no doubt continue for a long time, but gradually people will want to build their own schedule as they either save broadcast programmes or use catch-up services or download programmes from the appropriate website to watch when they want. High-definition TV is in its early days, but the World Cup in 2006 was used as a platform to launch it to the UK public, as well as TV services to mobile phones and the internet. 3D TV transmissions were broadcast for several of the World Cup 2010 games. No doubt other advances in technology will quickly follow. The ability to receive TV on the move on phone handsets or tablet-style computers will also change the way we consume broadcasting.

The government's plans to turn off the analog signal and rely totally on digital were well advanced at the time of writing with Wales and the north west of England entirely digital and the rest of the country due to follow within two years.

Ofcom reviewed the Broadcasting Standards Commission Code of Practice during its early days and drew up a new code that it issued in 2005 (http://www.ofcom.org.uk/tv/ifi/codes/).

This was one of the recommendations of the DCMS Select Committee back in 2003, and an obligation under the Communications Act 2003. It reviewed its code in 2009 in the light of five years of adjudications. It made some changes to take account of the problems it had faced with TV competitions, especially those that relied on viewers or listeners phoning in votes or answers to quizzes. Many of these had been on premium phone lines that remained open after the latest time for entry, taking the viewer's money for the call, but not entering them into the competition or counting their vote. More than 20 serious complaints along these lines were upheld by Ofcom with fines totalling millions being levied as punishment.

Election 2010

The coalition government formed after the 2010 election produced a programme that contained very little of the plans the Conservatives had talked of before the election to reform Ofcom and the BBC trust. The National Audit Office will be given access to the BBC's accounts 'to ensure transparency' but few other changes in broadcasting are proposed at the time of writing. The coalition does intend to enable partnerships between local newspapers, radio and television stations in order to 'promote a strong and diverse local media industry.' This will presumably be done by relaxing the cross-media ownership laws that presently limit newspapers from owning radio or TV and vice versa.

Chapter 16

Codes of conduct as a regulatory system

This chapter looks at the uses of codes of conduct, including:

- The development of codes of conduct

- Styles of code

- Elements of codes of conduct

Many countries have codes of conduct for journalists: Kantian-style universal directives that oblige journalists to behave in a certain way. Codes are designed to cover the main ethical problems faced by journalists in gathering information for stories; dealing with their contacts and sources; how they go about publishing, broadcasting and presenting the information gathered and how they guarantee the quality of the information, including dealing with complaints that arise.

As I have explained before, Kantian-style codes of categorical imperatives work well for journalists as deciding matters of ethics on grounds of consequence is rarely appropriate as we hardly ever have full access to all the information required to measure whether it would be right to publish this story or that on the basis of the greatest utility. The best we could hope for is to measure the consequences of breaking such Kantian rules as: *always tell the truth* or *the public has a right to be informed and journalists have a duty to see that they are*. Codes of conduct allow the key ethical issues to be previously debated and the generally correct path to be previously identified.

It is interesting to draw comparisons between the different codes of conduct of the PCC, Ofcom, the BBC and the NUJ, as they highlight the differences in approach to journalism by print journalists, broadcast journalists, publishers and broadcasters. They also help expose the distorting effect that results from treating journalism as a marketable product rather than something that should be made available to people as part of some democratic responsibility. The other regulatory bodies in the UK do not have such far-reaching codes, and I will mention them when applicable.

Both the PCC Code and the NUJ Code are printed in full in Appendices 1 and 2 respectively. The *BBC Editorial Guidelines* is a long and very detailed document and so excerpts are used in the appendices as comparisons. The entire document is available on the World Wide Web at http://www.bbc.co.uk/guidelines/editorialguidelines/guidelines accessed 14/10/10. Ofcom's Code is also lengthy and is available at http://www.ofcom.org.uk/tv/ifi/codes/bcode/ but an edited version is in the appendices. It came into force in July 2005 but was updated in 2009 and republished in December of that year. Several other codes are also published in the appendices of this book for comparison, but all the European codes can be found at http://www.uta.fi/ethicnet/ or at http://www.mediawise.org.uk/display_page.php?id=40.

Virtually all democratic societies insist on some standards of ethical behaviour from their media. Consequently, many countries now have codes of conduct, upheld by professional or cross-industry bodies or, in some instances, by a legally appointed tribunal. Essentially, a code of conduct is a list of dos and don'ts to guide journalists through the maze of moral problems they face from day to day, and, as Nigel G.E. Harris points out: 'one of the most noteworthy features of codes for journalists is just how wide is the range of countries in which they have been adopted. They are found not just in Western Europe and North America, but in countries as diverse as Egypt, South Korea, Jamaica, Mali and Venezuela' (1992: 62). But, as this chapter explains, the content and types of issue covered by codes vary a great deal and their use and effectiveness have varied in the many countries in which they operate. However, before looking at the codes themselves we need to look at some of the fundamental issues that underlie them.

Personal codes versus public codes

Most people have their own personal code against which they can measure their behaviour. Some people's codes are pretty basic, whereas others have a much stricter personal code. Whatever a person's code is, it has to be self-policing; if it is breached, only he or she will know. Since people generally have a good idea about the motivation of their behaviour and most of the circumstances involved in a particular problem, they can act as both prosecutor and judge to determine whether this act or that breaches their personal code. However, codes which are externally regulated – that is, public codes – are more complex. It is no longer a question of acting as your own judge and jury.

A public code involves trying to work to a universal statement which is universally applied; if it is wrong for one person to do something under certain circumstances, then it must be wrong for another person to do the same thing under the same circumstances. This is obviously different from a personal code where an action I may well consider to be wrong would be considered perfectly acceptable by someone else. Because I work for Global News Corporation, for instance, I might consider it morally wrong to be disloyal to my employer by covering a story about corruption in GNC. However, a reporter from another news organisation could cover the same story with enthusiasm. Of course, I might consider any corruption to be wrong and would attempt to cover such a story for my news organisation. I might then be dismissed or be obliged to resign for damaging my employer's business.

For the universal application of moral codes, everyone has to be clear about and accept what the code has to say. Because of this, codes tend to be limited to areas of general agreement and phrased in a way that covers all circumstances. So, for instance, a code could stipulate that it is wrong that I should *lie* to get a story about GNC corruption, whichever company I worked for.

Moral basis of codes

Codes of conduct are usually described as being deontological. They are based on the duties contained within them. Anyone following a code of conduct does not need to identify the consequences that flow from their action in order to see that they are behaving morally. The mere fact that their motive is to behave morally and that they follow the code of conduct previously laid down is sufficient for them to be seen as behaving morally. This flows from Kantian categorical imperatives. Universal laws can be drawn up identifying what is generally agreed to be moral behaviour for that group of professionals. A series of clauses is usually produced obliging a journalist to tell the truth, or report only in a straightforward manner. A typical clause would say: 'Journalists must not engage in intimidation, harassment or persistent pursuit' (PCC 2006). This is clear and unambiguous. It is universal and has no qualifications. All journalists are obliged to follow this clause of the code and there can be no exceptions. That fits in well with Kantian theory of moral obligation. There is a universal law, it does apply in all circumstances and a journalist can adhere to it without any fear of behaving immorally – except that further up, the code says: 'It should not be interpreted so . . . broadly that it constitutes an unnecessary interference with freedom of expression or prevents publication in the public interest.' There clearly may be times when a journalist knows that publication in the public interest is vital for a story, but that that might mean harassment of a contact. Yet if the clause of the code is truly Kantian, there should be no way the journalist can avoid fulfilling the clause without bending or even breaking the clause. The PCC (and other code-making organisations) realise this and most journalistic codes have a public interest defence written into them. The PCC says: 'There may be exceptions to the clause marked * where they can be demonstrated to be in the public interest.' Clauses so marked include the one on harassment as well as those on privacy, children, reporting of crime and clandestine devices.

These rule-based codes serve a number of useful purposes for professionals. They save time, ensuring there is no need to reinvent the wheel at every moral dilemma. A consequentialist has to weigh the evidence at every decision, but a deontologist can just follow the rules. If the rules says 'Thou shalt not steal', then it's easy to follow: one just does not steal. This makes life quite a bit easier; no need to worry about whether you will get away with it, if you will be spotted, if you can make your escape, where to hide the stolen goods and if you will be able to sell them.

Another important function of codes of conduct is the important public relations role they have. They are often introduced to reassure the public that a profession has standards of practice and to imply, at least, that professionals who transgress those standards will be disciplined. Many professions and trades have raced to introduce codes of practice over the past few years in the light of rising consumer consciousness: 'Written codes of ethics suggest that the mass media, and the men and women who produce them, are virtuous servants of society. They imply unified allegiance to professional standards of performance' (Gordon et al. 1998: 65).

A trade or profession feels better able to fend off public criticism if it has a code of practice it can produce to wave at the public in times of crisis. Whether it is travel agents replying to criticisms following a large number of complaints from dissatisfied holiday-makers or insurance companies fearing high levels of claims and complaints following a big storm, the calming influence of a code of practice is very important. A company finds that being able to claim that all will be dealt with according to the code of practice deflects criticism in a way that is difficult to achieve by any other method. It allows decisions to be delayed while tempers cool and, more importantly, the issues are forgotten (and maybe even forgiven) by the wider public. No industry has failed to notice that codes of practice can add an aura of respectability and fairness without necessarily forcing any real need for responsibility. It is almost impossible to achieve this in any other way. Even government has seen the benefit of introducing codes, such as the citizen's charter.

A code of conduct also allows debate. The PCC now reviews its code on an annual basis. The NUJ reviewed its code recently, agreeing a new one in 2007; Ofcom reviewed its code in 2009, making changes for its new code launched in December 2009. In these cases, people know what the code is (or can easily find out) and involve themselves in the debate. If an issue springs up then all can look at the code and see how it serves the journalist in that ethical dilemma and the code can be adjusted if required.

Just as the code allows debate, so it allows education. For new practitioners, students and even seasoned professionals, identifying a code of practice can help develop an understanding of the issues identified in a code and encourage consideration of how best to apply the elements of the code. Having identified what the industry generally thinks is appropriate behaviour, it is easy to school others into the correct stance.

Framing codes of conduct

Writing a code of conduct is not easy if it is to fulfil its aims. It should be short and easy to remember. A long code will be one that is accessed only at times of difficulty. The *BBC Editorial Guidelines* are excellent, but no one could remember them all and they need to be accessed in order to get the BBC's view on an issue. The PCC Code and the NUJ Code are much shorter and so the principles involved can be easily remembered and applied in everyday situations.

A good code needs to be unambiguous. No one is able to spend time agonising over what a code clause means, with a deadline rushing towards them. It needs to say clearly and concisely what is expected of the professional so that there is no need for a debate over every story. This universalisation was identified as an important element of a categorical imperative by Kant and it is no surprise that a good clause should be qualified as little as possible.

A code that is clear and unambiguous is also important when it comes to policing. A regulatory body such as the PCC needs to be able to decide whether a publication has breached the code and not be deciphering what the code means. A clear code makes policing much easier. As with all rules and law, a regulatory authority cannot tell why someone adhered to or broke the code of conduct (although they might be able to make a good guess) but the advantage of a code is that, properly written, a professional is bound to have behaved ethically if they follow the code. For instance, it is very difficult to castigate someone for upholding a rule that says they should keep promises.

There might well be good reasons for breaking a promise, but it is much more difficult to justify breaking a promise than it is to justify sticking by a rule to keep your promises whatever the final outcome happens to be. In the same way, while we might tell what some people call white lies to our friends about how they look, no one can accuse us of being immoral if we say we always tell the truth.

Codes of conduct

The development of codes

The first codes of conduct were drafted in the USA in the early part of the twentieth century. Britain and other European countries followed in the 1920s and 1930s. The British NUJ Code was first suggested in 1935 and eventually launched in 1936 (Bundock, 1957). However, one of the first European countries to start to develop a code was Sweden.

> The Publicists Club [of Sweden], which was founded in 1874 with journalists, newspaper editors and other publishers as its members, had, on a number of occasions in the beginning of the 1900s, served as a self-appointed tribunal to hear complaints against newspapers.
>
> (Nordlund 1991: 2)

The Swedish Press Council was formed on 16 March 1916 at a joint meeting of the Board of Publicists Club, the Swedish Newspaper Publishers Association and the Swedish Journalists Association (now the Swedish Union of Journalists).

In the early stages, codes were relatively brief, consisting of a few paragraphs or so and covering some basic principles. However, with the massive growth of television and radio broadcasting during and after the Second World War, codes came to be seen as more important. Separate codes were set up for print and broadcast journalists in the UK and many other countries. Although the basic moral principles underlying the type of information to be used and how it is gathered remain much the same for print and broadcast journalists, their application, as we will see later in this chapter, is often very different.

In Britain, independent television and radio were, until recently, covered by three regulatory bodies: the Independent Television Commission (ITC) for TV or the Radio Authority for radio which dealt with broadcasting licences and produced guidelines for commercial broadcasters; the Broadcasting Standards Council (BSC) which adjudicated on complaints of taste and decency; and the Broadcasting Complaints Commission (BCC) which looked most closely at ethical issues as they affect journalists. The Broadcasting Act 1996 combined the BCC and the BSC into a new Broadcasting Standards Commission that started work in January 1998 with a new code of practice. All this was swept away with the Communications Act 2003. This handed all these powers to the Office of Communications (Ofcom) which now has the power to allocate licences for TV and radio and other communication channels as well as providing a framework for complaints and contents codes for broadcasting in all its forms, including the internet.

Broadcasting codes, which had always needed to be longer and more detailed than print codes because of the legislative structure they were obliged to work within, began to grow and what had been just a few paragraphs in the early codes often became several pages with many detailed clauses. The main reason for this was that professional media bodies were determined to account for every situation that could arise that might result in public outrage. However, conversely, the more complex the codes became the easier it became for the media to wriggle around the words therein. It is difficult to convince people determined to stamp out 'media excesses' that a short code is often better as a method of control than the long, detailed rambling one that many codes have now become.

A short code has the advantage of being easier for journalists to remember and use. They are able to measure directly their performance against the principles contained in the code and quickly realise when they are straying from the straight and narrow. For instance, 'thou shalt not steal' only becomes difficult to operate when it is hedged with a number of sub-clauses detailing what is meant under specific circumstances by 'thou', 'shalt' and 'steal'. Similarly, in journalism, if a code says 'journalists shall not represent comment as fact' all journalists would be able to use that to measure their behaviour even though they would not all come to the same conclusions in similar cases. One person's comment might be seen only as analysis, and interpretation by another.

Codes are often now more concerned with practicalities than with principles. The Swedish code of conduct, for instance, consists of 19 short paragraphs covering many of the main issues. The British NUJ Code of Conduct (Appendix 2) covers most issues in 14 fairly terse paragraphs. The British PCC Code of Practice (Appendix 1), however, requires a weighty 45 paragraphs in 16 clauses with 6 paragraphs of introduction to cover fewer issues. The Ofcom code, introduced in July 2005, has 10 sections, each of which typically has 15 clauses and as many as 28 in some cases (http://www.ofcom.org.uk/tv/ifi/codes/bcode accessed 14/4/10). This again makes it a code that can only be used as a reference source. It is too long for anyone to remember and therefore be fully aware of all the ground it is trying to cover.

The outcome is that the longer codes are now too long to be of use to editors and journalists who do not have time to refer to the code every time an issue comes up. Editors and journalists then have to rely on an understanding of the basic ethical principles, something they were rarely given during training. A short direct code, which they would have time to use, would give journalists guidance on the issues.

Building codes

There tends to be a fair measure of agreement worldwide about what should be in a code and these elements are usually grouped into two main types of clauses. These are either rights-based or functions-based. The rights-based clauses deal with such things as privacy, confidential sources and accuracy: what people have a right to expect from journalists. The functional elements outline how journalists should behave in order to perform well as journalists. This would also include accuracy and how the information is presented. The main elements of a code are as follows:

- Gathering information.
- Dealing with contacts and sources.
- Publishing the information.
- Presentation of the information.
- Guaranteeing its quality.
- Dealing with complaints.

These can be split into rights-based elements and functions-based elements.

Rights-based elements of codes

These spring from the human rights that underpin democratic societies and are accepted by the European Convention and the United Nations Declaration on Human Rights.

Freedom of expression is the first right that most journalists consider. This gives the media the right to publish material and the freedom of the media springs from this. However, most journalists and journalism codes take this further, converting this right into a duty for the practitioner. Not only does the journalist, and by extension, the media, have a right to free expression, but the citizen has a right to receive such outpourings of free expression. From this many people claim the public have a right to know. However, this is not a right that can be guaranteed and is really a shorthand way of saying that people have a right to receive information, should anyone be interested in presenting it to them. From this we can make it an ethical duty of journalists to be the ones to ensure they do receive such information and that it is a journalist's job to protect the freedom of the media. So, many codes have the duty to defend press freedom contained within them. The PCC's Code, for instance, talks about 'protecting both the rights of the individual and the public's right to know' (http://www.pcc.org.uk/cop/practice.html accessed 8/4/10). The NUJ's Code also has a clause insisting that journalists protect freedom of the press: 'A journalist at all times upholds and defends the principle of media freedom, the right to freedom of expression and the right of the public to be informed' (NUJ Rulebook, 2009).

Privacy is another human right that is now also protected within codes of conduct. However, it is entirely possible that employing one's right to freedom of expression could easily breach another's right to privacy. A mechanism needs to be developed that allows the balancing of these rights. The public interest will be discussed later.

Presumption of innocence and fair trial are other rights that need to be balanced against freedom of speech. If someone is to get a fair trial and be presumed innocent until that has happened, then there may need be limits put on what is written about that person before their trial. Comments about whether they are believed to be innocent or guilty could easily prevent them getting a fair trial and certainly prevent them being presumed innocent, but preventing their publication could interfere with freedom of expression.

Liberty and security are rights that might limit the reporter's pursuit of an interview and might also lead to a reporter being careful about the publication of addresses or information about a person's whereabouts. The right not be discriminated against, and the right to a reputation are other rights that are often included within a code of conduct. In the case of the UK, reputation, presumption of innocence, fair trial and discrimination are all included in the law.

Functions-based elements of codes

Truth and accuracy are the first functions-based elements of a code. Freedom of expression and freedom to receive information do not contain a right to only receive truthful information. It is up to the consumer to sort out which source can be trusted and therefore which information is truthful. The same is true about comment. However, it is clear that an ethical journalist will be one who is aiming to tell the truth and to minimise subjective reporting by avoiding comment. The taking of bribes, protecting sources and methods of news-gathering are all matters for the individual reporter to work on with the help of the code because these also obviously affect the truthfulness of the reporter and the trustworthiness of their reporting. However, these are functional elements of ethics, not rights-based – there can't be a right not to take bribes, nor can there be a right for people to expect reporters not to take bribes. People can expect reporters not to take bribes because good reporters tell the truth and cannot tell the truth if they are taking bribes or being influenced in other ways.

Taste and decency also covers a range of issues which are not rights-based but clearly need to be considered. Print codes rarely mention taste and decency. The ability to print pictures or text that might cause offence is so widely open to interpretation and is so dependent on social pressure, audience and community mores that newspapers and magazine codes such as that of the PCC ignore the issue. This is not the case for broadcasters who have to be much more careful about what they transmit. This fits with the general view that TV and radio are piped into people's homes and that representations of nudity, sex, bad language and violence should be carefully edited. The UK's obscenity laws also limit what can be published and so there has been a long tradition in the UK about the publication of material that might offend. Other countries take a different view about what is acceptable to be broadcast. Some European countries are far more liberal in their interpretation of what is acceptable than the UK, while the USA is often far more conservative than even the UK. Some Muslim countries are more prepared to show pictures of violence and death than the UK, but less prepared to show nudity and sex.

Public interest

All codes require a mechanism that allows practitioners to balance the constraints they face under the code with their right to freedom of expression. Freedom of expression allows journalists to say what they want, but limits must be arranged to avoid invading someone else's privacy, reputation, right to a fair trial, or to prevent them being offended by what we publish, without a good reason.

That mechanism is the 'public interest' – a poorly defined device that allows practitioners to consider breaching the rights of individuals or groups for the wider benefit of the public at large. These can be difficult decisions to make and it is at this point that we switch from the deontological approach and need to start analysing the consequences of our actions. We start to insert caveats: it is wrong to invade someone's private life *unless* it is in the public interest. This requires the practitioner to attempt to measure whether the damage done to the individual is outweighed by the benefit to the majority. Some codes try to identify what we mean by the public interest. The PCC Code, for instance, says:

1 The public interest includes, but is not confined to:
   (i)   Detecting or exposing crime or serious impropriety.
   (ii) Protecting public health and safety.
   (iii) Preventing the public from being misled by an action or statement of an individual or organisation.
2 There is a public interest in freedom of expression itself.

(http://www.pcc.org.uk/cop/practice.html accessed 8/4/10)

So, if a reporter decides that the only way to expose the unhygienic practices of a food processing plant (a danger to the public that could lead to the illness and possible death of many of the customers of the plant) is to get a job in the plant by deceit and film the illegal practices (thus breaching the terms and conditions of the new employment), then those immoral acts of deceit and breach of contract must be justified in some way and the only way available for the journalist is to show that they are in the public interest. The public interest is to bring the company's shoddy practices into the public domain so that the public can decide for themselves whether to eat food produced in a way that is a danger to their general health and safety. Without the defence of public interest, all that has happened is that the reporter has indulged in a series of immoral, perhaps illegal, practices by getting a job by deceit, lying to his new 'employer', breaching his duty of confidentiality and potentially defrauding money (in wages). This is a lot of immoral behaviour to be justified by the public interest.

Although codes are there to be changed by circumstance, any change to a code means that the way practitioners will behave is changed. It is also not always possible to determine how a seemingly small change might alter the behaviour of the whole industry. For instance, the redefining of clauses about children in the PCC's Code over a period of about thirteen years has led to a quite clear change in the way that the media covers issues surrounding children. The PCC had been particularly effective in protecting the privacy of children (Frost 2004: 101–14). However, this, combined with fears of paedophile attacks and antisocial behaviour has meant that media coverage of children as achievers and role models has almost disappeared in the UK.

Codes and professionals

Codes of conduct are introduced into any professional area to give moral guidance. 'They serve an important purpose by setting standards against which conduct can be measured and evaluated' (Gordon et al. 1998: 69). It has been argued above that to be effective, a good code needs to offer easy guidance to the people who actually need to use it. But, as we have seen, as codes have developed they have become longer and more complex and one of the problems journalists face is not so much whether they abide by the code of conduct (either the NUJ's Code of Conduct or the PCC's Code of Practice), but whether they know what it says. It is easy to be dismissive of a code of conduct if it is too long and contains complex and difficult-to-follow clauses about ethical matters that rarely interfere with the average journalist's business. For instance, a clause about gaining interviews only by straightforward means is more likely to be remembered, and therefore acted on, than more detailed, but often less used, clauses about seeking permission of an authorised person before entering a hospital (see Appendix 1). Imagine a journalist bursting into a private nursing-home bedroom wearing a borrowed white coat and trying to obtain an interview from a seriously ill patient while pretending to be a doctor. He or she would be less likely to breach a code clause discussing interviewing only in straightforward ways than a specific clause banning the interviewing of people in hospitals without the authority of hospital personnel. The first clause goes to the heart of the issue whereas the second might merely spark a debate about who an authorised person may be.

Exhibit 16.1 Amendments to the PCC Code of Practice

By June 2006 the British PCC Code of Practice had been amended almost thirty times since its inception in 1991 to include:

- 1992: Additional paragraph in preamble on the reprinting of adjudications.
- 1993: Clause on listening devices.
- 1993: Requirement for swift cooperation by editors inserted in preamble.
- 1993: Long-lens cameras included in privacy clause.
- 1993: Definition of private property inserted.
- 1993: Addition to editor's responsibility in harassment clause.
- 1993: Reference to private property definition added to harassment clause.

▶

- 1994: 'Responsible official' changed to 'responsible executive' in hospital clause.
- 1995: Addition of rules to prevent jigsaw identification in child sex cases.
- 1995: Alteration to definition of private property.
- 1995: Alteration to wording of clause on children in sex cases.
- 1996: Separation of payment to witnesses and payment to criminals.
- 1997: Rewritten sections, particularly on intrusion and privacy, following the death of Diana, Princess of Wales in 1997.
- 1998: Accuracy extended to cover photo manipulation.
- 1999: Change in wording on privacy of children as victims and witnesses.
- 2003: Witness payments in trials.
- 2004: Another substantial rewrite in June as part of the new proposal for 'permanent evolution' of the code.
- 2005: The inclusion of transgender people in the discrimination clause.
- 2006: A clause on suicide added.
- 2007: The Code is expanded to cover online versions of publications.
- 2007: A clause is added to prevent the unauthorised removal of documents or photographs and to prevent accessing digitally held private information.
- 2009: Account taken of complainant's own public disclosures in privacy cases.
- 2009: Journalists obliged to identify themselves and whom they represent.
- 2009: Editors now obliged to demonstrate that they reasonably believed the publication was acting in the public interest.

The PCC Code Committee seeks views from the public every year as part of its review of its code.

Exhibit 16.2 Amendments to Ofcom Code of Practice

Ofcom started taking complaints in 2004 using the old ITC and BSC codes.

It launched its new code in July 2005. It amended this in December 2009, to firm up the code clauses on competitions. This followed a number of code breaches by various broadcasters in dealing with competitions and phone voting.

Keeping it simple gives the journalist more chance to think about the issues in real situations and less chance of ignoring the issues altogether in an attempt to wriggle around weak wording. A study of recent regulatory authority breaches of codes shows that a significant number are caused by ignorance rather than wilfulness. Reasonable training about basic issues linked with a short easy-to-remember code are the best tools for ensuring compliance to accepted standards.

Chapter 17

Press regulation systems in the UK and Ireland

This chapter outlines the regulatory systems in use in the UK and Ireland, including:

- The Press Complaints Commission

- The Teenage Magazine Advisory Panel

- The Press Council, Ireland

- The Internet Watch Foundation

Regulatory authorities

There are several regulatory mechanisms in the UK and Ireland designed to control the press:

- Press Complaints Commission
- Press Council of Ireland
- National Union of Journalists
- Teenage Magazine Arbitration Panel
- Internet Watch Foundation

The press in both the UK and Ireland is regulated by self-regulatory bodies, professional bodies such as the NUJ and possibly internal company regulation through a code of conduct or an ombudsman.

Press Complaints Commission

The PCC was set up following the first Calcutt report in 1991 solely to resolve complaints. Calcutt's recommendation that the Commission should not become involved in press freedom issues was regretted by the old Press Council. It felt that to seek to adjudicate on complaints that were not measured against the need for press freedom was to leave the media vulnerable to censorship. Despite these regrets, the old Press Council shut its doors in December 1990 and the PCC took up the reins in January 1991 under the leadership of Lord McGregor of Durris who had chaired the 1974–77 Royal Commission on the Press and was chairman of the Advertising Standards Authority.

The PCC is funded by Pressbof (the press standards board of finance), a body set up by newspaper publishers' organisations after the publication of the Calcutt Report. It raises finance from publishers to pay for the PCC and appoints the PCC's chairman. It also appoints the Editors' Code Committee that draws up the Code of Practice, that is ratified by Pressbof for use by the PCC in its adjudications.

The members of the Press Complaints Commission are selected by an Appointments Commission, which has five members: the PCC chairman, three members nominated by the PCC chairman and the chairman of Pressbof. The nominated members each serve for four years.

There are seventeen members of the Commission including the chairman. Seven of these are the press members, who should be working editors or senior journalists in executive positions. The remainder are independent members who cannot be involved with, or interested in, the business of publishing newspapers, periodicals or magazines. Since 2003, the new independent members have been appointed following an open advertising procedure. Press adverts invite people to apply for the position and the appointments committee makes the final decision.

The PCC does not normally initiate enquiries and does not require a legal waiver from complainants. Under the old Press Council, a legal waiver had prevented complainants going on to sue the newspaper through the courts, using a council judgment in their favour as evidence. The PCC judges complaints against a code of practice drawn up by a committee of editors nominated by Pressbof.

How the PCC works

The PCC is a lay committee, with a small professional secretariat to service it. As well as dealing with complaints, the PCC advises editors before publication. According to Lord Wakeham, who took over as chairman of the PCC in January 1995, more and more editors sought the advice of the PCC on particular stories or the approach to particular stories before publication during the 1990s. The hotline to the PCC was established shortly after Wakeham took over at the PCC, allowing editors to contact the PCC and discuss stories before publication to get a feel for the PCC's view. McGregor had not been keen on the idea, as he feared it smacked of prior restraint. This pre-publication advice continued during Sir Christopher Meyer's chairmanship, and staff at the Commission advise that it is an important part of their work these days with the chairman Baroness Buscombe (appointed in 2009), explaining on Radio 4's *Media Show* in early 2010 that in her office there was a huge file of such contacts from editors about stories that remained unpublished following PCC advice.

When the PCC receives a complaint they consider whether it is a potential breach of the code of practice. If it is, they will then seek to resolve the complaint, conciliating between the complainant and the publication. If this is not possible or the complaint concerns a potentially very serious breach of the code, the Commission will adjudicate, deciding whether to uphold the complaint or reject it.

The PCC also has an important role to play in providing material about self-regulation and the Code of Practice for trainee journalists and students. It lists several speakers on its website who will visit colleges or local community groups to discuss the PCC and its role. It also holds occasional open days in major cities around the country, puts advertisements in newspapers and magazines, using space donated by the publishers and participates at conferences. A helpline is also available to the public on 0845 600 2757 (0131 220 6652 in Scotland, 0292 039 5570 in Wales). An average of 120 calls a week were received in 1995, and in the 2005 report the PCC said it still deals with hundreds of calls, including a number of requests for journalists from newspapers and magazines to desist from asking questions, following or photographing people. The PCC offers general guidance to editors on its website (http://www.pcc.org.uk/EditorsCodeofPractice/UnderstandingEditorsCode.html accessed 22/4/10). This includes such matters as refugees and asylum seekers, court reporting or paedophiles.

How to complain

The PCC issues guidance on its website to would-be complainants. A complaint should be sent to the Commission, where a decision is taken on whether the matter presents a possible breach of the Code of Conduct. It is here that the importance of the Code becomes clear. Only if the Code is potentially breached can a complaint be considered.

The editor of the publication is then sent a copy of the complaint and it is suggested that he or she deals with it direct. This can often be done with a correction, some form of right of reply or an apology. If the matter is resolved to everyone's satisfaction at this stage, the PCC would not normally pursue it further. If the situation is not resolved, the Commission would seek to resolve the complaint by mediation. If this fails then the PCC would go on evaluate the case. First it will decide of there has been a breach of the code of practice. If there has then the PCC will decide whether the publication has taken or offered sufficient remedial action such as a correction, or an apology. If the PCC believes that the publication has offered sufficient remedial action then it will consider the case resolved. Only if there is insufficient remedial action, or such action is not feasible will the PCC uphold the complaint with a public ruling. This ruling must be published by the publication concerned and is also published on the PCC's website. These are the only penalties that the PCC is able to impose, although it has managed to obtain small amounts of compensation in one or two isolated cases.

The PCC attempts to deal with complaints as quickly as possible. It will normally only deal with complaints made within one month of publication or within one month of a reply from an editor to whom a complaint had been made. It will also not normally deal with third-party complaints, that is, complaints made by someone not directly involved in the complaint. The PCC will approach the subject of the story, if it does decide to follow up a third-party complaint, to seek his or her cooperation and will normally drop the proceedings if that person does not wish to become involved. If the complaint is about a story that involves litigation, then the PCC will normally wait until proceedings are over before proceeding with the complaint.

Types of complaint

All figures in this section are abstracted from the appropriate PCC annual report or biannual report. The PCC received 37,000 complaints in 2009 (this dwarfed the 4,698 complaints in 2008 – 358 more than in 2007). The vast majority of these concerned a column in the *Daily Mail* written by Jan Moir concerning the death of Boyzone singer Stephen Gately (see Table 17.1). The Gately column caught the attention of the twitteratti leading to thousands of complaints being made to the PCC. The Commission eventually decided that despite the column's shortcomings, the *Mail* was entitled to publish such a column although it was also right to publish a subsequent apology.

The number of complaints made to the PCC have climbed steadily over the years since 1991 and the Commission has consistently said that it believed the increase in complaints over the past 20 years was due to increasing awareness of the Commission rather than falling standards, a claim it repeated in its 2008 annual report (PCC 2009: 26). No attempt was made by the Commission in its 1998 annual report to explain the substantial fall in complaints that occurred in that year (down from 2,944 to 2,505).

The majority of complaints were not given a hearing by the PCC for a variety of reasons. Of those that did receive a PCC decision an average of 19.6 per cent were resolved whilst an average of only 1.9 per cent were adjudicated. The PCC's definition of resolved covers several different outcomes and it defines resolved as used in Table 17.2 as: 'complaints resolved to the express satisfaction of those complaining or those complaints in which the Commission judged that an offer of remedial action by the editor was sufficient to remedy any possible breach of the Code of Practice.' The PCC deems a case to be resolved when 'the PCC has been able to negotiate a resolution with the publication concerned that is satisfactory to the complainant' (http://www.pcc.org.uk/cases/index.html). It does this by a correction or an apology; a follow-up piece or letter from the complainant; a private letter of apology from the editor; an undertaking as to future conduct by the newspaper; or the annotation of the publication's records to ensure that the error is not repeated.

Over the past ten years there has been a gradual shift in emphasis from adjudication to resolution with the number of adjudications reducing over the years in both absolute and relative terms and the number of resolutions increasing (see Figure 17.1) with the PCC identifying in its 2006 report a 400 per cent increase in resolutions over the previous ten years while overall complaints increased by about 20 per cent. In its 2009 report, the PCC goes further in answer to its critics who say that very few of the thousands of complaints received are actually acted upon. New chairman Baroness Peta Buscombe writes:

> The PCC receives thousands of emails and letters every year, but many do not raise substantive issues and cannot be taken forward. It would be wrong to use these as the base figure for any comparison. Last year we made over 1600 individual rulings. In those cases, we required remedial action or criticised the editor over 40% of the time. The real figure that matters is 2 in 5, not 1 in 250.
>
> (http://www.pcc.org.uk/review09/letter_from_chairman/)

Table 17.1 Complaints made to PCC

	1991	1992	1993	1994	1995	1996	1997	1998	1999	2000	2001	2002	2003	2004	2005	2006	2007	2008	2009
No prima facie breach of code	347	584	704	914	1026	897	914	954	942	857	921	711	593	549	554	484	592	837	993
Disallowed as from third party	0‡	107	114	87	77	146	335	205	0	0	157	163	581	138	160	649	142	72	155
Resolved with editor	142	182	207	158	417	384	520	546	638	513	1345	1062	1426	417	565	2448	603	675	516
Disallowed for delay	46	64	97	85	91	110	93	112	0	0	153	155	80	65	31	13	0	10	3
Outside remit	137	232	447	427	800	1125*	593	689	0	0	403	502	630	632	909	472	560	0	777
Adjudicated – upheld or partly upheld	40	32	33	37	28	25	38	34	25	22	19	18	9	8	4	15	19	20	18
Adjudicated – rejected	27	51	52	43	33	40	43	35	20	35	17	6	12	22	16	16	17	17	17
Resolved		45	190	149	152	99	120	111	144	96	171	152	276	160	368	253	561	263	550
Complaints made to PCC	1,520	1,963	1,782	2,091	2,508	3,023	2,944	2,505	2,427	2,225	3,033	2,630	3,649	3,618	3,654	3,325	4,340	4,698	37,000+

PRESS COMPLAINTS COMMISSION

Source: All figures are from the appropriate PCC Annual Report with the exception of the figures for resolution and adjudication which are calculated from the website.

Notes:

From 2005 PCC issued biannual rather than monthly reports so some figures are January to January and some are April to April.

* Includes Euro 1996 complaints.

‡ Third-party complaints were not listed separately.

2009 total complaints includes more than 22,000 complaints about Jan Moir's column in the *Daily Mail* concerning the death of Stephen Gately.

Table 17.2 Fate of complaints to the PCC

Total complaints received 1991 to end of 2009	54,439	
Not pursued by complainant	1,783	3.3%
No case under the code	13,908	25.5%
Outside remit	11,093	20.4%
Disallowed for unjustified delay	1,419	2.6%
Third-party complaints	3,672	6.7%
Complaints not formalised*	10,733	19.7%
Resolved	10,673	19.6%
Adjudicated	1,016	1.9%

*This category was introduced only in 2004 and so covers just six years. The percentage is still a percentage of *all* complaints

During 2009, the PCC made significant changes in the way it presents its statistics, moving away from identifying the number of complaints it receives, which the 2009 report now characterises as contacts rather than complaints. It considers complaints rather than contacts so that although 25,000 may have contacted the PCC about the Jan Moir case, this is only one complaint. It then splits those complaints into two categories: complaints it could deal with (738) and complaints it couldn't, which include initial e-mail and letter contacts not followed through (2,600), complaints outside the PCC's remit (777) third-party complaints (155) and matters of taste (196). Of the complaints it could deal with, 609 were resolved, 111 received sufficient remedial action and 18 received public censure.

Resolution is used for complaints that, although of importance to the complainants, are generally relatively minor in the scheme of things. Almost always such complaints concern accuracy, occasionally combined with another element of the Code of Practice. Of the 3,954 resolved cases listed by the PCC on their website, 96.6 per cent concern accuracy.

Three typical examples of PCC resolutions selected at random in 2010 include:

- *A man* v *The Sunday Times*: A man complained to the Press Complaints Commission that the newspaper had linked him to a story about airport security when it was not genuinely relevant and the details reported were inaccurate. The newspaper did not accept that there had been a breach of the Code. However, the complaint was resolved when the newspaper took out the offending paragraph from the online article and the PCC negotiated the removal of the reference to the complainant's name in the Google link to the piece. The newspaper also took steps to ensure that online searches for the complainant's name did not show the article as a result.
- *Reza Esfandiari* v *The Times*: Reza Esfandiari complained to the Press Complaints Commission that the newspaper had published an online article which appeared to doubt the legitimacy of Mohsen Rezai's success during elections in Lali, Iran. The complainant provided statistics which showed that Mr Rezai had indeed won the election. The complaint was resolved when the newspaper agreed to amend the sentence in question to make clear that – while Mahmoud Ahmadinejad was predicted to win a two-thirds majority – it was, in fact, Mr Rezai who won in Lali by a similar margin.

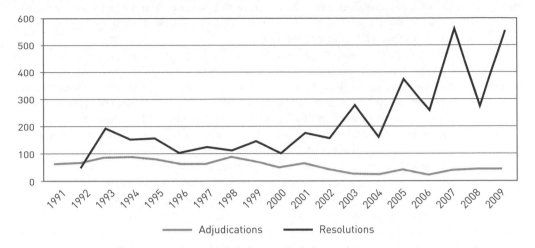

Figure 17.1 Adjudications and resolutions

- *Ms Gillian Lafferty* v *Mail on Sunday/Daily Mail*: Ms Gillian Lafferty, aunt of Niamh Lafferty, complained to the Press Complaints Commission that coverage of her niece's death in the newspapers contained inaccuracies and intruded into her family's grief. The complaint was resolved when – after the *Mail on Sunday* had published an apology to the Lafferty family in regard to a separate complaint from a family member – the newspapers each wrote private letters of apology to the complainant and her family.

Most complaints that are resolved end with the editors concerned publishing an apology, correction or, occasionally, offereing the complainant an opportunity to reply or changing or annotating the online version. The PCC sees this as a success area and says in its 2005 report:

> The most notable headline figure, in terms of complaints statistics for 2005, is not the 3,654 complaints the PCC received over the course of the year, although that is (by 5 complaints) the highest in the Commission's history. It is the increase by more than 40% in the number of complaints that were resolved following offers from publications: the highest ever number of resolved complaints in the fifteen-year history of the PCC.
> (http://www.pcc.org.uk/assets/111/PCC_Annual_Review2005.pdf accessed 23/7/06)

Adjudications are where the whole PCC makes a decision on whether the publication complained about has breached the PCC's Code of Practice. Newspapers and magazines that come under the PCC's jurisdiction are obliged to publish these adjudications; it is the only sanction that the PCC has. Nearly all publications, and certainly all major publications, come under the PCC's jurisdiction, paying fees to Pressbof for the Commission's upkeep although, embarrassingly, Express Newspapers did not for a period pay their subscriptions. There were also 92 complaints not followed through in 2009 because the complaint concerned a publication that did not subscribe.

The number of adjudications that are upheld sits fairly typically at around 50 per cent of those considered year on year, although there are some marked differences with 2003–2006 providing very few upheld adjudications.

Figure 17.2 shows how adjudications have fallen from a high in 1993, when there were 1,782 complaints, despite 2009 producing more than double the number of complaints (after ignoring the complaints concerning Stephen Gately). Only a fifth of the number of complaints dealt with in 2004 were upheld compared to that in 1998. This decrease in adjudications is illustrated very clearly in Figure 17.2. Resolution of a complaint means the publication has provided a correction, an apology or a reader's letter, all things that the publication could have done at the first complaint from a reader without the involvement of the PCC.

The really interesting part about complaints is that although the PCC dealt with 1,416 complaints from the 37,000+ contacts in 2009, hardly any of these complaints were of any real substance. Either we have an excellent press that belies the complaints that are constantly made about its performance or the PCC has very little impact on the standards of the UK press. To follow through on this its worth examining in detail the type of complaint the PCC considers.

In every year of PCC operation the majority of the complaints received were about accuracy with the average running at 64 per cent by 2009 (see Table 17.3). Fewer complaints about accuracy are adjudicated, largely because this is the easiest group to deal with by resolution: 96.6 per cent of resolved cases concern accuracy, only 56 per cent of adjudicated cases concern accuracy.

On average, 18 per cent of complaints made concern privacy: 11.4 per cent privacy, 2.5 per cent harassment and 4.1 per cent intrusion into private grief. Privacy is, while not the most numerous, certainly the most contentious of complaints made to the PCC. Not surprisingly, the percentage of resolutions concerning privacy, harassment and intrusion is lower than this at 12.9 per cent while almost half of adjudications concern privacy, harassment and intrusion at 48.7 per cent. The Commission has always been concerned about privacy intrusions, as has Parliament, the public and media campaigners. The PCC appointed Professor Robert Pinker as the Privacy Commissioner in 1995 to investigate privacy complaints but he was not replaced in this role following his semi-retirement in 2004. The PCC said: 'The Commission is especially vigilant in cases involving intrusion into privacy, and brings instances of severe or calculated breach of the Code to the attention of publishers in order that the need for appropriate disciplinary action may be considered' (PCC, 1995: 7).

The other areas that bring significant levels of complaint are children and discrimination. Although only 2.1 per cent of complaints received concern children; more than 10 per cent of those adjudicated involve children. Discrimination on the other hand, attracts 7.1 per cent of all complaints but only 0.3 per cent are resolved and 5.1 per cent adjudicated. This is because many are not deemed to be in breach of the Code as they are made by third parties or are not stories that discriminate against a specific individual (see Table 17.3).

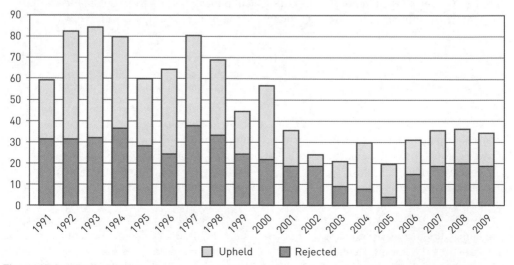

Figure 17.2 Adjudications

Although the Culture, Media and Sport Select Committee in its 2003 report called on the PCC to publish statistics of complaints against publications, this is something the PCC has consistently refused to do. It published general statistics about the number of complaints about national and regional papers and magazines, but not individual newspapers.

Statistics of adjudications collected over the lifetime of the PCC to early 2010 show that *The Sun* newspaper has consistently attracted the most complaints although only 40 per cent are upheld. *The Sun* is closely followed by its News International stablemate the *News of the World*. Not surprisingly, national daily and Sunday titles lead the league table. No regional newspaper has had more than six complaints adjudicated (see Table 17.4).

Things look slightly different when it comes to resolutions (see Table 17.5). Here the *Daily Mail* leads the table by a very long way with *The Sun* its closest rival, followed by the *Mirror* and the *Daily Express*. The majority of national daily and Sunday publications have between 50 and 100 resolutions, while magazines and regional papers more typically have 10 to 20.

Third-party complaints

The PCC is only obliged to consider complaints from those directly affected. However, the Commission may decide to consider a complaint from a third party. It would normally do so only when the issue was of public interest. Because of the way the PCC looks at complaints, the decision on whether it is a third-party complaint is not taken until it is decided whether there is a prima facie breach of the Code.

Table 17.3 Types of complaint

Type	Received	Resolved	Adjudicated
Accuracy	64.0%	96.6%	56%
Privacy	11.4%	11.7%	33%
Misrepresentation	1.7%	0.1%	8.4%
Children	2.1%	2%	10.1%
Harassment	2.5%	0.3%	8.1%
Discrimination	7.6%	0.3%	5.1%
Right of reply	2.0%	0.9%	4.6%
Intrusion	4.1%	0.9%	7.6%
Payments to criminals	0.3%	0	3.8%
Innocent relatives (reporting of)	0.7%	0.7%	3.5%
Hospitals	0.3%	3.6%	2.7%
Confidential sources	0.2%	0	0.8%
Sexual assaults	0	6.0%	0.3%
Finance	0.1%	1.9%	0.1%
Payments to witnesses	0	0.3%	0.4%

Table 17.4 Complaints league table as at April 2010

Publication	Total complaints	Upheld	Part upheld	% Upheld	Rejected	Resolved
The Sun	60	24	1	40.0	35	0
News of the World	53	17	5	32.1	28	2
Mail on Sunday	50	16	3	32.0	28	1
Daily Mail	45	7	2	15.6	34	2
Daily Mirror	45	13	5	28.9	26	1
Evening Standard	35	10	2	28.6	21	2
Sunday Times	34	12	0	35.3	22	0
Daily Star	29	10	1	34.5	16	2
Sunday People	26	9	1	34.6	16	0
Sunday Mirror	23	10	1	43.5	10	1
Daily Express	22	6	2	27.3	14	0
Daily Telegraph	21	5	1	23.8	13	2
Sunday Mail	21	8	2	38.1	10	1
Daily Record	16	5	2	31.3	9	0
Today	16	11	0	68.8	5	0
The Times	14	2	0	14.3	11	0
Sunday Telegraph	13	2	0	15.4	9	2
The Guardian	12	2	1	16.7	9	0
The Independent	10	3	0	30.0	7	0
Daily Sport	9	9	0	100.0	0	0
Sunday Sport	9	9	0	100.0	0	0
Sunday Mercury, Birmingham	8	6	1	75.0	1	0
Sunday Express	7	2	1	28.6	4	0
Independent on Sunday	7	2	0	28.6	5	0
The Observer	7	4	0	57.1	2	0
The Sun, Scotland	6	1	2	16.7	3	0
The News, Portsmouth	6	1	1	16.7	4	0
Scotland on Sunday	6	2	0	33.3	4	0
Sunday World	6	3	0	50.0	3	0

Hello!	6	4	0	66.7	2	0
Bedfordshire on Sunday	6	5	0	83.3	1	0
Yorkshire Evening Post	5	1	0	20.0	4	0
Evening Times, Glasgow	5	1	0	20.0	4	0
Bristol Evening Post	5	2	0	40.0	3	0
Manchester Evening News	5	3	1	60.0	1	0
OK! Magazine	5	3	0	60.0	2	0
Standard Recorder	4	1	0	25.0	3	0
Press And Journal, Aberdeen	4	1	0	25.0	3	0
Derby Evening Telegraph	4	1	0	25.0	3	0
Sunday Sun	4	1	1	25.0	2	0
Woman	4	2	1	50.0	1	0
Evening Chronicle	4	2	1	50.0	1	0
Chat	4	3	1	75.0	0	0
Luton on Sunday	4	3	1	75.0	0	0
The Voice	4	3	0	75.0	1	0
FHM Magazine	4	3	0	75.0	0	1
Evening Argus, Brighton	4	4	0	100.0	0	0
Bella	4	4	0	100.0	0	0
The Herald, Plymouth	3	0	0	0.0	3	0
Southern Daily Echo	3	0	1	0.0	2	0
Evening News, Edinburgh	3	0	0	0.0	3	0
Scottish Sun	3	0	0	0.0	3	0
Daily Post, Liverpool	3	1	0	33.3	2	0
The Journal (Newcastle)	3	1	1	33.3	1	0
Hertfordshire Mercury	3	1	0	33.3	2	0
News Shopper	3	1	0	33.3	2	0
PA	3	2	0	66.7	1	0
Private Eye	3	2	0	66.7	1	0
Evening Post, Reading	3	3	0	100.0	0	0
Business Age	3	3	0	100.0	0	0

Table 17.5 Newspaper resolutions league table

Top 40 publications by number of PCC resolutions, 1991 to April 2010		
1	Daily Mail	239
2	The Sun	180
3	Daily Mirror	106
4	Daily Express	104
5	News of the World	94
6	The Times	90
7	The Mail on Sunday	86
8	Evening Standard	80
9	The Guardian	63
10	The Daily Telegraph	62
11	The Sunday Times	57
12	Sunday Mirror	52
13	Daily Star	51
14	Daily Record	50
15	The People	46
16	Sunday Express	45
17	The Independent	38
18	Scottish Sun	37
19	The Sunday Telegraph	36
20	Sunday Mail	35
21	The Observer	28
22	Daily Sport	19
23	Metro	18
24	South Wales Echo	17
25	Daily Telegraph	15
26	Edinburgh Evening News	15
27	Press & Journal	15
28	The Scotsman	15
29	Express & Echo	14

30	Scottish Daily Mail	14
31	Take A Break	14
32	The Herald	14
33	Manchester Evening News	13
34	Sunday World	13
35	The Independent on Sunday	13
36	Today	13
37	Evening Chronicle (Newcastle Upon Tyne)	12
38	Hull Daily Mail	12
39	Lancashire Evening Telegraph	12
40	Liverpool Echo	12

The Commission prints copies of all its adjudications in a regular report. These used to be published monthly but in the last couple of years have been produced every two or even three months and finally, from 2006, every six months. This is partly because adjudications are now loaded on to the website as they are made and hard copy publication ceased at the end of 2009. There has been a significant change in the PCC's approach to third-party complaints, though, over the years. The PCC's traditional position of not taking third-party complaints became more and more difficult to sustain as the number of race complaints rose during the attacks on immigrants of the new millennium. Papers such as the *Daily Express* consistently ran stories portraying refugees in a way that many felt was racist, unfair and inaccurate. Slowly the PCC found itself obliged to accept more and more third-party complaints and finally it subtlely, and without publicity, redefined third-party to mean complaints involving a specific subject that had been brought by another. Complaints about accuracy made over stories that have no specific individual subject could now be complained about by third parties, the PCC's officers claimed. The Stephen Gately/Jan Moir case gave the PCC a particular problem after more than 25,000 third-party complaints were made; should they investigate even though the complaints were all third party? They were finally let off the hook when Gately's partner complained that the article was an intrusion into private grief.

Charter Compliance Panel

Another major change introduced in 2004 by the new chairman and flagged in the 2003 Select Committee's report was the Charter Compliance Panel and the Charter Commissioner. The Commissioner, and chairman of the Compliance Panel is Lt Gen Sir Michael Willcocks but at the time of writing the panel has no other members as it is in suspense pending the outcome of a review being carried out by the PCC.

The Compliance Panel is an independent audit committee that oversees the work of the PCC. It examines cases at random and produces a report and recommendations each year. It is not an appeal committee, but if complainants have complaints about the way their complaint was handled, they can write to the Charter Commissioner who will investigate and report any findings and recommendations to the PCC.

Websites

Pressbof decided in February 2007 that it should extend the remit of the PCC to cover editorial audio-visual material on newspaper and magazine websites. This was agreed after Pressbof decided there had been a significant step change in the industry with associated websites moving away from simply replicating the printed version of the newspaper or magazine and producing new and different material, often involving video or audio. Pressbof identified two key requirements for such material to be covered by the PCC:

1 that the editor of the newspaper or magazine is responsible for it and could reasonably have been expected both to exercise editorial control over it and apply the terms of the Code;
2 that it was not pre-edited to conform to the online or offline standards of another media regulatory body.

(http://www.pcc.org.uk/news/index.html?article=NDMyMg==)

They went on to decide nearly three years later that the PCC should expand its remit to cover online-only publications. There were three guidelines attached to this announcement:

The extension has been agreed on the following basis:

1 such publications must be recognisable as UK based newspapers or magazines which, if in printed form, would come within the jurisdiction of the PCC.
2 the publisher and editor must subscribe to the Editors' Code of Practice.
3 the publisher must agree to pay registration fees to PressBoF.

(http://www.pcc.org.uk/news/index.html?article=NDMyMg==)

Baroness Buscombe, Chairman of the PCC, said about the move:

We welcome the decision by the industry. The PCC needs this freedom to develop rapidly to meet the challenges and the opportunities presented by media convergence. One clear strength of the self-regulatory system is its flexibility to adapt to changing circumstances, while still providing a service that is free, fast, discreet and which involves the public in its decision-making.

Sanctions

The PCC's only sanction against a publication that breaches its code is to insist that they publish the PCC's adjudications. A number of critics, including the Culture, Media and Sport Select Committee have called on the PCC to introduce fines and possibly a financial compensation scheme (perhaps to charity) to punish errant publications, but the PCC has dismissed both of these on number of occasions. It says, in reference to a compensation scheme, that there is no evidence that complainants are seeking a financial award. This is probably true, but it doesn't mean that a financial punishment wouldn't be supported by complainants. However, the PCC fear this would slow up the process as more lawyers would be likely to become involved as publications strove harder to avoid such penalties – just what proponents of financial penalties had in mind. A suggestion that publications with poor complaints records should pay more to Pressbof for the PCC's upkeep was referred to Pressbof by the PCC.

Other sanctions could involve a front-page taster for the publication of an adjudication. The PCC promised to keep this under review.

Investigations and campaigns

The Select Committee and others have also called on the PCC to do more in terms of campaigns about press freedom and investigations into press involvement in major news stories such as the Bridgend suicides, the McCann abduction or the Ipswich murders.

Teenage Magazine Arbitration Panel

The Teenage Magazine Arbitration Panel was set up in 1996 to regulate the sexual content of magazines following concerns that teenage magazines contained overly-specific sexual content. It has produced guidelines in consultation with the industry and the Home Office.

TMAP aims to:

- provide an impartial forum for the adjudication of complaints;
- monitor adherence to the guidelines;
- promote its work among the general public;
- provide information and conduct research on the role of teenage magazines in the development of adolescents.

It covers *Bliss, Mizz, Sugar* and *Top of the Pops*. Other teenage magazines have closed since the formation of TMAP as this sector of the market has been hit by lower sales and increasing website use according to TMAP's 2007 annual report (http://www.tmap.org.uk/public/downloads/ TMAP_2007_AnnualReport_FINAL.pdf).

Complaints about content in teenage magazines should first be sent to the magazine, but if no satisfactory response is received, a complainant can write to TMAP. The chairman of TMAP, Dr Fleur Fisher, defends the organisation, saying it is 'the most closely regulated section of the magazine industry' (http://www.tmap.org.uk/cgi-bin/go.pl/news/article.html?uid=9726 accessed 25/7/06). Magazines are required to make it clear that any sexual contact under the age of 16 is illegal. However, TMAP is not overly busied by complaints, dealing with only one complaint in 2005 and then one in 2007. The 2005 complaint was against *Sugar* (12 April 2005) which carried an article about a young woman in Zambia who, having lost her father, was forced by her sister and cousin into prostitution at the age of 11 in order to feed the family. The complainant felt that the magazine had not made it clear that selling one's body for sex was illegal in the UK (but not in Zambia). TMAP upheld the complaint on that basis, saying that the article should have directly referred to underage sex being illegal in the UK. The panel also said:

> The Panel, in reaching their conclusion took into account a number of mitigating factors, most notably the general tone of the article which warned of the emotional and physical horrors of prostitution; that the article clearly set out the dangers of unprotected sex; and also the positive impact of charities which enable people to regain control of their lives. The Panel was keen to stress the importance of magazines reflecting the lives of young girls in other parts of the world, and that this article was praiseworthy in that respect. The Panel also noted that prostitution in Zambia is not illegal.
>
> (http://www.tmap.org.uk/cgi-bin/wms.pl/668 accessed 25/7/06)

In 2007, there was a complaint against *Sugar* magazine for an article headlined: *Sugar pulling guide – 6 secrets of sexiness*. However, the panel found that this did not breach the guidelines.

Competition Commission

The Competition Commission has only a very limited role in the regulation of the media in that it is obliged to look at potential purchases, mergers or takeovers of newspapers or magazines. There is special protection under the appropriate Act to ensure that such proposed takeovers are fully considered in the light of the public interest. Any such merger would be referred to the commission by the Secretary of State under the Fair Trading Act 1973.

National Union of Journalists

The NUJ was the first body in the UK to introduce a code of journalistic ethics. This was drawn up at the union's annual conference in 1936. The union introduced the Code into the rule book, making a breach of the Code a disciplinary offence. A journalist who is a member of the union could be reprimanded, fined or even expelled from the union for breaching the Code.

In 1986, the union set up an Ethics Council. Until 1979, the union had been a part of the Press Council but, after leaving over what it saw as the Council's failings, many members felt that the union should set up its own council. The Ethics Council was established for two reasons:

- To educate members and help promote better ethical standards.
- To hold hearings on complaints against members who were alleged to have breached the Code of Conduct.

(NUJ 1998: 16)

The second aim was always controversial. Many members argued that it was not the role of the union to discipline its own members, but others felt there was little point in having a code of conduct if it was not going to be upheld.

The anti-union stance of the government during the 1980s and 1990s led to a general weakening of union power and this played a part in reducing the role of the Ethics Council. No longer did journalists have to have an NUJ card in order to work in the more prestigious jobs in television and what used to be Fleet Street. This meant that breaching the NUJ Code, with the consequent risk of discipline and possible expulsion, was no longer the risk it once might have been. The union, too, was less inclined to deal harshly with members, as workers became less confident of the benefits of belonging to a union.

The rules were changed in the early 1990s after a number of attempts to remove the disciplinary role from the Ethics Council altogether. Now the Ethics Council will hear complaints about members who have allegedly breached the Code of Conduct, but only if they are made by another member. The Council no longer hears complaints lodged by members of the public. This has reduced complaints to a trickle. The Council has the power to decide that the Code of Conduct would be best promoted by resolving the complaint by educative rather than disciplinary means. But if a complaint hearing is held, and the member is found to be at fault, then the Ethics Council can reprimand that member or pass the case on to the National Executive Council with a recommendation to impose a stronger punishment, which can include fines of up to £1,000, suspension of membership or expulsion.

The Council has tended to concentrate on its educational and promotional role in the past ten years, giving talks to students in colleges and producing guidelines for journalists on a range of issues, from reporting on mental health issues to child abuse. It has also had informal talks with the PCC on issues of mutual concern, particularly the PCC's Code of Practice.

The union's 1998 annual conference changed the Code of Conduct, the first time that had happened for a number of years. The move, in line with the reaction of other regulatory bodies to the death of the Princess of Wales, was to strengthen the Code in the area of privacy. The conference also decided to back a call for a clause dealing specifically with the digital manipulation of pictures. Other changes followed in 2001 (privacy) and 2004 (children). The union carried out a major review of its Code in 2007, agreeing a completely new Code at its 2007 conference.

Press Council of Ireland

The Press Council of Ireland was launched in 2007 after four years of painstaking work by the Press Industry Steering Committee. Government plans for a new privacy law and libel law and a Ministry for Justice report calling for a statutory press regulator, all widely seen as a way of keeping the industry on track, gave spurs to the Committee and the Press Council was born. The Council promised to make the public interest paramount and so the managers and editors of the national and provincial newspapers, the magazine publishers, the UK newspapers circulating in Ireland and journalists through their trade union, the National Union of Journalists (NUJ), worked closely together to support independent scrutiny of the press's accuracy, fairness, its respect of privacy and all the obligations that stem from the privilege of enjoying a free press. The Steering Committee decided that the Swedish model was the closest to their preferred option and set up a Press Council with an associated news ombudsman.

The Council is funded by the industry and is set up with a majority of lay members appointed by an appointments committee. The new chairman of the council is Professor Thomas N. Mitchell, former Provost of Dublin University and he chairs a committee made up of 6 press representatives from the industry including the NUJ out of a total of 15 members; 210 publications are in membership. The system is designed:

- to provide the public with an independent forum for resolving complaints about the press;
- to resolve all complaints quickly, fairly and free of charge;
- to maintain the highest standards of Irish journalism and journalistic ethics;
- to defend the freedom of the press and the freedom of the public to be informed.

(www.presscouncil.ie)

The Press Council has statutory recognition under section 44 of the Defamation Act 2009. This recent piece of legislation in Ireland is designed to update the laws of libel and to give a stronger defence to publication in the public interest. This means qualified privilege now attaches to the reports and decisions of the Council and the ombudsman. It also offers a defence of reasonable publication to newspapers that subscribe to and follow the Press Council's Code of Practice and they can show the extent to which they follow the Press Council's Code and press ombudsman's decisions.

A complaint against a newspaper is made in the first instance to the press ombudsman, Professor John Horgan. For a complaint to be examined:

- it must breach the Code of Practice for Newspapers and Periodicals; and
- the person making the complaint must show that they have been directly affected by, and involved in, the article or behaviour in question.

The ombudsman's first move will be to attempt to resolve the case. If conciliation is not possible, the ombudsman will make a decision. He may refer significant or complex cases to the Press Council.

Should the complainant or the newspaper wish, they may appeal, but they must show reasonable causes, either in relation to significant new information, or to any error in procedures or in the application of the principles of the Code of Practice. If the council agrees there are sufficient grounds it will then hear the appeal. The ombudsman is not involved in this process and does not make any submission to the Council.

So far the Press Council has received 372 complaints in 2008 and 163 in the first half of 2009.

Internet Watch Foundation

The Internet Watch Foundation is an independent self-regulatory body with charitable status funded by voluntary contributions from the internet industry. It is governed by a board of ten consisting of an independent chair, six independent trustees, and three industry trustees. It was set up in 1996 to provide the UK internet hotline for the public and IT professionals to report criminal online content in a secure and confidential way.

The hotline service is designed to minimise the availability of content such as:

- child sexual abuse images hosted anywhere in the world;
- criminally obscene adult content hosted in the UK;
- incitement to racial hatred content hosted in the UK;
- non-photographic child sexual abuse images hosted in the UK.

Alliance of Independent Press Councils of Europe (AIPCE)

AIPCE is a loose network of independent media councils. It meets annually to discuss topical issues, to exchange ideas and to offer and receive advice. There is no formal membership and no central secretariat.

It does have a set of core beliefs and a website run by the UK PCC. Its aims are:

Table 17.6 Fate of Irish Press Council Complaints

Type of complaint	2008	2009
Outside remit	(81) 21.7%	(27) 16.6%
Miscellaneous	(5) 6%	(7) 25.9%
Out of time	(9) 11%	(5) 18.5%
Other regulatory authority	(13) 16%	(7) 25.9%
Third party	(17) 21%	(7) 25.9%
Pre 2008	(37) 46%	(1) 3.8%
Ruled out on first reading	(26) 7%	(10) 6.2%
Non-member publication	(45) 12%	(13) 8.0%
Breach of Code of Practice	(222) 59%	(113) 69.1%
Total	372	163

Table 17.7 Fate of adjudicated complaints

	2008	2009
Withdrawn		2 (6.4%)
Referred to Press Council	2 (4.1%)	3 (10.0%)
Upheld/part upheld	2 (100%)	1 (33%)
Not upheld	0 (0)	2 (66%)
Conciliated	12 (24.5%)	8 (26.0%)
Decided by press ombudsman	35 (71.4%)	17 (56.6%)
Sufficient action offered	4 (11.4%)	
Upheld/upheld in part	13 (37.2%)	
Not upheld	18 (51.4%)	
Appeals to Press Council	24	5
Upheld/part upheld ombudsman decision	10 (41.6%)	5 (100%)
Not upheld ombudsman decision	2 (8.3%)	0 (0%)
Insufficient grounds for appeal	12 (50%)	0 (0%)

Table 17.8 Principles of Code of Practice (percentage as cited by complainant)

	2008	2009 (to June)
Protection of sources		1
Children	2	4
Court reporting	3	3
Respect for rights	8	12
Fairness and honesty	10	14
Distinguishing fact and comment	11	11
Privacy	11	18
Incitement to hatred	20	8
Truth and accuracy	35	29

Source of Tables 17.6, 17.7 and 17.8: http://www.pressombudsman.ie/v1/publications/statistics2008.pdf and
http://www.pressombudsman.ie/v1/publications/Stats-first-half-2009-final.pdf

- that the regulation of editorial content in the media should be independent of government;
- that media content regulation, whether national or regional in its coverage, should be based on nations' differing cultures;
- that the writing of codes of journalistic ethics and their administration is the business of journalists and publishers, who take into account public feelings, and not the business of governments;
- that it is not possible to operate a universal code of ethics, and that the imposition of supranational codes and regulatory organisations, either at the European or global level, should be opposed.

News ombudsman

Ombudsmen are used by some newspapers and other news organisations. There is an organisation for news ombudsmen called the News Ombudsmen Organisation. Its president at time of writing was *The Observer*'s ombudsman, Stephen Pritchard. Ombudsmen are not particularly popular in the UK at the moment with only a handful of newspapers sporting one: *The Guardian* and *The Observer*, and the *Ipswich Star*, and that's about it. They are more popular as a regulatory solution elsewhere, though, and many American and Canadian newspapers have them, as well as papers in Sweden, the Netherlands and several other European countries.

Chapter 18

Broadcast regulation systems in the UK and Ireland

This chapter outlines the regulatory systems in use in the UK, including:

- UK media law
- The Office of Communications
- Regulation in the BBC
- Broadcasting Authority of Ireland

Although the press is self-regulated, a lot of media is regulated by the law. Broadcast media is in addition regulated by statutory bodies. This mixed regulatory power came about because of the history and development of media regulation. First, the law to provide basic civil rights protection for citizens then, as newspapers become more significant, further additions to the law. Then with the advent of broadcasting, initially publicly owned, a whole new field of regulation that even after the start of commercial broadcasting remains statutorily controlled. I have looked at the self-regulation that this spawned for the press and later the internet in the previous chapter. Now I turn to the law and statutory regulation of broadcasting.

The law

The law is used fairly extensively in the UK to regulate the media. The introduction of the Human Rights Act in 1998 guaranteed freedom of expression, thought and opinion for the first time in the UK and this extends to guarantee the freedom of the press, but it also gives a right to privacy for the first time and this has led to a developing area of law discussed elsewhere in this book.

The law has long been used in the UK, as elsewhere, to guarantee three human rights: the right to a reputation, the right to a fair trial and the right to presumption of innocence. The right to reputation is covered by the laws of defamation.

The law is the blunt instrument of regulation, as likely to damage those restricted by it as help those it was intended to support. It comes in two flavours: civil and criminal. The criminal law is prosecuted by the police and Crown Prosecution Service while civil offences require the injured party to pursue the case. The law is used as a regulator for a number of issues in the UK. Those covered by criminal law include: fair trial, obscenity and control of information particularly about children and state security. Reputation, confidential information and copyright are civil issues where the injured party must pursue their grievance direct to the courts.

Fair trial and the presumption of innocence are tightly protected by the law in the UK. Once an arrest has been made in criminal proceedings, there are very strict rules about what can be written until the trial and then there is careful control about what can be written during the trial. These rules are designed to ensure that juries come to the trial with no preconceived notions about the defendant. They also ensure that once the trial is under way, the media reports are fair and accurate. In that way, protection is offered under the law to the publication or broadcaster from libel suits while the accused is assured of a fair report that will not influence a jury. The law on what can and can't be reported is complicated and it is not my intention to cover it fully here – full details can be found in any good media law book such as Frances Quinn's *Law for Journalists* (2nd edn) – however, this is one area of UK law which attempts to control journalistic ethics.

Taste and decency is another area where limits are set by the Obscenity Acts. The Obscene Publications Act 1959 limits what can be written or displayed. The Act bars any material 'that tends to deprave and corrupt persons who are likely, having regard to all relevant circumstances, to read, see or hear the matter contained or embodied in it' (Obscene Publications Act 1959). This definition rarely troubles newspapers or TV and radio news broadcasts, so most taste and decency issues are not regulated by the law in the UK, but it is worth remembering that it is possible to face a charge of publishing obscene material. There are other areas of the law that often impinge on what an editor may publish in his or her newspaper, but many of these are rarely about the editorial. Adverts for psychics or patent remedies are controlled as are gambling and the sale of guns, but few of these are to do with journalistic ethical questions. The Newspaper Society's website has some excellent advice on these issues and is worth creating a shortcut to it on any editor's computer desktop.

Most of the other areas of legal restriction are covered by civil law. By far the most important of these, certainly in the UK, is the defence of reputation, a generally accepted human right. Protection of personal honour is upheld in virtually every country around the world in one way or another. Usually this is defended by the civil suit of libel. This allows the person whose reputation is under attack to sue in the courts. In the UK such a suit must prove that the complainant is the person mentioned in the story and that that story defames them in some way. This means they must prove that the words written or broadcast would tend 'to lower the claimant in the estimation of right-thinking members of society generally' (*Sim* v *Stretch* 1936 cited in Crone 2002: 3).

In the UK, the complainant does not need to prove the words are untrue, merely that they are defamatory. However, if the defendant can prove the defamatory words are true, that may be a defence to the suit. More usually, a publication would defend the alleged libel on the basis that the comments were based on true facts and were fair comment. The fair comment defence allows freedom of expression and opinion, provided the comments were made without malice. The law of libel in the USA is much more interested in whether malice was involved and the complainant not only has to prove that the words were defamatory, but also that the falsehoods were made maliciously. It is worth noting, that under the law, malice may mean that the remarks were made recklessly or without any regard to whether they were true or not. The law of libel in the UK has come under some attack in the UK over the past few years. Conditional fee agreements (CFAs) (also known as 'no win, no fee' cases) were introduced in section 58 of the Courts and Legal Services Act 1990 and allowed solicitors to take on cases without their client having to pay them. The Access to Justice Act 1999 (s. 27) amended the 1990 Act to allow success fees so that solicitors taking such cases could charge up to double the fee from the losing defendant. This made it worth lawyers taking on such cases, insuring a potential defeat with after-the-event insurance (ATE) on the basis that if they won, the premium was paid by the loser together with the fees and 100 per cent success fee. This had made libel cases very expensive and had a serious chilling effect on press freedom. Alongside this, as the internet became a standard way to publish, more and more foreign complainants were choosing to bring libel suits against publications from around the world in London. The UK's libel laws were seen as favouring the defendant making it better to sue in London. The issue became serious enough for several US states, including California and New York, to introduce legislation that would allow US courts in those states to block enforcement of judgments made in foreign courts if it were deemed not to offer the same level of protection for freedom of information as the state and US constitutions. The final problem for libel in 2010 was several cases brought by corporations or professional associations attempting to limit or gag critics from the academic or medical professions who were attempting to raise significant issues of concern. One of these was the British Chiropractic Association, which was seeking to sue Simon Singh, who had written a piece attacking the scientific basis for chiropractics. Eventually, after much expense, the Association dropped its suit. The government had picked up many of these concerns and the Culture, Media and Sport Select Committee had also considered the issues in its 2010 report. The Ministry of Justice attempted to reduce the size of success fees and had other plans, but the general election prevented them from completing. All major parties went into the election pledging to reform the law on libel.

Another area where the law has something to say on how journalists gather the news is the obtaining or protection of information. The Freedom of Information Act 2000 gives considerable rights to access information from public bodies including the government. On the other hand, the Data Protection Act 1989 limits access to information of a personal nature that is held about people. Because the Data Protection Act gives some protection for individuals, it is no longer so easy to get the names and addresses of those involved in accidents or admitted to hospital. The police and hospital authorities are prevented from giving out 'sensitive personal data' to journalists or a senior officer without the permission of the data subject. It has to be said that this is a clause that is widely used by many authorities as something to hide behind rather than as a protection of the individual, and information is often withheld improperly, with officers claiming this is because of the Data Protection Act. It is worth reminding ourselves at this point that the DPA does not prevent a journalist using such information if it can be obtained legally elsewhere: it is only a legal obligation on the data holder to keep the information secret; the information is not necessarily secret of itself. The law only requires that information collected for the purpose of record-keeping is used only for that one purpose and no other. So, a person admitted to hospital after a road accident might well have their data protected by the registering official and any other member of staff working at the hospital, but a visitor or relative who is prepared to give information would be exempt and can give the journalist the information he or she requires. However, the information must be collected legally, from a relative for instance. Information gathered illegally has been the subject of some concern and the Information Commissioner has called for journalists to be jailed for dealing in illegally gathered information.

Laws protecting the public or the state include the Official Secrets Act, the various Terrorism Acts, and other statutes designed to protect secure installations or the armed forces or security services. Terrorism Acts in the UK are not only designed to prevent acts of terrorism but also require journalists and others to pass information they receive to the authorities. This means it is an offence in the UK for a journalist to receive information about an alleged terrorist act without then informing the police about it.

The vulnerable are protected with the various pieces of hate legislation. Children are protected by a number of Acts, starting with the Children and Young Persons Act 1933. More recent Acts offer children anonymity through the courts whether they are witnesses, victims or the accused. Family courts, which deal with custody and such matters, until recently also carried out their work largely in private in order to protect the children involved. In 2009 the Ministry of Justice decided to open the courts to accredited media. The Ministry said that media would be able to attend all levels of family courts although the court would be able to restrict attendance if the welfare of the child required it. Launching the scheme, the then minister of Justice, Jack Straw, said:

> It is critical that family courts make the right decisions and the public have confidence they are doing so. A key part of building trust in the system is that people understand how it works. At the same time, we must protect the privacy of children and families involved in family court cases so they are not identified or stigmatised by their community or friends. These plans strike the right balance in providing a more open, transparent and accountable system while protecting children and families during a difficult and traumatic time in their lives.
>
> (http://www.justice.gov.uk/news/newsrelease161208b.htm)

The change is too new to evaluate its operation.

The Divorce Acts have limited the reporting of divorce in order to reduce the publication of salacious detail and there is also a limit on employment tribunals involving sexual misconduct for similar reasons. Under the Trade Union Reform and Employment Rights Act 1993, an employment tribunal can order that the employee or the employer, or both, or any other witnesses or parties to the case, cannot be identified. Anonymity is not automatic and each party will be given an opportunity to speak on the application. However, the press does not have the right to speak. Tribunal cases do sometimes contain evidence of sexual misconduct when a person, usually a woman, has left her job after being sexually harassed. Giving evidence of such conduct, which will have involved not only the conduct itself but the loss of a job, is a terrible ordeal and many former employees seek such a restricted reporting order when complaining of sexual misconduct. The law of confidence is another growing area of law used in the context of the media to protect against invasions of privacy.

Regulatory authorities

There are several regulatory councils in the UK and Ireland charged with controlling the broadcast media and guarding media standards. These are statutory bodies, regulated by statute:

- Office of Communications (Ofcom)
- The Competition Commission
- Broadcasting Authority of Ireland

Broadcasting

Regulation of broadcasting is far more complicated than that of the press as we might expect in a regulatory system supported by legislation. Broadcasting regulation has undergone a number of major changes over the past 20 years. The Broadcasting Act 1980 set up the Broadcasting Complaints Commission to adjudicate on complaints of unfair treatment in television and radio programmes or of 'unwarranted infringement of privacy'. The Broadcasting Standards Council was launched in 1988, at the peak of one of the outcries of moral outrage which has so characterised the 1980s and 1990s, to deal with complaints from viewers and listeners about decency. Before the introduction of these two bodies, complaints had been handled either by the BBC Complaints Panel or the Independent Broadcasting Authority, as appropriate. The Broadcasting Act 1990 changed that, introducing new regulatory and complaints authorities. Control of broadcasting was lodged with the BBC (through its Charter), the Independent Television Commission and the Radio Authority, while complaints and conduct were dealt with by the BCC and the BSC. The BCC was never very popular with broadcasters and few tears were shed when it was amalgamated with the BSC by the Broadcasting Act 1996.

Major changes were introduced in the early part of the twenty-first century with the introduction of a lighter-touch regulator to replace the ITC and the BSC. Ofcom, the Office of Communications, amalgamated several bodies: the ITC, the Radio Authority, the BSC, the Radiocommunications Agency and the Office of Telecommunications. This brought regulatory bodies for electronic communication in radio, TV and telephony all under the same authority. Only the BBC was able to stand outside this huge new regulator, although some control of BBC areas is lodged with Ofcom, which even has the power to comment on newspaper mergers and takeovers.

Ofcom

The Office of Communications, known as Ofcom, is the regulator for television and radio in the UK (with some exceptions in the case of the BBC). This body was constituted by the Office of Communications Act 2002 and gains its power from the Communications Act 2003. It took over from and combined a number of regulators that used to control radio, TV and telecommunications, including the Broadcasting Standards Commission, Oftel, the Independent Television Commission and the Radio Authority. Ofcom's future is not clear as the Conservatives had promised before the election to savagely reduce Ofcom's power, restricting it to narrow technical and enforcement roles. The coalition government had yet to say anything about its future at the time of writing, but Jeremy Hunt has been appointed minister for Culture, Media and Sport and he has spoken out strongly in the past for change including considerable deregulation, relaxing of cross-media ownership rules that prevent newspapers owning competing TV and radio stations, and vice versa, and the removal of many of Ofcom's powers.

The Communications Act says that the Secretary of State for Culture, Media and Sport should appoint at least three and no more than six members to the Ofcom board, including a chairman; in 2010, there was a board comprising the eight members, led by chairman Collette Bowe and deputy chairman Philip Graf, a former chairman of Pressbof. There is also an executive committee (Exco) with eleven members led by Ed Richards, the chief executive.

Ofcom regulates television, radio, any other broadcast medium, telephones (landlines and mobile) and any other high-speed data links. The convergence of technologies such as the internet, high-definition TV, mobile phones and data links have made distinctions between these seem highly artificial. We can now receive our TV over the web and our web on mobile phones as a matter of course and these technologies are becoming indistinguishable. We will simply receive high-quality digital data for display on high-definition screens or playback through high-quality audio systems. It is this convergence that drives the Communications Act 2003 and identifies Ofcom's duties. Ofcom is obliged to further the interests of:

- citizens in relation to communications matters; and
- consumers in relevant markets, where appropriate by promoting competition.

It is there to further the interests of citizen-consumers through a regulatory regime which, where appropriate, encourages competition. To do this, Ofcom says it will:

- encourage the evolution of electronic media and communications networks to the greater benefit of all who live in the United Kingdom;
- support the need for innovators, creators and investors to flourish within markets driven by full and fair competition between all providers;
- balance the promotion of choice and competition with the duty to foster plurality, informed citizenship, the protection of viewers, listeners and customers, and promote cultural diversity; and
- serve the interests of citizen-consumers as the communications industry enters the digital age.

The Act identifies two different types of audience: citizens and consumers. These two have very different requirements, although they may well often be the same people. The term 'citizens' is used to mean those who access broadcasting in its public service role, while 'consumers' is used to mean customers who make choices about their communication needs on the basis of payment for services used. Citizens require a public service broadcasting system that entertains, informs and educates and that is free at the point of reception. In order to serve these citizens, Ofcom needs to ensure that services are available in all parts of the country and that reception is acceptable virtually everywhere. It also needs to ensure that minority interests are reasonably catered for. In dealing with consumers, though, Ofcom can reasonably expect the market to operate and for high-cost services chosen by the customer to be paid for by subscription or some other direct form of payment as well as indirect payments such as advertising or sponsorship.

This means that Ofcom's key duties include:

- controlling the use for wireless telegraphy of the electromagnetic spectrum;
- ensuring the availability throughout the United Kingdom of a wide range of electronic communications services;
- ensuring the availability throughout the United Kingdom of a wide range of television and radio services which are of high quality and calculated to appeal to a variety of tastes and interests;
- the maintenance of a sufficient plurality of providers of different television and radio services.

Ofcom also has a duty to ensure standards are applied to provide adequate protection from offensive and harmful material, from unfair treatment in programmes and from unwarranted infringements of privacy (Communications Act 2003, section 3(2)). Ofcom also has a duty to improve the public's media literacy, by bringing about better public understanding of the media, including what is published, how it is selected and made available and its regulation and control.

Ofcom controls a wide range of the electronic spectrum including:

- radio and television in the UK;
- telephone lines including telephone numbers;
- data links;
- internet.

Ofcom is described as a light-touch regulator. It will only intervene when necessary, but will otherwise allow the market to operate. It consults widely and produces an annual plan, which is reviewed regularly. It will intervene when there is a specific statutory requirement, but the Communications Act 2003 is much vaguer about the need to intervene than previous Broadcasting Acts.

The BBC and the Welsh Authority, which controls S4C, are not directly connected to Ofcom.

One of Ofcom's major tasks over the past few years has been to oversee the move to digital TV and the switch-off of the analog system. At the time of writing, Ofcom's plans to switch over by ITV region are well advanced and Border, West Country, HTV Wales, Granada, HTV West, Grampian and Scottish Television are all now entirely digital. Yorkshire, Anglia and Central are due to follow in 2011 and Meridian, Carlton/LWT (London), Tyne Tees and Ulster in 2012.

Ofcom delegates some of its regulatory powers to various boards and committees. These include advisory boards for England, Wales, Scotland and Northern Ireland; advisory boards on the elderly and disabled people; the community radio fund panel; the radio licensing committee; the fairness committee; the election committee; the audit committee; the remuneration committee; the content board and the content sanctions committee.

The content board, which regulates TV and radio content, is chaired by Ofcom's deputy chairman and has twelve members appointed by Ofcom, four of whom represent each of the countries within the UK. The content board's role is to:

- examine the contents of anything that is broadcast or otherwise transmitted by means of electronic communications networks; and
- promote public understanding or awareness of matters relating to the publication of matter by means of the electronic media.

It also acts as an advisory board to the Ofcom board.

The Ofcom board has delegated the discharge of its functions in relation to content-sanctions cases to a committee known as the content sanctions committee, chaired by the chair of Ofcom's content board. The content sanctions committee considers cases referred to it by the executive for it to decide if there has been a breach of the relevant code or licence and to consider a penalty if a sanction is required. It will invite representation from the broadcaster, if a sanction is being considered. The committee consists of a maximum of five members, three from the content board and two from the Ofcom board.

Ofcom says it aims to deal quickly and simply with complaints about phones, internet service, TV/radio content, TV/radio advertising, digital TV availability and TV/radio interference.

The content sanctions committee has delegated powers to consider cases referred to it by the executive about broadcasts made on independent radio or TV. It decides on any sanction to be applied. Ofcom does not have the power to prevent a broadcast before transmission, but it can levy a sanction against a breach of the Code. This could be a fine, suspension or revocation of the licence for serious and/or repeated or deliberate offences. The content sanctions committee has a number of duties:

- to consider content or content-based cases referred to it by the executive for consideration of a statutory sanction (including cases involving the BBC and S4C);
- where the sanction under consideration includes a financial penalty or shortening or revocation of a licence, to invite oral representations from licensees;
- to decide whether to impose a statutory sanction and at what level, in accordance with Ofcom's penalty guidelines;
- to settle and approve decision letters to licensees;
- where such decisions are to be published, to settle and approve any press releases in consultation with the director of communications or by delegation to the chairman, as appropriate.

(http://www.ofcom.org.uk/about/csg/ocsc_index/ocsc_tor2/ accessed 21/12/06)

The content sanctions committee's decisions are taken in line with the penalty guidelines, but there is no right of appeal to Ofcom once the decision has been made. The chairman of the content board is also the chairman of the content sanctions committee. The Broadcast Code is published under ten section heads covering: under-eighteens; harm and offence; crime; religion; impartiality and accuracy; elections; fairness; privacy; sponsorship; and commercial references. Ofcom can take complaints about all broadcasters but not complaints about accuracy or impartiality on BBC TV and radio. Ofcom can only take a complaint about a programme once that programme has been broadcast. It has no power of prior restraint. Once a complaint has been made, either on the form available online, or by post or phone, Ofcom will investigate. Ofcom aims to resolve complaints as fast as possible. The fairness committee deals with complaints referred to it by the executive either on grounds of complexity or where one of the parties is dissatisfied with decisions of the executive.

Ofcom deals with a large number of complaints about a huge amount of transmitted TV and radio programmes. As can be seen by Table 18.1 only a small number of these are adjudicated and a decision reached. As with the PCC, many of the complaints are about issues that do not breach Ofcom's Broadcasting Code. Unlike the PCC, many of the complaints concern the same programme. This explains the huge differences in the total number of complaints year on year. Years with complaints about programmes such as *Jerry Springer the Opera* or the complaints about Russell Brand/Jonathan Ross and Andrew Sachs can show an increase in complaints by the tens of thousands. As far as it is possible to judge, the normal background level of complaints is not hugely dissimilar to the PCC, about 5,000–6,000, and Ofcom upholds an average of 108 standards complaints and 11 fairness and privacy complaints. Of course the majority of these complaints concern radio and TV programmes that are entertainment only, such as dramas, soap operas or films. The majority of finacial penalties imposed by Ofcom concern misrun competitions or phone-in voting programmes. Complaints about news programmes are much rarer with adjudications for news and current affairs programmes averaging just over 30 a year.

This makes quite an interesting comparison with the breakdown of complaints for all programme types which are much more heavily dominated by complaints about material that might cause harm and offence, especially to children.

The average of complaints up until April 2010 is shown in the unnumbered table on page 302.

Ofcom issues a new complaints bulletin every two weeks, each typically containing between seven and 15 complaints.

Ofcom reviewed its Broadcasting Code in 2009 following a number of complaints about competitions that had been improperly run or phone-in votes where phone calls were still being accepted,

Table 18.1 Complaints to Ofcom from annual reports

	2004/5	2005/6	2006/7	2007/8	2008/9
Total complaints	4185	14227	5575	67742	27549
Standards (closed cases)	1146	1086	3448	12532	12965
In breach	74	63	58	135	211
Resolved	54	109	75	25	43
Not in breach	1018	914	3315	12372	12711
Sanction imposed	3	16	15	11	30
Broadcasters sanctioned	3	5	4	9	18
Total fine imposed	527,500	160,000	4.21m	2.145m	6.8575m
Fairness and privacy	190	202	184	194	238
Adjudicated by fairness committee	67	18	29	27	17
Upheld	17	11	14	14	9
Not upheld	50	7	15	13	8
Adjudicated by executive		184	155	167	221
Upheld		8	13	9	14
Not upheld		44	38	38	7
Resolved	11	7	7	7	10
Not entertained	112	125	97	113	160

but the votes were no longer being counted. Ofcom upheld a number of complaints and imposed sanctions on a number of broadcasters for breach of the Code, but it considered this to be an area where additional changes were required to the Code and these were introduced at the end of 2009. They also produced a new election code in readiness for the forthcoming 2010 general election.

Ofcom and the BBC

Ofcom is responsible for some areas of the BBC's work. It has the power to regulate the following:

- protecting the under-eighteens;
- harm and offence;
- crime;
- religion;
- fairness;
- privacy.

Complaints can go to the BBC, but complainants can also complain to Ofcom. Two of the biggest complaints (in terms of numbers) that Ofcom have had to deal with concerned BBC programmes. *Jerry Springer the Opera* upset a number of Christian groups across the country who campaigned

Table 18.2 Ofcom news and current affairs adjudications

	2004	2005	2006	2007	2008	2009
Total complaints	30	33	48	22	16	33
Adudications	29	27	43	21	15	31
Upheld	12	1	14	12	6	10
Resolved	2	15	4	2	2	1
Not upheld	15	11	25	7	7	20
Code breach type (percentage)						
Children	1.0	2.6	2.0	1.5	0	2.0
Harm and offence	1.0	3.6	1.5	2.6	1.5	1.5
Crime	0	0	0	0	0	3.0
Religion	0	0	0	0	0	0
Impartiality and accuracy	0	9.1	0	4.5	0	0
Elections	0	0	0	0	0	3.0
Fairness	46.7	39.4	56.3	27.3	50.0	33.3
Privacy	36.7	12.1	27.1	18.2	6.3	27.3
Sponsorship	0	3.0	0	13.6	18.8	6.1
Commercial references	3.32	0	2.1	0	6.3	3.0

	All complaints	News and current affairs only
Children	27.3%	9.2%
Harm and offence	22.2%	11.7%
Crime	0.3%	0.5%
Religion	0.6%	0
Impartiality and accuracy	1.4%	2.6%
Elections	0.3%	0.5%
Fairness	22.6%	43.4%
Privacy	12.2%	24.5%
Sponsorship	5.3%	4.6%
Commercial references	6.0%	2.6%

to prevent the programme being shown and then complained about it after transmission. Ofcom minutes show that they received a total of 8,860 complaints (2,849 e-mails, 1,747 other contacts and 4,264 e-mails from one particular group). The BBC received many more direct to their editorial complaints unit. Ofcom was also asked by the BBC governors to consider its own finding. After careful consideration, Ofcom concluded that the prgramme was appropriately scheduled, on-air warnings were adequate, it was agreed that it was a satire on television and concluded by 9–2 that it had not humiliated groups in a gratuitous way. It considered that swearing and offensive language was justified by the context and had been transmitted at an appropriate time. It finally agreed, by 9–2, that it had not breached the Code.

In the Russell Brand/Jonathan Ross case, in which the pair made a spoof phone call to actor Andrew Sachs making offensive and humiliating comments about his granddaughter on air during the Russell Brand Show on Radio 2 in October 2008, the BBC was found to have breached the Code and that there were six underlying flaws in the BBC's compliance systems. Ofcom fined the BBC £150,000.

British Broadcasting Corporation

The BBC is Britain's most easily identified public service broadcaster, with an aim to inform, educate and entertain. With the renewal of its Royal Charter and Agreement on 1 May 1996, the BBC was required to draw up a code on a range of ethical issues. The Charter also placed a duty on the BBC board of governors to ensure that the BBC's employees and programme-makers comply with it, giving the governors similar powers to those then held by the Independent Television Commission. A new Charter was introduced in December 2006. This took the changes further and the government's proposals for the new Charter are discussed further on in this chapter.

The Agreement, a formal contract between the BBC and the Secretary of State for National Heritage (now Culture, Media and Sport), runs concurrently with the Royal Charter and explains how the BBC is to meet its broad objectives and duties. It formally guarantees its editorial independence in programme content, scheduling and management. It also means the licence fee will remain the primary source of finance for the BBC for the duration of the Charter.

The twelve members of the board of governors are appointed by the Queen in Council to monitor the BBC's performance and standards against set objectives. A new chairman of the board of governors, Michael Grade, and Director-General, Mark Thompson, took up office in 2004 following the resignation of Greg Dyke and Sir Christopher Bland over the Hutton Report.

The BBC's executive committee, whose members also sit on the broader-based board of management, is led by the Director-General Mark Thompson, who had previously been chief executive of Channel 4. He had previously worked at the BBC for more than 20 years, becoming Director of Television in 2000.

The new BBC Charter replaced the governors with the BBC trust and the executive committee with the executive board. The trust's role is to set the overall strategic direction for the BBC, while the executive board runs the BBC.

Regulation in the BBC

The *Editorial Guidelines*, the BBC's ethical 'bible', contains thirty-seven different sections, but the main ones that concern us are contained in the BBC's 'Values and Standards, Issues in Factual Programming and Politics'. They cover the following issues: impartiality and accuracy, fairness to contributors, privacy and the gathering of information, taste and decency, violence, imitative and antisocial behaviour, portrayal of children in programmes, and conflicts of interest. 'Issues in factual programming' include interviewing, reporting crime, relations with the police, confidentiality and the release of programme material, terrorism and national security, Northern Ireland, and material from outside sources. 'Politics' covers politics, Parliament and politicians, broadcasting during elections, and opinion polls. Finally, 'commercial issues in programmes' include commercial relationships, support services, covering outside events, on-air references to products, services and publications, using free or reduced-cost facilities, competitions, prizes and coverage of the National Lottery, premium-rate telephone services, charities, and charity appeals. All recorded programmes are required to complete a compliance form that shows the programme was made in compliance with the editorial guidelines.

The BBC takes complaints about its programmes through its editorial complaints unit. This investigates alleged breaches of the editorial guidelines. If the ECU upholds the complaint, it will instruct the programme to take action to correct the error and prevent the same mistake happening again (http://www.bbc.co.uk/guidelines/editorialguidelines/page/guidelines-accountability-principles accessed 14/10/10). The BBC answered just over 18,000 complaints in February 2010. Very few were complaints about breaches of the *Editorial Guidelines*, many were simply comments or matters of concern to viewers or listeners. Comments concerned the use of a new 'spidercam' in coverage of the six nations rugby match; changes to the billed schedule to accommodate Olympic coverage; or compaints about an *EastEnders* storyline that implied Lucas had killed 'Sugar' the dog. There were also complaints about leading the News at Six and Ten on 19 February with coverage of Tiger Woods' public apology. The ECU aims to deal with most complaints within twenty working days.

Trust's editorial standards committee

The trust's editorial standards committee (ESC) is responsible for fulfilling the Charter requirement 'to ensure that complaints are properly handled by BBC management'. It considers appeals from complainants about programmes transmitted, or material carried, by the BBC's domestic public services on radio, television and online. If a complainant is unhappy about the response made by the ECU, then he or she can appeal to the ESC. The ESC reports its activities to the trust and is required to handle complaints promptly and ensure they are investigated rigorously and impartially. Where a complaint is upheld, the BBC not only apologises for the breach in programme standards but takes remedial action to guard against the breach occurring again and/or to discipline individuals responsible for the breach. The BBC now has a code of practice on complaints that came into force in February 2005 (http://www.bbc.co.uk/complaints/complaints_process.shtml#code).

Editorial Guidelines

The BBC's *Editorial Guidelines* have developed out of the old producer guidelines and were published in 2005. They are now very firmly an online resource, available to producers, journalists and the public alike at http://www.bbc.co.uk/guidelines/editorialguidelines/edguide/. They are advertised as the distillation, if not the wisdom, of generations of producers and editors. The guidelines are structured around a number of headings, such as:

Accuracy
Impartiality
Harm and offence
Fairness, contributors and consent
Privacy
Reporting crime and anti-social behaviour

Children and young people as contributors
Politics, public policy and polls
War, terror and emergencies
Religion
Re-use and reversioning
Editorial integrity and independence from external interests
Conflicts of interest
External relationships and funding
Interacting with our audiences
The law
Accountability (also includes Ofcom Broadcasting Code and other codes/statements)
(http://www.bbc.co.uk/guidelines/editorialguidelines/guidelines accessed 14/10/10)

Each of these hyperlinks leads into a detailed set of sub-headings which themselves offer considerable advice in a wide variety of areas. This is not a code of conduct: it's too long and requires continual reference, but as easy-to-access, sound advice on professional moral issues, the guidelines are an excellent resource for BBC staff and other professionals working in the media. While many of them are advisory, some are mandatory, and all would be taken into consideration should a journalist breach them in a way that could lead to disciplinary proceedings. Serious breach of the *Editorial Guidelines* could be a dismissal matter for a BBC employee.

The BBC's future

As commercial stations struggle to provide news and local news providers such as newspapers make savage cuts, local and regional news provision seems under threat. One way to contine to assure a local news provision is for the BBC to be more involved. This is now the centre of a major political debate. The election in 2010 will determine who ends up directing the BBC for its final six years under the existing Charter, but the Conservatives have already made it clear that they would prefer to make a clearer division between the kind of TV available on commercial TV and the public service offering that the BBC should provide.

Those who believed strongly in the importance of public service broadcasting and its importance in providing a plurality of broadcasting and a wider range of information, education and entertainment wanted to minimise change to those elements involving the digital switchover. However, there were many people who wanted to reduce considerably the BBC's programme-making ability, claiming that where programmes were popular, the market should dominate and that the BBC's role should be relegated to specialist programmes aimed at minority groups.

Elections

Elections require particular care for broadcasters to ensure impartiality and fairness as required by the Communications Act. Ofcom has section 6 of its code all about elections, including the need to name all candidates standing in a constituency in any are or constituency report and an insistence that all candidates are offered equal opportunities to take part in programmes about their constituency or area. The BBC issued extensive guidelines in the 2010 general election which covered similar ground but also laid down rules on the uses of polls, vox pops and SMS/text messaging.

European Broadcasting Union

The EBU is an association of broadcast organisations, which was formed in 1950 by west European broadcasters to assist with the negotiation of broadcasting rights for sporting events and programme exchanges. It now operates the Eurovision and Euroradio networks and has 74 members active in 54 countries in Europe, North Africa and the Middle East. As well as providing services, the EBU also represents its members' interests to the European Parliament from its office in Brussels.

The union's legal department helps the different services to adopt common positions on regulatory and legal pressures in their home countries and abroad.

Broadcasting Authority of Ireland

The Broadcasting Authority of Ireland (BAI) was established on 1 October 2009 following the enactment of the Broadcasting Act 2009.

The objectives of the BAI are similar to those of Ofcom in the UK and are:

- To ensure that the number and categories of broadcasting services made available in the state best serve the needs of the people of the island of Ireland, bearing in mind their languages and traditions and their religious, ethical and cultural diversity.
- To ensure that the democratic values enshrined in the Constitution especially those relating to rightful liberty of expression, are upheld.
- To provide for open and pluralistic broadcasting services.

The BAI has a board and two statutory committees to deal with compliance and contract awards. Any viewer or listener can complain to the Broadcasting Authority of Ireland under any of the following categories:

- objectivity and impartiality in news;
- fairness, objectivity and impartiality in current affairs;
- harm and offence or anything likely to promote, or incite crime, or tending to undermine the authority of the state;
- privacy of an individual;
- harmful or offensive material such as the portrayal of violence and sexual conduct shall be presented with due sensitivity and with due regard to the impact of such programming on the physical, mental or moral development of children.

Chapter 19

The experience abroad

This chapter looks at some of the regulatory methods used in other countries:

■ The different approach taken in the USA

■ A brief examination of some Western European countries

■ Some of the systems used to overcome problems of cross-border working

Methods of regulation vary widely throughout the world with a steady gradation of control, starting with countries which allow journalists a fairly free hand and ending with countries that have almost total state control. The two main types of regulation revolve around those countries with democracy and constitutions and those without. However, the state of development of a nation will have an affect on the level of regulation and the expectation of the style of journalism, with those that are fully developed normally being more critical of government than those where support of the nation, its people and achievements is seen as more important. While there are always exceptions, the key blocks with regard to press freedom and journalism ethics are the Western world: US, Canada, Europe and Australia. Eastern Europe and much of Asia now has a free press, but it is not always willing to challenge government. Finally, there is Africa, the Middle East, South America and China where controls are often much more stringent and where democracy and consequently press freedom is much harder to find.

International protection

All EU countries are signatories to the European Convention on Human Rights. This is used by the European Court of Human Rights as the basis for the rights of citizens in Europe. It is now included in British law through the Human Rights Act 1998. There are two main clauses in the Convention that concern us here. One is about freedom of expression and the other involves invasion of privacy (Exhibit 19.1).

The Council of Europe has also looked at the subject of the media and drafted its own resolution. This does not have specific power on its own, though, and is merely an expression of policy (Exhibit 17.2).

The other international code which supports the right to freedom of expression and contains the individual rights of citizens is the UN Declaration on Human Rights. This also contains two clauses, one on privacy and one on freedom (Exhibit 17.3).

Although a large number of countries are signatories to the Declaration, it does not always mean that they adhere to it.

Constitutional protection

America and some European countries have full and effective constitutions which guarantee, among other things, the freedom of the press or a more general freedom of expression. By and large these countries are more likely to accept the protection of some citizens' rights, in areas such as privacy, in the knowledge that press freedom is secured by the constitution.

Exhibit 19.1 The European Convention on Human Rights

8. All persons have the right to respect for his private and family life, for his abode and his correspondence ...
10. (1) Anyone has the right to freedom of expression. This right includes freedom of opinion and freedom to receive or communicate information or ideas without interference from public authorities and regardless of borders. This article does not prevent states from subjecting radio or television broadcasting or cinema enterprises to a system of authorisations.

---

(2) The exercise of these freedoms with their accompanying duties and responsibilities may be subjected to certain formalities, conditions, restrictions or sanctions defined by law, which constitute measures necessary in a democratic society to national safety, territorial sovereignty or public safety, defence of order and prevention of crime, protection of health or morals, protection of the reputation or rights of others, in order to prevent the divulging of confidential information or in order to guarantee the authority and impartiality of judicial power.

Exhibit 19.2 The Council of Europe Resolution 1003 (1993)

7. The media's work is one of 'mediation', providing an information service, and the rights which they own in connection with freedom of information depend on its addressees, that is the citizens.
8. Information is a fundamental right which has been highlighted by the case law of the European Commission and Court of Human Rights relating to Article 10 of the European Convention on Human Rights and recognised under Article 9 of the European Convention on Transfrontier Television, as well as in all democratic constitutions. The owner of the right is the citizen, who also has the related right to demand that the information supplied by journalists is conveyed truthfully, in the case of news, and honestly, in the case of opinions, without outside interference by either the public authorities or the private sector.
9. The public authorities must not consider that they own information. The representativeness of such authorities provides the legal basis for efforts to guarantee and extend pluralism in the media and to ensure that the necessary conditions are created for exercising freedom of expression and the right to information and precluding censorship ...
15. Neither publishers nor proprietors nor journalists should consider that they own the news. News organisations must treat information not as a commodity but as a fundamental right of the citizen.

The US constitution is one of the most obvious examples. The First Amendment to the constitution is precise and thoughtful: 'Congress shall make no law ... abridging the freedom of speech, or of the press.' This gives journalists in the USA considerable support, more than enough for them to feel confident about allowing protections for ordinary citizens. The privacy laws in the USA allow far less invasion than in Britain. There are four different types of complaint that can be made about invasions of privacy in the USA:

- Intrusion, phone tapping or trespassing without consent.
- False light – resembles libel or malicious falsehood in that it attempts to prevent the circulation of untrue stories.
- Misappropriation – a person's name or likeness is used without consent.
- Embarrassment – an objection to the publication of private information.

(Dill 1986: 135)

Exhibit 19.3 The United Nations Declaration on Human Rights

12. No-one shall be subjected to arbitrary interference with his privacy, family, home or correspondence, nor to attacks upon his honour and reputation. Everyone has the right to the protection of the law against interference or attacks ...
19. Everyone has the right to freedom of opinion and expression. This right includes freedom to hold opinion without interference and to seek, receive and impart information and ideas through any media regardless of frontiers.

Public interest is a defence against a charge of invading privacy. Indeed, the burden is on the person claiming privacy to prove that there is no public interest in the story. This is rarely easy to do and consequently there are few successful embarrassment cases. Nevertheless, an attempt at protection does exist (ibid.: 136).

In a case cited by Barbara Dill (ibid.: 132), the first woman ever to be elected president of a student body was later found to be a transsexual. The woman had gone to great lengths to keep this secret and when it was publicised by the *Oakland Tribune* she was devastated and brought a suit against the paper. She won and was awarded $775,000 (including $525,000 punitive damages and $25,000 against the writer of the article personally). However, this was later overturned on appeal, on a technicality, and when a new trial was ordered, the college's insurance company ordered the paper to make an offer, which was accepted. There can be no doubt that if this story were translated to Britain, the *Star* or *The Sun*, uncovering a confidence of this sort, would have no hesitation about publishing it – and not in a small gossip-style column but as a major lead story.

In another case cited by Dill, a woman was taken to hospital for a pancreas problem that had led to her eating enough for ten people but still losing 25 lb in a year. Her picture was taken without her consent in hospital. The subsequent story and picture were used by a paper. The court ruled that although the story may have been newsworthy, her name was not. The case was not helped by the strong-arm tactics used by the news agency that gathered the story. If this case had happened in the UK, although the PCC's Code would have been breached, in that the picture should not have been taken in the hospital without permission, the story (and name) would certainly have been used with a picture if it could have been obtained in some other way.

If the law on privacy were the same in the UK as it is in the USA, it could present a major problem for the UK press. One only has to consider the number of times in recent years that photographs have been published of major celebrities showing more than they had intended while manoeuvring in and out of cars in short skirts. The laws on trespass and intrusion are also very limiting. Taping interviews without permission, trespassing or using trickery are all potentially illegal. Trespass is not often a problem as it is difficult to bring a case, provided the journalist leaves when asked by a person with suitable authority.

America was one of the first countries in the world to have a code of conduct. Nelson Antrim Crawford, in *The Ethics of Journalism*, identifies the first as being the Kansas Editorial Association's Code of Ethics for the Publisher, written in 1910 (Crawford, 1969). This sets out codes of practice for advertising departments, circulation and news. Many of the early codes varied from being mission statements for the paper to being disciplinary codes. They covered everything from drinking on duty, to dealing with customers, to truth, and objectivity. A large number of early US codes are published in Crawford's *The Ethics of Journalism* and they are well worth reading, if only to enjoy their diversity. Many newspapers in the USA still have codes, although most of them are more like mission statements.

The Society of Professional Journalists in the USA, which has a membership of about 13,500, has a code of conduct which it borrowed from the American Society of Newspaper Editors in 1926. It wrote its own code in 1973 (the SPJ was still known as Sigma Delta Chi in those days) and revised it in 1984 and 1987. Its present version was adopted in September 1996 after a lengthy debate among its membership, part of which was conducted on the internet. The code is substantially different from UK codes in its presentation but is not all that different in content. The code does underline some of the differences I have mentioned before: presumption of innocence in criminal law is covered in this code, for instance. The code also recognises that the people the media come into contact with have rights. 'Minimise harm' is one of the duties expressed in the code. The code says: 'Journalists should recognise that private people have a greater right to control information about themselves than do public officials and others who seek power, influence or attention. Only an overriding public need can justify intrusion into anyone's privacy.' The code also calls on journalists to 'Show good taste. Avoid pandering to lurid curiosity' (http://spj.org/ethics/code.htm).

In many ways the code is much more high-minded than those on offer in the UK, yet in other ways it is more practical: 'Journalists should always question sources' motives before promising anonymity' (http://spj.org/ethics/code.htm), it says, like an old and wise news editor warning an enthusiastic trainee journalist. It's good advice, but is it ethics? There is more excellent advice about accepting gifts or bribes, but there is little in the code that a UK journalist would disagree with in principle. This is not the only code in existence. In the Associated Press (AP) Managing Editors' Code we find another theme that crops up in US codes time and time again. They are much more concerned about lobbying government to ensure they maintain free access to information than in the UK. It is ironic that it was Margaret Thatcher who pushed a private member's bill to give the media access to public meetings, yet as Prime Minister she privatised all of these institutions, thus ensuring their meetings were once again held in secret.

The Managing Editors say in their code: 'The newspaper should fight vigorously for public access to news of government through open meetings and records' (http://www.apme.com/html/ethics.html). This, of course, is in a country which has a Freedom of Information Act, allowing journalists free access to all public documents.

The Radio–Television News Directors' Association also has a code of conduct (http://web.missouri.edu/~jourvs/rtcodes.html). Again it includes the right to a fair trial but, interestingly, this code talks about the need to be impartial. None of the print codes felt this was necessary. With no laws limiting broadcasters' right to say what they like (because of the First Amendment), it was felt necessary to put this in a code of ethics. In the UK of course, the law has already included this. But why did broadcasters in the USA feel obliged to make it an ethical issue when the print journalists did not, especially in a country where television is seen as having many of the qualities of the tabloids in the UK? American journalists seem, from the outside at least, to take ethics more seriously than their UK counterparts. There are a number of books, codes have been around since the 1920s and the subject is taught seriously in journalism schools. Yet their laws are a lot more straightforward. The freedom of the press is protected by the constitution and freedom of information is guaranteed. There are few restrictive laws, with the exception of privacy and defamation. There is no Press Council, however, or other body to police the codes of conduct on a federal basis. News councils do exist though. The Minnesota News Council, for instance, has been in existence since 1971. It attempts to promote media fairness by encouraging the public to 'insist upon responsible reporting and editing'. It holds public hearings on ethical complaints and has the support of the local media. The complaints hearing has local media representatives sitting on it with a sitting justice of the state supreme court as chairperson. According to its internet website, the News Council offers the following services:

- Public hearings on complaints brought by individuals or organisations named in a story who feel damaged by it (selected third-party complaints are also accepted if they are of compelling public interest and raise a significant ethical question).
- Public forums on topics of media ethics.
- Private forums to facilitate communication between the media and organisations and communities experiencing trouble in working with the media.
- Mediation assistance between the public and media.
- Public speaking to civic and educational groups.
- It publishes a quarterly newsletter, *NEWSWORTHY*.
- It transmits a cable television programme, *NEWSWORTHY*, premièred in August 1996 and broadcast on the Twin Cities regional cable channel.

(http://www.news-council.org/trial/newsworthy_tv.html)

Other news councils have come and gone, so these voluntary, self-styled organisations depend entirely on the enthusiasm of the small group determined to run them and the support, or lack of it, of the local media.

Countries with no constitutional protection of freedom

Let us now move on to countries which, although they do not have constitutional freedom of expression, seem in many respects to be very similar to America. Sweden was the first European country to become involved in regulating journalism ethics. It set up its first press council in 1874. Sweden's code of conduct is not enormously different from that of the PCC. It is much more straightforward, though, spelling out the issues with little of the fine rhetoric of the US codes. The approach of the Swedish journalist is very different from that of the UK journalist. With few laws to consider, the Swedes take their code of ethics very seriously. It is difficult to tell why this might be. Perhaps they are more responsive to social pressures? Perhaps they are less concerned with gossip? Perhaps there is less competition? Certainly the press compensation funds which allow for state support of newspapers may remove some of the market pressure faced by UK journalists.

Sweden has a media council supported by all sectors of the industry. It deals with complaints from the public and measures them against a code of conduct. It is slightly unusual in that it has a media council and not just a press council. It also has an ombudsman who can take up complaints on behalf of a reader or viewer.

Dutch journalists also seem to take ethics very seriously. They too have very few laws limiting the media, and think hard about their ethics. Interestingly, although Sweden has a strong code of ethics, which journalists support strongly, journalists in the Netherlands have opposed having such a code. There is a general acceptance of the 'Bordeaux' Code of the International Federation of Journalists (see Appendix 5). Their collective view, according to Huub Evers, an author and lecturer in journalistic ethics at one of the journalism schools in the Netherlands, is that codes are too restrictive. A detailed code, covering all the issues a journalist needs to know, is too inflexible to work in everyday practice (see Chapter 16 on working with codes). The editors-in-chief of a number of Dutch papers did try to formulate a code in the mid-1990s, but this was rejected by most journalism groups within the Netherlands and the Press Council continues to discuss complaints case by case and make a declaration of principle. According to Dr Evers, the Council's reputation is growing. Adjudications of the Dutch Press Council are printed in the union's journal, *The Journalist*. Several Dutch newspapers also have news ombudsmen and these are useful ways of dealing with readers' complaints.

Legal controls

Some countries, of course, go further and require legal controls of some areas of media work. Italy takes a different approach to regulation from most other European countries. It has a code of conduct and, like America, there is strong constitutional protection for the rights of the citizen and personal honour, including the right of ownership of a person's own image. This means that in certain circumstances a person needs to give permission before his or her photograph may be used in the media. There is also a limited amount of freedom of information. This is mainly at a local level. In addition, the law enforces the journalist's right to protect sources. The journalist is obliged 'to respect professional secrecy with regard to sources of information, when this is required by its confidential nature' (Ordine dei Giornalisti 1993: 7).

There is strong legal protection for the code of conduct through professional registration. A journalist may only work in Italy if he or she is a member of the Ordine dei Giornalisti and is listed on the Professional Register. This professional body ensures that only properly trained people, who have passed their professional exams, taken before a committee of five journalists and two magistrates appointed by the court of appeal in Rome, may be listed on the register and hold a press card. No one under the age of twenty-one can become a journalist. Breaching the code of ethics may mean a member being expelled and their livelihood removed: 'A member can be removed from the professional register if his [sic] conduct has seriously compromised professional decorum in such a way that his continuation in the professional register or lists is incompatible with the dignity of the profession' (Ordine dei Giornalisti 1993: 14). Journalists may only re-apply for membership after five years. A warning, reprimand or suspension is a more usual punishment.

Professional registration for journalists is an uncommon approach around the world because of the damaging effect that having only professional journalists writing for publication can have on press freedom. Such limiting of access to the media must also limit its ability to provide a range of ideas and opinions. 'Journalism is not a profession. It is the exercise by occupation of the right of free expression available to every citizen. That right, being freely available to all, cannot in principle be withdrawn from a few by any system of licensing or professional registration' (Robertson 1983: 3). This concern has not escaped the Italians and a referendum was held in June 1997 to decide whether professional registration should stay. The Radical Party in Italy opposes registration because it says it limits press freedom. A number of journalists, many of them influential in the Italian unions, oppose change. They say that more pressure could be put on journalists by proprietors and editors to write biased copy. It would be easier to buy in political viewpoints. A limit on entry into the profession gives Italian journalists more freedom to write what they want than journalists in the rest of Europe. 'Journalists have the unsuppressible right of freedom of information and criticism, limited by compliance with legislation designed to safeguard the privacy of others, the irrevocable obligation to respect the substantial truth of the facts, and respect for the obligations imposed by honesty and good faith' (Ordine dei Giornalisti 1993: 7).

There are other countries which pick up specific laws to control areas of journalistic work. All of these areas tend to appear in codes of conduct, but individual countries consider them important enough to be singled out. They cover the following subjects:

- Privacy
- Presumption of innocence
- Children
- Protection of personal honour
- Confidential sources

- Media silence
- Reality TV

Privacy

Privacy is one of the areas of considerable difference in journalistic practice around the world. In some places there is protection of privacy for all but the most public of figures. The right to respect for privacy is enshrined in the European Convention on Human Rights but its application varies enormously in the individual states across Europe. Italy, Finland and France, for instance, have privacy legislation while Britain, Ireland, Sweden and the Netherlands do not. Generally this is protection from invasion of privacy but some countries also protect from publication. Germany is one country that is leading the way on privacy legislation and several of the recent decisions on privacy in Germany will have a direct effect on the interpretation of privacy law elsewhere in Europe, including the UK. The Princess Caroline of Monaco case in 2004, for instance, starts to put limits on privacy in what might be described as public places (see Chapter 6 for fuller details). In Finland it is a criminal offence to publish information about a private citizen.

Laws preventing phone-tapping, bugging and other forms of invasion of privacy are common throughout Europe. Less common are laws allowing complainants to take action about a published invasion of their privacy. France enforces the right to a private life through article 9 of its civil code: 'Each has a right to respect for his private life' (http://www.uta.fi/ethicnet/). Finland enforces the right to privacy in its criminal code, making it an offence to spread information, an insinuation or an image depicting the private life of another person which was conducive to causing suffering. In a 2010 case before the European Court of Human Rights several Finnish publications sought to overturn criminal convictions on the grounds that they breached their right to free expression. The case involved a public figure who, together with his mistress, returned to the marital home, sparking a fight with his wife which led to him being given a conditional prison sentence and his mistress being fined. The publications named the man and his mistress and used her picture. The domestic courts found that as she was not a public figure, the fact that she was the girlfriend of a public figure was not sufficient to justify revealing her identity. The European Court felt that the consequences for the applicants were severe enough for there to be a violation of article 10. However, the case shows the wide variation of approach. A similar case in the UK would not lead to a privacy suit.

The right to respect for privacy is in the US Bill of Rights and so is also protected under the constitution alongside freedom of the press.

Presumption of innocence

One of the areas of ethics which varies widely across Europe is coverage of court cases and in particular the rights of defendants to protect their reputations. A Swedish journalist, for instance, would be very cautious about naming a person accused of a crime, and facing trial. While this can be partly ascribed to the different legal system, which means that the case can be heard in full before a lower and a higher court, leading to possible prejudice of the case at the higher court, the main thrust of ethical argument in Sweden seems to be the protection of civil rights. Only after the trial and a finding of guilt might a Swedish journalist consider using the convict's name. In Britain the name is used automatically and the assumption would be that it is the right thing to do. Naming the person is not seen as an invasion of privacy or a secondary punishment, but an assurance that justice is done. In April 1996, the then Lord Chief Justice, the Rt Hon Lord Taylor of Gosforth, spoke to a Commonwealth Judges and Magistrates' Association Symposium which was considering allowing TV cameras into courts. He said: 'It is crucial in a democracy that justice is administered in public: "Justice must not only be done, but must be seen to be done."' Although he opposed the idea of cameras in courts as putting too much pressure on witnesses and defendants, he said: 'It is healthy that the media, and through them the ordinary citizen, should observe closely and critically how public institutions and services are run.'

The Lord Chancellor, Lord Mackay of Clashfern, agreed, although with reservations. In a letter to all judges in 1997, he expressed his concern at the standard of some press reporting of judicial decisions, while restating his belief that the criminal justice system is, and should be, the subject of public scrutiny. Recommending that before passing sentence in cases which might attract media attention, judges should produce a written note of their sentencing remarks for distribution, he said: 'It is unfair to the individual judge concerned, as well as to the public's perception of the judiciary as a whole, if criticism by the media is based not on the facts as laid before the judge but on a markedly different account of the situation.' The Press Complaints Commission described the Lord Chancellor's initiative as a 'useful recommendation'.

The Netherlands follows the same route as Sweden's. Court cases are covered, but reporters talk about a '28-year-old man from Amsterdam' or maybe '28-year-old A.B. from Amsterdam'. The Dutch also believe that defendants' chances of rehabilitation should not be harmed by identifying them.

Yet things are changing. In line with the move away from 1960s' liberalism into the more authoritarian approach of the 1990s, both the Swedes and the Dutch are reconsidering their views. Already, some cases in both countries have led to people being named and there are moves to allow TV cameras into courts in the Netherlands. Cameras are not actually banned at the moment, but it requires the judge's approval in each case and this is rarely granted. The new law, if passed, would allow cameras in unless the judge refused. Since that would presumably require the judge to have a specific reason for refusal, this is a complete change-about for the Netherlands. It seems that as society becomes more concerned with punishing the guilty than rehabilitating them, the journalistic ethic will change. Already, reporters from those countries, which a few years ago would not have considered naming suspects or convicts and would have been horrified at the suggestion that they should, are prepared to consider the principle case by case. If TV cameras are introduced into the Dutch courts on a regular basis, then it is extremely unlikely that anonymity will continue for long, although editors generally would prefer to continue that tradition. A report of the practice of news ombudsmen in the Netherlands puts the view of the ombudsman for *Rotterdams Dagsblad* when asked by readers why suspects' names are not stated in full: 'norms pertaining to the privacy protection of suspects and convicts "are shifting slightly" but a shift towards the standards prevailing in countries such as England and Belgium does not seem to be imminent as yet. "Thank goodness", he comments' (Evers at al. 2010: 49). Similar sentiments appear in the section looking at decisions of the ombudsman of *The Volkskrant* with the ombudsman declaring: 'Over recent years, the editors have been increasingly sloppy in their consideration for the privacy of perpetrators and victims' (ibid: 68).

Children

Children are protected in many countries around the world in two main ways: by taste and decency and by privacy. Germany, for instance, has strong laws to protect the young from corruption. The 'Gesetz über die Verbreitung jugendgefährdender Schriften 1961' (Law on the dissemination of publications endangering the young) established an examining board of twelve members who may list a publication which is considered to be of a violent, pornographic or racist nature. Although daily newspapers and political periodicals are not covered, if a publication appears on the list twice in the same year, it may be removed from circulation for up to a year.

Protection of personal honour

Defamation or protection of personal honour is enforced in some fashion practically everywhere in the world, with 158 of 168 countries reviewed by campaign group Article 19 in 2009 having criminal defamation laws and only 10 having only civil laws. Criminal libel can lead to heavy fines or even jail sentences. In addition many countries have what is known in many South American countries as desacato – insult laws. Variations of desacato or defamation are used fairly widely around the world as a way of preventing or punishing criticism of the government and individual ministers or other significant public figures. According to Article 19, Desacato laws are prevalent across the Central and South American region, granting special protection for the reputations of public officials which is not available to other members of society. As recognised by the Inter-American Court, this is contrary to democratic principles which would usually expect political and public figures to tolerate more, not less, public scrutiny and offer less privacy. Descato laws remain in place in Bolivia, Brazil, Colombia, Cuba, Ecuador, El Salvador, Guatemala, Haiti, Uruguay and Venezuela although Paraguay, Costa Rica, Peru and Chile have abolished them over the past ten years.

In Asia, defamation is often used to stifle criticism of the leadership and a number of people have been imprisoned for criminal defamation in the Philippines while in Malaysia and Singapore, civil defamation with uncapped fines as a penalty have left defendants bankrupt, encouraging wide self-censorship. Many European countries also provide special protection for public officials and symbols. The Middle East also has its fair share of countries prepared to jail for defamation with Iran leading the way.

Several European countries offer protection of personal honour under their constitutions and this spills through into their codes of ethics. The International Federation of Journalists' Code of Conduct, for instance, says: 'The journalist shall regard as grave professional offences the following: plagiarism, malicious misrepresentation, calumny, slander, libel, unfounded accusations' (International Federation of Journalists' Declaration of Principles on the Conduct of Journalists, http://www.uta.fi/ethicnet/). This is picked up in quite a few European codes as a quick look through http://www.uta.fi/Ethicnet/ will confirm. In the UK there are no codes of ethics which pick up this point and the issue tends to be left entirely in the domain of defamation. If someone's personal honour is called into question, their only recourse is to sue.

Confidential sources

Legal protection for confidential sources exists in the UK to the extent of section 10 of the Contempt of Court Act 1981 which says a court may not oblige a person to disclose a source of information unless it is necessary in the interests of justice, national security or the prevention of crime. The US also recently introduced such protection – known as shield law – in 2007 to give some protection to journalists seeking to protect confidential sources. Similar laws exist in Canada and also several Western European countries.

Media silence

Another debate that has cropped up in Europe concerns voluntary 'media silences'. A spate of incidents in the Netherlands sparked off this debate. Nine divorced fathers, in completely separate incidents over a space of a year, killed their children and then in most cases killed themselves. Academic research in the Netherlands by a child psychologist suggested that the media coverage was sparking other such incidents. In other words, reading about the events of an earlier case was likely to provoke another. The US psychologist David Philips has done similar work which also

claims to prove this link. As a result, there were calls for a media silence on
ignored these calls but did alter the way they used the stories, putting them in
than on the front page and not using photographs. Apart from not being entir
argument, the editors also thought that it was their duty to inform people.
have been heard of locally, and indeed several of the cases happened only streets from each other,
suggesting that any copycat effect did not require the newspapers.

Reality TV

This is another ethical dilemma that is yet to hit Britain in a big way. Although we do have some
programmes which contain footage from surveillance cameras or police car cameras, and there are
a few programmes that have unplanned interviews which can involve invasion of offices or homes,
there are not many such programmes. But in other parts of Europe, such as the Netherlands, reality
TV can be a problem. In the Netherlands, freelance camera teams often film road accidents and
similar incidents as they happen. As only the more exciting footage is screened on TV, there are
suggestions that such footage is sometimes elaborated. It is also important that victims are recognisable. This involves some close-ups of road accident victims which viewers found too excessive.
Some protests followed.

Death and torture

Imprisonment, torture and death is the fate of journalists in some countries. While this isn't always
at the hands of government agencies, there are plenty of countries where those seeking power find
it useful to suppress free speech.

More than 1,100 journalists and media staff have been killed in the line of duty over the past
12 years with 139 dying in 2009, according to the International Federation of Journalists:

- 2009 – 139
- 2008 – 109
- 2007 – 172
- 2006 – 153
- 2005 – 154
- 2004 – 129
- 2003 – 92

In 2009 the Philippines topped the shameful league with 37 deaths, 32 of them brutally massacred
by a militia on Mindanao Island in a group of 57 victims mutilated and dumped in shallow
graves. Mexico came next with 13 dead, followed by Somalia 9, Russia 6, Iraq 5 and Colombia and
Palestine 4 each according to the IFJ. Reporters Sans Frontières, another organisation campaigning
for journalists' safety, records a similar number. Murder is fairly rare in the British Isles but Martin
O'Hagan was shot and killed by terrorists in Northern Ireland in 2001 (http://www.guardian.
co.uk/obituaries/story/0,3604,560952,00.html accessed 19/7/06). Surprisingly, he was the first
journalist to be killed in the Province since 1969, although not the first to be threatened. It was
criminals who were behind the murder of Irish journalist Veronica Guerin in June 1996. She had
become famous for stories about Ireland's drug barons and eventually she paid for her success.

Hundreds of journalists are routinely jailed around the world with hundreds more attacked
or threatened. Such regulatory methods are much more likely in some countries than others.
RSF identifies Eritrea, North Korea, Turkmenistan, Iran, Burma, Cuba, Laos, China, Yemen and

.am as the ten countries with the worst press freedom record in the world (http://en.rsf.org/
.ss-freedom-index-2009,1001.html)

Suspension of publication is another tool used regularly by governments as a way of crushing
dissent and preventing freedom of the media whether legal or illegal. Police searches or attacks on
newspapers or broadcast stations is a tactic widely used to scare journalists, oblige self-censorship
or prevent publication or broadcast. In early 2010 Iran suspended publication of daily newspaper
Eternad. The licence of weekly *Iran Dokht* was cancelled by the Press Surveillance Commission for
'non-compliance with the Press law' while journalists being held by the intelligence ministry were
being pressured to publicly ask for forgiveness from the supreme leader. Iran is far from alone in
using such methods and countries such as Belarus, Zimbabwe, the Philippines and Liberia are all
examples of countries using violence against journalists in an effort to reduce criticism.

There are, of course, some countries which avoid violence by using the law to restrict the media,
jailing journalists, supporting censorship and the closure of newspapers and broadcast stations or
variations on these themes.

In Turkey, for instance, Baris Yarkadas, editor of online publication *Gercek Gündem*, in 2010
faced five years in prison for a comment insulting the president posted on the site by a reader.
In Algeria in 2009, the government banned distribution of three French publications – *L'Express*,
Marianne and *Journal du Dimanche* – in the run up to a presidential election.

Global code of ethics

A global code of ethics was suggested at a World Association of Press Councils meeting in Istanbul
in 1998 and the European Commission has suggested a pan-European code. This has not received
any support within the industry in the UK and the PCC is strongly opposed. Speaking at a meeting
of the Commonwealth Press Union in 1998, Lord Wakeham, the then PCC chairman, said a code
could 'end up doing much mischief and be misused by those who seek to bring in often draconian
controls against the press through the back door, under the guise of a respectable international
body' (PCC 1998: 3). He pointed out that it would be impossible to produce a global code of
conduct that would be acceptable to all societies without curtailing the freedom to report in many
of them.

Cross-border collaborations

The European Broadcasting Union is one such body, and is the largest professional association of
national broadcasters in the world with 74 members in 54 countries. It was founded in Western
Europe in 1950 and negotiates broadcasting rights for major sporting events, operates the Eurovision
and Euroradio networks, organises programme exchanges and coordinates co-productions.

TV Without Frontiers is a European Directive aimed at determining jurisdiction for European
broadcasters to ensure that it is clear which set of laws apply to which broadcaster when national
borders are crossed. For instance BBC 1 can be received in Ireland, Holland and some other
European countries and so jurisdiction can be significant, so the TVWF Directive guarantees
freedom of reception and no restriction of retransmission.

Chapter 20

The future

This chapter examines some of the issues that might change the way we view some ethical or regulatory problems in the future. It discusses the issues involved in:

- Citizen journalism and the increase of audience input

- The rise in interactivity produced by the internet

- The impact that convergence of media will have for journalists

A number of issues will concern the media in the future. It is probable that none of these will change the basic moral problems that face journalists in their daily work, but it is possible that they will make decision making more difficult. Working across international borders, for instance, emphasises the differences in moral approach between cultures and the use of the internet will add other problems. Interactivity is an important new element of the internet. The consumer changes from the passive reader or viewer of what is offered to someone who can actively track down the information he or she requires and respond instantaneously by e-mail and even become a news-gatherer in their own right. Citizen journalism, through weblogs and personal websites and what the NUJ describes as witness contributors will become more and more a feature of future news-gathering operations. The consumer can supply his or her own slant on the news directly to the supplier faster and more efficiently than ever before. Journalists at BBC online are often alerted to stories by readers e-mailing for information on a breaking story. This developing interactive element is seen by many as the most important facet of the internet when it comes to journalism. It should allow more input from a vast range of sources, most of which are more likely to be pushing their own viewpoint. With this wider range of available material, the filtering process, if only in terms of time available to read all this information, will become more difficult.

Citizen journalism is also growing with many people producing weblogs that put their view of the news with their own commentary. These are often accessed by professionals and are used as starting points for stories. They are even lifted wholesale by some sources: an unethical process as well as being one that breaches copyright laws in most of the Western world.

Citizen journalism has grown at such a pace through the first few years of the new millennium that journalists have been facing a major change on the way breaking stories are gathered. Many people throughout the world have mobile phones, many of which are capable of taking reasonable quality video or still pictures. These can then be sent direct to the news desks of major newspapers or broadcasters. This is described by the NUJ as witness contributions, to distinguish those who have stumbled on a newsworthy event and would like to see their pictures used in the newspapers and possibly earn a fee, from those would-be journalists who write blogs and columns or take pictures and publish on the internet. Already several major news and picture agencies have widened their scope to help witness contributors find a market for their pictures. Cavendish Press, a big Manchester-based news agency invites celebrity-watchers to send in pictures with the promise of big money:

> If you have caught THAT picture of a breaking news event, your favourite celebrity, wacky weather, or the cuddliest creatures, we could make you thousands. It doesn't matter if your picture is taken on a mobile phone, digital camera or professional camera gear, please download them onto your PC and send them to us NOW. The quicker you send them in to us, the bigger chance there is for more cash.
>
> (http://www.cavendish-press.co.uk/sell-your-pictures.asp)

Another agency, Mrpaparazzi, offers a similar service on http://www.mrpaparazzi.com. Cavendish Press offers photographers a 60/40 split of any sales and warns photographers that:

> Cavendish Press will not syndicate any pictures submitted which could be seen to invade or abuse another person's privacy or cause unlawful harassment, abusive, threatening, harmful, obscene, profane, sexually oriented, racially offensive or otherwise objectionable annoyance which could give rise to civil or criminal liability against Cavendish Press. We strictly adhere to codes outlined in the Press Complaints Commission http://www.pcc.org.uk/cop/practice.html. We will not syndicate any submitted photograph(s) which have been manipulated or doctored in anyway prior to submission to Cavendish Press.
>
> (ibid.)

This is a phenomenon that can only grow. As cameraphones become more and more sophisticated, so the quality of video and still pictures will improve and with virtually everyone on the planet owning such a camera, their willingness to consider sending pictures of the latest news direct to newsrooms will grow. All newsrooms accept such pictures and most national newspapers and broadcasters actively encourage the sending of such pictures. There are concerns about the ethics of such pictures and about the health and safety of contributors. One amateur, whose video of a major fuel depot blaze in the south of England was later played by several of the major news broadcasters, could be heard on the playback commenting on how dangerous this was and hoping that nothing else exploded. In other incidents, pictures of road accidents or suicides were sent to news desks without any warning being given to those receiving the pictures of their horrific nature. There is also the risk that celebrities, often the subject of such snatch pictures, will now have no real privacy at all. Any trip into the open world will put them at risk of being photographed. Magazines such as *Heat* are always keen to get interesting pictures of celebrities. If there is not a free-for-all, it is likely that it will only have been prevented by the courts or Parliament agreeing to limit such pictures by allowing a general growth of a tort of privacy. Already some lawyers in the USA boast that they are able to prevent such pictures of high-profile clients there.

This phenomenon only differs to what has happened since the media began, in terms of its scale. Cheap and sophisticated hardware means everyone now has access to the equipment needed to take pictures and send them quickly to news desks. Twenty years ago, only a few people had the cameras and facilities to get film or prints to a news desk in time for it to be of significant value. The change in technology was firmly highlighted by the terrorism bombs in London on 7 July 2005. Pictures were sent through to news desks that would not have been possible for professional photographers to obtain. Quick-thinking passengers evacuating the bombed underground trains were able to take videos of their escape and send them to news desks. Professional news people were not able to get anywhere near the scene and so virtually all the good pictures were taken by amateurs. It was a watershed moment.

It has caused a lot of concern among journalists, many of whom see it as a threat to their livelihoods. However, it follows in a long tradition. War correspondents, for instance, were often army officers, sending dispatches back from a front that was almost impossible for a professional journalist to reach or too expensive for a newspaper to send a correspondent to. Journalists are still going to be required to produce the routine reports or to provide updates and background material once the initial story has been broken. There is little chance that bloggers or witness contributors are likely to be interested in extending their journalism into the everyday work of the professional. These changes are also likely to fit into the developments that many in the industry will require in order for it to remain profitable. The general view among business leaders is that things will become more difficult for the media over the next few years and the recession has made things even more difficult. Greater demands on shrinking advertising budgets will lead to tighter margins. This means that journalist processors will be controlling material from amateurs who do not have a firm grasp of ethics. Pictures and copy will have to be checked more carefully to ensure they were gathered in accordance with the appropriate code of practice.

Many people see the present grip on the media by a small number of moguls as being broken by the internet and growing interactivity. I am sceptical enough to believe that where big money and control are involved, the reverse is more likely to be true. We may well fall into the hands of an even smaller, more powerful group of moguls. Already there is evidence that consumers find the sheer quantity of information that is available overwhelming, and turn to portal sites for assistance. Portal sites are internet sites whose sole purpose is to direct the consumer to sites of specific interest. If you are interested in media ethics (and you may not be by now), then there are several portal sites which would guide you on to other sites about media ethics. Many portal sites are now growing up. They usually have their own material and then direct the consumer on to specialist sites for in-depth information.

Many of these have been developed by existing mainstream news providers. The BBC, Electronic Telegraph, and the Guardian online are such sites. Some have developed out of the new technology industries, but aim to do the same thing: Yahoo and MSN are two such portals. They provide information content of their own, filtered and tailored in a traditional way, and provide access to an indexed range of additional sites.

These sites will grow in importance. Despite the claims that the 'me paper' (an online 'newspaper' filtered from original sources only by criteria decided by the reader) will take over on the internet, the reverse seems likely to be the case. Most people access online news from sources they trust – usually the brands that they have grown up trusting. This is why the BBC online, Guardian unlimited, the Daily Telegraph online and the Washington Post online are the sort of sites that are doing well and are likely to continue to hold their readers' loyalty. Newer sites are being used, but even then they tend to be either new but corporate brands, such as AOL or Yahoo, or highly specialist sites selected for their expertise. These brands now use reader-counting technology to determine which stories are the most popular. News desks press reporters to get stories similar to those that prove to be popular in a constant bid to gain more readers/viewers. Advertising is starting to follow the stories that draw readers from the news home page. Soon all news sites will be gathering news by directly measuring the reader response because that will lead to more advertising revenue. This aim to use popular stories has always been a part of the media but until the internet, there was no easy way to measure story types and the readers'/viewers' reaction to them. Circulation and viewing figures didn't come in until days after the product was finished and left to gather dust. Links to particular stories rather than a range of stories were impossible. Now, there can be instant feedback, leading the newsdesk to seek to build more information from a popular story to get it riding higher up the popularity index. Alongside this desire to only carry stories that are extremely popular at the expense of important but duller stories is the risk to truth. The need to get stories up on the webpage quickly has meant that many news providers now see the website as a way of providing a Beta version of the story, an early draft of what may finally appear in the newspaper or broadcast and the updated web page. This can lead to an approach where fact checking and a respect for truth take second place to getting the story to readers. This again has always been the risk inherent in journalism, but although traditional deadlines have always been tight, there have always been deadlines; an opportunity to take a decision about whether the story stands up and should run with as much information as is available or whether it should be delayed until all are confident of its accuracy. Now the temptation is to run with what you have on the basis that it can be updated every time new information becomes available.

Cross-border working

As the journalist becomes more international, so working across borders seems less and less unusual. Traditionally the journalist's forays abroad tended to be for spells as a foreign correspondent or to cover a war or election in a particular spot for a short period before returning home. Technology is making it much easier for the journalist to research a foreign country from their desk, as well as making it more likely for them to be working for a multinational employer on a multinational publication. Moving news on to the World Wide Web ensures that journalists will be working for a multinational audience. It's also much more likely that international reporting will be carried out with reporters working to film or video feeds being sent from the site of incidents without the reporter actually being there at all.

This raises several ethical points as well as making the regulatory system more difficult. Something illegal in one country may be legal in another but highly unethical in a third. Covering courts, for instance, is an important part of the media's business in Britain. Naming the accused, their alleged crime and defence is seen as an important part of ensuring that justice is seen to be done. While some people might argue that some of the more unsavoury details of court cases should not appear in the media (much of the detail of the Rosemary West trial was voluntarily suppressed by many papers as being unsuitable for a family newspaper), hardly anyone in this country opposes the view that the media should publish details of major trials to ensure that public justice is done. Yet in Sweden, journalists are horrified at the idea of naming the accused during trials. Even in important trials, the normal practice is not to name the accused until after a finding of guilt, and often not even then. Journalists will need to be even more aware of the systems in other countries if they are working globally. The coverage of the McCann case from Portugal and the more recent case of a mother arrested over the deaths of her two children in Spain show the difficulties of working to the laws and ethics of another country when often the film or pictures and even copy are provided by freelances or agencies from that country working as a home reporter.

If a reporter is obliged to put together a report based entirely on video sent from the scene of major story, they can have no idea about what sort of editing process has already gone on. The Haitian earthquake, for instance, saw many reports compiled from home bases using video sent from the scene. Stories of violence and looting were grossly exaggerated or even manufactured according to some commentators because video scenes were either misinterpreted at home or were exaggerated by their provider in a bid to ensure their use and then that line was over-developed at home. This sort of problem is not new. Journalists travelling to the scene of a major story are not always able to see the full story for themselves as they are often being shown around by a fixer employed for their local knowledge and language skills, but who of course will choose to take them to the sorts of places that will give the correspondent the story the fixer knows he or she wants regardless of how accurate or fair that is. The difficulty of the increasing use of technology is that while it is a cheap way of covering such stories – often the only way if the story is somewhere remote with poor travel links and a difficult political situation – the reporter has no way of knowing what is missing from the material being sent.

The internet

The internet has changed journalism and the provision of news, comment and analysis for ever. It can be an incredibly powerful tool providing instant information at your fingertips together with comment and analysis that allows you to read or view what others are thinking and to debate and discuss but, like all man-made things, it is also capable of harm and contains an enormous amount of propaganda, lies, spite and malicious nastiness. Blogs are often just opportunities to attack people unfairly and the ability to criticise without having to face the person you are attacking often tempts people to be viciously unpleasant in their criticisms. Condemnation often seems to be the norm on the internet.

This can mean that offence often moves into causing harm and journalists using the internet as a research tool need to be very careful about how they use the information they gather, depending on the source.

Internet material is much easier to access than traditional methods, but it is also much more difficult to be certain that one is getting the most up-to-date information. The use of the internet as a research tool is becoming more important in many newsrooms, although journalists, in the UK at least, lag well behind other researchers in this area. The burden of proof for any source is more difficult on the internet as the element of trust and credibility is not there. Even if a site carries the name of a large company, there is no guarantee it is an authorised site. Many sites are now being set up to attack the credibility of a company. A disgruntled ex-employee or former customer can easily set up a site with a credible name to give damaging hoax information about the company. All internet information needs to be treated with caution unless one is confident about the site.

All too often, internet information only gives one side of the story. Information on the Net is only there because copyright owners want to put it there. Whether it is information they have painstakingly gathered to expose government corruption, or a multi-coloured presentation on the latest model of a car put out by its manufacturer, it must all be treated with the same scepticism that should be used about any source.

Sad 'anoraks' no longer scribble their pet obsessions in green ink on jagged-torn pages of lined exercise books. Their reports are now as superbly presented on the Net as any corporate presentation. This slickness appears to add veracity where none exists. Much material on the Net comes from unofficial or commercial sources and needs to be treated with suspicion. The rise in conspiracy theories can probably be laid at the door of the internet as anyone with a campaign, no matter how ridiculous, can not only find an audience of potentially millions but also sufficient people to take the idea seriously to give it some authority. Credibility and balance is difficult to measure on the internet without seeking additional sources. See Case study 20.1.

Case study 20.1 Small fish in a big pond

Because internet material is self-generated but widely available, a small organisation can put out masses of material and make itself appear to be a big player with more influence than its real power base. A number of organisations have now seen that this is an ideal way to contact young, literate, moderately wealthy individuals. Cult religions, political and religious extremists, as well as small but financially strong pressure groups, are starting to use the internet to attract this key audience which is growing by the thousands every day. For instance, creation–evolution theory has attracted support among fundamentalist Christians in the US southern states before and since the Scopes monkey trial. A law proposing equal time for creation-science and evolution-science in Arkansas schools was opposed by individual plaintiffs, who included the resident Arkansas Bishops of the United Methodist, Episcopal, Roman Catholic and African Methodist Episcopal Churches, the principal official of the Presbyterian Churches in Arkansas, other United Methodist, Southern Baptist and Presbyterian clergy, as well as several persons who sued as parents and friends of minor children attending Arkansas public schools. Organisations included the American Jewish Congress, the Union of American Hebrew Congregations, the American Jewish Committee, the Arkansas Education Association, the National Association of Biology Teachers and the National Coalition for Public Education and Religious Liberty. The plaintiffs won their case to have evolution taught as the main theory of human development in those schools. Yet a quick search on the internet using the word 'creation' produced more than thirty websites in favour of creation-biology compared with only fifteen for evolution. A small but vocal and determined minority had been able to build up their pet theories to appear far more widely believed than they really are.

The issue of credibility of information and trust on the internet is an important one for the public relations industry. Practitioners want to be able to find a way to assure journalists and customers that the information is accurate. The question of credibility is also important for journalists. Many traditional newspaper and broadcast organisations now have very sophisticated websites. The importance of the validation of information being put out under the banner of, say, the BBC, *Guardian* or *Daily Telegraph* cannot be overestimated. This is one of the main reasons why the big players will eventually dominate on the Net as far as news services are concerned. Why get your news from Joe Bloggs' website when you can go direct to the BBC or the *Daily Telegraph* and get a validated service from a provider you already trust? The move by some of the key players to switch to paid for content on the web could have an impact here. Although users are now used to getting material free, there may still be a feeling of valuing something that costs. In other words, if you have to pay for content, then users will see it as being more trustworthy and so the provider will need to make sure that it is more trustworthy. It may also help limit the advertising link with editorial being able to survive in its own right.

Some organisations are seeking to put together a regulation body to validate websites by ensuring they stick to a code of conduct. The anarchic background from which the World Wide Web sprang makes it very resistant to this sort of change. Most users are more concerned about the risk of censorship than they are about validating the information on the Web. Some others are keen to set up a standard that bloggers and others can adhere to if they wish. It would be entirely voluntary but allow those who stuck to it to identify basic standards. The PCC and Ofcom now regulate websites that are associated with subscribing news providers and the PCC also allows news websites to be become subscribing members if they wish. Such sites would be able to say that they adhered to the PCC's Code of Practice.

Many governments are keen to bring in regulation, particularly over pornography on the Net. There are now numerous software systems designed to allow parents to prevent their children accessing sexually explicit sites. The rise in the number of crimes including sexual assault and murder following the grooming of young people on the internet by predatory adults has reached near moral panic status, but the threat is real and CEOP (Child Exploitation and Online Protection), an agency of the British police, now has a button on many social network sites that those who fear they may be being groomed can hit to report the contact. Facebook's refusal to carry the button has brought it a lot of criticism and has thrown Facebook's privacy policies firmly into the public arena.

Copyright

Concerns over copyright have already led some commercial operators to start withdrawing their intellectual property from the internet and led to the passing of the Digital Economy Act in the dying days of the Labour government in 2010. The Act attempts to address the issue of online infringements of copyright. Pictures of film stars or of scenes from cult favourites, which had been spread liberally on the Net for the enjoyment of fans, are now being withdrawn as they start to appear in publications both on and off the Net. *The X Files* TV show, for instance, had built up a large internet-based following, possibly because its fans were young, moneyed and technologically literate. So damaging did the copyright infringements become, with pictures and scripts being passed around the Net, that Fox Television issued a cease-and-desist order in the USA against an unofficial site which Fox claimed had been using copyright material. In a 2006 employment tribunal case, a photographer claimed he was made redundant from the *Jewish News* because he refused to be involved in the illegal downloading of pictures from the internet for use in the paper (Lagan 2006: 8). The Digital Economy Act attempts to identify such breaches of copyright by allowing copyright holders to search for breaches and then contact the ISP which must by law notify the subscriber of the copyright infringement report. The idea is that subscribers who infringe copyright could be identified by a code number which would show whether they were serious repeat offenders. If they were a court order could be sought and further action taken.

Much material is being placed on the Net by organisations in the hope of attracting journalists. The UK government, for instance, now puts out most of its information to the press and public this way and charges freelance journalists for sending out hard copy of press releases. Many commercial organisations, such as film and video distributors and fashion houses, also distribute press information this way. Details on major film releases, along with pictures and star interviews, might be just the ticket for a local paper hoping to flesh out its review pages. While this sort of PR work is only a technological update of the old press handout, there is a greater temptation to use the already keyed-in copy rather than write a new piece from scratch using the handout as notes.

Multi-media journalism

As technology develops, so the old divisions between radio, TV and press grow narrower. Journalists already work in all three fields at once on the internet and this development will continue with journalists using whatever medium they think is best to support the message being transmitted. This will almost certainly combine with some level of interactivity with the consumer, probably linked with digital TV. At the time of writing digital TV was only just developing from a sophisticated way of providing us with more channels, and therefore more programmes, with higher quality transmission to a system with added value and interactivity. But the cabling of the UK, combined with the power of the internet, opens all sorts of possibilities.

Interactivity means that advertisers, publishers and broadcasters will be able to build up complex databases on our likes and dislikes and feed us information, advertising and programming, both passive and active, that are tightly targeted at our individual needs and desires. This already happens to a limited extent through the post. Junk mail is becoming much more tightly focused to our needs and wants. Digital TV and the internet can take this a stage further. This may well mean that the present regulatory councils will need to be adjusted and it will become important to have a multi-media ethics council that is able to consider the problems of broadcasters, advertisers and publishers. With statutory regulation largely in place for broadcast, but desperately avoided by publishing, this will cause some friction. Will the government of the day be prepared to give up statutory regulation? Will the publishers be prepared to take on statutory regulation? Will TV broadcast on the internet be regulated by the Broadcasting Act or will it be unregulated? With the growth of cable, satellite and digital broadcasting, the old argument for regulated, impartial TV and radio will become less compelling and many of the present conglomerate owners, who are also the driving forces behind the new communication methods, will be pressing for more open forms of regulation or even total deregulation. This will lead to interesting dilemmas. For instance, how can children, or indeed anyone who might be offended, be protected from unacceptable material containing bad language, nudity or violence if there is no longer a watershed and if we can all watch or read whatever we want from comedies to pornography on whatever device we want, whether that's mobile phone, TV or computer wherever we happen to be, even in a public space such as a train or restaurant?

There are also social problems. If we all have a machine that receives calls, shows video, accesses the internet anytime, anywhere, will our relationships with others change? We can see hints of that now with tables of people in restaurants all on the phone to others outside the group, at much the same time.

The biggest change that is likely to come though is a growth in interactivity. Readers' pictures, readers' letters have existed almost since newspapers began, but the internet and mobile phone technology make them easily accessible to all. Blogs and citizen journalism will grow although I personally doubt if blogs will ever be anything more than readers' letters, even if they do enable some people with something important to say to gain access to an audience much more easily than would be the case today.

Archive

Another issue that has grown in significance over the past few years and will only become more important is archive material on the web. Stories on the web form a superb archive of material published by the news provider over the years that can easily be mined for specific information. While it has always been possible to research newspaper archives for data, this has been cumbersome and time consuming, meaning that such research is normally only carried out for very good reason. Now archive searches are quick and easy. This means that any error in the archive, or any invasion of privacy will easily be discovered and so newspapers and so websites are having to reconsider their policies about archive material. For instance, say a person was arrested in connection with a series of serious crimes. A report appears in the local paper and in the website. A few weeks later the charges are withdrawn as the person arrested is found to have no involvement at all. Yet every time someone searches that person's name, the arrests come up on Google or Yahoo. Of course this emphasises the importance of news organisations following through with stories and publishing the withdrawal of the charges so those would also show up on the search. But this is not the only reason why people want to revisit website reports that may show them in a bad light. Newspapers and broadcasters are being increasingly bombarded with requests to 'unpublish': to remove references to people involved in stories. This is not about errors; most news organisations now accept that errors on websites need to either be deleted or tagged with the correction. The main concern now is legitimate, accurate stories that may make life very difficult for the person in an age when searching is so easy.

The main options for a website are:

- delete or edit the item;
- take the whole page down;
- block search engines from accessing the page; or
- tag the page with a correction.

Google explains how to block access to search engines on http://googlepublicpolicy.blogspot. com/2009/07/working-with-news-publishers.html. This can be done either at the time of loading or at a pre-determined specific date so that the search engine will remove the page from the index on a certain date.

According to Kathy English, public editor of the *Toronto Star*, requests to unpublish are becoming more frequent (2009: 6). The problem with unpublishing is that archives are a matter of public record and to remove or to delete them would be a form of censorship. This has led to considerable reluctance by some editors to even consider it. The Rehabilitation of Offenders Act in the UK requires that minor criminal charges are not mentioned after a certain amount of time has passed and it is this issue of how long misdemeanours are held online that is troubling some editors as it perhaps gives the most difficult balance between public interest and potential personal harm and according to English, Gatehouse Media, which owns hundreds of weeklies in the United States, is piloting a policy where minor misdemeanours are removed from the website six months after initial publication.

According to the BBC (http://news.bbc.co.uk/1/hi/programmes/click_online/8447742.stm), France is proposing a right-to-forget law to deal with this issue, giving net users the right to have old information about them deleted.

Privacy

Privacy is an area where many say that things are changing, as mentioned back in Chapter 6. Many at the forefront of the social media revolution believe that people expect less privacy now and are happy to share information. Mark Zuckerberg, CEO and co-founder of Facebook, told the Cruncie Awards in San Francisco in 2010 that: 'people have really gotten comfortable not only sharing more information and different kinds, but more openly and with more people.' He identified this as reflecting changing attitudes among the general public and a shift in the general view on privacy. However, just a couple of months into 2010, Zuckerberg had to admit that Facebook had 'missed the mark' with its privacy controls and new privacy controls were added at the end of May. Despite this Zuckerberg still believes that we should have only one public identity: 'The days of you having a different image for your work friends or co-workers and for the other people you know are probably coming to an end pretty quickly … having two identities for yourself is an example of a lack of integrity.' This might be fine for a successful 20-something who heads his own international company straight out of college but is not the reality of most people's lives. However, he is not alone in thinking that privacy is an overrated concept and that Facebook and other social network sites have spelt the end of privacy. Quite a few social network supporters believe the way forward is far more openness, a transparency in our private lives that would make for greater integrity because we would no longer take duplicity as the norm, double standards as the way we work. We would no longer hide behind masks, but would show everyone our true face.

The trouble is that few people seem to really believe this. The evidence is that although we are all extremely interested in the lives of others through gossip magazines, revelatory newspapers and reality shows, we are not so keen to allow others to invade our privacy uninvited. More and more people seem to expect more privacy in their lives, particularly about their identity. A number of complaints to both the PCC and Ofcom concern people's identity. They expect to be asked permission to have their photographs taken or to be videoed. They expect to be informed before their name or address is used in the newspaper or broadcast, as identified above, they expect to be able to erase the record when things are published about them that they would prefer to keep private even though they are truthful and a matter of public record (Frost 2010). An examination of the complaints record of the PCC and Ofcom suggest that despite the views of Zuckerberg and other social network leaders, most people are even keener on keeping their lives private than they were before Facebook was invented. It is as though the social network sites have sensitised people to the need for privacy, leading them to understand that knowing about others but keeping secret themselves alters their relative social power. Whether it is their health or home life, the wish of many people to 'be on the telly' seems to have been replaced with a wish to be famous, but only for the manufactured personality of celebrity that they can control. It seems likely that in contrast to Zuckerberg's wish for a single public face that is identical to our private face, the complete reverse will be true with us all having at least two highly distinct faces; one for public use and one for family.

Protecting reputation

Libel and the protection of reputation has become a big issue over the past few years in the UK. The increase in cases run as conditional fee agreements – no win, no fee – has meant that many journalists have feared an increase in the so-called 'chilling effect', where journalists fear to write stories because of the high risk of a libel suit that is bound to cost the newspaper money, win or lose. The outgoing Labour government of 2010 was intending to make changes to the arrangements for CFAs, reducing the success fee that barristers could claim from 100 per cent to 10 per cent, but lost the election before they could. The new coalition government is less determined, but has said it will look into it.

Another issue connected with reputation is the way London has become the tourist capital of the world, with foreign nationals choosing to sue here because of the claimant-friendly laws. It is easier to sue for libel here than in many countries, because people in the public eye elsewhere often have to prove malice in order for a case to succeed in another country. That is not the case in the UK, where all that needs to be proved is that the words written or broadcast were defamatory about an identifiable person.

The final problem with UK libel laws is the single publication rule. This piece of English law means that every publication of a libel resets the clock as a new publication. The courts have judged that an internet publication is a new publication, effectively removing the protection contained in the Defamation Act 1996 that means a writ must be issued within one year of publication. With most material now published on the internet, the single publication rule, combined with the enthusiasm to sue in London means that anyone defamed on the internet can sue in London with high hopes of success.

The coalition government has promised to investigate the problems surrounding libel, saying: 'We will review libel laws to protect freedom of speech.' The coalition government has promised a number of other changes in the future that may well effect journalism in the UK for the better. A Freedom Bill is planned and although some details are available in the coalition government's programme the original LibDem Freedom Bill on which this promise is based calls for 20 measures to 'restore fundamental rights'. These include scrapping the ID card scheme, restoring the right to protest in Parliament Square and abolishing the control order scheme.

Of direct effect on journalism, though, they also promise to:

- Restore a public interest defence for whistleblowers.
- Strengthen freedom of information.
- Scrap ministerial veto on blocking release of Cabinet minutes.
- Introduce safeguards against misuse of anti-terror legislation.

PCC Code of Practice

The Press Complaints Commission is charged with enforcing the following Code of Practice, drawn up by the Editors' Code of Practice Committee, which was framed by the newspaper and periodical industry and was ratified by the PCC in September 2009.

The Code

All members of the press have a duty to maintain the highest professional standards. This Code sets the benchmark for those ethical standards, protecting both the rights of the individual and the public's right to know. It is the cornerstone of the system of self-regulation to which the industry has made a binding commitment.

It is essential that an agreed code be honoured not only to the letter but in the full spirit. It should not be interpreted so narrowly as to compromise its commitment to respect the rights of the individual, nor so broadly that it constitutes an unnecessary interference with freedom of expression or prevents publication in the public interest.

It is the responsibility of editors and publishers to implement the Code and they should take care to ensure it is observed rigorously by all editorial staff and external contributors, including non-journalists, in printed and online versions of publications.

Editors should co-operate swiftly with the PCC in the resolution of complaints. Any publication judged to have breached the Code must print the adjudication in full and with due prominence, including headline reference to the PCC.

1 Accuracy

   (i)   The Press must take care not to publish inaccurate, misleading or distorted information, including pictures.

   (ii)   A significant inaccuracy, misleading statement or distortion once recognised must be corrected, promptly and with due prominence, and – where appropriate – an apology published.

   (iii)   The Press, whilst free to be partisan, must distinguish clearly between comment, conjecture and fact.

   (iv)   A publication must report fairly and accurately the outcome of an action for defamation to which it has been a party, unless an agreed settlement states otherwise, or an agreed statement is published.

2 Opportunity to reply
   A fair opportunity for reply to inaccuracies must be given when reasonably called for.

3 *Privacy

   (i)   Everyone is entitled to respect for his or her private and family life, home, health and correspondence, including digital communications. Editors will be expected to justify intrusions into any individual's private life without consent.

   (ii)   It is unacceptable to photograph individuals in private places without their consent.

   Note – Private places are public or private property where there is a reasonable expectation of privacy.

4 *Harassment

(i)   Journalists must not engage in intimidation, harassment or persistent pursuit.

(ii) They must not persist in questioning, telephoning, pursuing or photographing individuals once asked to desist; nor remain on their property when asked to leave and must not follow them. If requested, they must identify themselves and whom they represent.

(iii) Editors must ensure these principles are observed by those working for them and take care not to use non-compliant material from other sources.

5 Intrusion into grief or shock

(i)   In cases involving personal grief or shock, enquiries and approaches must be made with sympathy and discretion and publication handled sensitively. This should not restrict the right to report legal proceedings, such as inquests.

*(ii) When reporting suicide, care should be taken to avoid excessive detail about the method used.

6 *Children

(i)   Young people should be free to complete their time at school without unnecessary intrusion.

(ii) A child under 16 must not be interviewed or photographed on issues involving their own or another child's welfare unless a custodial parent or similarly responsible adult consents.

(iii) Pupils must not be approached or photographed at school without the permission of the school authorities.

(iv) Minors must not be paid for material involving children's welfare, nor parents or guardians for material about their children or wards, unless it is clearly in the child's interest.

(v)   Editors must not use the fame, notoriety or position of a parent or guardian as sole justification for publishing details of a child's private life.

7 *Children in sex cases

1. The press must not, even if legally free to do so, identify children under 16 who are victims or witnesses in cases involving sex offences.

2. In any press report of a case involving a sexual offence against a child:
    (i)   The child must not be identified.
    (ii) The adult may be identified.
    (iii) The word 'incest' must not be used where a child victim might be identified.
    (iv) Care must be taken that nothing in the report implies the relationship between the accused and the child.

8 *Hospitals

(i)   Journalists must identify themselves and obtain permission from a responsible executive before entering non-public areas of hospitals or similar institutions to pursue enquiries.

(ii) The restrictions on intruding into privacy are particularly relevant to enquiries about individuals in hospitals or similar institutions.

9 *Reporting of crime

(i) Relatives or friends of persons convicted or accused of crime should not generally be identified without their consent, unless they are genuinely relevant to the story.

(ii) Particular regard should be paid to the potentially vulnerable position of children who witness, or are victims of, crime. This should not restrict the right to report legal proceedings.

10 *Clandestine devices and subterfuge

(i) The press must not seek to obtain or publish material acquired by using hidden cameras or clandestine listening devices; or by intercepting private or mobile telephone calls, messages or emails; or by the unauthorised removal of documents or photographs; or by accessing digitally-held private information without consent.

(ii) Engaging in misrepresentation or subterfuge, including by agents or intermediaries, can generally be justified only in the public interest and then only when the material cannot be obtained by other means.

11 Victims of sexual assault
The press must not identify victims of sexual assault or publish material likely to contribute to such identification unless there is adequate justification and they are legally free to do so.

12 Discrimination

(i) The press must avoid prejudicial or pejorative reference to an individual's race, colour, religion, gender, sexual orientation or to any physical or mental illness or disability.

(ii) Details of an individual's race, colour, religion, sexual orientation, physical or mental illness or disability must be avoided unless genuinely relevant to the story.

13 Financial journalism

(i) Even where the law does not prohibit it, journalists must not use for their own profit financial information they receive in advance of its general publication, nor should they pass such information to others.

(ii) They must not write about shares or securities in whose performance they know that they or their close families have a significant financial interest without disclosing the interest to the editor or financial editor.

(iii) They must not buy or sell, either directly or through nominees or agents, shares or securities about which they have written recently or about which they intend to write in the near future.

14 Confidential sources
Journalists have a moral obligation to protect confidential sources of information.

15 Witness payments in criminal trials

(i) No payment or offer of payment to a witness – or any person who may reasonably be expected to be called as a witness – should be made in any case once proceedings are active as defined by the Contempt of Court Act 1981.

This prohibition lasts until the suspect has been freed unconditionally by police without charge or bail or the proceedings are otherwise discontinued; or has entered a guilty plea to the court; or, in the event of a not guilty plea, the court has announced its verdict.

*(ii) Where proceedings are not yet active but are likely and foreseeable, editors must not make or offer payment to any person who may reasonably be expected to be called as a witness, unless the information concerned ought demonstrably to be published in the public interest and there is an overriding need to make or promise payment for this to be done; and all reasonable steps have been taken to ensure no financial dealings influence the evidence those witnesses give. In no circumstances should such payment be conditional on the outcome of a trial.

*(iii) Any payment or offer of payment made to a person later cited to give evidence in proceedings must be disclosed to the prosecution and defence. The witness must be advised of this requirement.

16 *Payment to criminals

(i) Payment or offers of payment for stories, pictures or information, which seek to exploit a particular crime or to glorify or glamorise crime in general, must not be made directly or via agents to convicted or confessed criminals or to their associates – who may include family, friends and colleagues.

(ii) Editors invoking the public interest to justify payment or offers would need to demonstrate that there was good reason to believe the public interest would be served. If, despite payment, no public interest emerged, then the material should not be published.

The public interest

There may be exceptions to the clauses marked * where they can be demonstrated to be in the public interest.

1. The public interest includes, but is not confined to:
    (i) Detecting or exposing crime or serious impropriety.
    (ii) Protecting public health and safety.
    (iii) Preventing the public from being misled by an action or statement of an individual or organisation.
2. There is a public interest in freedom of expression itself.
3. Whenever the public interest is invoked, the PCC will require editors to demonstrate fully how the public interest was served.
4. The PCC will consider the extent to which material is already in the public domain, or will become so.
5. In cases involving children under 16, editors must demonstrate an exceptional public interest to override the normally paramount interest of the child.

NUJ Code of Conduct

Members of the National Union of Journalists are expected to abide by the following professional principles:

A journalist:

1 At all times upholds and defends the principle of media freedom, the right of freedom of expression and the right of the public to be informed.
2 Strives to ensure that information disseminated is honestly conveyed, accurate and fair.
3 Does her/his utmost to correct harmful inaccuracies.
4 Differentiates between fact and opinion.
5 Obtains material by honest, straightforward and open means, with the exception of investigations that are both overwhelmingly in the public interest and which involve evidence that cannot be obtained by straightforward means.
6 Does nothing to intrude into anybody's private life, grief or distress unless justified by overriding consideration of the public interest.
7 Protects the identity of sources who supply information in confidence and material gathered in the course of her/his work.
8 Resists threats or any other inducements to influence, distort or suppress information.
9 Takes no unfair personal advantage of information gained in the course of her/his duties before the information is public knowledge.
10 Produces no material likely to lead to hatred or discrimination on the grounds of a person's age, gender, race, colour, creed, legal status, disability, marital status, or sexual orientation.
11 Does not by way of statement, voice or appearance endorse by advertisement any commercial product or service save for the promotion of her/his own work or of the medium by which she/he is employed.
12 Avoids plagiarism.

The NUJ believes a journalist has the right to refuse an assignment or be identified as the author of editorial that would break the letter or spirit of the code. The NUJ will fully support any journalist disciplined for asserting her/his right to act according to the code.

Code of Practice for Press Council of Ireland

The Code of Practice is intended as work in progress and it is expected that it will continue to evolve in light of experience and in response to changes in public opinion and perceptions. It will form the basis for adjudications by the Press Ombudsman and Press Council of Ireland for Irish newspapers and periodicals.

It comprises elements from the Code of Practice of the British Press Complaints Commission, the Statement of Principles of the Australian Press Council, and the Publishing Principles of the German Press Council. Account has also been taken of the Ethics Code of the US-based National Conference of Editorial Writers, of NUJ and Journalists' Codes in a number of countries around the world, and of the concerns of the Irish Commission on the Newspaper Industry, 1996.

You can complain about any article you see in any Irish newspaper or periodical that you think may breach this Code. You can also complain about the behaviour of a journalist that you think may breach the Code. We cover all publications that are members of the National Newspapers of Ireland (daily and Sunday newspapers, also Irish editions of UK newspapers), the Regional Newspapers Association of Ireland (provincial newspapers) and the Periodical Publishers Association of Ireland (Irish-published magazines).

Preamble

The freedom to publish is vital to the right of the people to be informed. This freedom includes the right of a newspaper to publish what it considers to be news, without fear or favour, and the right to comment upon it.

Freedom of the press carries responsibilities. Members of the press have a duty to maintain the highest professional and ethical standards.

This Code sets the benchmark for those standards. It is the duty of the Press Ombudsman and Press Council of Ireland to ensure that it is honoured in the spirit as well as in the letter, and it is the duty of publications to assist them in that task.

In dealing with complaints, the Ombudsman and Press Council will give consideration to what they perceive to be the public interest. It is for them to define the public interest in each case, but the general principle is that the public interest is invoked in relation to a matter capable of affecting the people at large so that they may legitimately be interested in receiving and the press legitimately interested in providing information about it.

Principle 1 – Truth and Accuracy

1.1 In reporting news and information, newspapers and periodicals shall strive at all times for truth and accuracy.

1.2 When a significant inaccuracy, misleading statement or distorted report or picture has been published, it shall be corrected promptly and with due prominence.

1.3 When appropriate, a retraction, apology, clarification, explanation or response shall be published promptly and with due prominence.

Principle 2 – Distinguishing Fact and Comment

2.1 Newspapers and periodicals are entitled to advocate strongly their own views on topics.

2.2 Comment, conjecture, rumour and unconfirmed reports shall not be reported as if they were fact.

2.3 Readers are entitled to expect that the content of a publication reflects the best judgment of editors and writers and has not been inappropriately influenced by undisclosed interests. Wherever relevant, any significant financial interest of an organization should be disclosed. Writers should disclose significant potential conflicts of interest to their editors.

Principle 3 – Fairness and Honesty

3.1 Newspapers and periodicals shall strive at all times for fairness and honesty in the procuring and publishing of news and information.

3.2 Publications shall not obtain information, photographs or other material through misrepresentation or subterfuge, unless justified by the public interest.

3.3 Journalists and photographers must not obtain, or seek to obtain, information and photographs through harassment, unless their actions are justified in the public interest.

Principle 4 – Respect for Rights

Everyone has constitutional protection for his or her good name. Newspapers and periodicals shall not knowingly publish matter based on malicious misrepresentation or unfounded accusations, and must take reasonable care in checking facts before publication.

Principle 5 – Privacy

5.1 Privacy is a human right, protected as a personal right in the Irish Constitution and the European Convention on Human Rights, which is incorporated into Irish law. The private and family life, home and correspondence of everyone must be respected.

5.2 Readers are entitled to have news and comment presented with respect for the privacy and sensibilities of individuals. However, the right to privacy should not prevent publication of matters of public record or in the public interest.

5.3 Sympathy and discretion must be shown at all times in seeking information in situations of personal grief or shock. In publishing such information, the feelings of grieving families should be taken into account. This should not be interpreted as restricting the right to report judicial proceedings.

5.4 Public persons are entitled to privacy. However, where a person holds public office, deals with public affairs, follows a public career, or has sought or obtained publicity for his activities, publication of relevant details of his private life and circumstances may be justifiable where the information revealed relates to the validity of the person's conduct, the credibility of his public statements, the value of his publicly expressed views or is otherwise in the public interest.

5.5 Taking photographs of individuals in private places without their consent is not acceptable, unless justified by the public interest.

Principle 6 – Protection of Sources

Journalists shall protect confidential sources of information.

Principle 7 – Court Reporting

Newspapers and periodicals shall strive to ensure that court reports (including the use of photographs) are fair and accurate, are not prejudicial to the right to a fair trial and that the presumption of innocence is respected.

Principle 8 – Prejudice

Newspapers and periodicals shall not publish material intended or likely to cause grave offence or stir up hatred against an individual or group on the basis of their race, religion, nationality, colour, ethnic origin, membership of the travelling community, gender, sexual orientation, marital status, disability, illness or age.

Principle 9 – Children

9.1 Newspapers and periodicals shall take particular care in seeking and presenting information or comment about a child under the age of 16.

9.2 Journalists and editors should have regard for the vulnerability of children, and in all dealings with children should bear in mind the age of the child, whether parental or other adult consent has been obtained for such dealings, the sensitivity of the subject-matter, and what circumstances if any make the story one of public interest. Young people should be free to complete their time at school without unnecessary intrusion. The fame, notoriety or position of a parent or guardian must not be used as sole justification for publishing details of a child's private life.

Principle 10 – Publication of the Decision of the Press Ombudsman / Press Council

10.1 When requested or required by the Press Ombudsman and/or the Press Council to do so, newspapers and periodicals shall publish the decision in relation to a complaint with due prominence.

10.2 The content of this Code will be reviewed at regular intervals.

BBC Code of Ethics

The BBC has one of the most comprehensive codes of ethics for journalists and broadcasters in the world. It is too long to publish here in full and I only give the index below but it is available on the Web at http://www.bbc.co.uk/editorialguidelines/

The BBC's Editorial Values
Using the Guidelines
Accuracy
Impartiality
Harm & Offence
Fairness, Contributors & Consent
Privacy
Reporting Crime & Anti-Social Behaviour
Children and Young People as Contributors
Politics, Public Policy and Polls
War, Terror & Emergencies
Religion
Re-use and Reversioning
Editorial Integrity & Independence from External Interests
Conflicts of Interest
External Relationships and Funding
Interacting with our Audiences
The Law
Accountability
   Appendix 1: Ofcom Broadcasting Code
   Appendix 2: Code of Conduct for Competitions and Voting
   Appendix 3: Statement of Policy on Alternative Finance
   Appendix 4: Framework for Funding Prizes and Awards

International Federation of Journalists

Declaration of Principles on the Conduct of Journalists

Adopted by the Second World Congress of the International Federation of Journalists at Bordeaux on 25–28 April 1954 and amended by the 18th IFJ World Congress in Helsingör on 2–6 June 1986.

This international Declaration is proclaimed as a standard of professional conduct for journalists engaged in gathering, transmitting, disseminating and commenting on news and information and in describing events.

1   Respect for truth and for the right of the public to truth is the first duty of the journalist.

2   In pursuance of this duty, the journalist shall at all times defend the principles of freedom in the honest collection and publication of news, and of the right of fair comment and criticism.

3   The journalist shall report only in accordance with facts of which he/she knows the origin. The journalist shall not suppress essential information or falsify documents.

4   The journalist shall use only fair methods to obtain news, photographs and documents.

5   The journalist shall do the utmost to rectify any published information which is found to be harmfully inaccurate.

6   The journalist shall observe professional secrecy regarding the source of information obtained in confidence.

7   The journalist shall be aware of the danger of discrimination being furthered by the media, and shall do the utmost to avoid facilitating such discrimination based on, among other things, race, sex, sexual orientation, language, religion, political or other opinions, and national or social origins.

8   The journalist shall regard as grave professional offences the following: plagiarism, malicious misrepresentation, calumny, slander, libel, unfounded accusations, acceptance of a bribe in any form in consideration of either publication or suppression.

9   Journalists worthy of that name shall deem it their duty to observe faithfully the principles stated above. Within the general law of each country the journalist shall recognise in professional matters the jurisdiction of colleagues only, to the exclusion of every kind of interference by governments or others.

Ofcom Broadcasting Code

The Code was updated in October 2009 and is too lengthy to publish in full here but covers the following principles:

- The Legislative Background to the Code
- How to use the Code
- Section 1: Protecting the Under-Eighteens
- Section 2: Harm and Offence
- Section 3: Crime
- Section 4: Religion
- Section 5: Due Impartiality and Due Accuracy and Undue Prominence of Views and Opinions
- Section 6: Elections and Referendums
- Section 7: Fairness
- Section 8: Privacy
- Section 9: Sponsorship
- Section 10: Commercial References and Other Matters
- Appendix 1: Extracts from the Communications Act 2003
- Appendix 2: Extracts from the Audiovisual Media Services Directive (Directive 89/552/EEC, as amended by Directive 97/36/EC and by Directive 2007/65/EC)
- Appendix 3: European Convention on Human Rights Articles 8, 9, 10 and 14
- Appendix 4: Financial Promotions and Investment Recommendations
- Cross-promotion Code

(http://www.ofcom.org.uk/tv/ifi/codes/bcode/ accessed 8/2/2010)

Broadcasting Authority of Ireland
2–5 Warrington Place
Dublin 2
Tel: 01 644 1200
Fax: 01 644 1299
Email: info@bci.ie
Web: www.bci.ie

Still using the Code of the Broadcasting Commission of Ireland.

Content principles

General Community Standards
Due Care
Protection for Children
Assessment

Content rules

Violent Programme Material
Sexual Conduct

Coarse and Offensive Language
Persons and Groups in Society
Factual Programming – News, Current Affairs and Documentaries
Children's Programming
Drugs, Alcohol and Solvent Abuse
Imitative Behaviour

(http://www.bai.ie/pdfs/BCI_Code_Prog_Stands_Mar07.pdf)

TMAP Guidelines

TMAP Guidelines for Coverage of Sexual Subject Matter in Teenage Magazines

1.1 The guidelines are the outcome of discussions between publishers of teenage magazines (represented through the Periodical Publishers Association [PPA]), retailers of teenage magazines (represented by, among others, the British Retail Consortium [BRC], National Federation of Retail Newsagents [NFRN], the Multiple Newsagents Association [MNA]) and magazine editors (represented by the British Society of Magazine Editors [BSME]).

1.2 The guidelines cover the editorial content of teenage magazines. The final arbiter of the meaning and interpretation of the Guidelines is the Teenage Magazine Arbitration Panel (TMAP), to whom any complaints relating to alleged infractions of the Guidelines should be addressed.

1.3 There is a separate code of practice relating to advertisements, which is produced by the Advertising Standards Authority (ASA), which is the final arbiter in the meaning of the code of practice. The ASA deals with complaints about advertisement content.

2.1 The guidelines apply to magazines published more than once a year when it is apparent that young people aged under 16 comprise 25 per cent or more of the total readership.

2.2 A list of such titles will be drawn up on the basis of the latest available figures over a 12 month period, using the reports of the Youth Target Group Index survey (Youth TGI) or other figures or bases accepted by the TMAP.

General principles and procedures

3.1 Readers will always be encouraged to take a responsible attitude to sex and contraception, and where relevant to seek advice from General Practitioners and other professionals.

3.2 If sex is being discussed, then safer sex will be highlighted and encouraged wherever relevant.

3.3 Where under-age sex or sexual abuse is discussed it will be clearly stated as illegal. Under-age sex will be discouraged and the age of consent clearly stated.

3.4 Editorial advice will be given in good faith, with relevant professional organisations contacted for guidelines and named within the editorial if appropriate.

3.5 Readers will be encouraged to seek support from parents, guardians or other responsible adults wherever relevant. The emotional consequences of sexual activity will be highlighted where relevant.

3.6 The editorial content of the magazines will reflect the typical concerns of the magazine's readership, with advice given to provide readers with relevant and responsible answers to their concerns.

3.7 It is recognised that magazines have an important role to play in the field of sex education for, and emotional development of, teenagers.

Implementation and assessment

4.1 Publishers of teenage magazines containing subject matter on sexual issues are responsible for ensuring that editorial policies for their magazines fall within the guidelines.

4.2 Editorial policies with regard to the publication of subject matter on sexual issues will be formally recorded by the publishers. All editorial staff employed to work on such subject matter will be instructed on the magazine's editorial policy and informed of any changes to that policy if relevant.

4.3 Editorial instruction will incorporate clear examples of appropriate and inappropriate editorial treatment of subject matter on sexual issues.

4.4 Each magazine will appoint an independent consultant of good standing to advise the editor on an ongoing basis with regard to sexual, emotional and moral issues.

4.5 An annual audit will be conducted by TMAP to ensure published material (those titles listed as a result of 2.2, plus any other titles apparently aimed at the defined readership) falls within the Guidelines.

4.6 All teenage magazines containing problem pages will ensure that published letters are based on genuine letters received by those magazines.

4.7 All published responses to letters on problem pages will be provided by relevant, professionally qualified advisors. Relevant qualifications will be approved by the TMAP.

Retail display

5.1 Publishers will advise distributors and retailers of the appropriate display category of their magazines.

5.2 Distributors and retailers should ensure that displays of magazines reflect the perceived age of purchasers, as communicated by publishers.

Addresses for regulatory bodies

British Broadcasting Corporation
Broadcasting House, London, W12 7RJ
Tel: 144 (0)208 743 8000
http://www.BBC.co.uk

National Union of Journalists
Headland House, 308–312 Gray's Inn Road, London, WC1X 8DP
Tel: 144 (0)207 278 7916 Fax: 144 (0)207 837 8143
e-mail: Acorn.house@nuj.org.uk
http://www.nuj.org.uk

Ofcom
Riverside House, 2a Southwark Bridge Road, London, SE1 9HA
Tel: 144 (0)207 981 3000 Fax: 144 (0)207 981 3333
http://www.ofcom.org.uk

Press Complaints Commission
Halton House, 20/23 Holborn, London EC1N 2JD
Tel: 144 (0)207 831 0022 Fax: 144 (0)207 831 0025
http://www.pcc.org.uk

Press Standards Board of Finance
Merchants House Buildings, 30 George Square, Glasgow, G2 1EG

European Broadcasting Union
17A Ancienne Route
1218 Grand-Saconnex
Switzerland
Tel: 141 (0)22 717 2111
Fax: 141 (0)22 747 4000

Defence Press and Broadcasting Advisory Committee
Secretary: Andrew Vallance
Floor 1 Spine H 21
Ministry of Defence
Main Building
Whitehall
London SW1A 2HB
020-7218-2206
e-mail: secretary@dnotice.org.uk

My ethics blog

My ethics blog is an occasional look at ethical issues as they arise, giving background information, analysis and views.
http://ethics-regulation.blogspot.com/

Alliance of Independent Press Councils of Europe

The Alliance of Independent Press Councils of Europe has no formal membership structure. However, the following European organisations participate in the Alliance's conferences:

- **Armenia** – Baku Press Club
  Website: www.ypc.am/eng/
  Email: pressclub@ypc.am
- **Azerbaijan** – Press Council
  Website: www.presscouncil.az
  Email: bakupressklub@azintex.com
- **Belgium** – Raad voor de Journalistiek
  Website: www.rvdj.be
  Email: rvdj@skynet.be
- **Bosnia & Herzegovina** – Press Council
  Website: www.vzs.ba/ba/
  Email: info@vzs.ba
- **Bulgaria** – National Council for Journalism Ethics
  Website: www.mediaethics-bg.org
  Email: office@mediaethics-bg.org
- **Cyprus** – Media Complaints Commission
  Website: www.cmcc.org.cy
  Email: epidideo@cytanet.com.cy
- **Denmark** – Press Council
  Website: www.pressenaevnet.dk
  Email: sekr@pressenaevnet.dk
- **Estonia** – Press Council
  Website: www.eall.ee/pressinoukogu (Publishers)
  Website: www.asn.org.ee (Journalists)
- **Finland** – Press Council
  Website: www.jsn.fi
  Email: nina.porra@jsn.fi
- **France** – Association pour la Prefiguration d'un Conseil de Presse
  Website: www.apcp.unblog.fr
  Email: nath.dolle@gmail.com
- **Germany** – Press Council
  Website: www.presserat.de
  Email: info@presserat.de
- **Hungary** – Center for Independent Journalism
  Website: www.cij.hu
  Email: ilona.moricz@cij.hu
  – Association of Content Providers
  Website: www.mte.hu
- **Ireland** – Press Ombudsman and Press Council
  Website: www.presscouncil.ie
  Email: info@pressombudsman.ie
- **Italy** – Press Ombudsman and Press Council
  Website: www.odg.it
  Email: femasel@tin.it

- **Kosovo** – Press Council
  Email: presscouncil.kosovo@gmail.com
- **Luxembourg** – Press Council
  Website: www.press.lu
  Email: secretariat@press.lu
- **Malta** – Press Club and Press Ethics Commission
  Website: www.maltapressclub.org.mt
  Email: joeavella@onvol.net
- **Moldova** – Press Council
  Website: www.consiliuldepresa.md
  Email: secretariat@consiliuldepresa.md
- **Netherlands** – Raad voor de Journalistiek
  Website: www.rvdj.nl
  Email: raad@rvdj.nl
- **Norway** – Press Complaints Commission
  Website: www.presse.no
  Email: pfu@presse.no
- **Russia** – Public Collegium for Press Complaints
  Website: www.presscouncil.ru
  Email: collegium@ruj.ru
- **Spain** – Information Council of Catalunya
  Email: manuel.pares@uab.es
- **Sweden** – Press Ombudsman and Press Council
  Website: www.po.se
  Email: po@po.se
- **Switzerland** – Press Council
  Website: www.presserat.ch
  Email: info@presserat.ch
- **UK** – Press Complaints Commission
  Website: www.pcc.org.uk
  Email: will.gore@pcc.org.uk
- **Ukraine** – Journalistic Ethics Commission
  Website: www.cje.org.ua
  Email: taras@kuzmov.com

While maintaining a European focus, AIPCE has welcomed to its meetings various representatives from the following regulatory authorities:

- **Botswana** – Press Council
  Email: pcbotswana@yahoo.com
- **Israel** – Press Council
  Website: www.m-i.org.il
  Email: moaza@m-i.org.il
- **Peru** – Press Council
  Website: www.consejoprensaperuana.org.pe
  Email: consejopp@amauta.rcp.net.pe

- **Sri Lanka** – Press Complaints Commission
  Website: www.pccsl.lk
  Email: pccsl@pccsl.lk
- **Thailand** – Press Council
  Website: www.presscouncil.or.th
  Email: chavaron@inet.co.th
- **Zambia** – Media Council
  Email: benmwale1@yahoo.ca
  Email: mecoz@yahoo.co.uk

Glossary

Broadcasters Television and radio equivalent of newspaper proprietors.

Consumers A collective term used to refer to readers of publications, viewers of TV, listeners to radio, internet surfers, teletext viewers and other information receivers. By this term I mean they are consuming the information provided by a journalist, not that they are necessarily buying the product, whether it is a publication or a broadcast.

Hard news A term used by journalists to mean stories that have immediate impact and drama. They must be topical. Plane crashes, deaths, political decisions, stock market crashes, murder, court verdicts and anything which involves shouting 'stop the press' is hard news.

Information Used in its widest sense to mean anything that is printed by magazines or newspapers or transmitted in news and current affairs programmes by radio and television or over electronic systems as part of the editorial content. In this context it can mean 'hard news', 'soft news', analysis, comment, opinion, conjecture, and so on.

Publish Includes broadcast as well as publication in the traditional senses.

Reader Used as a general term to mean receivers of the message when this is transmitted by print.

Soft news This is a term used by journalists to define stories that do not have immediate impact. Often such stories have more of a manufactured feel to them as a PR agency or a journalist has tried to build them up into a hard news story – known as giving the story a harder edge. Soft news stories are likely to be about people, possibly showbiz, certainly gossipy, or about events which do not have immediate impact. Often soft news stories are used as features, and many features are soft news stories.

Bibliography

Allport and Postman (1947) *The Psychology of Rumor*. Holt, Rinehart and Winston, New York.

Amnesty International (2003) *Refugees and Asylum Seekers: A Guide for Journalists in Scotland*. Amnesty International, Edinburgh.

Andre, J. (1992) 'Censorship: Some Distinctions', in Elliott D. Cohen (ed.) *Philosophical Issues in Journalism*. Oxford University Press, Oxford.

Anthony, S. (1973) 'Anxiety and Rumor', in *Journal of Social Psychology* 40 (3), 597–620.

Archard, D. (1998) 'Privacy, the Public Interest and a Prurient Public', in M. Kieran (ed.) *Media Ethics*. Routledge, London.

Aristotle (1976) *The Ethics of Aristotle* (translated by J.A.K. Thompson). Penguin Classics, London.

Aristotle (1980) *The Nicomachean Ethics* (translated by W.D. Ross). Oxford University Press, Oxford.

Banks, D. and Hanna, M. (2010) *McNae's Essential Law for Journalists* (20th edn). Oxford University Press, Oxford.

BCC (1981–96) *BCC Report*. HMSO, London.

BBC (1996) *BBC Producers' Guidelines*. BBC, London. http://www.bbc.co.uk/info/editorial/prodgl/contents/html

BBC (1999) *The Changing UK*. BBC, London.

Bell, M. (1998) 'The Journalism of Attachment', in M. Kieran (ed.) *Media Ethics*. Routledge, London.

Belsey, A. and Chadwick, R. (1992) *Ethical Issues in Journalism and the Media*. Routledge, London.

Benn, P. (1998) *Ethics*. University College London Press, London.

Bertrand, Claude-Jean (2001) *M*A*S Transaction*. Hampton Press Inc., Cresskill, NJ and London.

Bertrand, Claude-Jean (2003) *An Arsenal for Democracy*. Hampton Press Inc., Cresskill, NJ.

Blackburn, S. (2005) *Truth: A Guide for the Perplexed*. Penguin, London.

Bleyer, W.G. (1913) *Newspaper Writing and Editing*. Constable and Co., London.

Bok, S. (1982) *Secrets*. Oxford University Press, Oxford.

Booker, C. and North, R. (2007) *Scared to Death: From BSE to Global Warming – Why Scares are Costing Us the Earth*. Continuum International Publishing Group, London.

Broadcasting Act (1981) HMSO, London.

Broadcasting Act (1996) HMSO, London.

Broadcasting Standards Commission (1998) *Annual Review*. BSC, London.

Broadcasting Standards Commission (1998) *Codes of Guidance*. BSC, London.

Broadcasting Standards Council (1994) *A Code of Practice* (2nd edn). BSC, London.

Broder, D. (1983) 'Newsmen Work for the Reader', *International Herald Tribune*, 21 July.

Browne, C. (1996) *The Prying Game*. Robson Books, London.

Bruschke, J. and Loges, W.E. (2004) *Free Press vs. Fair Trial: Examining Publicity's Role in Trial Outcomes*. Lawrence Erlbaum Associates, Mahwah, NJ.

Bundock, A. (1957) *A History of the NUJ*. Oxford University Press, Oxford.

Burden, P. (2008) *News of the World? Fake Sheiks and Royal Trappings*. Eye Books, London.

Calcutt, QC, Sir David (1993) *Review of Press Self Regulation*. HMSO, London.

Carey, P., Armstrong, N., Lamont, D., & Qartermain, J. (2010) *Media Law* (5th edn). Sweet & Maxwell, London.

Carey, P. and Sanders, J. (2004) *Media Law* (3rd edn). Sweet & Maxwell, London.

Christians, C.G., Rotzoll, K.B. and Fackler, M. (1998) *Media Ethics: Cases and Moral Reasoning* (5th edn). Longman, New York.

Cohen, E.D. (ed.) (1992) *Philosophical Issues in Journalism*. Oxford University Press, Oxford.

Cohen, S. and Young, J. (eds) (1973) *The Manufacture of News: Deviance, Social Problems and the Mass Media*. Constable, London.

Cohen-Almagor, R. (2001) *Speech, Media and Ethics*. Palgrave, Basingstoke.

Cohen-Almagor, R. (2006) *The Scope of Tolerance: Studies on the Costs of Free Expression and the Freedom of the Press*. Routledge, London.

Committee on Privacy (1972) *The Report of the Committee on Privacy*. HMSO, London.

Committee on Privacy and Related Matters (1990) *Report of the Committee on Privacy and Related Matters*. HMSO, London.

Concise Oxford English Dictionary (1964). Oxford University Press, Oxford.

Cooley, Thomas (1888) *Law of Torts* 29 (2nd edn).

Crawford, Nelson Antrim (1969) *The Ethics of Journalism*. Greenwood, New York (originally published 1924).

Crissell, A. (1997) *An Introductory History of British Broadcasting*. Routledge, London.

Crone, T. (2002) *Law and the Media* (4th edn). Focal Press, London.

Curtis, L. and Jempson, M. (1993) *Interference on the Airwaves*. Campaign for Press and Broadcasting Freedom, London.

Davies, N. (2008) *Flat Earth News*. Chatto & Windus, London.

Department of National Heritage (1995) *Privacy and Media Intrusion: The Government's Response*. HMSO, London.

Dhavan, R. and Davies, C. (1978) *Censorship and Obscenity*. Martin Robertson, London.

Dill, B. (1986) *Journalist's Handbook on Libel and Privacy*. Free Press, New York.

Dunbar, R. (1992) 'Why Gossip is Good for You', *New Scientist* 2 (11), 2–31.

English, K. (2009) *The Longtail of News: To unpublish or not unpublish*. APME: Toronto.

Evers, H., Harmen, G. and van Groesen, J. (2010) *The News Ombudsman: Watchdog or Decoy?* AMB, Diemen.

Franklin, B. (1999) *Newsak and News Media*. Routledge, London.

Frost, Chris (2000) *Media and Self-Regulation*. Pearson, London.

Frost, Chris (2002) 'Source Credibility: Do We Really Believe Everything We Read?' *Aslib Proceedings*, 54 (4), 222–8. AIM, London.

Frost, Chris (2003) *Designing for Newspaper and Magazines*. Routledge, Abingdon.

Frost, Chris (2003) 'The Press Complaints Commission: Privacy and Accuracy', *Ethical Space: the Journal of the Institute of Communication Ethics*, 1 (1), 32–8. Troubador, London.

Frost, Chris (2004) 'The Press Complaints Commission: A Study of Ten Years of Adjudications on Press Complaints', *Journalism Studies* 5 (1), 101–114. Routledge: Abingdon.

Frost, Chris (2006) 'Press Complaints Commission: Ten Years of Self-regulation', in Keeble, R. (ed.) *Communication Ethics Today*. Troubador, London.

Frost, Chris (2010) 'The Development of Privacy Adjudications by the UK Press Complaints Commission and Their Effects on the Future of Journalism', *Journalism Practice*, 4(3). Routledge: Abingdon.

Frost, Chris (2010) *Reporting for Journalists* (2nd edn). Routledge, Abingdon.

Fuller, J. (1996) *News Values*. University of Chicago Press, Chicago.

Galtung, J. and Ruge, M. (1973) 'Structuring and Selecting News', in Stanley Cohen and Jock Young (eds) *The Manufacture of News: Deviance, Social Problems and the Mass Media*. Constable, London.

Garneau, G. (ed.) (1993) *Free Press Threat in Europe*. Garneau, Paris.

General Council of the Press (1954–63) *The Press and the People*. GCP, London.

Gilbert, H. (1977) *The Nature of Morality: An Introduction to Ethics*. Oxford University Press, Oxford.

Glasser, T. L. (1992) 'Objectivity and News Bias', in Elliott D. Cohen (ed.) *Philosophical Issues in Journalism*. Oxford University Press, Oxford.

Gluckman, M. (1963) 'Gossip and Scandal', *Current Anthropology* 4 (3), 307–15.

Gordon, D.A., Kittross, J. and Reuss, C. (1998) *Controversies in Media Ethics*. Longman, New York.

Hadley et al. (1950) *The Kemsley Manual of Journalism*. Cassell, London.

Halberstam, J. (1992) 'A Prolegomenon for a Theory of News', in Elliott D. Cohen (ed.) *Philosophical Issues in Journalism*. Oxford University Press, Oxford.

Halstead, P. (2005) *Human Rights*. Hodder Arnold, London.

Hamelink, C. (2000) *The Ethics of Cyberspace*. Sage, London.

Harcup, T. and O'Neill, D. (2001) 'What is news? Galtung and Ruge revisited', *Journalism Studies* 2 (2), 261–80.

Harcup, T. (2007) *The Ethical Journalist*. Focal Press, London.

Hare, R.M. (1995) *The Language of Morals*. Clarendon Press, Oxford.

Hargrave, A.M. (1991) *Taste and Decency in Broadcasting*. BSC, London.

Hargreaves, I. (2003) *Journalism: Truth or Dare?* Oxford University Press, Oxford.

Hargreaves, R. (2002) *The First Freedom: A history of Free Speech*. Sutton Publishing, Stroud.

Harman, H. (2006) 'A Right to Report … or a Right to Privacy?' *Press Gazette*. 23 June, London.

Harris, G. and Spark, D. (1997) *Practical Newspaper Reporting*. Focal Press, Oxford.

Harris, Nigel G.E. (1992) 'Codes of Conduct for Journalists', in *Ethical Issues in Journalism and the Media*. Routledge, London.

Hartley, John (1982) *Understanding News*. Routledge, London.

Hausmann, C. (1987) *The Decision-making Process in Journalism*. Nelson-Hall, Chicago.

Hermes, J. (1995) *Reading Women's Magazines*. Polity Press, Cambridge.

House of Commons (1951) *Report of the Broadcasting Committee 1949*. HMSO, London.

House of Commons (1962) *Report of the Broadcasting Committee 1960*. HMSO, London.

House of Commons (1977) *Report of the Committee on the Future of broadcasting*. HMSO, London.

House of Commons Culture, Media and Sport Committee (2003) *Privacy and Media Intrusion*. Stationery Office, London.

House of Commons Culture, Media and Sport Committee (2010) *Press Standards, Privacy and Libel*. Stationery Office, London.

Hudson, G. and Rowlands, S. (2007) *The Broadcast Journalism Handbook*. Pearson Longman, Harlow.

Innes, J. C. (1992) *Privacy, Intimacy and Isolation*. Oxford University Press, Oxford.

ITC (1992) *Annual Report and Accounts*. ITC, London.

ITC (1993) *Annual Report and Accounts*. ITC, London.

ITC (1994) *Annual Report and Accounts*. ITC, London.

ITC (1995) *Annual Report and Accounts*. ITC, London.

ITC (1996) *Annual Report and Accounts*. ITC, London.

ITC (1997) *Annual Report and Accounts*. ITC, London.

ITC (1998) *Annual Report and Accounts*. ITC, London.

Kant, I. (1948) *Groundwork of the Metaphysics of Morals* (translated by H.J. Paton). Routledge, London.

Kant, I. (1990) *Foundations of the Metaphysics of Morals* (translated by Lewis White Beck). Prentice-Hall, Englewood Cliffs, NJ.

Kant, I. (1993) *Grounding for the Metaphysics of Morals* (3rd edn) (translated by James W. Ellington). Hackett Publishing Company Inc., Indianapolis, IN.

Keeble, R. (2009) *Ethics for Journalists* (2nd edn). Routledge, London.

Kieran, M. (1998) *Media Ethics*. Routledge, London.

Kieran, M., Morrison, D. and Svennevig, M. (2000) 'Privacy, the public and journalism', *Journalism*, 1 (2), 145–69. Sage, London.

Klaidman, S. and Beauchamp, T.L. (1987) *The Virtuous Journalist*. Oxford University Press, Oxford.

Koch, T. (1990) *News as Myth*. Greenwood Press, New York.

Lagan, S. (2006) 'Photographer Unfairly Sacked for Refusing to Use Illegal Pictures', *Press Gazette*, 30 June, London.

Lambeth, E. (1992) *Committed Journalism*. Indiana University Press, Bloomington, IN.

Leapman, M. (1986) *The Last Days of the Beeb*. Allen & Unwin, London.

Lewis and Short (1900) *Latin Dictionary*. Clarendon Press, Oxford.

Lord Chancellor's Department (1993) *Consultation Paper on the Infringement of Privacy*. HMSO, London.

Lord Chancellor's Department (1996) *Payment to Witnesses*. HMSO, London.

Mansfield, F.J. (1935) *The Complete Journalist*. Pitman, London.

Mansfield, F.J. (1943) *Gentlemen, the Press!* Turner and Dunnett, London.

Mark's Gospel (1989) The Holy Bible, New revised standard version. Oxford University Press, New York.

Martin, K. (1947) *The Press the Public Wants*. The Hogarth Press, London.

Matelsk, M.J. (1991) *TV News Ethics*. Focal Press, London.

McKay, J. (1999) *Manuals For Courtesans*. The Association for Journalism Educators Conference, London.

Matrix Chambers (2002) *Privacy and the Media: The Developing Law*. Matrix Chambers, London.

Meyer, P. (1987) *Ethical Journalism*. University Press of America, Lanham, MD.

Mill, J.S. (1991) 'What Utilitarianism is', in *On Liberty and Other Essays*. Oxford University Press, Oxford.

Mill, J.S. (1998) *Utilitarianism* (edited by Roger Crisp). Oxford University Press, Oxford.

Millar, C. (2006) 'Quiet Wedding, Cheryl?' *Evening Standard*, 13 July, London.

National Heritage Committee (1993) *Report on Privacy and Media Intrusion*. HMSO, London.

Nietzsche, F. (1973) *Beyond Good and Evil* (translated by R.J. Hollingdale). Penguin Books, Harmondsworth.

Nordlund, S. (1991) An address to the Stockholm Symposium on Press Councils and Press Ethics, June 1991.

Norman, R. (1983) *The Moral Philosophers: An Introduction to Ethics*. Clarendon Press, Oxford.

NUJ (1930–1978) *The Journalist*. NUJ, London.

NUJ (1970–1976) *Minutes of the NEC*. NUJ, London.

NUJ (1998) *Rule Book*. NUJ, London.

NUJ (2005) *NUJ Rulebook 2005*. NUJ, London.

O'Malley, T. (1994) *Closedown*. Pluto Press, London.

O'Malley, T. and Soley, C. (2000) *Regulating the Press*. Pluto, London.

Ordine dei Giornalisti (1993) Regulation Governing the Profession of Journalism (Law No. 69 of 3 February 1963).

Overbeck, W. (2000) *Major Principles of Media Law*, Harcourt College, Fort Worth.

Paine, T. (2000) *Common Sense and the Rights of Man*, Phoenix Press, London.

Paine, R. (1967) 'What is Gossip About: An Alternative Hypothesis', in *Man 2* (June), 278–85.

Parent, W.A. (1992) 'Privacy, Morality and the Law', in Elliott D. Cohen (ed.) *Philosophical Issues in Journalism*. Oxford University Press, Oxford.

PCC (1991) *Annual Report*. Press Complaints Commission, London.

PCC (1992) *Annual Report*. Press Complaints Commission, London.

PCC (1993) *Annual Report*. Press Complaints Commission, London.

PCC (1994) *Annual Report*. Press Complaints Commission, London.

PCC (1995) *Annual Report*. Press Complaints Commission, London.

PCC (1996) *Annual Report*. Press Complaints Commission, London.

PCC (1997) *Annual Report*. Press Complaints Commission, London.

PCC (1998) *Annual Report*. Press Complaints Commission, London.

PCC (1999) *Annual Report*. Press Complaints Commission, London.

PCC (2000) *Annual Report*. Press Complaints Commission, London.

PCC (2001) *Annual Report*. Press Complaints Commission, London.

PCC (2002) *Annual Report*. Press Complaints Commission, London.

PCC (2003) *Annual Report*. Press Complaints Commission, London.

PCC (2004) *Annual Report*. Press Complaints Commission, London.

PCC (2005) *Annual Report*. Press Complaints Commission, London.

PCC (published regularly since 1991) *Report Nos 1–39*. Press Complaints Commission, London.

Pendleton, J. (1890) *Newspaper Reporting*. Elliot Stock, London.

Philo, G. (ed.) (1996) *Media and Mental Distress*. Glasgow Media Group, Glasgow.

Ponsford, D. (2006) 'Privacy Puzzler After Cole Nets Libel Win', *Press Gazette*, 30 June, London.

Potter, J. (1989) *Independent Television in Britain. Vol. 3 Politics and Control*. Macmillan, London.

Press Council (1953–90) *The Press and the People. Annual Report of the Press Council*. Press Council, London.

Press Council (1991) *Press at the Prison Gates. Press Council Booklet No. 8*. Press Council, London.

Prichard, H.A. (1949) *Moral Obligation*. Oxford University Press, Oxford.

Prichard, H.A. (1968) *Moral Obligation and 'Duty and Interest'*. Oxford University Press, Oxford.

Quinn, F. (2009) *Law for Journalists* (2nd edn). Pearson Longman, Harlow.

Radio Authority (1991–98) *Annual Report and Financial Statement*. Radio Authority, London.

Randall, D. (1996) *The Universal Journalist*. Pluto Press, London.

Reed, T.A. (1876) *The Reporter's Guide*. Pitman, London.

Reporters Without Borders (2002) *Freedom of the Press Throughout the World*. RSF, Paris.

Richards, I. (2005) *Quagmires and Quandaries: Exploring Journalism Ethics*. University of New South Wales Press, Sydney.

Robertson, G. (1983) *People against the Press*. Quartet, London.

Robertson, G. and Nicol, A. (2002) *Media Law* (4th edn). Penguin, London.

Rosentiel, T. and Mitchell, A. (2003) *Thinking Clearly: Cases in Journalistic Decision-making*. Columbia University Press, New York.

Rosnow, R.L. and Fine, G. (1976) *Rumor and Gossip: The Social Psychology of Hearsay*. Elsevier, London.

Ross, W.D. (1930) *The Right and the Good*. Oxford University Press, Oxford.

Royal Commission on the Press (1949) HMSO, London.

Royal Commission on the Press (1962) HMSO, London.

Royal Commission on the Press (1977) HMSO, London.

Rozenberg, J. (2004a) *Privacy and the Press*. Oxford University Press, Oxford.

Rozenberg, J. (2004b) 'Caroline Wins Legal Ban on Paparazzi Pictures', *The Daily Telegraph*, 25 June, London.

Sanders, K. (2003) *Ethics and Journalism*. Sage, London.

Schlesinger, P. (1978) *Putting Reality Together: BBC News*. Constable, London.

Sergeant, J. (2001) *Give Me Ten Seconds*. Macmillan, London.

Shakespeare, W. (1993) *Othello*. Addison Wesley Longman, Harlow.

Shannon, R. (2001) *A Press Free and Responsible*. John Murray, London.

Shibutani, T. (1966) *Improvised News*. Bobbs-Merrill, IN.

Sinclair, R. (1949) *The British Press*. Home and Van Thal, London.

Singer, P. (1994) *Ethics*. Oxford University Press, Oxford.

Smith, Z. (2006a) 'Journalists Hit back at Clarke's "Poison" Slur', *Press Gazette*, 1 May, London.

Smith, Z. (2006b) 'Trust in the British Media Rockets: But It's Still Lower Than Other Countries', *Press Gazette*, 1 May, London.

Snoddy, R. (1993) *The Good, the Bad and the Unacceptable*. Faber & Faber, London.

Spacks, P.M. (1986) *Gossip*. University of Chicago Press.

Sparks, C. and Tulloch, J. (eds) (2000) *Taboid Tales*. Rowman & Littlefield, London.

Stephenson, H. and Bromley, M. (1998) *Sex, Lies and Videotape*. Addison Wesley Longman, London.

Taylor, J. (1999) *Body Horror*. Manchester University Press, Manchester.

Tebbutt, M. (1995) *Women's Talk? A Social History of Gossip in Working Class Neighbourhoods, 1880–1960*. Scolar Press, Aldershot.

Times/Mirror Center for the People and the Press (1994) *Eight Nations, People and The Press Survey* (published 16 March 1994), Washington DC.

Tomlinson, H. and Thomson, M. (2004) *New Law Journal*, London. http://www.carter-ruck.com/articles/280504_NewModelPrivacy.html

Tracey, M. (1998) *The Decline and Fall of Public Service Broadcasting*. Oxford University Press, New York.

Venables, J. (1993) *What is News?* ELM Publications, Huntingdon.

Wacks, R. (1995) *Privacy and Press Freedom*. Blackstone Press, London.

Warburton, N. (1998) *Philosophy: The Classics*. Routledge, London.

Ward, G. (1997) *Mental Health and the National Press*. Health Education Authority, London.

Warren and Brandeis (1890) 'The right to privacy', *Harvard Law Review*, 4, 193.

Wellings, K. and Field, B. (1996) *Stopping Aids: Aids/HIV Public Education and the Mass Media in Europe*. Longman, Harlow.

Welsh, T. and Greenwood, W. (1995) *Essential Law for Journalists*. Butterworths, London.

Whitaker, B. (1981) *News Limited: Why You Can't Read All About It*. Minority Press Group, London.

Williams, B. (2002) *Truth and Truthfulness*. Princeton University Press, NJ.

Wilson, J. (1996) *Understanding Journalism*. Routledge. London.

X, George (1997) 'Leave My Child Alone', in Mike Jempson (ed.) *Child Exploitation and the Media*. Smallwood Publishing, London.

Internet sites of interest

UK Parliament: http://www.parliament.uk

European codes of conduct can be found at: http://www.uta.fi/ethicnet/

The Department of Culture, Media and Sport: http://www.DCMS.gov.uk

The BBC: http://www.bbc.co.uk

BBC Producers' Guidelines: http://www.bbc.co.uk/info/editorial/prodgl/index.htm

Open Media Research Institute: http://www.omri.cz/index.html

Journalism UK: http://www.octopod.demon.co.uk/journ_UK.htm

Journalism news: http://bcn.boulder.co.us/campuspress/sjmc/journnews.html

European journalism: http://www.demon.co.uk/eurojournalism/

Ofcom: http://www.ofcom.org.uk

Press Complaints Commission: http://www.pcc.org.uk

National Union of Journalists: http://www.nuj.org.uk

Reporters Sans Frontières: http://www.rsf.org

European Broadcasting Union: http://www.ebu.ch/

Index